This is a thoughtful, wise, detailed and cogent study of an issue that remains critically important today: the peaceful settlement of the Israeli/Palestinian conflict and the governance of Jerusalem. It shows how effective diplomacy could work if given a chance, and points the way to a better place.

Bob Rae, Mediator, Parliamentarian and 21st Premier of Ontario

This densely worded publication is a valuable mine of information, ideas, approaches and reflections on the problem of the future of Jerusalem and its role in any peace agreement. Irrespective of whether one agrees with the concept of a Special Regime for the Old City or not, the wealth of data and range of views it contains is unsurpassed and will constitute an essential resource for any scholar working on contemporary issues in Jerusalem. The editors have worked hard in making available the background research as well as the policy products themselves that resulted from the Initiative. It is a comprehensive and remarkable addition to the literature.

Mick Dumper, Professor in Middle East Politics, University of Exeter

The Old City of Jerusalem is the epicenter of the Arab-Israel conflict, where religion, politics, and violence meet. This volume, the first of three, seeks to deconstruct and demystify the issues required to resolve the Jerusalem problem. It offers a viable, hard-headed and creative way to approach the challenges of governance and sovereignty. Practitioners must read these volumes if they hope for success in advancing the Middle East peace process.

Daniel Kurtzer, Woodrow Wilson School of Public and International Affairs, Princeton University; former U.S. ambassador to Egypt and Israel

TRACK TWO DIPLOMACY AND JERUSALEM

Track Two Diplomacy and Jerusalem is the first in a series of three books which collectively present the work of the Jerusalem Old City Initiative, or JOCI, a major Canadian-led Track Two diplomatic effort, undertaken between 2003 and 2014. JOCI's *raison d'être* was to find sustainable governance solutions for the Old City of Jerusalem, arguably the most sensitive and intractable of the final status issues dividing Palestinians and Israelis.

Track Two Diplomacy and Jerusalem includes a series of studies that place JOCI within its historical setting and explains the theoretical context of Track Two diplomacy. The book then proceeds to present the Initiative's culminating documents, which outline in detail its proposed Special Regime governance model. Until now, the proposals have remained unpublished and available only to a limited audience of key stakeholders.

Presenting the information in an accessible format, this book will contribute positively to the wider conversation on Jerusalem, especially with respect to the long-standing conflict over control and governance of this holy city. It will therefore be of value to several audiences, from the policy-making community to the various traditions found in academia.

Tom Najem is Project Manager of the Jerusalem Old City Initiative and Associate Professor in the Department of Political Science, University of Windsor, Canada.

Michael J. Molloy is Co-Director of the Jerusalem Old City Initiative and Adjunct Professor at the University of Ottawa's Graduate School of Public and International Affairs, Canada.

Michael Bell is Co-Director of the Jerusalem Old City Initiative, Adjunct Professor at the University of Windsor and Senior Fellow at the Norman Paterson School of International Affairs at Carleton University, Canada.

John Bell is Co-Director of the Jerusalem Old City Initiative and Director of the Middle East and Mediterranean Programme at the Toledo International Center for Peace, Spain.

UCLA CENTER FOR MIDDLE EAST DEVELOPMENT (CMED) SERIES

Series Editors
Steven Spiegel, UCLA
Elizabeth Matthews, California State University, San Marcos

The UCLA Center for Middle East Development (CMED) series on Middle East security and cooperation is designed to present a variety of perspectives on a specific topic, such as democracy in the Middle East, dynamics of Israeli-Palestinian relations, Gulf security, and the gender factor in the Middle East. The uniqueness of the series is that the authors write from the viewpoint of a variety of countries so that no matter what the issue, articles appear from many different states, both within and beyond the region. No existing series provides a comparable, multinational collection of authors in each volume. Thus, the series presents a combination of writers from countries who, for political reasons, do not always publish in the same volume. The series features a number of sub-themes under a single heading, covering security, social, political, and economic factors affecting the Middle East.

TRACK TWO DIPLOMACY AND JERUSALEM

The Jerusalem Old City Initiative

Edited by Tom Najem, Michael J. Molloy,
Michael Bell and John Bell

Routledge
Taylor & Francis Group

LONDON AND NEW YORK

First published 2017
by Routledge
2 Park Square, Milton Park, Abingdon, Oxon OX14 4RN

and by Routledge
711 Third Avenue, New York, NY 10017

Routledge is an imprint of the Taylor & Francis Group, an informa business

British Library Cataloguing in Publication Data
A catalogue record for this book is available from the British Library

Library of Congress Cataloging in Publication Data
Names: Najem, Tom, editor.
Title: Track two diplomacy and Jerusalem : the Jerusalem Old City Initiative / edited by Tom Najem, Michael Molloy, Michael Bell, John Bell.
Other titles: UCLA Center for Middle East Development series ; 11.
Description: Milton Park, Abingdon, Oxon ; New York, NY : Routledge, 2017.|
Series: UCLA Center for Middle East Development ; 11 | Includes bibliographical references and index.
Identifiers: LCCN 2016012344| ISBN 9781138666733 (hardback) | ISBN 9781138666740 (pbk.) | ISBN 9781315619231 (e-book)
Subjects: LCSH: Jerusalem–International status. | Jerusalem–Politics and government. | Arab-Israeli conflict–1993—Peace. | Conflict management–Middle East. | Track two diplomacy.
Classification: LCC DS109.95 .T73 2017 | DDC 956.05/4–dc23
LC record available at https://lccn.loc.gov/2016012344

ISBN: 978-1-138-66673-3 (hbk)
ISBN: 978-1-138-66674-0 (pbk)
ISBN: 978-1-315-61923-1 (ebk)

Typeset in Bembo
by Taylor & Francis Books

CONTENTS

LIST OF ILLUSTRATIONS

Figures

Maps

Table

Boxes

ACKNOWLEDGEMENTS

When we began to work on the project that became the Jerusalem Old City Initiative back in 2003, we had no idea that we were setting out on a decade long journey. In the course of that decade, which involved dozens of trips to Jerusalem and the region, and countless meetings, we had the great privilege of working with a large number of talented men and women whose kindness and patience made the work a pleasure.

In the course of this Initiative, we consulted close to two hundred individuals and dozens of institutions in Israel, the Palestinian territories, the Arab world, Europe, the United States and Canada. To all those who gave us their time, ideas and perceptions, we are deeply grateful.

We quickly realized that to tackle such a complex and politically fraught subject as the Old City of Jerusalem, we needed to count on the knowledge, wisdom and political acumen of people who knew much more about the topic than we did. Our success was built on their knowledge, their political judgement, and their willingness to travel along with us on that long journey.

Many of these people were initially cautious about engaging in another Track Two initiative dealing with possibly the most difficult of the issues dividing Israelis and Palestinians. However, the idea that the key to resolving the problems posed by the Old City might be found thinking through a special governance regime, had its own attraction. We were encouraged to find people from both sides coming to regard the JOCI project as their own.

We would like to acknowledge the enormous contribution made by these people, who we have come to regard as highly valued partners and, in many cases, friends. At the last formal meeting of our regional and international partners, we found many of the participants reluctant to see the project end, signalling that it had become as important to many of them as it was to us.

That being said, we do not claim that every element that found its way into our proposal had the unanimous approval of those whose contributions we acknowledge in the pages below. At the end of the day the JOCI team takes responsibility for the choices made.

Early in the process we encountered Ambassador Arthur Hughes of the Middle East Institute. Art was with us at the critical Istanbul meeting and participated vigorously in both the Security and Governance Working Groups, where his deep Middle East experience and his diplomatic skills helped to shape the conclusions of both. Beyond that, the esteem and respect he commands in Washington and his wide network of contacts enabled him to guide us through the Washington labyrinth and gain access to critical American political figures and influential public servants. Art became the voice of JOCI in Washington and an essential member of our team.

We were also fortunate that two distinguished and exceptionally knowledgeable Jerusalemites, Nazmi al-Jubeh and Daniel Seidemann joined the JOCI family early and, despite occasional misgivings about the directions we were taking, contributed to virtually every aspect of the work. Indeed, their contributions, insights and ideas are dotted throughout the volumes.

Ambassador Daniel Kurtzer and the late Shira Herzog provided wise counsel and, at critical moments in the process, injected creative ideas that illuminated the way forward.

Academics Menachem Klein and Salim Tamari provided thoughtful critiques of our ideas as they emerged.

The Jerusalem Old City Initiative's Security Working Group, chaired by Michael Bell, was spearheaded by General John de Chastelain, former RCMP Deputy Commissioner Roy Berlinquette, and Ambassador Art Hughes. JOCI recruited a highly expert security team of Israelis and Palestinians; notable among these were Pini Meidan-Shani, Moty Cristal and Issa Kassassieh and several others who, for various reasons, asked not to be identified. The regional teams also included Arieh Amit, Jibrin al-Bakri, Reuven Berko, Yasser Dajani, and Peri Golan.

The Jerusalem Old City Initiative's Governance Working Group, chaired by Mike Molloy, was spearheaded by David Cameron, Art Hughes and Jodi White, with important contributions from Shira Herzog, Tim Donais and Lara Friedman. Regional team leaders included two distinguished veterans of the Middle East peace process, Gilead Sher and Hiba Husseini, with specialized legal expertise being provided by Mazen Qupty and Jonathan Gillis. We also drew heavily on the expertise of the Jerusalem Institute for Israel Studies including Ruth Lapidoth, Ora Aheimer, Israel Kimhi and of the Palestinian think tank, Al Mustakbal Foundation.

Expertise on the hypersensitive Holy Sites was provided by Michael Dumper and Marshall Breger while Trond Bakkevig, convenor of the Council of Religious Institutions of the Holy Land, facilitated a dialogue between the JOCI team and key Muslim, Jewish and Christian leaders.

At a critical moment in the process, senior Israeli and Palestinian members signalled the need to review the basics of our proposals from a political perspective. Thus was born the London Caucus consisting of Gilead Sher, Pini Median-Shani, Ambassador Manuel Hassassian, Yasser Dajani and Moty Cristal among others.

A more profound understanding of some of the issues that a Special Regime would have to deal with was undertaken within three separate projects on archaeology, property and economic implications. Lynn Swartz Dodd provided insights into the archaeological issues; Anneke Smit and David Viveash delved into the complex and murky world of private property in the Old City; economists Ephraim Kleiman and Nadiv Halevi teased out the economic implications of a Special Regime.

A project of this magnitude required the cooperation and assistance of a wide variety of institutions. This undertaking would not have been possible without the generous financial assistance of the then named Department of Foreign Affairs and International Trade (Global Affairs Canada), the Canadian International Development Agency (CIDA), and the International Development Research Centre (IDRC). We also received assistance at critical junctures from the Centre for International Governance Innovation (CIGI) in Waterloo, the Woodrow Wilson School for Public and International Affairs at Princeton University, Search for Common Ground, and the Toledo International Centre for Peace in Madrid. For the support of all these, we are most grateful.

Rosemary Hollis of Chatham House arranged a particularly useful workshop that helped us to understand the business of creating institutions in areas emerging from conflict. Emma Murphy helped to organize a meeting at Durham University that marked the launch of JOCI as an actual Track Two exercise.

We wish to express our gratitude to the Canadian embassies in Tel Aviv, Washington and Amman; the Canadian representative office in Ramallah; the Canadian High Commission in London; the permanent missions of Canada to the United Nations in New York, Geneva and to the European Community in Brussels. The staff members of these various missions were invariably supportive and helpful.

It is important to note that none of our funders, at any time, approached us with views or advice respecting the direction of our work. We alone are responsible for JOCI's content and recommendations. Needless to say, any shortcomings are ours and ours alone.

Early institutional support was provided by the Munk Centre for International Studies at the University of Toronto, which published our initial *Discussion Document* in their MCIS Briefing Series. We are appreciative of the support of Janice Stein, Marketa Evans and Sebastian Bouhnick.

The University of Windsor is the institutional home of the Jerusalem Old City Initiative. The University was a major source of funding, accommodation and administrative support. President Alan Wildeman, Vice President Academic Neil Gold, and the Dean of the Faculty of Arts and Social Sciences Cecil Houston, recognized both the possibilities and the significance of what JOCI was attempting to do and were unstinting in their constant support. For this we are most grateful.

JOCI is situated in the Department of Political Science, where its faculty members including Abdel Salam Sidahmed and Roy Amore provided us with a high level of expertise on religious matters. The JOCI Project Manager's team included a blend of staff members and talented graduate students. They included Rachelle Badour, Derek Barker, Crystal Ennis, Felicia Gabrielle, Jonathan Nehmetallah, Giovanna Roma, Remy Sirls and Shayna Zamkanei.

A special note of thanks to all who have assisted in preparing the volumes to publication, most especially to Jo Molloy and Giovanna Roma both of whom spent countless hours over the years doing the often thankless but essential tasks associated with editing a work of this magnitude. We also appreciate the efforts (and patience) of Joe Whiting, senior acquisitions editor at Routledge, who took a strong interest in this project some time ago, and continued to provide unwavering support through to publication. Finally, a special thanks to Steven Spiegel and Elizabeth Matthews for also seeing value in the project and including it in their excellent UCLA series on Middle East Security and Cooperation.

CONTRIBUTORS

Tom Najem is Project Manager of the Jerusalem Old City Initiative and Associate Professor of Political Science at the University of Windsor. He is a specialist in the field of international relations and comparative politics of the developing world, with a specialization in the Middle East and North Africa. From 2002 to 2012, Najem served as Department Head of Political Science at the University of Windsor. He has also lived and worked in the Middle East and North Africa and held previous academic appointments in Morocco and at the University of Durham, UK. His latest publications include *Africa's Most Deadly Conflict: Media Coverage of the Humanitarian Disaster in the Congo and the United Nation's Response, 1997–2008* (Wilfrid Laurier University Press, 2012), and *Lebanon: The Politics of a Penetrated Society* (Routledge, 2011).

Michael J. Molloy is Co-Director of the Jerusalem Old City Initiative, Adjunct professor at the University of Ottawa's Graduate School of Public and International Affairs, President of the Canadian Immigration Historical Society, and an expert on global refugee affairs. He was a senior official in the Canadian Department of Foreign Affairs and International Trade (DFAIT) and Citizenship and Immigration Canada, the Canadian Ambassador to Jordan (1996–2000), and the Canadian Coordinator for the Middle East Peace Process at DFAIT (2000–2003). A founding member of the Multilateral Refugee Working Group (the Middle East Peace Process), he has worked on the Palestinian refugee issue since the early 1990s and acted as Senior Advisor for the Canadian delegation to the Multilateral Refugee Working Group. Molloy was also a member of the Canadian team sent to select Ugandan Asian expellees in 1972, oversaw implementation of the refugee provisions of the 1976 Canadian Immigration Act, and coordinated the movement of 60,000 Indochinese refugees to Canada in 1979–1980. A career foreign service officer, he served in Japan, Lebanon, the USA, Geneva, Jordan (twice), Syria and Kenya.

Michael Bell is Co-Director of the Jerusalem Old City Initiative and served as the Paul Martin Senior Scholar on International Diplomacy at the University of Windsor from 2005 to 2013. Currently, he is an Adjunct Professor at the University of Windsor and Senior Fellow at the Norman Paterson School of International Affairs at Carleton University. He has served in the Middle East for many years, first as Canada's Ambassador to Jordan (1987–1990), then to Egypt (1994–1998), and Israel (1990–1992, 1999–2003), and he was also the Executive Assistant for Middle East Affairs to the Honourable Robert Stanfield (1978–1979), Director of the Middle East Relations Division (1983–1987), Director General for Central and Eastern Europe (1992–1994), and Fellow at the Weatherhead Centre for International Affairs at Harvard University (1998–1999). Former Ambassador Bell was also appointed as Chair of the International Reconstruction Fund Facility for Iraq (IRFFI) Donor Committee (2005), and the Senior Scholar of Diplomacy at the Munk Centre for International Studies at the University of Toronto (2003–2005). His comments on Middle East affairs are often sought out by the press, and he is a regular contributor to the *Globe and Mail*.

John Bell is Co-Director of the Jerusalem Old City Initiative, Director of the Middle East and Mediterranean Programme at the Toledo International Center for Peace (Spain), and former Middle East Director with Search for Common Ground, Jerusalem. He was a Canadian and United Nations diplomat, serving as Political Officer at the Canadian Embassy in Cairo (1993–1996), member of Canada's delegation to the Refugee Working Group in the Peace Process (1992–1993), Political Advisor to the Personal Representative of the Secretary-General of the United Nations for southern Lebanon (2000–2001), Advisor to the Canadian Government during the Iraq crisis (2002–2003), and Consultant to the International Crisis Group on Jerusalem. Bell was also a spokesperson for the Canadian Department of Foreign Affairs, and Communications Coordinator for the Signing Conference for the International Treaty to Ban Landmines (1997). He is often asked to comment about the Middle East and has written numerous pieces for magazines and newspapers worldwide.

Roy Berlinquette has been a Member of the Military Police Complaints Commission since 2007, and in this last capacity, served as Panel Member on the Afghanistan Public Interest Hearing and has made decisions on many conduct and interference complaints. Berlinquette was a Member of the Office of the Oversight Commission on Police Reform for Northern Ireland (2001–2007) and has thirty-six years' experience with the Royal Canadian Mounted Police (RCMP), where he has held numerous positions, most notably Deputy Commissioner of the North West Region (1997–2000). He was also a principal for a company specializing in risk management, comptrollership and investigations, in Ottawa.

David Cameron was Chair of the Department of Political Science at the University of Toronto at the time of the JOCI project, and is currently Dean of the

Faculty of Arts and Science. As an expert on federalism and decentralized government, Cameron was named the Director of Research of the Pepin-Robarts Task Force on Canadian Unity in 1977, and worked with the Government of Canada as an advisor in the Federal-Provincial Relations Office, as well as the Coordination Group working on the Quebec Referendum (1979). He later went on to become Assistant Secretary to Cabinet for Strategic and Constitutional Planning, and Assistant Undersecretary of State, Education Support. He was appointed Deputy Minister of Intergovernmental Affairs for the Ontario Government (1987) and the Ontario Representative to the Government of Quebec and Special Advisor on Constitutional Reform to then Premier David Peterson (1989). Cameron was a chief negotiator during the Charlottetown constitutional discussions, and has advised numerous international governments on constitutional reform and governance management. He was a Halbert Fellow at the Hebrew University of Jerusalem. Cameron has won numerous awards including the Governor General's International Award for Canadian Studies (2002). His numerous publications include *Citizen Engagement in Conflict Resolution: Are There Lessons for Canada in International Experience?* (University of Toronto Press, 1997).

John de Chastelain is a retired Canadian soldier and diplomat, and Companion of the Order of Canada. He was Canada's Chief of Defence Staff twice, the Commandant of the Royal Military College of Canada (1977–1980), and in 1985, was appointed Commander of the Order of Military Merit. In 1993, General de Chastelain was appointed Canada's Ambassador to the United States after which he was asked to serve as Chief of Defence, for the second time. He became Chair of the Independent International Commission on (Arms) Decommissioning in 1997, which led to the Belfast Agreement (1998). He is a recipient of many honours and awards including the title Officer of the Order of Canada (1993), Royal Military College Club of Canada's Birchall Leadership Award (2006), the Vimy Award, and in 2010 he was inducted into the Wall of Honour at the Royal Military College of Canada. He has honorary degrees, in Law, Conflict Resolution, Education, and Military Science.

Marketa Evans is a specialist in international political economy and was the Executive Director of the Munk Centre for International Studies at the University of Toronto, during her involvement with the JOCI project. She went on to become the Extractive Sector Corporate Social Responsibility Counsellor for the Canadian Department of Foreign Affairs and International Trade. From 2009 to 2013, she was a special advisor to the Canadian Minister of International Trade, and Director of Strategic Partnerships (2008–2009) at Plan International Canada – a leading development NGO. Evans currently serves as Vice President of Strategy at the United Way of Greater Toronto.

Arthur Hughes is a senior advisor and the Washington Coordinator for the Jerusalem Old City Initiative, a Scholar at the Middle East Institute's Public Policy

Centre in Washington, D.C., and board member of the Foundation for Middle East Peace. He has over forty years' experience in peacekeeping, diplomacy and the military, and was a career American Foreign Service Officer from 1965 to 1997. His most senior positions include Ambassador to Yemen (1991–1994), Deputy Assistant Secretary of State for Near Eastern Affairs (1994–1997), Director General of the peacekeeping operation the Egypt-Israel Multinational Force and Observers (1998–2004), Deputy Chief of Mission at the U.S. Embassy in Israel (1986–1989), Deputy Chief of Mission at the U.S. Embassy in Israel, and Deputy Assistant Secretary of Defense for Near East and South Asia (1989–1991). Former Ambassador Hughes was also a Lieutenant in the U.S. Army in Germany, is a graduate of the Infantry and the Intelligence Schools, and has won numerous awards including the Presidential Distinguished Service Award and the State Department Career Achievement Award.

Peter Jones is Associate Professor at the University of Ottawa's Graduate School of Public and International Affairs and a leading expert on Track Two diplomacy and security. Previously, the scholar-practitioner was Senior Policy Advisor to the National Security Advisor to the Prime Minister of Canada for five years, was an analyst for the Security and Intelligence Secretariat of the Privy Council of Canada, and also worked at the Department of Foreign Affairs and the Department of Defence. In the 1990s, Jones led the Middle East Security and Arms Control Project at the Stockholm International Peace Research Institute (SIPRI) in Sweden. He has led several Track Two dialogues in the Middle East and South and Southeast Asia. Jones is a fellow at several research institutions, including the Center for Trans-Atlantic Relations at the Paul H. Nitze School of Advanced International Studies of the Johns Hopkins University, and The Regional Centre for Conflict Prevention of the Jordan Institute for Diplomacy in Amman, Jordan, and is currently an Annenberg Distinguished Visiting Fellow at the Hoover Institution at Stanford University. He recently published *Track Two Diplomacy: In Theory and Practice* (Stanford University Press, 2015).

Menachem Klein is Professor of Political Science at Bar-Ilan University, Israel, and is an expert on the Israeli-Palestinian Peace Process, divided cities, and Jerusalem. In 2000, he was an adviser on Jerusalem Affairs and Israel–PLO Final Status Talks for the Minister of Foreign Affairs, Professor S. Ben-Ami, and a member of the advisory team operating in the office of Prime Minister Ehud Barak. His latest publications include *Lives in Common: Arabs and Jews in Jerusalem, Jaffa and Hebron* (Hurst, 2014), and *The Shift: Israel–Palestine from Border Conflict to Ethnic Struggle* (Hurst and Columbia University, 2010).

Giovanna Roma was a research associate at the Jerusalem Old City Initiative at the University of Windsor from 2013 to 2015. Prior to this, she worked at the Centre for European Studies, housed at Carleton University. Giovanna's research interests are wide-ranging and include conflict resolution and Track Two diplomacy; the Middle East and North Africa; Europe and the European Union; and anti-corruption and good governance.

Jodi White is the President and Founder of Sydney House Consultants, Distinguished Senior Fellow at both the Norman Paterson School of International Affairs and the Arthur Kroeger College of Public Affairs at Carleton University, and at the time of the JOCI project, was also the Director and Secretary-Treasurer of Action Canada (2010–2014). Most notably, White was the Chief of Staff to the Minister of Foreign Affairs from 1984 to 1988 and became the Chief of Staff to the Prime Minister of Canada in 1993.

MAPS

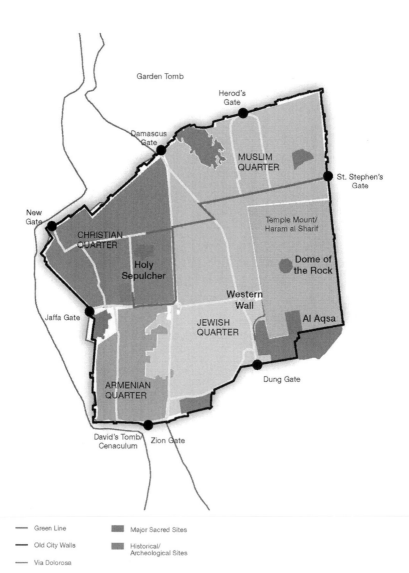

Garden Tomb

Herod's
Gate

Damascus
Gate

MUSLIM
QUARTER

St. Stephen's
Gate

New
Gate

CHRISTIAN
QUARTER

Temple Mount/
Haram al Sharif

Dome of
the Rock

Holy
Sepulcher

Western
Wall

Jaffa Gate

JEWISH
QUARTER

Al Aqsa

ARMENIAN
QUARTER

Dung Gate

David's Tomb/
Cenaculum   Zion Gate

— Green Line

— Old City Walls

— Via Dolorosa

▩ Major Sacred Sites

▩ Historical/
Archeological Sites

MAP 0.1 The Old City
Courtesy of Terrestrial Jerusalem

MAP 0.2 Israel, The West Bank and map of Jerusalem
© Shaul Arieli

INTRODUCTION

In the fall of 2011, the venerable American magazine *The Atlantic*, in association with the S. Daniel Abraham Centre for Middle East Peace produced a four-part series on the long standing Israeli–Palestinian conflict titled 'Is Peace Possible?'[1] which looked at various proposals to resolve each of the four final status issues – borders, security, refugees and Jerusalem. The Jerusalem Old City Initiative's Special Regime governance model was presented as one of three promising options for resolving the conflict over the Old City of Jerusalem.[2]

The authors of *The Atlantic* series noted the Special Regime's distinct advantages over other proposals, including: 1) maintaining the geographical, historic and religious integrity of the Old City; 2) requiring only minimal cooperation between the two sides; 3) providing a mediating intervening force; 4) protecting full access to Holy Sites; and 5) potentially diffusing sensitive questions of sovereignty. *The Atlantic* publication was but one of a number of references made in influential outlets in recent years of the suitability that the Special Regime model brings to resolving the conflict over the control and governance of Jerusalem's Old City.[3]

Track Two Diplomacy and Jerusalem: The Jerusalem Old City Initiative is the first in a series of three books which present in detail the work of the Jerusalem Old City Initiative, or JOCI. A major Canadian-led Track Two diplomatic effort, it was based at the University of Windsor, in Windsor, Ontario, Canada and took place between 2003 and 2014. JOCI's *raison d'être* was to find sustainable governance solutions for the Old City of Jerusalem, arguably the most sensitive and intractable of the final status issues dividing Palestinians and Israelis.

It is certainly not difficult to understand the enormous sensitivity that surrounds any discussion regarding the governance of Jerusalem's Old City. While less than one square kilometer in size, the Old City figures deeply in the collective consciousness of the world's three great monotheistic faiths, containing as it does sites of exceptional holiness for Jews, Muslims and Christians alike. Control over this highly contested space is therefore of great concern not only to Israelis and Palestinians, but also to the international community, including stakeholders of the various religious traditions.

The modern State of Israel has controlled the Old City since the June 1967 Arab–Israeli War and subsequently annexed it, though this act was not recognized by the international community. Palestinian Arabs, who form the majority of the approximately 35,000 residents, also lay claim to the Old City and demand its inclusion in a future Palestinian state. It is highly unlikely that either side in the dispute will accept or acquiesce to the other's maximalist position on the Old City, ensuring continuing stalemate on this issue, and thus, almost certainly, on the wider conflict between Palestinians and Israelis.

The Jerusalem Old City Initiative was conceived by three former Canadian diplomats – Michael Bell, Michael J. (Mike) Molloy and John Bell – in the wake of the failure of the Camp David talks in 2000, which reportedly had collapsed in large part over the question of Jerusalem. Indeed, a colleague intimately associated with the Camp David talks noted the two sides were simply not adequately prepared to tackle the issue of Jerusalem. Thus, the collapse of the peace talks at Camp David and subsequently at Taba in 2001 meant that the much needed ground work on the issue of Jerusalem fell to civil society, including to those working in the context of what Joseph Montville termed Track Two diplomacy, or unofficial diplomacy.

The three former Canadian diplomats had extensive experience dealing with the Palestinian–Israeli conflict, and the Initiative was founded out of their deep interest in the profound symbolic needs embodied in the Old City, and in an attempt to find functional governance alternatives that would meet the needs of Palestinians, Israelis and believers around the world. They understood the degree of work that needed to be done on the issue and, within the context of a relatively unique Track Two framework, they along with Israeli, Palestinian and international partners embarked on a project that ultimately saw the development of the Special Regime governance model.

The Jerusalem Old City Initiative unfolded in three more or less distinct phases – 1) the conceptualization of a governance model for the Old City; 2) the development and articulation of its proposals referred to as the Special Regime; and 3) the advocacy and transfer of the model to the official diplomatic community in the hopes of contributing to a resolution to the conflict.

Phase one, the pre-Track Two period, took place between 2003 and 2005, and consisted of identifying the needs of stakeholders (symbolic, religious, security, economic, political and social) and posited a set of alternatives to meet them. During this period, the JOCI team concluded that an effective and empowered third party presence was imperative in the Old City, and became convinced of the need to maintain its physical integrity. This contrasted, for example, with the Geneva Accords which recommended dividing the Old City and implementing a complex set of management mechanisms. Sustainability was seen as the *sine qua non* for success. Out of this the Special Regime concept crystallized.

This first phase of the Initiative consisted of research, network building and conceptualization. There were intensive consultations with a broad set of interlocutors – Palestinians, Israelis and internationals – to define needs and explore the feasibility of a third party presence in the Old City. This led ultimately to the publication in December 2005 of the *Jerusalem Old City Discussion Document: New Directions for Deliberation and Dialogue*, which is presented in its original form in this volume. The *Discussion Document* explored alternatives, sketched out the issues and made suggestions for a way forward that were flexible enough to elicit discussion and interest. The culmination of this phase, a meeting held in Istanbul, Turkey in December of 2005, brought together approximately 25 Jerusalem experts from various disciplinary traditions to discuss and debate the ideas found in the *Discussion Document*. Those participants – Israeli, Palestinian and international – had extensive experience in the various issues impacting Jerusalem, and many were seasoned participants in previous Track Two initiatives or, indeed, at some point in their careers, in official diplomacy. The Istanbul meeting, held over two days, proved a key turning point in the history of JOCI with wide agreement amongst participants that the Special Regime concept merited further development to be undertaken in the context of a Track Two framework.

Phase two of the Initiative took place between 2006 and 2010, and consisted of the detailed development of the Special Regime governance model. JOCI morphed into a Track Two initiative, formally establishing an academic and administrative home in the Department of Political Science at the University of Windsor. The Department Head, Dr. Tom Najem, joined the team as project manager. A framework was developed, and funds were raised to carry out the Initiative.

The Track Two framework implemented by the JOCI team to develop the Special Regime model was more or less straightforward, but characterized by a flexibility designed to deal with unfolding political dynamics, and the needs of its regional partners. Working groups were established consisting of a careful balance of Palestinian, Israeli and international specialists tasked with developing the specificities of a Special Regime governance model. These working groups were provided with additional support through the commissioning of research papers on a host of governance, security and related issues. Ideas generated by the working groups were tested in various forums with key stakeholders. A further level of support came from a high-level group of Israeli and Palestinian individuals, known as the London Caucus (not to be confused with the London track referred to in Chapter 4), whose main role was to review the fundamental principles underpinning JOCI and offer political advice.

Out of phase two came the three key documents which form the basis of the Special Regime governance model. The overall structure of a Special Regime and its specific responsibilities were described in *The Governance Discussion Document: A Special Regime for the Old City of Jerusalem*. The security arrangements of the Special Regime, identified at the Istanbul meeting as a high priority, are described in *The Jerusalem Old City Initiative Security Assessment*. Finally, the text of the preceding documents were integrated and further refined in the more succinct *Mandate Elements for the Old City Special Regime*, which was designed to serve as a working text for the negotiating table. All three documents are presented here in their original forms and, at over 36,000 words combined, offer a highly detailed and developed model of governance.

Phase two culminated in May of 2010 when the Initiative formally unveiled its proposals at the Mayflower Hotel in Washington, D.C. The event, which was co-sponsored by the Middle East Institute, attracted nearly 300 participants, as well as global media from North America, the Middle East and Europe – several of which reported widely on what became known as the 'Canadian peace plan'.[4]

The Washington event initiated the third and final phase of the Jerusalem Old City Initiative (2010–2014). This phase consisted primarily of advocacy but also saw continuing work on three critical issues (property, archaeology and economic implications), and led to the publication of three in-depth studies. Those studies are found in the third book of this series: *Contested Sites in Jerusalem: The Jerusalem Old City Initiative*.

Readers familiar with Track Two diplomacy recognize the great variety of projects that fall under this moniker. The projects and their processes, aims and goals vary considerably. The Jerusalem Old City Initiative fell under a specific type of Track Two which some academics refer to as 'Hard Track Two'. The ultimate aim of this unofficial diplomacy is to develop proposals or to generate ideas, which can be transferred to the official negotiations (Track One) with the aim of contributing to the resolution of a particular conflict.

From the outset, this was the aim of JOCI founders and the Initiative was designed to further this goal. This ambitious objective permeated the design of the project, engagement with key regional and international experts, and advocacy designed to ensure that the product reached key stakeholders. With respect to the latter, this involved the targeted dissemination of the JOCI documents and concepts through a series of conferences and consultations in North America, Europe and, most importantly, Israel, the Palestinian Territories and the neighbouring countries.

A detailed discussion of the somewhat complex concept of transfer is included in this first volume. Suffice it to say, the proposals reached key stakeholders including those in the Palestinian, Israeli and American governments. By the fall of 2013, a formal peace process under US tutelage was underway, and JOCI was able to channel its ideas into this process. As one of the founders of the Initiative noted at the time, by doing so, our work is now complete.

Purpose and organization of the series

Purpose

With the formal completion of the Initiative, the next logical progression was to disseminate the extensive body of work generated by the Jerusalem Old City Initiative to a wider audience.

Three main reasons guide our decision to publish the volumes.

First and foremost, we wish to present to the wider public the Special Regime governance model in its entirety. Until now the proposals remained unpublished and available only to a limited audience of key stakeholders. This approach is in keeping with the traditional practice of Track Two exercises, especially those dealing with highly sensitive areas, and is par for the course for advocacy and transfer strategies. With this publication, however, we hope that the proposals will reach a significantly larger audience, and will contribute positively to the wider conversation on Jerusalem, especially with respect to the longstanding conflict over control and governance of this holy city.

Second, we want to make available the previously unpublished studies that the Jerusalem Old City Initiative commissioned in aid of its work over the past decade. The more than two dozen studies, written largely by our Israeli, Palestinian and international partners, served various functions but all provided a critical source of information and helped to inform the development of the Special Regime governance model. These papers provide historical background and regional perspectives on governance and security matters, as well as on Holy Sites, property, archaeology and economics. Further studies were written to explain how the Special Regime would deal with particularly sensitive issues in the areas of property and archaeology.

Both collectively and individually, these previously unpublished papers are informative and provide important insights into key aspects of the Old City. Publication of these papers will give the readers context in which to understand how the Special Regime idea developed. Each paper in its own right becomes a contribution to the literature on Jerusalem, and will, we hope, be of value to current discussions on Jerusalem, and to the research community for years to come.

Our third and final reason for publishing the series is to provide readers with a detailed academic account of JOCI, an influential and recent Track Two initiative dealing with the Israeli–Palestinian conflict. To date no account of the Initiative has been written and, in the pages which follow, a theoretical and historical milieu is provided in order to contextualize this decade-long project, and in particular, to place it within the literature on conflict resolution and Track Two diplomacy.

These books were designed to appeal to several audiences, from the policy-making community to the various traditions found in academia. With respect to the latter, those that work in the areas of conflict resolution, and the Palestinian–Israeli conflict will find their contents particularly useful. The general public with a strong interest in the Israeli–Palestinian conflict, especially with particular reference to Jerusalem, may also find the volumes of interest.

Organization

At the end of a decade of intensive work on the Old City the Initiative had generated enough material for three books.

The present volume includes a series of studies that place JOCI within its historical setting and the theoretical context of Track Two diplomacy. It then proceeds to present the Initiative's culminating documents, which outline in detail the Special Regime governance model.

The second book, *Governance and Security in Jerusalem: The Jerusalem Old City Initiative,* presents studies that were written for JOCI by our regional and international partners. These include background papers to situate the socio-economic, security and governance conditions in the Old City before proceeding to a series of papers which look at governance options and security studies for a Special Regime. It is worth re-emphasizing that these papers by our Palestinian, Israeli and international partners were highly influential in informing the development of the Special Regime model.

The third and final book, *Contested Sites in Jerusalem: The Jerusalem Old City Initiative,* includes studies by regional and international partners in the areas of Holy Sites, archaeology, property and economics. As with the studies in the second book, the studies on Holy Sites in particular informed the Special Regime model. Further, the papers on archaeology, property and economics were written after the completion of the Special Regime model and were intended to address in depth how a Special Regime would deal with each of these three important areas.

This first book is divided into two parts: the first deals with the theoretical, historical and comparative context, the second presents the Special Regime proposals. Part I includes Chapters 1 through 5, with the first chapter providing the theoretical foundations in which to situate the Jerusalem Old City Initiative. Written by Peter Jones, Professor of Political Science at the University of Ottawa and leading scholar-practitioner of Track Two diplomacy, the chapter defines Track Two diplomacy, provides a succinct historical account of the field, and develops a helpful framework in which to contextualize and critically examine Track Two processes, particularly with respect to the degree of impact such processes have had on resolving conflict.

Using the foundations laid out in Jones' chapter, Chapter 2 provides a historical account of the Jerusalem Old City Initiative, focusing in particular on its origins, its main players, and the process in which the proposals were developed. Written by David Cameron, the Dean of the Faculty of Arts and Social Sciences at the University of Toronto, and a key member of the Governance Working Group and contributing author to two of the three Special Regime documents, the chapter offers readers a first-hand account of the JOCI process and the products developed.

Chapter 3 addresses one of the most fundamental issues in Track Two exercises, that of transferring the ideas developed in unofficial processes to policy makers and negotiators in hopes of influencing and contribution to the outcome of a conflict. Co-authored by Tom Najem, Professor of Political Science at the University of Windsor and Project Manager of JOCI, the chapter provides a first-hand account of how JOCI succeeded in transferring its ideas to a strategic audience, including to the most important actors in the Israeli–Palestinian conflict, thereby reaching levels that would be the envy of many Track Two processes.

Chapters 4 and 5 complete Part I by offering a comprehensive comparative study of the historical impact of Track Two processes on official negotiation (Track One) with respect to Jerusalem. Professor Menachem Klein of Bar Ilan University, who wrote these chapters, is a leading authority on Jerusalem, and has been an active participant in numerous Track Two and Track One processes including those dealing specifically with Jerusalem. The chapters' contents allow for a comparison of the impact of JOCI with those of other Track Two initiatives.

Part II presents the JOCI Documents – the Special Regime governance proposals – in their original form at the time of their completion.

Chapter 6, the first chapter of Part II, contains the *Discussion Document* written by the JOCI Directors in 2005, which laid the basic foundations for the three subsequent publications: The Mandate (Chapter 7), The Governance Document (Chapter 8) and the Security Document (Chapter 9). Collectively, these documents form the nucleus of the Special Regime governance model.

Finally, an epilogue takes stock of the Jerusalem Old City Initiative Special Regime governance model, restating its major contributions (especially on sovereignty, and a third party element) and its utility for future negotiators. It stresses the inherent flexibility of the model and argues that it can be adopted as a whole, or in part. Further, the epilogue states that the model could also be used as a foil to debate and develop other models of governance for the Old City; indeed, a process that is being undertaken by regional and international groups currently working on Jerusalem.[5]

A detailed explanation of the organizational breakdown of the second and third books will be given in their respective introductions.

We wish to make a final point on the organization of these three books, and in particular on how readers could approach them. Despite their massive size, the volumes were organized in a manner that, we hope, will make them accessible to various audiences. The volumes could be read as a whole, or for their individual sections, and in some cases, even individual chapters.

As a whole, the series offers what is perhaps the most comprehensive account of a complex and long running Track Two exercise available, explaining the process through a theoretical, historical and comparative context, and providing not only the finished product (the Special Regime model), but also the numerous studies developed by partners that fed into the development of the final product.

The books can also be read for their individual parts, and as such offer a comprehensive reference tool.

However the reader wishes to approach the work, we hope that in addition to our own governance model, the plethora of studies found in the series will contribute to a greater understanding of the complexity of the issues surrounding Jerusalem's Old City, and the possibilities of addressing them in a manner that will be of benefit to all of Jerusalem's stakeholders.

Notes

1 *The Atlantic* and the S. Daniel Abraham Center for Middle East Peace, 'Is Peace Possible,' last modified 14 November 2011, http://www.theatlantic.com/special-report/is-peace-possible.

2 The other two were the territorial sovereignty model (e.g. Geneva) and the hybrid model – another means of introducing a third party role.

3 See Chapter 3 of this volume for a more detailed account of media coverage of JOCI.

4 See Patrick Martin, 'A Canadian solution to unite the Old City', *The Globe and Mail*, 6 March 2009; Avinash Gavai, 'Ban Ki-Moon speech throws light on Canada-UN relationship', *Embassy*, 19 May 2010; Hilary Leila Krieger, 'Special Regime for sharing J'lem', *The Jerusalem Post*, 6 May 2010.

5 See the conclusion in Chapter 3 of this volume for details.

PART I

The theoretical and historical background to the Jerusalem Old City Initiative (JOCI)

1

TRACK TWO DIPLOMACY AND THE JOCI PROJECT

Some points to look for

Peter Jones

Introduction

'Track Two diplomacy' usually refers to informal processes, often aimed at helping to develop ideas that might assist in resolving conflicts. These processes are frequently carried out by academics or others (such as retired officials) who have some sort of tie to their respective government or national/ethnic leadership. Beyond this, Track Two defies easy categorisation. At some level of abstraction, virtually any process involving private citizens talking about international problems could be considered Track Two. Moreover, many Track Two processes take place in confidence. It is a difficult topic to nail down, much less to subject to critical scrutiny.

This chapter will lay a foundation for the rest of the volume by exploring what Track Two is, where it came from and what the key practical and theoretical questions are surrounding it.[1] As such, the chapter is not so directly concerned with the Jerusalem Old City Initiative (JOCI) as are other chapters in this book. But what this chapter offers is a set of ideas and concepts against which the JOCI project can be compared as to how it was run and why it evolved the way it did.

It should be noted at the outset that there is no set way for any Track Two project to run; there is no template and no 'right and wrong' of how to do Track Two. One of the things that will become apparent in this chapter is that the discipline has evolved through trial and error and is often characterised as much by an *ad hoc* approach as anything else. Case studies are very important to the development of the concepts and the literature and the JOCI project offers an important case for further discussion.

Thus the purpose of this chapter is not to suggest a means whereby JOCI can be 'graded' as to how well it followed an immutable set of Track Two rules. There are no such rules. The objective here is to offer some concepts and ideas which have arisen out of a history of Track Two (and to explore that history) as a means of helping us to use the JOCI experience to further develop our ongoing understanding of what Track Two is and how it works. This chapter thus asks a series of questions about how the JOCI project 'stacks up' against a set of issues which, collectively, define the way in which the field is studied.

Before beginning the discussion, it is worth noting broadly that Track Two finds itself between different traditions of social science. Many elements of the 'realist' school tend to favour explanations of international affairs which stress interest-based bargaining, the competition for power between states and zero-sum games. Social-psychological and constructivist theories tend to stress interpersonal relations, community building and the development of norms.[2] While neither realism nor constructivism is as definitive as presented here, most Track Two is more comfortable in the latter tradition. Track Two tends to stress interpersonal, social-psychological dynamics aimed at increasing each side's understanding of the underlying factors motivating the other's position, and its own, as a tool to open up possibilities for cooperative problem solving. Almost by definition, it is difficult to quantify such processes according to traditional academic research criteria.

Track Two diplomacy: the origins and development of the term[3]

The term Track Two diplomacy was coined in 1981 by Joseph Montville, an American Foreign Service Officer.[4] Montville used the term to denote unofficial conflict resolution dialogues. He was keen to persuade his diplomatic colleagues that such dialogues should be better understood by diplomatic professionals. He defined Track Two as:

> [...] unofficial, informal interaction between members of adversarial groups or nations with the goals of developing strategies, influencing public opinion, and organising human and material resources in ways that might help resolve the conflict.[5]

Importantly, there was no particular magic about the term Track Two diplomacy. Montville merely noted that, if official diplomacy might be called 'Track One', then unofficial attempts to resolve differences might be called 'Track Two'. There is a simplicity to this term, but it also, unfortunately, implies that such discussions could be construed as a form of diplomacy. With very rare exceptions they are not: practitioners of Track Two diplomacy are not diplomats. That title belongs only to those who officially represent their countries.[6] While some Track Two processes may be closely related to, and sponsored by, official diplomacy and while officials may take part in various Track Two processes, in their private capacities, such processes cannot substitute for official interactions between states and should not try to.

Track Two background[7]

It is difficult to pinpoint exactly when Track Two began. General discussions of international affairs by interested public elites began at least before World War I in the form of the various 'peace societies'. In retrospect, much of this was naïve, and would not be considered Track Two by those active in the field today. Following World War II, a private group called 'Moral Rearmament' convened a number of retreats involving prominent German, French and, later, British citizens with the aim of promoting reconciliation between these societies.[8] In the Asia–Pacific region an international non-governmental organisation (NGO) called the Institute of Pacific Relations (IPR) was 'a pioneering channel of unofficial diplomatic dialogue' from 1928 to 1961.[9]

Intensive and ongoing Track Two took place between the superpowers during the Cold War. The Pugwash and the Dartmouth Conferences opened avenues for dialogue on strategic stability and security. Sometimes tacitly encouraged by the governments of the United States of America (US) and the Union of Soviet Socialist Republics (USSR), and occasionally barely tolerated, these dialogues produced ideas which featured in later arms control agreements. They also provided a mechanism whereby leading figures could meet to discuss broader issues.[10]

Most people who are active in the field today believe that what we now largely know as Track Two, in its sense as unofficial facilitated dialogues intended to help develop ways to resolve conflicts, first arose in its present form in the mid-1960s. Professor John Burton, a former Australian diplomat, and colleagues at University College in London and elsewhere convened a process to help resolve a dispute between Malaysia, Singapore and Indonesia. Drawing upon contacts in the region, Burton decided to try to resolve a dispute between the three countries over boundaries. With United Kingdom (UK) government support, Burton invited small teams which had government connections to London for a series of quiet workshops during 1965–1966. Using facilitation techniques designed to draw out all participants on the underlying aspects of the dispute rather than trading exchanges over their official positions, Burton and his colleagues assisted the participants in developing potential solutions. These ideas were subsequently incorporated into an agreement between the countries. Though the exact extent to which the process contributed is debated, it played a role.[11]

Burton and his colleagues labelled their method 'controlled communication'. They believed that it constituted a new method consisting of informal workshops, chaired by a neutral third party who facilitated the protagonists' mutual analysis of problems with the aim of helping them to develop solutions not apparent through traditional diplomatic techniques.[12]

Since Burton's pioneering efforts, an active scholar-practitioner community has arisen.[13] Herbert Kelman, a Harvard-based political psychologist who has been a leading figure in informal discussions between Israelis and Palestinians, ran one of the best known such projects.[14] During the course of his work and research, Kelman and colleagues developed a refinement of Burton's Controlled Communication, which they referred to as 'Interactive Problem Solving'.[15] Kelman defined this model as:

an academically based, unofficial third party approach, bringing together representatives of parties in conflict for direct communication. The third party typically consists of a panel of social scientists that, between them, possess expertise in group processes and international conflict, and at least some familiarity with the conflict region. The role of the third party … differs from that of the traditional mediator. Unlike many mediators, we do not propose (and certainly, unlike arbitrators, we do not impose) solutions. Rather, we try to facilitate a process whereby solutions will emerge out of the interaction between the parties themselves. The task of the third party is to provide the setting, create the atmosphere, establish the norms, and offer the occasional interventions that make it possible for such a process to evolve.[16]

In 1993, Fisher produced a further refinement under the term 'Interactive Conflict Resolution'.[17] Fisher's Interactive Conflict Resolution (ICR) has both a focused and a broad dimension:

[i]n a **focused** manner, Interactive Conflict Resolution is defined as involving small-group, problem-solving discussions between unofficial representatives of identity groups or states engaged in destructive conflict that are facilitated by an impartial third party of social-scientist practitioners. In a **broader** manner, ICR can be defined as facilitated face-to-face activities in communication, training, education, or consultation that promote collaborative conflict analysis and problem solving among parties engaged in protracted conflict in a manner that addresses basic human needs and promotes the building of peace, justice and equality.[18]

The concepts of focused and broader Track Two are an important contribution. They introduce the notion that Track Two can have much broader aims than the immediate resolution of a specific dispute between two parties; that Track Two can be aimed at laying the groundwork for a broader societal reconciliation. These concepts also introduce the notion that the best path to the discussion of a specific conflict may sometimes lie in a wider discussion of relations in an attempt to frame the dialogue differently so that, when the two sides do arrive at the specific issue, they do not do so from entirely different perspectives.

Recurring themes

These concepts, and others, developed what may be termed a classic approach to Track Two. While there are subtle differences, a reading of the various histories and concepts reveals that they tend to share certain characteristics:

- They emphasise small, informal dialogues, which the literature refers to as 'Problem Solving Workshops', between people from the various sides of a conflict, which are usually facilitated by an impartial third party.[19]

- Though the dialogues are unofficial, it is generally expected that the participants will have access to decision makers at home, and/or be able to influence the development of thinking in their societies on the conflict.
- These dialogues are not meant to be meetings where the current positions of the conflicting sides are debated, but rather workshops where the participants step back from official positions to jointly explore the underlying causes of the dispute in the hope of jointly developing alternative ideas.
- These dialogues are ongoing processes, rather than one-off workshops.
- Most practitioners tend to emphasise the value and importance of addressing the deep-seated, psychological aspects of disputes as being at least as important as discussion of any specific differences.
- While not exactly secret, the dialogues are conducted quietly and the so-called 'Chatham House Rule' is applied. This is done in order to create an atmosphere within which outside-the-box thinking can flourish and participants are not afraid to propose and explore ideas that could not be entertained by an official process or one in which exchanges might be repeated in the press.

Such processes can lead to a number of results. Amongst these are:

- changed perceptions of the conflict and the 'other';
- opening new channels for communication between adversaries who had few other means of communicating (and, in some cases, no means of communicating);
- the identification and development of new options for future negotiation;
- in the case of those Track Two dialogues devoted to subjects other than conflict resolution, such as regional security, the creation of communities of experts who have developed and are conversant with possible new approaches to the issue under discussion;
- preparing the ground for the transition of ideas developed in Track Two to the official track; and
- the development of networks of influential people who can work to change views in their countries and regions.

Expanding definitions

Meantime, others have developed models which illustrate different aspects of Track Two. The concept of 'multi-track diplomacy' developed by Diamond and McDonald[20] identifies nine discrete tracks.[21] The authors explore the functions of each and the relationship between them which constitute the system as a whole. At about the same time, a retired US diplomat named Harold Saunders was developing an idea he called 'Circum-negotiation', which also stressed the need to conceive of a peace process as comprised of multiple tracks of dialogue which must interact if true reconciliation and peace is to be achieved, though Saunders believes that this interaction is more organic than the systemic approach favoured by Diamond and McDonald.[22] Saunders went on to develop an idea of 'Sustained

Dialogue', a belief that true reconciliation and peace can only arise from a repeated series of interactions over a long period of time, designed to allow the participants to break down stereotypes and jointly construct more positive images and narratives as a basis for reconciliation.[23]

S.A. Nan and others have developed a concept known as 'Track One and a Half'.[24] This refers to unofficial dialogues, where all or most of the participants from the conflicting sides are officials, or non-officials but acting under something approaching instructions from their respective governments. However, they participate in their private capacities, and rely on an unofficial third party to facilitate the process, usually in strict secrecy. The essential element is that this is close to an official process, but one which the two parties do not wish to refer to as such, often because of issues relating to recognition.

Another approach to the various kinds of Track Two comes from a study of Track Two in the Middle East. Four authors (two Israelis and two Palestinians) divided Track Two into two broad categories: 'hard' Track Two and 'soft' Track Two.[25] Hard Track Two is similar to Track One and a Half: its objective is to try to produce an agreement. Soft Track Two is oriented towards broader discussions aimed at familiarising the two sides with each other, but without necessarily having an expectation of an agreement – though some soft Track Two projects aim at a joint paper or book. In some ways, hard and soft Track Two share characteristics with Fisher's focused and broad dimensions of Interactive Conflict Resolution.

In reality, of course, the development of Track Two has not been linear. Different scholars and practitioners have stressed different aspects of the idea.[26] Some have delved into the psychological aspects of conflict and consequently consider Track Two to be a venue to help those in conflict address deep-seated emotional and psychological issues.[27] These people are not necessarily looking to achieve an agreement (though they are not opposed to finding one, to be sure) but rather aim to set the stage for broad societal reconciliations.[28] Others stress the more realist goal of producing an agreement between the leaderships in conflict as the key objective of Track Two.[29]

Track Two is not without critics. Some officials are concerned that amateurs may damage the diplomatic process, though others hold that Track Two can be a useful adjunct to diplomacy.[30] Some scholars, meanwhile, question whether Track Two is a discipline, arguing that poor analytical standards of what makes successful interventions have created a field which lacks academic credibility and official legitimacy. They also worry that a lack of standards as to what qualities and training the third party must possess raise the spectre of poorly prepared individuals attempting this role and doing damage.[31] Still others, often retired officials, question whether the desire of social scientists to scientifically determine the efficacy of Track Two can ever be achieved in real world circumstances.[32] Lastly, others note that serious study of the field is underway, to the extent that the need which many of the processes have for confidentiality allows.[33]

As this brief exploration of various terms and concepts illustrates, the field of Track Two is a fluid one. The terminology is far from fixed, and the same terms can be used to mean quite different things. For my own purposes, I define the term Track Two diplomacy as: *unofficial dialogues, generally between two antagonistic parties, and often facilitated by an impartial third party and involving individuals with some close connections to their respective official communities, focused on cooperative efforts to explore new ways to resolve differences over, or discuss new approaches to, policy-relevant issues.*[34]

The JOCI project

So what, from all these points and definitions, was the JOCI project? More importantly, what did its third party and regional participants *think* it was and how did this evolve as it went along? Was it so close to the official process as to be an example of Track One and a Half or hard Track Two? Or was it further removed, and therefore more a case of soft Track Two or Fisher's broad Interactive Conflict Resolution? Did the third party see its role in terms of the ideas laid by Kelman in his definition of Interactive Problem Solving, or did they have a different sense of their purpose? How did this evolve as they went along? What objectives did the founders of the JOCI project have at the outset, and how did they change as the project evolved? Did those engaged in the process conceive of their efforts as following a pre-set pattern of how such a project should evolve? Did they look to the literature on Track Two to make determinations of how they should approach issues and problems?

One way to organise thinking around how to evaluate a Track Two project is to consider it in terms of key issues which confront the field. Though there are several of these, the following seem particularly important in evaluating the JOCI process.

Ripeness or readiness?[35]

A first concern is the question of how to determine the optimal moment for a third party to initiate a Track Two process. Much research has gone into the idea of 'ripeness'. This concept holds that there is an optimal moment to intervene when both sides perceive themselves to be in a 'mutually hurting stalemate', but one where they can also perceive a possible way out through compromise.[36] Others have taken ripeness and applied it to a 'cycle' of conflict phases. They have found that specific kinds of Track Two processes are more likely to succeed in the low, rising and declining phases of a conflict, while the high intensity conflict phase tends to be where official diplomacy alone has the best chance of success. They have also found that, in some cases, Tracks One and Two should be utilised in a sequenced manner, whereas simultaneous application is called for in other cases.[37]

Still others, such as Pruitt, argue that the issue is not so much when a conflict may be ripe for resolution, but rather when the participants (or some of them) are 'ready' to begin to talk. Ripeness may thus be more relevant to Track One (or perhaps Track One and a Half, or hard Track Two), while readiness embraces the question of whether credible people are ready to begin informal discussions aimed at exploring ways to reframe the dispute in both practical and psychological terms, as called for in soft Track Two.[38] Bartoli's study of the Community of Sant'Egidio's role in facilitating the talks to end Mozambique's civil war captures the concept of readiness. In his article, 'Mediating Peace in Mozambique', Bartoli explains:

> [i]n the debate over timeliness we tend to underestimate the power of the mediation itself – the transforming power of the experience of adversaries talking with one another and with others in a setting which is conducive to constructive dialogue. Therefore, it is probably useful to say that violent conflicts are always ripe to end. [...] Often the debate over ripeness neglects the fact that there is a very different perception of the same war by rich and poor [...] For the weakest, ripeness is always 'now.'[39]

For the JOCI project, it would be useful to know whether the third party believed at the outset that the situation regarding the Old City of Jerusalem was somehow ripe for a resolution of this issue. If so, why? If not, why not? How did this determination influence the way the project was set up and run? If the sense was more that the project was operating under the aegis of readiness, what were the expectations or hopes of how the project might use the readiness of some to discuss this issue to assist in the creation of ripeness as regards its possible resolution?

Ethics and Track Two

A second area where the JOCI project could shed light on the questions that surround Track Two is the ethical issues and responsibilities which arise in the field. There are several dimensions to the question of ethics. For example, it is often the case that a Track Two process will include representatives of those who have been fighting. Either or both sides will have engaged in questionable activities. Sitting down with such people raises the issue of 'shaking hands with the devil'. Moreover, some of those at the table may be looking for amnesty as part of a settlement. Should a third party facilitate discussions which may help them to achieve this, or which may be a ruse to help achieve other nefarious ends? This is, at the least, distasteful, and, at the most, potentially immoral. And yet, one cannot end a conflict without talking to those involved in the fighting and, more importantly, encouraging them to talk to each other. Much will depend on the specific context of each situation.

Another aspect of ethics is the responsibilities of the third party. Much research has been done on this question.[40] My own list of ethical points which arise from experience as a third party includes:

- *first, do no harm* – you are entering a complex situation where the consequences of mistakes are generally higher for the regional participants than for you; sensitivity, caution and humility are called for and the third party should resist the temptation to use the forum as a vehicle to experiment with different conflict resolution techniques, especially without the informed consent of the regional participants;

- *be in it for the long haul* – it is unfair to persuade those in situations of conflict to come to the table if you do not intend to be there for as long as it takes;
- *you are not there to export your solution, but to help them find their own* – you may have strong views as to how the problem should be solved, but what matters is whether the regional participants can jointly develop *their* own solution and your role is to help them do so, not to foist your ideas onto them;[41]
- *you are not alone* – avoid the tendency to think that your activity is, in itself, going to 'make peace'; real peace is the product of a multi-level, multi-year process of which your activity is likely but a small part;[42] and
- *honesty and right intention* – you must be scrupulously honest with the participants about your background, funding, intentions and what you can deliver.

The participants from the conflict also have ethical responsibilities. Again, my own list would include:

- *respect and listening* – the parties should be prepared to respect each other's right to hold divergent views, and to listen without hectoring or interrupting;
- *maintaining the confidentiality of the process* – in those Track Two processes which require secrecy to succeed, this is a basic ethical and procedural requirement;
- *right intention* – be there because you genuinely want to explore whether a resolution may be possible, not because you want to appear to be willing to consider one, even as you prepare for more fighting;[43] and
- *be honest about what you can deliver* – be honest about whether you think you can bring your leadership or society along rather than raising false expectations.

Did those who structured and ran the JOCI project have a discussion of ethics as such? What were the results? More generally, how did they incorporate ethics into their project framework? Were their expectations in this regard met or were there surprises along the way?

Transfer

A third area of research surrounds the question of how best to ensure the proper 'transfer' of the results of Track Two processes into the official diplomatic realm, or to civil society, depending on the objectives of the Track Two project in question. Thus, transfer means the business of how the results of Track Two dialogues make their way into the official process, and into the broader dialogue in each society. In reviewing the scholarly work on transfer one notes an evolution of thinking that is associated with specific authors who often wrote about personal experiences.[44]

In Burton's first effort in Southeast Asia in the 1960s, transfer was predicated on the assumption that the ideas generated would make their way through to the official process because Burton had included people who were from the official process or had very close links to it. Thus, he spent little time planning for a later transfer of ideas or outcomes to the official process. Burton's concept of transfer held that the ability to get new ideas directly to decision makers was central; if one could get ideas to the key decision makers, then conflicts could be resolved.

Kelman and others began to consider transfer as an issue in the early 1970s. They stated that a central goal of Interactive Conflict Resolution was to influence Track One and acknowledged that transfer was complex and difficult; that Track Two practitioners have to think seriously about and plan for it. Kelman and his colleagues identified two basic elements of transfer: the changes in individual perceptions, attitudes, etc., that the participants in the Problem Solving Workshop (PSW) experience; and how these changes affect the policy-making process on both sides.[45] Kelman developed further ideas on how transfer takes place and identified key ways in which Track Two assists Track One and also transfers its results to Track One:

- development of cadres of people who may take part in future official negotiations;
- provision of specific substantive inputs into a negotiation process, or even discussions about the possibility of negotiations; and
- developing a political environment in which negotiations may be possible.[46]

The problems which PSW participants can have when trying to transfer their new insights to their home audience have come to be known as the issue of 're-entry'. This is defined as the issue of how those who have participated in PSWs, and whose attitudes have been altered by the experience, are affected when they re-enter their own side. The great majority of their compatriots will not have been through the PSW experience and will not have had the opportunity to have their attitudes to the other side transformed. This is true both in terms of re-entry amongst one's professional peers and the re-entry amongst the general public, although the specific issues attending both are different. Will the PSW participants revert to their previous attitudes, or will they attempt to introduce into their domestic debates the notion that change is possible? How can Track Two processes be designed to promote the latter?

Mitchell, writing in the early 1980s, went into the issue of re-entry in detail.[47] He distinguished between two separate, but related, levels of transfer. The first is the question of the internal effectiveness of a PSW process – how the perspectives and views of the participants are changed by the workshop process itself. The second is the question of the external effectiveness of the PSW – how the broader nature and course of the conflict are influenced by the ideas that come out of the PSW and how the participants in the PSW can contribute to this. Mitchell acknowledged that objective factors on the ground influence how much decision makers are prepared to use the results of Track Two, even if they are disposed to do so. This leads to the recognition, alluded to in the fourth of my ethical considerations, that real peace is made as a result of a complex and interlocking web of factors, and that Track Two, however important in getting a dialogue going, is but one of these.

Mitchell also pondered the related question of the ideal relationship between the participants in a Track Two and their governments and its impact on transfer. He noted that, the closer the participants are to their officials, the more likely they will be to be able to transfer the results. But he also noted that such people may be more likely to be influenced by official policy to the point that their ability to 'think outside the box' (to be willing to develop and propose significant changes to existing policy) may also be compromised because they are either afraid to compromise their standing by promoting very different ideas, or simply less able to think differently than the environment they identify so closely with. Conversely, Mitchell argued that people further away from power might well be more willing to develop new and novel ideas for resolving the conflict, but will be less likely to be able to effectively transfer them to officials because they will be regarded as outsiders. This problem, which has also been noted by others who study Track Two,[48] has implications for whom one recruits to participate in such exercises. The ideal are people with close connections to the intended target of transfer, but who are also intellectually and morally prepared to think 'outside the box'. Such people can be rare, however, and so one seeks to recruit a mixture of people who, between them, have access but also include those who will push the overall group along in its consideration of new ideas.

In the late 1990s, Fisher developed a schematic model of transfer.[49] This model depicts the likely lines of transfer between Track Two and key official constituencies. It locates Track Two closer to 'Inter-societal Relations' (civil society) than to Track One, but shows the paths by which Track One actors can be affected by Track Two through the diffusion of ideas from the 'bottom up'. The exact mode of transfer will, of course, depend on the specific circumstances, but Fisher's model represents an important attempt to lay out the key issues and actors. As to exactly how transfer happens, Fisher looked into a variety of mechanisms, from personal contacts between Track Two participants and senior officials, often based on many years of established relations; memos and working papers; and more public approaches, such as op-eds, speeches and interviews.

Fisher's model is thus a useful tool with which to understand transfer dynamics and it has stimulated much follow-on work and consideration of the issue. But its use in reality (as with the use of any political science model in reality) requires an intimate knowledge of the individual parties – their characteristics and asymmetries. It also requires a well-developed sense of the fluid dynamics of the discussions; of the way in which events flow and circumstances change over the life of a project.

Obviously, some of the mechanisms by which transfer is effected are designed to be private and some public, which raises the question of when it is appropriate to break silence. This is a serious matter, as a Track Two intended to try to get official policy to change may regard it as necessary to maintain secrecy in order to give officials time to ponder far-reaching ideas for policy changes in private and without having to respond to public calls for change. On the other hand, in situations where officials are unlikely to be able to change policy, or to want to, a more public transfer strategy may be useful in order to try to generate a groundswell of pressure for change. Fitzduff and Church, in their study of how NGOs affect change on a policy level, refer to strategies aimed at quietly influencing elites as *insider* strategies, while those aimed at influencing a wider audience are *outsider* strategies.[50] In their study of Track Two in the Israeli–Palestinian case, and particularly Track Two aimed at bringing about a change in official positions (or aimed at *insider* audiences as Fitzduff and Church would have it), Agha *et al.* have noted the importance of the existence of a senior official inside the government, whom they call a 'mentor' to the Track Two effort. This is an individual who is willing to shield the participants in the Track Two from criticism of their actions, to act as a buffer between the senior-most Track One leadership and the Track Two (especially in situations where the Track Two deals with an explosive issue), to guide the Track Two participants in understanding what the critical problems are and what the 'traffic will bear' in terms of appetite for change, and to steer the results through the political and bureaucratic maze.[51]

Other key issues have arisen over the years as we have further developed our understanding of transfer. For example, Çuhadar, in a study of how transfer worked in various Israeli–Palestinian Track Two projects,[52] noted that transfer can actually happen in three directions: upwards (to officials); downwards (to civil society); and sideways. The latter observation, which is new, speaks to the idea that Track Two projects can transfer ideas and people to each other, especially in long-standing conflicts where there are likely to have been several Track Twos on similar issues over time. This speaks to a notion that transfer must be considered as a long-term process whereby an accumulation of Track Two projects on a given issue has the effect of inculcating a new way of looking at problems into an influential body of people. This is in contrast to being a discrete and time-limited interaction over the results of a specific Track Two project between the participants and officials.

As to the question of when transfer might be most effective, Capie, writing about Track Two in Southeast Asia, has posited that moments when Track One is looking to take up the ideas proposed by Track Two are actually relatively rare.[53] He identifies such moments as being those of what he calls 'Structural Opportunity' – moments when officials are actively looking for new ideas, often as a result of a crisis (real or perceived). But such moments of structural opportunity are not, in themselves, enough for a Track Two to succeed in getting its ideas across. The Track Two must actually have sound ideas to propose at those moments and it must have influential proponents for those ideas who will be listened to by the officials. In other words, it is necessary for the Track Two to have developed and refined its proposals, and to have prepared a cadre of proponents of those ideas over a lengthy period in order to be ready to take advantage of the moment of structural opportunity when it appears.

Another person who has looked into a specific matter of transfer is Chataway, who looked at the role of the convenor of a Track Two process, sometimes known as the 'third party', in transfer.[54] It is usually assumed that the lead in transfer will be taken by the regional participants in the Track Two, and this is usually the case; after all, they have the regional contacts and local credibility. Chataway found, however, that there are specific circumstances when the third party can be an effective agent of transfer. These circumstances might include instances when the third party has unusual personal credibility with the intended target of the transfer. Or perhaps when the ideas are considered so new that the regional participants look to the third party to take the lead in order to shield them from the negative consequences of the first exposure of a potentially unwelcome idea to its intended audience. In other words, the third party takes upon themselves the risks which may attend putting new ideas onto the agenda, thereby protecting the participants with some of the risks associated with re-entry as was discussed earlier.

Yet another issue identified by those who have looked at the question of transfer in Track Two is known as 'asymmetric transfer'. There are at least two dimensions to this issue. First, there is a question of circumstances in which one of the parties to the dispute has significantly more power than the other. How, in such circumstances can the Track Two project convince the more powerful party to accept the need to consider changes in their policies? In such circumstances, Mitchell believes that the key lies in transfer strategies which seek to persuade the more powerful actor (which Mitchell calls the 'lion') to cost out the future in such a way as to recognise that continuation of the conflict will bring about costs which will eventually grow to unsustainable levels. It may be better in these circumstances to accept the need for change now, while the lion can still dictate (to some extent, at least) the terms of the interaction.[55]

The second aspect of asymmetry and transfer has to do with the problem of how each side can know that transfer on the other side is taking place with the same degree of efficiency as it is on one's own. What if one side has real access to senior decision makers, but the other does not – even though it may claim to? This is a potentially serious problem. If one side convinces its leadership that the other is serious about real change, only to then find out that the other side does not really have the access it claimed to, credibility will vanish and potentially good ideas can be lost. Çuhadar provides specific examples of cases where this has happened, either because of competing channels on one or both sides, or because one side had vastly different access to its decision makers than the other did.[56] It is therefore necessary for the third party to keep a close eye on transfer, even in those cases where the regional participants will take the lead on it.

How did those who ran the JOCI project deal with the issue of transfer? Did they have a plan at the outset, or were they more inclined to let the process take its course and see what could be done when the project had a product? Were they interested in private transfer to the officials (*insider*) or transfer designed to stimulate a more public debate (*outsider*), or had they thought this through? Had they identified the need for mentors and sought out such people? Did they have strategies to identify and deal with issues such as re-entry and asymmetry? Were ideas about transfer updated as the process went along? What criteria were used and why?

Measuring the effectiveness of Track Two

Finally, there is the question of developing ways to measure the success of Track Two. Much thought has been given to this question over the years.[57] Some argue that one cannot assess Track Two without indicators of success against which to judge results; the field needs to establish indicators of what success means and how it is measured.[58] Certainly those who fund projects want to measure the results in some tangible way. Others believe that, while efforts should be made to develop ways of assessing Track Two, highly specific measurements are difficult for most projects, as they do not lead to specific outcomes but are intended to open up new avenues of dialogue. What those dialogues may achieve is hard to discern at the outset. The accomplishment is therefore, to at least some extent, the process itself.

Many issues arise when considering the question of evaluation. For example, there is the issue of why an evaluation is being done; different constituencies may have different reasons for wanting an evaluation done. The funder may be interested in seeing if the money was well spent (though this raises a host of definitional questions in itself – what exactly does 'well spent' mean?). Conflict resolution experts may want to do an evaluation of a project to determine whether different techniques of facilitation might have been more or less effective. Experts on the history of the specific conflict may wish to evaluate what contribution different ideas discussed in the Track Two project made to the development of ways forward, and so on.

Another issue is that of the timescale of the evaluation. In most cases, tangible outcomes of any particular Track Two project may not be apparent until much later, when the ideas generated have filtered into the official process, perhaps through other Track Two dialogues.[59] Of course, some projects do have goals which can be measured – the concept of hard Track Two introduced earlier often relates to quite specific discussions of specific matters. But these are a relative rarity in the field; most often the contributions of a Track Two dialogue will not be felt for years, and only in a diffuse way. How then can any particular Track Two project's contribution be evaluated?

Kelman et al.'s lengthy pre-Oslo Israeli–Palestinian workshops exemplify the challenge posed by the issue of 'measuring' Track Two. Though it would be difficult to trace a linear path between these workshops and Oslo, many Oslo participants had been through the Kelman process and many of the ideas which underlay the Oslo agreement had been developed in the Kelman meetings. It would have been impossible for the years that the Kelman process was underway prior to Oslo to have pointed to specific outcomes that could be 'measured' because it was only after Oslo that analysts could point retrospectively to such a relationship.[60] This is one of the enduring difficulties of the field.

As a practitioner I have found it critical to evaluate each project *on its own terms*. In reviewing the voluminous literature on the question of evaluating Track Two interventions, a number of commonalities emerge from the various methodologies proposed:

- They tend to stress the need for the Track Two project *itself* to establish its own goals and then develop ways to measure them, rather than being measured against goals established by outside agencies;
- They recognise that the projects should be evaluated against their own objectives and methodologies, rather than against different Track Two projects which may be active at the same time on the same issue – this means that each project is sufficiently unique that detailed comparisons between projects are not useful, although generalised comparisons may be possible for descriptive purposes; and
- They recognise that evaluation must take place over time, and that Track Two projects go through different phases, each of which will require a different approach within the overall evaluation process.

This approach requires great intellectual honesty on the part of the organisers and participants in a process. The alternative, attempts by outside agencies, and particularly funders, to introduce cross-cutting criteria which allow different projects to be compared to each other should be approached with great care. Comparisons run the risk of skewing projects towards goals not originating with the participants themselves.

Has the JOCI project been able to measure its impact and effectiveness, or is it too soon? Were there benchmarks for evaluation established at the outset of the JOCI project, and what were they? How were they assessed as the project went along? What might we look for in future years as signposts that the JOCI project has had an enduring impact?

Conclusion

Taken together, the questions explored in this chapter constitute much, though not all, of the research agenda of Track Two diplomacy. My own view is that hard and fast rules in each of these areas that will apply across all cases are not going to be found. But this does not mean that study of specific cases, such as the JOCI project, is without utility. By understanding previous cases, practitioners of Track Two and officials can better understand options for structuring such processes to assist in moving intractable conflicts forward.

In terms of the JOCI project, and of Track Two as it has applied to the issue of Jerusalem generally, it will be interesting to see if lessons can be drawn in each of these areas. But it is also likely that any conclusions drawn will be tentative and subject to reappraisal as time goes forward. This is the nature of the study of Track Two.

Notes

1 For more on these questions see the author's *Track Two Diplomacy: In Theory and Practice* (Stanford, CA: Stanford University Press, 2015); and *Canada and Track Two Diplomacy* (Toronto: The Canadian International Council, 2008).

2 For a brief review of the main theories of international relations see S.M. Walt, 'One World, Many Theories', in *Foreign Policy* (Spring 1998). For a review of how they apply to Track Two see Jones, *Track Two Diplomacy*, Chapter 2.

3 This section is drawn from Jones, *Track Two Diplomacy*, Chapter 1.

4 The term was first mentioned in W.D. Davidson and J.V. Montville, 'Foreign Policy According to Freud', in *Foreign Policy* 45, Winter (1981–82), but is generally attributed to Montville.

5 J.V. Montville, 'Transnationalism and the role of Track Two Diplomacy', in *Approaches to Peace: An Intellectual Map*, ed. W.S. Thompson and K.M. Jensen (Washington, DC: US Institute of Peace, 1991).

6 For more on this argument see Jones, 'Track II Diplomacy and the Gulf Weapons of Mass Destruction Free Zone', in *Security and Terrorism Research Bulletin*, 1 (Dubai: Gulf Research Center, October 2005): 15–17.

7 For more on the background of the field see: Jones, *Track Two Diplomacy*, Chapter 1; R.J. Fisher, 'Historical Mapping of the Field of Inter-active Conflict Resolution', in *Second Track/Citizen's Diplomacy: Concepts and Techniques for Conflict Transformation*, eds. J. Davies and E. Kaufman (Lanham, MD: Rowman & Littlefield, 2002); and C.R. Mitchell, 'From Controlled Communication to Problem Solving: The Origins of Facilitated Conflict Resolution', *The International Journal of Peace Studies*, 6, no. 1 Spring, 2001.

8 Moral Rearmament changed its name to Initiatives of Change International in 2001. More on its history can be found at http://www.iofc.org/en/abt/history. Accessed 21 July 2016.

9 The quote is from L.T. Woods, 'Letters in Support of the Institute of Pacific Relations: Defending a Nongovernmental Organisation', in *Pacific Affairs* 76, no. 4 (Winter, 2003–2004). For more on the IPR see P.F. Hooper (ed.), *Rediscovering the IPR: Proceedings of the First International Research Conference on the Institute of Pacific Affairs* (Honolulu: Centre for Arts and Humanities, University of Hawaii, 1994).

10 See M. Evangelista, *Unarmed Forces: The Trans-national Movement to End the Cold War* (Ithaca, NY: Cornell University Press, 1999); and G.E. Schweitzer, *Scientists, Engineers and Track Two Diplomacy: A Half-Century of U.S.-Russian Inter-academy Cooperation* (Washington, DC: National Research Council of the National Academies, 2004). Pugwash was awarded a share of the 1995 Nobel Peace Prize for its work in promoting disarmament during the Cold War years.

11 See C. Mitchell, 'Ending Confrontation Between Malaysia and Indonesia: A Pioneering Contribution to International Problem Solving', in *Paving the Way: Contributions of Interactive Conflict Resolution to Peacemaking,* ed. R.J. Fisher (New York: Lexington, 2005), 19–40; R.J. Fisher, 'Historical Mapping of the Field of Inter-active Conflict Resolution', in *Second Track/Citizen's Diplomacy: Concepts and Techniques for Conflict Transformation,* eds. J. Davies and E. Kaufman (Lanham, MD: Rowman & Littlefield, 2002), 65–66, especially; R.J. Fisher, *Interactive Conflict Resolution* (Syracuse, NY: Syracuse University Press, 1997), 19–36.

12 For more see A.V.S De Reuck, 'Controlled Communication: Rationale and Dynamics', *The Human Context* 6, no. 1 (1974); and J.W. Burton, *Conflict and Communication: The Use of Controlled Communication in International Relations* (London: MacMillan, 1969).

13 For an overview history of the development of this field see Fisher, 'Historical Mapping'.

14 See H.C. Kelman, 'Interactive Problem-solving: Informal Mediation by the Scholar Practitioner', in *Studies in International Mediation: Essays in Honor of Jeffrey Z. Rubin*, ed. J. Bercovitch (New York: Palgrave MacMillan, 2002). For a comprehensive analysis of Israeli–Palestinian Track Two see, H.S. Agha, A. Feldman, A. Khalidi, and Z. Schiff,

Track II Diplomacy: Lessons from the Middle East (Cambridge, MA: The MIT Press, 2004). For more on H.C. Kelman see Fisher, 'Historical Mapping', 67–68, and Fisher, *Interactive Conflict Resolution*, 56–74.

15 H. Kelman, 'The Interactive Problem-Solving Approach', in *Constructive Conflicts: From Escalation to Resolution,* eds, C.A Crocker and F.O. Kreisberg (New York: Rowman & Littlefield, 1996).

16 H.C. Kelman, 'Interactive Problem Solving as a Tool for Second Track Diplomacy', in *Second Track/Citizens' Diplomacy*, eds, J. Davies and E. Kaufman, 82.

17 R.J. Fisher, 'Developing the Field of Interactive Conflict Resolution: Issues in Training, Funding and Institutionalisation', in *Political Psychology* 14 (1993).

18 Fisher, *Interactive Conflict Resolution*, 7–8, emphasis added.

19 For more on the origins and theory of the Problem Solving Workshop, see Jones, *Track Two Diplomacy*, Chapter 5.

20 L. Diamond and J. McDonald, *Multi-track Diplomacy: A Systems Approach to Peace 3rd ed.* (West Hartford, CT: Kumarian Press, 1996).

21 The nine 'tracks' are: Track One – Government; Track Two – Nongovernment/Professional; Track Three – Business; Track Four – Private Citizen; Track Five – Research, Training, Education; Track Six – Activism; Track Seven – Religion; Track Eight – Funding; Track Nine – Communications and the Media.

22 See H. Saunders, 'Pre-negotiation and Circum-negotiation: Arenas of the Peace Process', in *Managing Global Chaos: Sources of and Responses to International Conflict*, eds. C. Crocker, F.O. Hampson and P. Aall (Washington, DC: United States Institute of Peace Press, 1996).

23 H. Saunders, *A Public Peace Process: Sustained Dialogue to Transform Racial and Ethnic Conflicts* (New York: St. Martin's Press, 1999).

24 For More on Track One and a Half, see: S.A. Nan, D. Druckman, and J.E. Hoor, 'Unofficial International Conflict Resolution: Is There a Track One and Half? Are There Best Practices?' *Conflict Resolution Quarterly* 27, no. 1 (2009); S.A. Nan, 'Track One and a Half Diplomacy: Contributions to Georgia-South Ossetian Peacemaking', in *Paving the Way,* ed. R.J. Fisher (2005); S.A. Nan, *Complementarity and Co-ordination of Conflict Resolution Efforts in the Conflicts over Abkhazia, South Ossetia and Transdniestria* (Ph.D. diss., George Mason University, 1999); and J. Mapendre, *Consequential Conflict Transformation Model, and the Complementarity of Track One, Track One and a Half and Track Two Diplomacy* (Atlanta, GA: The Carter Center, 2000).

25 See Agha *et al.*, *Track II Diplomacy*, 3–5 and *passim* for a discussion of this idea.

26 See Fisher, 'Historical Mapping'.

27 For example, L.W. Doob's research into the psychological aspects of Track Two is prominent in any history of the field. For more see: L.W. Doob, 'A Cyprus Workshop: An Exercise in Intervention Methodology', *Journal of Social Psychology* 94, no. 2 (1974); L.W. Doob, *Interventions: Guides and Perils* (New Haven CT: Yale University Press, 1993); and Fisher, *Interactive Conflict Resolution*, 37–55. In addition to L.W. Doob's work in this area, E. Azar developed the notion that intractable conflicts are based on deep social and psychological divisions between societies which must be reconciled if peace is to be achieved. He called these rifts 'Protracted Social Conflicts' and developed a model of intervention to address the broader needs of reconciliation. See E. Azar, 'From Strategic to Humanistic International Relations', in *Thinking the Unthinkable: Investment in Human Survival*, ed. N. Jamgotch (Washington, DC: University Press of America, 1978). For more on Azar see Fisher, *Interactive Conflict Resolution*, 77–97.

28 For a vision of Track Two as primarily a mechanism for broader reconciliations see J. Davies and E. Kaufman, 'Second Track/Citizen's Diplomacy: An Overview', in *Second Track/Citizens' Diplomacy*, eds. J. Davies, J and E. Kaufman, 1–14.

29 These are often the goals of Track One and a Half and hard Track Two.

30 See C.J. Chataway, 'Track II Diplomacy from a Track I Perspective', in *Negotiation Journal* (July 1998). See also R.J. Fisher, 'Coordination Between Track Two and Track One Diplomacy in Successful Cases of Prenegotiation', in *International Negotiation*, 11

(2006): 65–89. Former US Secretary of State G.P. Shultz comments on how he was somewhat suspicious of Track Two while in office, though he has come to view it differently since leaving government, in his *Foreword* to Jones, *Track Two Diplomacy*, ix.

31 See N.N. Rouhana, 'Interactive Conflict Resolution: Issues in Theory, Methodology, and Evaluation', in *International Conflict Resolution after the Cold War*, eds. D. Druckman and P.C. Stern (Washington, DC: National Academy Press, 2000), and N.N. Rouhana, 'Unofficial Third-Party Intervention in International Conflict: Between Legitimacy and Disarray', in *Negotiation Journal* (July 1995).

32 H. Saunders *et al.*, 'Interactive Conflict Resolution: A View for Policy Makers on Making and Building Peace', in *International Conflict Resolution after the Cold War*, eds. D. Druckman and P.C. Stern (Washington, DC: National Academy Press, 2000).

33 See Fisher, *Interactive Conflict Resolution* and his edited volume *Paving the Way*.

34 The definition appears on page 24 of Jones, *Track Two Diplomacy*.

35 For more Ripeness and Readiness as they relate to Track Two, see Jones, *Track Two Diplomacy*, 66–71.

36 See I.W. Zartman, 'Ripeness: The Hurting Stalemate and Beyond', in *International Conflict Resolution after the Cold War*, eds. D. Druckman and P.C. Stern (2000). Of course, the concept of ripeness is far more sophisticated and nuanced than considerations of space will allow for presentation here.

37 See C.A. Crocker, F.O. Hampson, and P. Aall, 'Multiparty Mediation and the Conflict Cycle', in *Herding Cats: Multiparty Mediation in a Complex World*, eds. C.A. Crocker, F.O. Hampson, and P. Aall (Washington, DC: United States Institute of Peace Press, 2003).

38 For more on 'Readiness' see D.G. Pruitt, 'Readiness Theory and the Northern Ireland Conflict', in *American Behavioural Scientist* (2007): 50, and D.G. Pruitt, *Whither Ripeness Theory?* Working Paper no. 25 (Fairfax, VA: Institute for Conflict Analysis and Resolution, George Mason University, 2005), www.gmu.edu/departments/ICAR/wp_25_pruitt.pdf.

39 A. Bartoli, 'Mediating Peace in Mozambique: The Role of the Community of Sant'Egidio', in *Herding Cats,* eds. C.A. Crocker, F.O. Hampson, and P. Aall, 250.

40 See, for example, Rouhana, 'Unofficial Third Party Intervention', 266–267; L.A. Fast, R.C. Neufeldt and L. Schirch, 'Towards Ethically Grounded Conflict Interventions: Re-evaluating Challenges in the 21st Century', in *International Negotiation* 7 (2002); B. Barry and R.J. Robinson, 'Ethics in Conflict Resolution: The Ties That Bind', *International Negotiation* 7, no. 2 (2002); and 'Conflict Resolution and the Ethics of Intervention', in O. Ramsbotham, T. Woodhouse and H. Miall, *Contemporary Conflict Resolution 3rd Edition* (Cambridge: Polity Press, 2011), 317–331.

41 Though facilitators may sometimes introduce ideas aimed at helping the two sides to develop their own thinking, particularly at the beginning of a process, the objective should not be to get the two sides to adopt a facilitator's preconceived idea of how the conflict should end.

42 Conflicts are resolved by the protagonists, not by those who intervene – however important they are in assisting a dialogue. For an analysis of Track Two as part of a larger peace process, see H. Saunders, 'Pre-negotiation and Circum-negotiation: Arenas of the Peace Process', in *Managing Global Chao*, eds. C. Crocker, F.O. Hampson and P. Aall (1996).

43 Although, in reality, many participants, at least at the outset, will keep all options open.

44 The succeeding paragraphs draw on Jones, *Track Two Diplomacy,* Chapter 6; and R.J. Fisher, 'Introduction: Analysing Successful Transfer Effects in Interactive Conflict Resolution', in *Paving the Way* (2005).

45 H.C. Kelman, 'The Problem Solving Workshop in Conflict Resolution', in *Communication in International Politics*, ed. R.L. Merritt (Urbana, IL: University of Illinois Press, 1972). See also Fisher, 'Introduction: Analysing Successful', 5.

46 H.C. Kelman, 'Contributions of an Unofficial Conflict Resolution Effort to the Israeli-Palestinian Breakthrough', in *Negotiation Journal* 11, no. 1 (1995).

47 C.R. Mitchell, *Peacemaking and the Consultant's Role* (Westmead: Gower, 1981). See also Fisher, 'Introduction: Analysing Successful', 5.

48 See, for example, H.C. Kelman, 'Evaluating the Contributions of Interactive Problem Solving to the Resolution of Ethnonational Conflicts', *Peace and Conflict* 14 (2008): 33; Fisher, *Interactive Conflict Resolution*, 202–204. For the implications of this problem to Track Two in the Asia Pacific region see H.J. Kraft, 'The Autonomy Dilemma of Track Two Diplomacy in Southeast Asia', *Security Dialogue* 31, no. 3 (2000).

49 Fisher, *Interactive Conflict Resolution*, 202.

50 See M. Fitzduff and C. Church (eds), *NGOs at the Table: Strategies for Influencing Policies in Areas of Conflict* (New York: Roman and Littlefield, 2004).

51 For more on 'mentors' and Track Two see, Agha *et al.*, *Track II Diplomacy*, 4–6.

52 See E. Çuhadar, 'Assessing Transfer From Track Two Diplomacy: The Cases of Water and Jerusalem', *Journal of Peace Research* 46, no. 5 (2009).

53 See D. Capie, 'When Does Track Two Matter? Structure Agency and Asian Regionalism', *Review of International Political Economy* 17, no. 2 (2010).

54 See C. Chataway, 'The Problem of Transfer from Confidential Interactive Problem Solving: What is the Role of the Facilitator?' *Political Psychology* 23, no. 1 (2002).

55 See C.R. Mitchell, 'Persuading Lions: Problems of Transferring Insights from Track Two Exercises Undertaken in Conditions of Asymmetry', *Dynamics of Asymmetric Conflict* 2, no. 1 (2009).

56 Çuhadar, 'Assessing Transfer From Track Two Diplomacy', 647 and 650.

57 For more on the issue see: Jones, *Track Two Diplomacy,* 154–164; Jones, 'Filling a Critical Gap or Just Wasting Time?'; H. Lewis, 'Evaluation and Assessment of Interventions', in *Beyond Intractability,* eds. G. Burgess and H. Burgess (Boulder, CO: Conflict Research Consortium, University of Colorado, September 2004), last modified July 2, 2008, www.beyondintractability.org/essay/evaluation; P.C. Stern and D. Druckman, 'Evaluating Interventions in History: The Case of International Conflict Resolution', *International Studies Review* 2, no. 1 (2000): 33–63; C. Church, and J. Shouldice, *The Evaluation of Conflict Resolution Interventions: Framing the State of Play* (Letterkenny, Ireland: Browne, 2002); C. Church and J. Shouldice, *The Evaluation of Conflict Resolution Intervention, PART II: Emerging Practice and Theory* (Letterkenny, Ireland: Browne, 2003); M. Deutsch and J.S. Goldman, 'A Framework for Thinking About Research on Conflict Resolution Initiatives', in *The Handbook of Conflict Resolution: Theory and Practice 2nd ed.*, eds. M. Deutsch, P.T. Coleman, and E.C. Marcus (San Francisco, CA: Jossey-Bass, 2006), 825–848; H.C. Kelman, 'Evaluating the Contributions of Interactive Problem Solving to the Resolution of Ethnonational Conflicts', *Peace and Conflict* 14 (2008): 29–60; E. Çuhadar, B. Dayton, and T. Paffenholz, 'Evaluation in Conflict Resolution and Peacebuilding', in *Handbook of Conflict Analysis and Resolution*, eds. D.J. Sandole, S. Byrne, I. Sandole-Staroste, and J. Senehi (New York: Routledge, 2009): 286–299; and T.P. D'Estree, L.A. Fast, J.N. Weiss, and M.S. Jakobsen, 'Changing the Debate about "Success" in Conflict Resolution Efforts', in *Negotiation Journal* (2001): 101–113.

58 A point forcefully made by N.N. Rouhana in both his articles cited earlier in this chapter.

59 For more on this line of reasoning see Saunders, 'Pre-negotiation and Circum-negotiation' and D.D. Kaye, *Talking to the Enemy; Track Two Diplomacy in the Middle East and South Asia* (Santa Monica, CA: RAND Corp, 2007): 105–107.

60 For more on H.C. Kelman's process, which was not the only Israeli–Palestinian process active before the Oslo Process, but which is widely regarded as one of the most influential, see Kelman, 'Evaluating the Contributions of Interactive Problem Solving'. The fact that the Oslo Process has not lived up to its promise – or, perhaps more accurately, that the Oslo participants have not lived up to *their* promises – is not a reflection on Kelman's process.

References

Agha, H.S., A. Feldman, A. Khalidi, and Z. Schiff. *Track II Diplomacy: Lessons from the Middle East.* Cambridge, MA: MIT Press, 2004.

Azar, E. 'From Strategic to Humanistic International Relations'. In *Thinking the Unthinkable: Investment in Human Survival*, edited by N. Jamgotch. Washington, DC: University Press of America, 1978.

Bartoli, A. 'Mediating Peace in Mozambique: The Role of the Community of Sant'Egidio'. In *Herding Cats: Multiparty Mediation in a Complex World*, edited by C.A. Crocker, F.O. Hampson, and P. Aall. Washington, DC: United States Institute of Peace Press, 2003.

Barry, B. and R.J. Robinson. 'Ethics in Conflict Resolution: The Ties That Bind'. *International Negotiation* 7, no. 2(2002): 137–142.

Burton, J.W. *Conflict and Communication: The Use of Controlled Communication in International Relations*. London: MacMillan, 1969.

Capie, D. 'When Does Track Two Matter? Structure Agency and Asian Regionalism'. *Review of International Political Economy* 17, no. 2(2010): 291–318.

Chataway, C.J. 'The Problem of Transfer from Confidential Interactive Problem Solving: What is the Role of the Facilitator?' *Political Psychology* 23, no. 1(2002): 291–318.

Chataway, C.J. 'Track II Diplomacy from a Track I Perspective'. *Negotiation Journal* 14, no. 3 (1998): 269–287.

Church, C. and J. Shouldice. *The Evaluation of Conflict Resolution Intervention, PART II: Emerging Practice and Theory*. Letterkenny, Ireland: Browne, 2003.

Church, C. and J. Shouldice. *The Evaluation of Conflict Resolution Interventions: Framing the State of Play*. Letterkenny, Ireland: Browne, 2002.

Crocker, C.A., F.O. Hampson and P. Aall, 'Multiparty Mediation and the Conflict Cycle'. In *Herding Cats: Multiparty Mediation in a Complex World*, edited by C.A. Crocker, F.O. Hampson and P. Aall. Washington, DC: United States Institute of Peace Press, 2003.

Çuhadar, E., B. Dayton and T. Paffenholz. 'Evaluation in Conflict Resolution and Peacebuilding'. In *Handbook of Conflict Analysis and Resolution*, edited by D.J. Sandole, S. Byrne, I. Sandole-Staroste and J. Senehi. New York: Routledge, 2009.

Çuhadar, E. 'Assessing Transfer From Track Two Diplomacy: The Cases of Water and Jerusalem'. *Journal of Peace Research* 46, no. 5(2009): 641–658.

Davidson, W.D. and J.V. Montville. 'Foreign Policy According to Freud'. *Foreign Policy* 45 (1981–82): 145–157.

D'Estree, T.P., L.A. Fast, J.N. Weiss and M.S. Jakobsen. 'Changing the Debate about "Success" in Conflict Resolution Efforts'. *Negotiation Journal* 17, no. 2(2001): 101–113.

De Reuck, A.V.S. 'Controlled Communication: Rationale and Dynamics'. *The Human Context* 6, no. 1(1974): 14–80.

Deutsch, M. and J.S. Goldman. 'A Framework for Thinking About Research on Conflict Resolution Initiatives'. In *The Handbook of Conflict Resolution: Theory and Practice 2nd Edition*, edited by M. Deutsch, P.T. Coleman and E.C. Marcus, 825–848. San Francisco, CA: Jossey-Bass, 2006.

DiamondL. and J. McDonald. *Multi-track Diplomacy: A Systems Approach to Peace 3rd Edition*. West Hartford, CT: Kumarian Press, 1996.

Doob, L.W. *Interventions: Guides and Perils*. New Haven, CT: Yale University Press, 1993.

Doob, L.W. 'A Cyprus Workshop: An Exercise in Intervention Methodology'. *Journal of Social Psychology* 94, no. 2(1974): 161–178.

Evangelista, M. *Unarmed Forces: The Trans-national Movement to End the Cold War*. Ithaca, NY: Cornell University Press, 1999.

Fast, L.A., R.C. Neufeldt and L. Schirch. 'Towards Ethically Grounded Conflict Interventions: Re-evaluating Challenges in the 21st Century'. *International Negotiation* 7, no. 2 (2002): 185–207.

Fisher, R.J. 'Coordination Between Track Two and Track One Diplomacy in Successful Cases of Prenegotiation'. *International Negotiation* 11, no. 1(2006): 65–89.

Fisher, R.J. (ed.) *Paving the Way: Contributions of Interactive Conflict Resolution to Peacemaking.* New York: Lexington, 2005.

Fisher, R.J. 'Historical Mapping of the Field of Inter-active Conflict Resolution'. In *Second Track/Citizen's Diplomacy: Concepts and Techniques for Conflict Transformation*, edited by J. Davies and E. Kaufman. Lanham, MD: Rowman & Littlefield, 2002.

Fisher, R.J. *Interactive Conflict Resolution.* Syracuse, NY: Syracuse University Press, 1997.

Fisher, R.J. 'Developing the Field of Interactive Conflict Resolution: Issues in Training, Funding and Institutionalisation'. *Political Psychology* 14, no. 1(1993): 123–138.

Fitzduff, M. and C. Church (eds) *NGOs at the Table: Strategies for Influencing Policies in Areas of Conflict.* New York: Rowman and Littlefield, 2004.

Hooper, P.F., editor. *Rediscovering the IPR: Proceedings of the First International Research Conference on the Institute of Pacific Affairs.* Honolulu: Centre for Arts and Humanities, University of Hawaii, 1994.

Jones, P. *Track Two Diplomacy: In Theory and Practice.* Stanford, CA: Stanford University Press, 2015.

Jones, P. *Canada and Track Two Diplomacy.* Toronto: The Canadian International Council, 2008.

Jones, P. 'Track II Diplomacy and the Gulf Weapons of Mass Destruction Free Zone'. In *Security and Terrorism Research Bulletin* 1. Dubai: Gulf Research Center, October 2005.

Kaye, D.D. *Talking to the Enemy; Track Two Diplomacy in the Middle East and South Asia.* Santa Monica, CA: RAND Corp, 2007.

Kelman, H.C. 'Evaluating the Contributions of Interactive Problem Solving to the Resolution of Ethnonational Conflicts'. *Peace and Conflict* 14, no. 1(2008): 29–60.

Kelman, H.C. 'Interactive Problem-Solving: Informal Mediation by the Scholar Practitioner'. In *Studies in International Mediation: Essays in Honor of Jeffrey Z. Rubin*, edited by J. Bercovitch. New York: Palgrave MacMillan, 2002.

Kelman, H.C. 'The Interactive Problem-Solving Approach'. In *Constructive Conflicts: From Escalation to Resolution*, edited by C.A. Crocker and F.O. Kreisberg. New York: Rowman & Littlefield, 1996.

Kelman, H.C. 'Contributions of an Unofficial Conflict Resolution Effort to the Israeli-Palestinian Breakthrough'. *Negotiation Journal* 11, no. 1(1995): 19–27.

Kelman, H.C. 'The Problem Solving Workshop in Conflict Resolution'. In *Communication in International Politics*, edited by R.L. Merritt. Urbana, IL: University of Illinois Press, 1972.

Kraft, H.J. 'The Autonomy Dilemma of Track Two Diplomacy in Southeast Asia'. *Security Dialogue* 31, no. 3(2000): 343–356.

Lewis, H. 'Evaluation and Assessment of Interventions'. In *Beyond Intractability*, editors G. Burgess and H. Burgess. Boulder, CO: Conflict Research Consortium, University of Colorado, September 2004. Last modified July 2, 2008. http://www.beyondintractability.org/essay/evaluation. (Last Accessed: 26 April 2016.)

Mapendre, J. *Consequential Conflict Transformation Model, and the Complementarity of Track One, Track One and a Half and Track Two Diplomacy.* Atlanta, GA: The Carter Center, 2000.

Mitchell, C.R. 'Persuading Lions: Problems of Transferring Insights from Track Two Exercises Undertaken in Conditions of Asymmetry'. *Dynamics of Asymmetric Conflict* 2, no. 1(2009): 32–50.

Mitchell, C.R. 'Ending Confrontation Between Malaysia and Indonesia: A Pioneering Contribution to International Problem Solving'. In *Paving the Way: Contributions of Interactive Conflict Resolution to Peacemaking*, edited by R.J. Fisher, 19–40. New York: Lexington, 2005.

Mitchell, C.R. 'From Controlled Communication to Problem Solving: The Origins of Facilitated Conflict Resolution'. *The International Journal of Peace Studies* 6, no. 1(2001): 59–67.

Mitchell, C.R. *Peacemaking and the Consultant's Role.* Westmead: Gower, 1981.

Montville, J.V. 'Transnationalism and the Role of Track Two Diplomacy'. In *Approaches to Peace: An Intellectual Map*, edited by W.S. Thompson and K.M. Jensen. Washington, DC: US Institute of Peace, 1991.

Nan, S.A., D. Druckman and J.E. Hoor. 'Unofficial International Conflict Resolution: Is There a Track One and Half? Are There Best Practices?' *Conflict Resolution Quarterly* 27, no. 1(2009): 65–82.

Nan, S.A. 'Track One and a Half Diplomacy: Contributions to Georgia-South Ossetian Peacemaking'. In *Paving the Way: Contributions of Interactive Conflict Resolution to Peacemaking*, edited by R.J. Fisher. New York: Lexington, 2005.

Nan, S.A. 'Complementarity and Co-ordination of Conflict Resolution Efforts in the Conflicts over Abkhazia, South Ossetia and Transdniestria'. Ph.D. diss., George Mason University, 1999.

Pruitt, D.G. 'Readiness Theory and the Northern Ireland Conflict'. *American Behavioural Scientist* 50, no. 11(2007): 1520–1541.

Pruitt, D.G. *Whither Ripeness Theory?* Working Paper, no. 25. Fairfax, VA: Institute for Conflict Analysis and Resolution, George Mason University, 2005. www.gmu.edu/depa rtments/ICAR/wp_25_pruitt.pdf. (Last Accessed: 26 April 2016.)

Ramsbotham, O., T. Woodhouse and H. Miall. *Contemporary Conflict Resolution 3rd Edition.* Cambridge: Polity Press, 2011.

Rouhana, N.N. 'Interactive Conflict Resolution: Issues in Theory, Methodology, and Evaluation'. In *International Conflict Resolution after the Cold War*, edited by D. Druckman and P.C. Stern. Washington, DC: National Academy Press, 2000.

Rouhana, N.N. 'Unofficial Third-Party Intervention in International Conflict: Between Legitimacy and Disarray'. *Negotiation Journal* 11, no. 3(1995): 255–270.

Saunders, H. *et al.* 'Interactive Conflict Resolution: A View for Policy Makers on Making and Building Peace'. In *International Conflict Resolution after the Cold War*, edited by D. Druckman and P.C. Stern. Washington, DC: National Academy Press, 2000.

Saunders, H. *A Public Peace Process: Sustained Dialogue to Transform Racial and Ethnic Conflicts.* New York: St. Martin's Press, 1999.

Saunders, H. 'Pre-negotiation and Circum-negotiation: Arenas of the Peace Process'. In *Managing Global Chaos: Sources of and Responses to International Conflict*, edited by C. Crocker, F.O. Hampson and P. Aall. Washington, DC: United States Institute of Peace Press, 1996.

Schweitzer, G.E. *Scientists, Engineers and Track Two Diplomacy: A Half-Century of U.S.-Russian Inter-academy Cooperation.* Washington, DC: National Research Council of the National Academies, 2004.

Stern, P.C. and D. Druckman. 'Evaluating Interventions in History: The Case of International Conflict Resolution'. *International Studies Review* 2, no. 1(2000): 33–63.

Walt, S.M. 'One World, Many Theories'. *Foreign Policy* 110(1998): 29–46.

Woods, L.T. 'Letters in Support of the Institute of Pacific Relations: Defending a Nongovernmental Organisation'. *Pacific Affairs* 76, no. 4(2003–2004): 611–621.

Zartman, I.W. 'Ripeness: The Hurting Stalemate and Beyond'. In *International Conflict Resolution after the Cold War*, edited by D. Druckman and P.C. Stern. Washington, DC: National Academy Press, 2000.

2

THE JERUSALEM OLD CITY INITIATIVE

An analytical history of the product

David Cameron

Introduction

The aim of this chapter is to give an account of the origins and unfolding of the Jerusalem Old City Initiative, focusing on its turning points and critical features, and its distinctive policy-formation approach.

JOCI fits into the general category of Track Two Middle East peacemaking efforts and, more specifically, Track Two efforts that relate specifically to Jerusalem and the Old City. Peter Jones in this volume offers a helpful discussion of Track Two diplomacy, particularly in the Middle East. While acknowledging the looseness of the notion, Jones points out that it typically involves informal processes (but not, in fact, diplomacy) undertaken by unofficial, non-governmental actors aimed at generating ideas to assist in the resolution of what is usually a two-party conflict. It 'tends to stress interpersonal, social-psychological dynamics aimed at increasing each side's understanding of the underlying factors motivating the other's position, and its own, as a tool to open up possibilities for cooperative problem solving'.[1]

Our discussion of JOCI will proceed as follows. After briefly introducing the architects of JOCI we will describe how it came into being and its early activities. Then we will outline the unfolding of the project itself, dividing the account into the following phases:

- Phase 1 – to December 2005 – preparing the discussion document
- Phase 2 – to November 2007 – preparing the security document
- Phase 3 – to November 2008 – preparing the governance document
- Phase 4 – to February 2010 – preparing the mandate document

We will conclude the chapter with a consideration of what has been accomplished.

For economy of presentation, we are defining the main phases of the project by reference to the preparation of the chief JOCI documents, but in reality the process was not nearly so tidy and linear as this representation might lead the reader to believe. For much of the life of JOCI, there was recurrent discussion about what other topics needed to be included – an exploration of the constitutive narratives of Palestinians and Israelis, a major examination of Holy Sites (within and possibly outside the walls of the Old City), an exploration of the political economy of the Old City and the Holy Basin. The ultimate shape of the project, as is reflected in this chapter, was not clear until well along in JOCI's life. The series of research and advisory papers commissioned by JOCI attests to the wide range of issues and topics canvassed at various points in the project. In addition, the next stage in the JOCI process was typically embedded in the latter part of the previous stage and emerged organically out of it; for example, work leading to the preparation of the governance document began 11 months prior to the completion of the security document.

It should be remembered as well that the overall process itself – which entailed repeated trips to the region, extensive consultations with a wide group of influential Israelis and Palestinians, and the production of successive drafts of any given document – typically dealt with more than one subject at a time. So the Jerusalem Old City Initiative is properly understood, not as a tightly organized enterprise that sequentially produced a series of documents, but rather as a fluid process, defining itself as it went, involving discussions and debate, research and policy work, published material, advocacy, and communication activity – all of it produced over time in successive iterations.

It is worth noting that I am not only the author of this chapter on the Jerusalem Old City Initiative, but also one of its active participants. I was invited to become a member of the Governance Working Group (GWG) in the autumn of 2006 and have been actively involved in it and in the preparation of the mandate paper since that time. It cannot, then, be expected that I will approach the recounting of this experience with the degree of distance typical of an uninvolved scholar or researcher. This chapter is an account of the JOCI experience, as understood by one of its participants. It is based on a review of the project archives[2] and a number of interviews with Michael Bell, Mike Molloy and John Bell – the architects of this initiative, whom I will often refer to as the troika; Tom Najem – then Chair of the Department of Political Science at the University of Windsor and manager of the initiative; and Ambassador Arthur Hughes – key participant in the security, governance and mandate processes. This chapter has been reviewed for accuracy with all of the above, in addition to consultation with John de Chastelain and Roy Berlinquette, key members of the security team.[3]

The architects of the project

The architects of the Jerusalem Old City Initiative are former Canadian diplomats – John Bell, Michael (Mike) Molloy and Michael Bell.

Michael Bell was, for most of the life of the project the Paul Martin (Sr.) Senior Scholar for International Diplomacy at the University of Windsor. Formerly the Chair of the Donor Committee of the International Reconstruction Fund Facility for Iraq, he spent 36 years in the Canadian Department of Foreign Affairs, serving as Ambassador to Jordan (1987–1990), Egypt (1994–1998), and Israel (1990–1992 and 1999–2003). He has also been Director of the Department's Middle East Relations Division (1983–1987) and Director General for Central and Eastern Europe (1992–1994). He retired from the public service in 2003.

Michael J. Molloy is an adjunct professor at the University of Ottawa's Graduate School of Public and International Affairs, and a former senior official at the Canadian Department of Foreign Affairs and at Citizenship and Immigration Canada. His involvement in Middle East affairs includes his roles as Canada's Ambassador to Jordan (1996–2000), Special Coordinator for the Peace Process (2000–2003) and Senior Advisor to the Canadian delegation to the Refugee Working Group in the peace process (1992–1996). Molloy has also served as Director General for Refugee Affairs at Immigration Canada (1989–1992) and Director General, Citizenship and Immigration Operations in Ontario (1994–96). He served in Tokyo, Beirut, Minneapolis, Geneva, Amman (twice), Damascus and Nairobi. He also retired from the public service in 2003.

John Bell is the Director of the Middle East and Mediterranean Program and Eurasia Program at The Toledo International Centre for Peace (CITPAX). He is the former Middle East Director for Search for Common Ground, a global conflict resolution NGO. He too is a former Canadian diplomat who served as a political officer at Canada's embassy in Cairo (1993–1996) and a member of Canada's delegation to the Refugee Working Group in the peace process (1992–1993). As a United Nations diplomat he was Political Advisor to the Personal Representative of the Secretary-General of the United Nations for southern Lebanon (2000–2001).

The origins of the project

Michael Bell and Mike Molloy met for lunch in Ottawa in the autumn of 2003. They had both retired in the summer of that year and had talked about working together on a project that would capitalize on their experience and interest in the Middle East. In the preceding three years, as Canadian Peace Process coordinator, Molloy had been exposed to a number of Track Two initiatives and had been impressed with their ability to address topics that were too sensitive for official intervention. Neither was clear on what they should do; they discussed the possibility of doing some work on borders, on a customs union, or on water management, but in their discussions they gradually began to focus on Jerusalem.

Jerusalem was obviously a critical issue in the Middle East conflict – manageable in scope, not technical in character – and Bell and Molloy believed that there was an opening or opportunity for some useful work to be done. They were surprised and, as former diplomats, disappointed that in preparation for the talks at Camp David in 2000, neither the Americans nor either of the parties to the talks, had sufficiently anticipated the challenges of Jerusalem. In 2003, the topic was too hot for Israeli or even US State Department people to work on seriously, and, while the Palestinians had Jerusalem experts in their Negotiation Support Unit, they were focused primarily on building up the Palestinian case.

Bell and Molloy invited John Bell to Ottawa in December 2003 to join the project. All three had worked together on the Multilateral Refugee Working Group, and the two Bells had served together in Cairo. John Bell, having completed a UN assignment in southern Lebanon, was in Toronto. The three settled fairly quickly on Jerusalem as the project focus and, at that meeting, went some distance towards defining the core elements of the project. It would address the Old City and possibly the surrounding Holy Basin and the Holy Sites therein; it would attend to the symbolic and spiritual dimensions of the conflict; and it would emphasize what they termed a 'needs-based' approach. Everyone knew what each side to the conflict *wanted*; the three believed that what was less known and little studied was what the respective *needs* were. The three were acutely aware that there was an element of risk in three outsiders choosing to tackle one of the hard-core issues in one of the world's most significant and intractable conflicts.

The initial idea was to examine issues and policy possibilities both within the walled city and in the Holy Sites beyond; the enterprise was at first called the Holy Basin Project. However, as the troika reflected further on the matter, they realized that there were notable advantages in restricting the project to the Old City. It had walls and thus an unequivocal definition of borders and territory; most of the Holy Sites – and the most important of them – were concentrated within the walls of the Old City; and it was a space within which Palestinians and Israelis were living in close and intense proximity. With the Temple Mount/Haram al-Sharif at its core, the walled city was at the very centre of the Israeli–Palestinian conflict.

The troika realized that they did not want to form an organization to house the project and face the transactional and administrative responsibilities attendant upon the management of such a project. They thus decided to locate JOCI at the Munk Centre at the University of Toronto, where Michael Bell was then a Senior Fellow. The decision to lodge the project with an existing organization – first in the Munk Centre and subsequently (from August 2005) in the Political Science Department at the University of Windsor – turned out to be of great benefit to the project because professional project standards, particularly financial management, could be provided by the host organizations without consuming large amounts of the time of the troika. The Human Security Fund at DFAIT awarded JOCI a grant, which permitted the first phase of the project to go forward. Dr. Marketa Evans, then the Executive Director of the Munk Centre, worked with the project and was helpful in providing both logistical support and project advice, pushing the team to clarify its plans and approach.[4]

The university link proved to be very important in the region because the troika were able to present themselves as former diplomats now doing quasi-academic research, which made it easier in many cases for their regional interlocutors to participate. What was in substance a policy and political process could be presented as a kind of research enterprise. Without the university association, it would have been tricky to have had two former Canadian ambassadors travelling around the region, poking their noses into highly sensitive Palestinian–Israeli issues. At the same time, the profile and reputation of Michael Bell and Mike Molloy in the region helped to ensure that people would answer their telephone calls and open their doors.

Early stages

The early stages of the project were characterized by reading, research and information gathering; project definition; initial fundraising; and regional consultations.

The DFAIT grant financed two long, hard trips to the Middle East – in May and September of 2004 – during which the troika had an opportunity to test out ideas and approach, solicit views, and explore the possible participation of various Israelis and Palestinians in the initiative. The project was beginning its work at a particularly troubled moment in Palestinian–Israeli relations: the Second Intifada was just winding down; Israeli politics was roiling with then Prime Minister Ariel Sharon's announcement in December 2003 of the government's unilateral Gaza disengagement plan; the separation barrier was under construction; Hamas leader, Sheikh Ahmed Yassin was assassinated on 22 March 2004; and finally, Yasser Arafat died in November of that year.

Each mission was two–three weeks long, and the troika met with somewhere around 100 people. The *Discussion Document* (December 2005), which grew out of these initial consultations, lists 144 people whom the group consulted – Palestinians, Israelis and internationals. Typically, the three of them would have five–six meetings each day. At the end of each day, they met to review what they had learned from the discussions and to prepare notes. At the time of the May mission, the troika was still thinking about working on the Old City and the Holy Basin, but as they drove around the Holy Basin, they realized the formidable security challenges associated with the broader approach and gradually scaled the project back to addressing the walled city exclusively. They were already thinking about a Special Regime of some sort by that point and were using the Geneva Accords as a foil.

Meetings during the May visit were crucial in confirming that they were onto something important and that their tentative approach had merit. Among many other meetings, the one with Gilead Sher – a busy lawyer who was the co-chief negotiator at the Camp David and Taba meetings – was telling. Sher expressed strong interest in the ideas presented by the troika, giving the latter an important boost of confidence at the time.

Between trips, the group had a study completed of all previous proposals for Jerusalem. They were encouraged to see how often previous attempts had suggested a Special Regime, or a special arrangement, or an international system of some sort, though no one appeared to have developed the idea extensively.

The troika came back from that first trip thoroughly saturated with information and ideas. After a short break, they, along with Marketa Evans, spent two tough days in Toronto working through the issues. They confirmed that they would restrict their approach to the Old City and that they would look to develop some sort of Special Regime. They began to think about a Governance Board of some kind. They had been subjected to vigorous questioning on the matter of sovereignty and recognized that they would need to find some way through that thicket of conflicting claims. The Geneva proposal to divide sovereignty inside the Old City was not persuasive to them because of the deep instability it would entail, but they realized that their project would have to address the matter in some fashion.

By the time of their second trip in the autumn of 2004, they had received further financial support, this time from the International Development Research Centre (IDRC). IDRC officials pushed them on their methodology, contending, among other things, that they needed to do a literature review, and suggested the commissioning of research papers which could feed into the policy-making process in which they were engaged. These ideas, particularly the latter, became an important dimension of the project overall.

Except for a few forays, the group stayed away from hardliners on both sides. It made no sense to them to seek to involve Hamas, which would have no interest in the goals of the project; the same thinking applied to the Israeli right wing, and for the same reason. Apart from that, they tried to reach everyone who worked on the subject, and were fairly successful in doing so. It was clear, after the two trips, that there was growing interest in the region in what the troika was doing. The Palestinians, with whom they interacted, while cautious, nevertheless were willing to continue their discussion with the team and encouraged them to proceed with its work. On the Israeli side, the Jerusalem Institute for Israel Studies, for example, expressed real interest, in part, it seemed, because of JOCI's extensive contact with Palestinians, something the JIIS at that time lacked.

Phase 1 – to December 2005: preparing the discussion document

A Chatham House meeting in November 2004 proved to be very helpful in advancing the work of JOCI. Mike Molloy had worked with Chatham House earlier in his career and was impressed with both their analytical rigor and their Track Two expertise. He asked them to set up a meeting of experienced people to advise the group on how they might proceed. The troika indicated the approach they were gradually developing and the Middle East Group at Chatham House organized the meeting at Minster Lovell in the Cotswolds. Chatham House brought together an impressive group of people with experience in Northern Ireland and the Balkans, relating to peace-building and post-conflict justice challenges, plus experienced soldiers who could speak to the security issues that would have to be dealt with in any peace arrangement for Jerusalem. The soldiers emphasized the importance of intelligence in the maintenance of security in troubled regions and the need to build public support from the ground up. The group also included Mick Dumper, from the University of Exeter, who has written extensively about Jerusalem. These discussions were very helpful in identifying a number of the key priorities, such as security, and in helping to shape the overall approach the team would utilize.

It was about this time that two things became evident. First of all, through trial and error, the team had settled on the method it would employ to do its work. As one of the troika said: 'test, test, test: consult, consult, consult'. A triangle of tools was developed and has been used throughout the project: a) continual consultation and discussion with actors in the region, sometimes without a precise agenda, sometimes with a draft document in hand, and usually in one-on-one meetings or in small groups of just two or three; b) the commissioning of research studies, undertaken chiefly by regional actors; and c) occasional larger meetings, bringing together Israelis, Palestinians and foreign actors. The triangle of tools did two things: it improved and refined the quality of the work the project produced; and it engaged regional actors in the life and work of the project, helping them to think through the issues in a non-threatening environment, and giving them something of a stake in its process and output. Just as the Canadian academic affiliation helped to establish the *bona fides* of the troika, so the commissioned research reports gave regional participants a non-controversial means by which they could participate in politically sensitive discussions.

A second thing became apparent at this point: the team had jelled. The three members of the core team had strong personalities, and often-conflicting ideas, but, by the early part of 2005, they had learned how to work together effectively, although not without occasional arguments, and had found themselves playing usefully congruent roles. Mike Molloy was the planner and chaired many of the meetings; he kept his eye on the process and on the overall progress being made. Michael Bell focused more on the substance of the work and was vigilant in testing and assessing the ideas and proposals that were being imported into the project. John Bell, particularly after he joined the NGO, Search for Common Ground, and moved to Jerusalem in February 2005, provided an indispensable regional presence, working closely with local actors, gathering their views and concerns, testing their tolerances, making sure the evolving project worked on the ground. John Bell's diplomatic skills, Lebanese background and fluency in Arabic were especially important in sustaining good relations with the Palestinians involved in the project. He was able to provide not only logistical support but the critical policy sensitivity that grew out of living day-to-day in the region.

By the summer of 2005 the team knew that they needed to set something of their own down on paper. By then they had accumulated several commissioned research studies, and in August, with the project relocated to the University of Windsor, they submitted a proposal to CIDA's Network for Peace fund to permit them to hold a conference and to establish more explicitly a network of interlocutors. In anticipation of what was to become the Istanbul meeting, the troika drafted their *Discussion Document*. The writing took place betweenSpecial Regime Court of Appeals August and October and was ready for publication just prior to the December 2005 Istanbul meeting. There had been some internal discussion about whether to hold off publication until after the meeting, but it was decided to proceed, in part, because the document was by design open and porous, and it invited comments on issues rather than stipulating positions.

The Jerusalem Old City Initiative Discussion Document: New Directions for Deliberation and Dialogue was published as a Munk Centre for International Studies Briefing in December 2005. Deliberately tentative, raising questions and exploring options, rather than asserting positions or declaring conclusions, the paper represented the state of development of the project, now called the Jerusalem Old City Initiative. It acknowledged the central position of sovereignty in the debate about the fate of the Old City, but sought to shift the focus to a consideration of possible practical arrangements that would address the needs of the parties to the conflict and offer a sustainable regime over the long term. This needs-based, bottom-up approach, it was suggested, might yield a practical institutional framework for governance, law and security, as well as a potential role for the international community, that would meet the social, property ownership, economic, political, religious and spiritual needs of the inhabitants of the Old City and of the larger Palestinian and Israeli communities. The approach, in the view of the authors, would be consistent with either a divided sovereignty model, along the lines of the Geneva Accords, or an indefinite postponement of the sovereignty issue in the Old City. The paper ends by saying that the Jerusalem Old City Initiative aims 'to encourage movement to the negotiating table by creating a network involving Israelis, Palestinians and serious third parties' to:

- create and disseminate knowledge about the Old City and the key negotiating issues;
- propose creative solutions to some of these critical issues;
- promote public education and engagement designed to improve mutual understanding;
- promote practical projects to improve living conditions in the Old City.

Prior to the Istanbul meeting, the administrative home of the JOCI project had shifted from the Munk Centre at the University of Toronto to the Department of Political Science at the University of Windsor. Michael Bell was taking up a position at Windsor as the Paul Martin (Sr.) Senior Scholar for International Diplomacy, and the Department was chaired by Professor Tom Najem, a Middle East specialist, so it made sense for JOCI to relocate there. The move also allowed for the creation of a more suitable organizational structure. Najem became the fourth member of the JOCI management team as the project's manager, responsible for academic standards and publications, grants and other fundraising, budget preparation, and overall accountability. Windsor gave the project strong support from then on, including financial backing when it was critically needed. As a consequence of this transition, both Marketa Evans of Munk and Tom Najem attended the Istanbul meeting.

The troika approached the Istanbul meeting – which included a group of two dozen people, predominantly prominent Israelis and Palestinians ('the A team', as one of those present put it) – with some trepidation. They anticipated a good deal of challenge and criticism, but, instead, found that the participants were surprisingly interested in talking about the substantive issues and ideas. The main item on the agenda was the *Discussion Document*. Participants appreciated the fact that the *Document*'s authors were humble and open to ideas. In addition to the *Discussion Document*, several background papers were presented. These included an architectural presentation on the Damascus Gate, which led to a full-fledged JOCI study on the Jaffa Gate; a presentation on legal and security issues; a discussion of the cultural background of the conflict; and a presentation on next steps, entitled *What to Focus On and How to Get There: Priorities, Projects, Studies, Processes.*

The Istanbul discussions were important for two reasons: they validated the work that the project had been doing and they clearly identified security as the next big item on the JOCI agenda. Furthermore, the meeting gathered the 'A teams' of Jerusalem experts on both sides for the first time since serious negotiations had been going on, before the Second Intifada. This, in itself, was an achievement for the JOCI effort. Going into the Istanbul meeting, the project directors were facing the dilemma about what to do next: governance, Holy Sites, property ownership, economic and social needs, a legal framework – there was a long list of possible priorities. At Istanbul, however, there was unanimity among the Palestinians and the Israelis: security should be the first priority. Without a foundation of confidence on questions of security and non-violence, it was felt, there was little prospect of any other elements of a Jerusalem settlement being addressed satisfactorily. Istanbul was important for another reason, too. Mark Bailey, Director General of Foreign Affairs for the Middle East and North Africa, attended and formed a strongly favourable view of the project and its potential, and was able to convince sceptics in Ottawa that JOCI merited support. DFAIT proved to be the most loyal and consistent supporter of JOCI; without the Department's support over many years it is unlikely that the project could have succeeded.

Phase 2 – to November 2007: preparing the security document

Prior to initiating Phase 2 the troika decided that Michael Bell would manage the activities of the Security Working Group (SWG) while Mike Molloy would take responsibility for Governance. John Bell, now located in Jerusalem would coordinate with Israeli and Palestinian participants and keep the dialogue going between visits and meetings.

On the basis of the strong message from the Palestinian and Israeli participants at Istanbul, the JOCI team began in early 2006 to tackle the issue of security. They decided that a serious study of the issue, conducted by people with expertise in the field, was needed, and that this work, as usual, should be done in close, continuing consultation with relevant Israelis and Palestinians. The core security group was recruited and composed of: John de Chastelain, former Chief of the Canadian Defence Staff and Chief Arms Decommissioner for Northern Ireland; Roy Berlinquette, a former Deputy Commissioner of the RCMP and a participant in the redesign of the Northern Ireland Police Service; and an American, retired Ambassador Arthur Hughes, formerly Director General of the Multinational Force and Observers in Sinai and an Adjunct Scholar at the Middle East Institute in Washington. Michael Bell asked de Chastelain, whom he knew, to participate. Berlinquette was suggested by a DFAIT officer. Hughes' name surfaced in the course of discussions Molloy and Michael Bell had in Washington with the Director of the Middle East Institute; as a result, he was invited to the Istanbul meeting, and then to join the Security Working Group.

By the time the security group began their work, the basic assumptions of the JOCI model were sufficiently clear that they could form the foundations upon which the security architecture would be constructed. It was assumed that the security arrangements for Jerusalem would be part of a comprehensive peace agreement between the Palestinians and the Israelis, which would establish a Special Regime for the Old City, treating it as a single unit under a single administrator with executive authority.

The security team developed its ideas through a series of consultative missions to the region during which they reviewed commissioned papers on various aspects of the issue and received verbal and written advice. On the Israeli side the group of security advisors included Pini Meidan-Shani, Peri Golan, Reuven Berko and Moty Cristal. Colonel Jibrin al-Bakri and Yasser Dajani provided expertise on the Palestinian side. Nazmi al-Jubeh and Daniel Seidemann helped the team develop an appreciation of the history and day-to-day reality of the Old City and the Holy Sites, both within and outside the walls. Issa Kassassieh and several very senior Palestinian officials offered advice and encouragement during the visits the team made to Ramallah. Internationally, the team benefitted from the advice of members of the RCMP, the Police Service of Northern Ireland and the EU Coordinating Office for Palestinian Police Support. Members of Canada's Department of Foreign Affairs offered ongoing assistance as well, as they did throughout all stages of the JOCI project.

A July 2006 workshop at Durham University, in England, proved to be critical to the JOCI project in general, as well as to the SWG, although the workshop did not unfold as intended. It was meant to be a major gathering of Israelis, Palestinians and international participants, but the 25 June 2006 abduction of Gilad Shalit, a soldier in the Israel Defence Forces, by Hamas, caused a crisis during which the Palestinians were unable or unwilling to travel. Since the Palestinians would not be attending the Durham workshop, the meeting planners determined that it did not make sense to go ahead with Israeli but not Palestinian representation, so the session was reconstituted with a smaller group of participants in the JOCI process, predominantly from outside the region. The project was running out of money; with the Canadian Conservative Party now in office as a result of their election victory in January 2006, it was less clear how the new Canadian government would view JOCI's work. It was a moment of great uncertainty for the project. Nevertheless the meeting at Durham turned out to be a difficult but very important event.

In addition to the JOCI team (the troika and Tom Najem), the three SWG members, as well as Daniel Kurtzer, a former US Ambassador to Israel and Egypt and a Princeton University professor, attended. In a very frank and freewheeling discussion, a series of topics were addressed, most of them related to security matters. Among them were: the general political context; an examination of Old City maps, the foundation of the security force's authority, security implications for governance and law, management of the gates to the Old City, funding questions, and an action plan.

Because of the absence of the full slate of Palestinians and Israelis, a candid self-evaluation of the process and results so far was possible. The participants realized that the effort to establish regional working groups on different topics was not working well; they were very difficult to organize and manage, and very often key participants would not or could not show up at scheduled meetings because of political developments on the ground. The JOCI team realized that it would be more effective to give people contracts to do the work that needed to be done; in that case, you were dealing with only one or possibly two people, and, if they were being paid for a service, it was likely that they would pay more attention to what was needed and when. In addition, one-on-one or virtually one-on-one consultations were better than bigger gatherings; they were easier to arrange and the project's interlocutors spoke in this context with a candour that could not be matched in the larger sessions. Thus the project methodology was further refined.

If the opportunity to make some midcourse corrections was one of the real benefits of Durham, another arose from Dan Kurtzer. It was Kurtzer who put forward the idea of a 'rolling draft', an informal document that would evolve over time, which listed in tentative and summary form the common understandings that had been reached to date in the project. This proved to be very helpful when the project moved to the governance stage of its work. Kurtzer sketched out, in very summary form, what the document might look like.

One significant challenge for the Security Working Group, voiced by a number of people, was how to combine security with the easy movement of Israeli and Palestinian citizens and others into and out of the Old City. Given the JOCI model, the gates of the Old City could become international border crossings. How could one reconcile the requirements of state security with the necessity of residents moving back and forth through the gates in the course of their daily lives? Or tourists and pilgrims, entering the Old City from the Israeli side, but wanting to go out the Palestinian gates to visit the Garden of Gethsemane and other Holy Sites in Palestine, and then go back to Israel by the same route? A failure to crack this nut would seriously compromise the credibility of the security proposals and undermine the viability of the developing JOCI model.

To address this question, the project recruited two young architects to do an intensive study of one of the gates – the Jaffa Gate – and propose a model that would address these concerns. Yehuda Greenfield-Gilat and Karen Lee Bar-Sinai, the two authors, completed an 80 page report in May 2007 which demonstrated how a relatively unobtrusive security facility could be built next to the Jaffa Gate that could process as many as 1,000–1,200 people per hour, into and out of the Old City via the Jaffa Gate, the maximum numbers under normal usage. They also showed how, with an additional but more obtrusive facility, double that number could be handled during 'massive population events'. Similar arrangements could be made at the other Old City gates.

The SWG, along with their interlocutors in the region, wrestled with a number of other key issues. Should there be an Old City police force, or a multilateral Police Service? Should there be Israeli and Palestinian police in the Old City and should they be armed? How long should the proposed security arrangements be expected to last? How would the Holy Sites be protected and who would protect them? Then there were more technical matters to sort out relating to training, the size of the force, and the question of integrated units. As the group met and talked with Palestinians and Israelis the answers to these questions gradually became clear, and are reflected in their report, the *Jerusalem Old City Security Assessment*.

A JOCI planning session was held in Windsor on 19th and 20th of September 2006 to coordinate the work of the SWG with the other emerging dimensions of the project. Art Hughes and Roy Berlinquette reported on the security work, and then there was a preliminary discussion of the planned Governance Working Group and what the scope of its mandate would be. As priority areas, the group identified: the specification of the mandate of the Jerusalem Special Regime; its functions and jurisdiction; its organizational structure; and the legal framework and related legal issues. Two other potential areas of study, which had been considered possibilities for some time, were also discussed: a possible project on narratives and cultural realities; and a possible study of the political economy of the Old City. There were, however, concerns raised about proceeding with either at that time. With respect to the narrative-culture proposal, there were doubts about what JOCI could usefully add to this debate and concern about whether such a project would assist in the JOCI search for middle ground or deepen the division between participating Israelis and Palestinians. With respect to the political economy idea, the point was made that this was likely to be a touchy subject, and that it might prove to be very difficult, not to say expensive, to carry out economic studies effectively in Jerusalem. As a result neither of these possible projects was initiated.

Over the course of the fall and winter of 2006–2007, the Security Working Group met frequently on its own, and engaged in extensive consultations in the region. Between the meetings there was a continual e-mail exchange of ideas. De Chastelain took responsibility for putting together a rough first draft of their report – which he called his 'straw man' – and this was circulated to Hughes and Berlinquette towards the end of March. After incorporating their input, the group sent the draft to the troika for review. Its basic shape held through to the ultimate publication of the report eight months later. This period involved extensive discussions with the Palestinian and Israeli participants in the security exercise and with others, both in the region and in Canada. The consultations culminated with a major session held in Istanbul in October 2007 involving the three members of the SWG, two of the troika (Michael Bell and John Bell), Tom Najem, and the

Israeli and Palestinian interlocutors with whom the group had worked most closely: Jibrin al-Bakri, Reuven Berko, Moty Cristal, Yasser Dajani, Manuel Hassassian and Pini Meidan-Shani. The Istanbul meeting reviewed such questions as the presence of Palestinians and Israelis in the Old City police force, the mandate of the proposed Old City Police Service, and entrance and exit from the Old City.

It was acknowledged and understood that the Security Assessment was a document reflecting the best judgement of the Jerusalem Old City Initiative, and not a consensus document reflecting the views of all who had been involved. The authors of the report noted that, from their reading of the papers produced by the Palestinians and Israelis and their consultation with both communities, there was not full agreement with the proposals contained in the *Jerusalem Old City Initiative Security Assessment*. They stated, however, their belief that the differences could be resolved and an effective security system for the Old City could be accomplished. A virtually final version of the *Security Assessment* was circulated 10 days after Istanbul and the document was published on 15 November 2007. It was released in revised form on 27 February 2008, with a slightly altered Annex A.

After its publication in November, Michael Bell and John de Chastelain joined Art Hughes in Washington on two occasions to convey the substance of the report and the rationale to staff at the Department of State, the National Security Council, Department of Defense and the CIA. The group also met with Congressional staffers and others.

The thinking reflected in the *Jerusalem Old City Initiative Security Assessment* was carried forward and ultimately embedded in the work of the GWG. This is not surprising, given that at a very early stage in the JOCI operation, broad choices were made about the nature of the model of governance that was to be proposed. That broad-gauge understanding then animated the work of both the security and the governance teams. In addition, Art Hughes participated as a member of both working groups, helping to establish coherence between the two efforts. Finally, the troika took a vigorous interest in what each of the working groups was doing and, in fact, offered direction and input all along the way.

Phase 3 – to November 2008: preparing the governance document

From very early on, the troika knew that a major part of this project was the need to address the question of how the Old City would be governed within the framework of a Special Regime. As early as September 2006, they began to scope out what would be involved in getting this part of the project done.

A work plan was put together in the course of the fall for the GWG. As stated in the document,[5] the aim for the GWG was to 'examine the options for a governance structure, possibly for a specified period (e.g. 15 years), that would involve a third party presence and mechanisms for Palestinian and Israeli input and participation'. It spoke of the appointment of an administrator with executive authority – 'an internationally reputed person nominated by the Quartet and acceptable to both parties, supported by a Council of Israelis and Palestinians'.

The document also spoke both of the issues to be addressed and of the process for moving the work forward. The issues included: the mandate of the Special Regime, its Source of Authority, its jurisdiction, its functions or scope of responsibility, and its structure. As for the process, it foresaw working with 'a team of Israelis, Palestinians and international experts in an iterative process, building on the work already produced to deepen knowledge and understanding through a process of meetings and studies to yield detailed governance options no later than December, 2008'.

During this period, the JOCI management team also identified the people they wanted to have as the core members of the GWG. They were: Art Hughes, who gradually shifted the focus of his JOCI work to governance, and increasingly became the overall project's Washington coordinator; Jodi White, then President of the Public Policy Forum; Marshall Breger, professor at the Columbus School of Law at the Catholic University of America; Michael Dumper, professor of Middle Eastern Studies at Exeter University; and David Cameron, professor and chair of the Department of Political Science at the University of Toronto. Breger and Dumper had been involved in JOCI before, as had Hughes; of the three, Hughes was most heavily and most constantly involved, while Marshall Breger participated more occasionally and as circumstances permitted, and Mick Dumper actively engaged from the beginning until April 2009. Lara Friedman, Government Relations Director for Americans for Peace Now, while not formally a member of the governance team, attended many of the meetings in Canada. She played a key role in helping to shape the governance discussion paper after the consultations had been completed. White and Cameron were new to the project. They were introduced to JOCI and to some of the people involved at a meeting in Ottawa, held on 15 January 2007, which focused primarily on security matters. Molloy took a hands-on approach as chair of the Governance Working Group, planning and chairing all of its meetings. The other members of the troika were fully involved throughout the process.

During the first GWG visit to the region in March 2007 to begin consultations, Michael Bell suggested to Cameron and White that they might consider developing a rolling draft of the sort Kurtzer had sketched out in Durham in July 2006. Working at the American Colony Hotel between meetings and consultation sessions, White and Cameron began to assemble what came to be known as *The Guiding Assumptions*. Starting as a document of three–four pages, the rolling draft grew to 14 pages by the end of the year and contained the main elements that would appear later in the Governance Document. The November version, for example, contained a foreword, a map of the Old City, an executive summary, and the following main sections: introduction, rationale, premises, Source of Authority, role of the administration, role of the parties, security requirements, holy sites, coordination, legal and regulatory frameworks, political economy and conclusion. The rolling draft proved to be an extraordinarily useful tool to try out ideas, assess the level of consensus on particular points, and test vocabulary and nomenclature without putting people on the spot or forcing them into defensive posture. Successive versions were distributed to the JOCI interlocutors in Palestine and Israel, and shared with officials in London and Washington. The rolling draft became more detailed and more substantial as time went on, as the comments and advice of those who reviewed it, including the London Caucus, were incorporated into the text. Ultimately it underpinned the *Mandate Paper and Governance Discussion Document* (see below).

As with the security component of the project, JOCI commissioned several research, information and policy papers, this time on the Holy Sites, dispute resolution, and aspects of governance in the Old City. These were reviewed as they became available and their findings fed into the governance discussions. In the course of 2007, there were half a dozen meetings of the GWG in Ottawa and the Middle East. By the end of that year, the group was ready to begin preparation of the governance discussion document.

The active preparation of that document was begun at a meeting of Mike Molloy, Michael Bell, Jodi White, Art Hughes and David Cameron. Molloy had assembled a 16-page rough draft composed of part of the Guiding Assumptions rolling draft, sections of the relevant research papers that the project had commissioned, pieces of his own writing, and other sources. At the start of the meeting, the group worked its way through a dozen key issues and principles that needed to be settled as a part of the drafting process. It then reviewed the rough draft, identified the soft spots, and assigned responsibility for further drafting to each member of the group. Towards the end of the meeting, there was an attempt to sketch out an organizational chart for what was then being called the Special Governance Authority. It was agreed that each member would submit his or her drafting suggestions to Molloy by 10 January 2008 who would bring it all together in a single paper for the meeting of a larger group at Windsor on 20–21 January 2008.

In attendance at the subsequent Windsor meeting were the troika and all members of the GWG. Molloy had produced what he called *Governance Discussion Document, Draft Minus 1, 18 Jan 08*. The 24-page draft reflected the contents of the Guiding Assumptions paper and was filled with questions, notes to the participants, and tentative assignments of further writing tasks. This was the document from which the final version grew. To ensure that the group was aware of some of the detailed input it had received in the course of the previous 12 months, Molloy provided a document called the *Governance Research Grid*, which displayed, in reference to the key elements of the governance document, the findings contained in the papers prepared by Israeli and Palestinian research teams. Finally, a volume of background material was provided to the members of the GWG, which contained the Guiding Assumptions rolling draft as of November 2007, two papers on the Holy Sites, and the Palestinian and Israeli governance research papers mentioned above. There was vigorous and wide-ranging discussion at Windsor, both about the substance of the discussion document and about its organization and presentation.

Perhaps the most important idea was the deceptively simple question about the Special Regime idea posed by Shira Herzog: were we looking at a Special Regime because of the nature of the *place* or because of the *people* who live there? According to Molloy who was chairing the meeting, this was a pivotal moment. A number of Israeli interlocutors were urging that the Special Regime should be a 'polis' or city state that would be responsible for a broad swath of issues affecting the lives of the inhabitants, essentially creating something close to a new citizenship. Others advocated what they called 'Special Regime light', a minimalist approach focused very tightly on Holy Site security. It became clear to a number of the participants that the Special Regime had everything to do with the extraordinary spiritual/nationalist attributes of the place and little to do with the mix of inhabitants. This insight became the test by which functions and responsibilities were either included under the Special Regime's mandate or left to the Israeli or Palestinian authorities.

Another important contribution to the process of thinking through the governance model emerged from a group referred to as the London Caucus, which met at the Washington Mayfair Hotel in London in November and December 2007. It arose out of a desire by some of the key regional players to pin down the main principles of the project and also create a useable policy document for dissemination to decision makers to begin the process of familiarizing them with JOCI's concepts. This small and close knit group was comprised of the troika and Moty Cristal, Gilead Sher and Pini Meidan-Shani on the Israeli side and Manuel Hassassian and Yasser Dajani along with a senior political figure on the Palestinian side. It was a rare occasion to assemble individuals of that calibre from both sides to tackle the hardest nut in the conflict, the Old City. As a result, the discussions of the London Caucus over the course of two meetings went a long way toward refining the language that describes the Special Regime and its basic principles, in a manner that satisfied both sides. The three-page document that emerged from an intensive discussion of the Guiding Assumptions paper contained language that served as a point of reference during later periods of reassessment and consolidation regarding key matters, including sovereignty, mandate, scope and purpose of the Special Regime.

Between the January 2007 Windsor meeting and the completion of the *Governance Discussion Document* in November 2008, there were a half dozen meetings in Windsor, Ottawa, London, Jerusalem, Ramallah and Madrid. There was the usual combination of team drafting sessions and consultations with Palestinians and Israelis on successive versions of the paper, with a view to gaining the broadest basis of acceptance of the document when it ultimately appeared and averting any surprises for the regional interlocutors. Hard issues had to be resolved in the course of these meetings. Most vexing were the following interrelated set of questions: How active ought the parties to be in the Governance Board? What role does the governance board play in the day-to-day operations of the Old City? What are the scope and authority of the Special Regime's Chief Administrator? How are the interests and aspirations of the residents of the Old City communicated to the Chief Administrator? More generally, how ought the lines of accountability in this system to be designed? Regional participants in the process and members of the JOCI team debated these matters vigorously both as the Guiding Assumptions were being developed and while the discussion document was being prepared.

By the time it was released in November 2008, the discussion document had grown to 48 pages, complete with a map and organizational charts. Starting with an overview of the proposed Special Regime, it lays out the proposed governance structure, the functions of the Special Regime, and the financial and economic dimensions of the arrangements.

The security and policing arrangements had been well worked out by the Security Working Group and they were fitted into the proposal of a Special Regime without too much difficulty or controversy. The guiding approach for the management of the Holy Sites was fairly clear as well; they would be left as much as possible to the traditional forms of community management that currently prevailed in the Old City while the critical role of the Special Regime would be the maintenance of peace and security in the Old City.

On balance, I think, it is fair to say that the ultimate choices relating to the structuring of the Special Regime were made with the principles of sustainability and workability uppermost in mind, tempered with the notion that the Special Regime should focus on the friction-generating features of the Old City (place) and leave the lives of the inhabitants (people), as much as possible, under the authority of the two states. The Geneva model of divided sovereignty was vulnerable on these points, in the judgement of the JOCI participants. It was assumed that the Special Regime would be put in place in an atmosphere of scant trust and limited mutual confidence. It was therefore important to ensure that the Special Regime was endowed with sufficient authority and autonomy that it could weather the storms that would inevitably break out en route. The Old City Board would have third-party international representation to keep the parties honest; it would be responsible for holding the Chief Administrator accountable for the implementation of the treaty provisions, but would have limited authority to intervene in the day-to-day management of the Old City.

Once his or her roles and responsibilities were established, the Chief Administrator would possess clear authority to administer the Old City on behalf of the parties, but only in the specific areas assigned. The administrator's primary role would be to keep the peace, and a professional Police Service composed of international members would be created to support this central objective. The other major role would be to see to the day-to-day practical well-being of the inhabitants and visitors to the Old City. The residents of the Old City, Israeli and Palestinian, would exercise their democratic rights as citizens within the framework of their respective states, but would not enjoy democratic rights in respect of the Special Regime itself; there would be no elected municipal council or Old City legislature. All of this was done with an eye to making the system work.

Consultations over these complex issues with the main interlocutors intensified through the spring and early summer of 2008 until both Palestinian and Israeli partners encouraged the team to compose a draft based on the consultations. The draft was passed back and forth a few times between the governance team and the troika over the summer. The team looked forward to polishing the paper over the fall when word came that members of the new US Administration's transition team were asking about the Initiative. The JOCI team went into high gear and the final version, *Governance Discussion Document: A Special Regime for the Old City of Jerusalem* was published on 8 November 2008.

Phase 4 – to February 2010: preparing the mandate document

As far back as March 2008, while the JOCI governance team and the troika were wrestling with defining the respective roles and responsibilities of the Old City Governance Board and the Chief Administrator, Art Hughes began raising the need for the project to articulate a specific mandate for the Old City Chief Administrator that might be embedded in the comprehensive peace treaty between the parties that would set the system up. In an e-mail dated 25 March 2008, Hughes put it this way: 'A lot of our effort has been to find a way to set up a governance structure that will make the Chief Administrator (CA) strong and relatively independent, without continuous ongoing interference by the Parties, but with legitimacy and accountability.' His solution was to propose 'a strong and very, very detailed mandate included in the Treaty and Associated Documents that would be the CA's instructions, responsibilities, obligations, authorities and rights. As part of the Treaty, the mandate would come directly to the CA from the Parties and comprise their commitment to the OCSR [the Old City Special Regime] and CA in a very clear and public way. This would also reinforce the Parties' vested interests in working to ensure success of the OCSR.'

During the final months as the governance discussion document was being completed, this contention began to make itself felt among the members of the governance team and the troika, leading to the conclusion that there was one more major piece of work to be done. Art Hughes and David Cameron were assigned to take the lead on this in late 2008, and produced a document dated 12 December 2008, in which the rationale for the initiative was laid out:

- 'The heart of the Special Regime is a Chief Administrator for the Old City with real powers and authorities assigned him by Israel and a new state of Palestine with their full commitment and support, also underpinned by the international community perhaps by a Security Council resolution.'
- 'The key to an effective Chief Administrator is a mandate that articulates in internationally binding form, as a part of the Treaty package, the powers, authorities and immunities assigned and granted him and his staff by the Parties jointly.'
- 'A clear and comprehensive mandate will help maximize the likelihood of success of a Special Regime. A model mandate will clarify to the Parties early-on the extent and nature of their joint commitment required to a Special Regime to ensure that it will work.'

The document indicated the areas that would need to be covered by the mandate statement:

1. Definition of the Special Regime, broadly put, its responsibilities and geographic limits.
2. The creation of an Old City Board by which the Parties appoint the Chief Administrator, receive his reports and provide oversight.
3. The appointment, role, responsibilities, authorities and powers of the Chief Administrator (including his ability to change laws, to create and hire staff and promulgate internal regulations) and also those reserved by the Parties to themselves.
4. The facilities, rights and immunities granted by the Parties to the Special Regime, its Chief Administrator, his staff and direct contractors.
5. Organization of the main bodies and elements of the Special Regime, e.g. technical staff for city services, Police Service.

Serious work on the mandate statement began in the early months of 2009. Hughes and Cameron hired then University of Toronto doctoral student, Luc Turgeon,[6] to gather material about relevant international cases to see whether there were any useful lessons to be identified. Turgeon provided information on the arrangements for the Saar Basin and the Free City of Danzig, both created by the Treaty of Versailles, the unimplemented efforts to establish a Free Territory of Trieste after World War II, the discussion relating to the internationalization of Jerusalem in the 1940s, and the regimes developed for Mostar and Kosovo arising out of the collapse of the former Yugoslavia. Hughes reviewed the structure and approach of several treaties relating to Palestine and Israel so that a familiar format could be established. Hughes took the lead in the early drafting.

Two features particularly characterized the work as it developed in the first half of 2009. First, it seemed useful to divide the content into two categories: a general statement of the critical elements that would go into the treaty itself; and a more detailed articulation of the provisions that would be located in an annex to the treaty. Second, Hughes and Cameron drafted the mandate statement in the treaty and the annex in language appropriate for use in the actual treaty document itself. Each of these features, as we will see, was discarded as the work moved forward later in the year.

The usual practice of drafting, circulating, testing and re-drafting proceeded during the early months, with telephone conferences, e-mail exchanges, a visit to the region in the middle of June, and a face-to-face get together of the troika, the mandate drafting team, as well as Tom Najem, Roy Berlinquette and Dan Kurtzer at the Royal York in Toronto on 15–16 July 2009. Perhaps the most critical meeting relating to the preparation of the mandate statement took place at the Mayfair Hotel in London, England, in mid-August. The troika and the mandate drafters (Cameron and Hughes) attended, with Molloy in the chair. Hiba Husseini participated from the Palestinian side. The Israeli participants were Gilead Sher and Pini Meidan-Shani. It proved to be a long and intense meeting, with the Israeli participants in particular expressing concern, mounting to alarm, about the impact the document would have if released in something like its present form.

Their anxiety rested on their belief that the mandate statement would be the only product from the whole JOCI process to which people would pay real attention and, in its present form, as a draft segment of a comprehensive peace treaty, every clause and phrase would be scrutinized. In its current form, it did not adequately reflect the regional input that had been offered. And since the elements of the proposal were inevitably presented in stark relief because of the format employed, the sometimes delicate understandings that had developed during the extensive consultations were lost from view. What is more, treaties are legal documents, and their drafting should be left to legal experts with specialized expertise in the field.

Two things resulted from these discussions. It was agreed that it would be preferable to back away from the style and language of a treaty, and describe the elements of the mandate in a more general and less formal way; it was suggested that the team think of the document as providing advice to the legal drafters of the treaty rather than effectively constituting the treaty provisions themselves. Partly with this in mind, and partly because the meeting participants did not think the segmentation worked, it was agreed that there should be just one document, a statement of the mandate elements, and not two (the treaty segment and the associated annex). This advice guided the work from August until its conclusion in February 2010. A document, reconfigured along these lines, was put together, discussed during a mission to the region in November 2009 and at a face-to-face meeting of the JOCI principals in early January 2010, again at the Royal York Hotel in Toronto, and the completed work was published in February 2010.

With this last task accomplished, there was recognition, both among members of the JOCI team, and among JOCI's interlocutors in the region, that the essential work of the Jerusalem Old City Initiative was done. In addition to all of the research and background studies, there are the three main policy products that form the corpus of the JOCI project. Since the early days, as we have seen, JOCI has devoted itself exclusively to working through a distinctive conception of the way in which the Old City might be managed in the light of a comprehensive peace agreement between Palestine and Israel. Jerusalem was, and is, one of the dauntingly challenging elements in the conflict and clearly will be one of the most difficult matters to resolve in any peace process. With its core documents on security, governance and the mandate of the Special Regime, the Jerusalem Old City Initiative has provided a coherent and detailed articulation of one possible approach to its resolution. With the substantive work effectively done, 2010 became the year in which the priority shifted decisively to explaining the work to decision makers and the broader policy community, especially in Washington, and to communicating the merits of the approach.

What has been accomplished?

Let us first characterize what kind of a process the Jerusalem Old City Initiative is. Clearly it falls into the general category of Track Two undertakings. No one asked the troika to do this; it was an unofficial, non-governmental enterprise, initiated by knowledgeable people who were not part of or direct participants in the conflict. Most of the work was done off the radar screen, employing the Chatham House rule. Its central purpose was to generate ideas and an approach to the resolution of the Jerusalem component of the general Israeli–Palestinian conflict. The process was highly informal and brought key actors from both sides together in utterly unofficial settings to explore the issues, understand the views of the other side, and, if possible, come to some informal understandings about how the Jerusalem component of the general conflict might be addressed.

It aspired to offer some ideas and support to political actors in two ways. First, working with key Palestinians, Israelis and internationals, JOCI sought to shape the ideas and attitudes of some of the people who might very well be directly involved in the peace negotiations when and if they occur. Second, JOCI attempted to provide a well worked out set of ideas, distinct from Geneva, which might be used as a model or a guide when the negotiators in a future peace process turned to the question of Jerusalem. The JOCI process continued for several years, with extensive opportunity to explore issues, test ideas, and adjust views in the light of further discussion – all of it with the aim of moving as far as possible in the direction of consensus. Its accomplishments need to be understood both in terms of the process it employed and the policy proposals it generated.

Peter Jones, elsewhere in this volume, raises a number of questions about Track Two and Track One and a Half processes; a brief consideration of these may help us to refine our understanding of JOCI as a form of Track Two initiatives. Jones raises the question of the extent to which the principals in the JOCI process self-consciously located themselves and their work within the larger rhythms of the dispute. As experienced Middle East hands, the troika had long since assimilated the context and rhythms of the conflict into their thinking, as well as the unfolding political realties with which it was associated. In addition, they developed their proposal on the hypothesis of a comprehensive peace agreement between Israel and a new state of Palestine; in that sense, the JOCI model is not time bound or dependent on the particular circumstances of the day, except insofar as the idea of a two-state solution is itself time bound.

As to the ethical principles framing the initiative, another issue raised by Jones, there was a clear desire on the part of the troika not to interfere or complicate in any way the efforts of the regional actors to achieve a mutually satisfactory settle-ment; JOCI was meant to feed some helpful new ideas into the process, not to disrupt it. With respect to the question of 'transfer', it is clear that the troika understood that their policy work, if it were to be regarded as a success, would have to be fed back into the political process and to inform broader citizen think-ing about the issue. Throughout the project, there were repeated discussions between the team members about communications, about the need to inform critical actors of what was being done, but to do it in a quiet, confidential way so that none would be put on the spot with a premature question or a request to speak in favour or against. There was also a sensitivity shown to the needs of the regional interlocutors with whom the JOCI team worked, recognizing that participation was tricky for some of them, and that, if they were to speak frankly, their desire for confidentiality had to be respected absolutely. This, I believe, was done. As for the 're-entry' of participants, changed by the Track Two experience, confronting their former, unchanged societies, this was a problem that never really arose, in large part because JOCI consistently attempted to deal with just one fragment, albeit a critically important one, of the larger conflict. Thus, while the participants may have been altered in their policy views on the question of how to deal with the Old City within the framework of a comprehensive peace agreement, they were at no risk of being transformed in their political outlook in ways that would alienate them from their home communities. The participants were considering policy alternatives within an assumed framework, namely, a comprehensive peace agreement based on a two-state solution, not attacking, transforming, or undermining the framework itself.

In concluding this chapter, let me say a few words about the overall achievements of the initiative. There are currently two main alternative approaches to the question of Jerusalem. The Geneva initiative deals with Jerusalem as part of a larger, comprehensive Track Two peacemaking exercise; JOCI deals with it alone. The troika was very conscious of the Geneva initiative and had a clear sense of the strengths and weaknesses of its way of handling the Jerusalem question as compared to the JOCI approach. In a nutshell, Geneva's principal virtue is that it settles the sovereignty question; its weakness is that its sovereignty solution, which entails the presence of two sovereign states, rubbing shoulders within the walled Old City, suffers in not meeting the criteria of stability and workability very well. That, at least, is the view of the JOCI team. Indeed, the JOCI working hypothesis is that it is highly unlikely that the two sides will be able to agree on sovereignty in the Old City, and that this might prove to be a significant impediment to reaching a peace settlement. The JOCI model assumes that the two parties might decide to hold that matter in suspension, and in the interim agree on practical arrangements for the governance of the Old City of Jerusalem, namely, a Special Regime in which a powerful Chief Administrator governs on their behalf. This model fails to settle the sovereignty question, but scores high on the stability and workability index. It is, then, useful to have a clear and carefully articulated alternative to Geneva to draw on if necessary, either in whole or in part.

The previous paragraph speaks to the product; it is also worthwhile to consider the process. JOCI involved scores of participants over several years whose views have shaped, and been shaped by, the extensive discussions that have taken place. Those who participated throughout have had the chance to sense the degree of consensus one might hope to achieve as well as the sticking points and problem areas that will require particular attention in any future talks. Many of the JOCI participants will be active players if and when serious negotiations actually get under way. There is clearly a benefit in their having travelled the JOCI road in advance. In addition, the effort of the team to brief policy makers in Washington and elsewhere means that the model is a known and available resource for those actors as well.

That the Jerusalem Old City Initiative was able to travel as far down the road as it has done, is owed in part to:

- The fact that it was a critical, but relatively neglected issue – in many ways, too hot to handle by people in the region themselves, acting on their own.
- The fact that its focus was clear and simple – the walled Old City of Jerusalem; it did not try to do a lot of things, but rather one thing – and well.
- The fact that the project was led by disinterested outsiders.
- The fact that it was Canadians, who are regarded as minor, neutral players in the region, who were leading the project.
- The fact that the Canadians leading the project had detailed knowledge of the region and its people.
- The fact that those leading the project had no personal or political stake in the outcome.
- The fact that the project was carried out in continuing consultation with key people in the region.

These were some of the factors that made it possible for JOCI to achieve what it did.

The Jerusalem Old City Initiative is an instance of what one might term policy development by the powerless. The troika held no power and had no place in the political or governmental structures of Palestine and Israel. They were not old Middle East hands from Washington. They were not officials from other interested third countries. They were former Canadian diplomats with a love of the region and a desire to make a contribution, but possessed of no leverage or control, or connection to powerful policy makers. Yet in a self-initiated project of a decade's duration, they were able to engage key Israeli and Palestinian actors in the region, and others, in sustained discussion about the future of Jerusalem, and, with their assistance, develop a policy alternative to the Geneva proposal. This has widened the policy space within which a solution might be found and has given future negotiators of Middle East peace a wider range of tested ideas from which to draw. It must be admitted that, for the moment, it is all about potential and possibility; whether the policy proposals embedded in the Jerusalem Old City Initiative will actually be utilized in some practical way is anyone's guess. But, given that we are talking about the Middle East peace process, pretty much the same point can be made about all of the other policy proposals on offer.

Notes

1 P. Jones, 'Track Two Diplomacy and the JOCI Project: Some Points to Look for', in *Track Two Diplomacy and Jerusalem: The Jerusalem Old City Initiative,* eds. T. Najem *et al.* (London: Routledge, 2016).
2 The JOCI archives are housed in the Department of Political Science at the University of Windsor, the home of the initiative. Material accessed included correspondence and

literature of the various working groups – e-mails and minutes of the various meetings and drafting sessions, as well as other documents related to the work of the Initiative.

3 The interviews conducted with the JOCI Directors, the Project Manager, and members of the Security Working Group took place over a span of three years (2010–2013), in Toronto, Ottawa and Windsor, as well as by phone and e-mail correspondence.

4 She was assisted by Sebastian Bouhnik, a doctoral student in the University of Toronto Political Science Department.

5 In a document dated 24 November 2006, *Governance Working Group, GWG Work Plan 1*, issued by the Chair of this working group, Mike Molloy.

6 Luc Turgeon is currently Assistant Professor at the School of Political Studies, University of Ottawa.

3

THE JERUSALEM OLD CITY INITIATIVE AND THE TRANSFER PROCESS

Tom Najem* and Giovanna Roma

Introduction

The Jerusalem Old City Initiative falls under the rubric of 'Hard' Track Two diplomacy, a concept discussed by Peter Jones in Chapter 1. While Hard Track Two initiatives may have several objectives in mind, the main one is to develop ideas and to share them with official diplomatic and policymaking circles in the hopes of influencing the resolution of a particular conflict.

As explained in the introduction to this volume, the Jerusalem Old City Initiative was successful in sharing its ideas (i.e. the Special Regime model) with a host of key stakeholders engaged in the Palestinian–Israeli conflict. These include: 1) primary Track One audiences – the US, the Israeli and Palestinian authorities; 2) influential public policy and political affairs organizations especially in the US context; and 3) influential media outlets.

The purpose of this chapter is to provide an account of the transfer process (i.e. the process by which ideas developed in Track Two are conveyed to Track One actors) undertaken by the Jerusalem Old City Initiative. Focus is on those key elements in the JOCI process that were instrumental in facilitating transfer, helping to reach official levels to which most Hard Track Two processes aspire. Particular emphasis is given to the role played by JOCI participants – the three founders and key American, Palestinian and Israeli partners – who, collectively, ensured that JOCI proposals reached targeted audiences.

Before proceeding with the main arguments of this chapter, a brief note on methodology. As with many of the academic studies on Track Two, the methodology for this chapter falls broadly within the tradition of the academic practitioner case study approach.[1] The authors of this chapter are in a unique position to comment on the JOCI transfer process. In particular, Najem is a member of the JOCI management team, with first-hand knowledge and access to information that would, otherwise, be unavailable. Further, it is worth noting that given the sensitive nature of the material, we have erred on the side of caution and chosen not to publish the names of many of the individuals that JOCI corresponded with or briefed.[2]

In writing this chapter we have also consulted with the three directors, as well as key partners in JOCI, especially former American diplomat Ambassador Art Hughes, who played an instrumental role in facilitating the transfer of JOCI ideas in Washington. The chapter's shortcomings, however, are ours alone.

In addition, we have benefitted from the small but growing academic literature on the transfer process.[3] Our preference, however, is to keep the chapter largely descriptive in nature. We have engaged elsewhere with the wider academic literature and the host of theoretical issues that this literature has generated.[4]

The JOCI transfer process – an explanation of success

The literature identifies several variables that may influence the transfer of ideas in Track Two diplomacy.[5] In the case of the Jerusalem Old City Initiative, success in transferring proposals to stakeholders is best understood within a framework that encompasses the following factors: 1) role of founders/facilitators; 2) quality of participants; 3) timing; 4) advocacy; and 5) product. While the role of the founders and participants is most important, all five factors are interrelated to a considerable extent and are thus essential in explaining the dynamics that allowed for JOCI to transfer its ideas to key constituents.

Having said this, it is important to state that transfer means that the ideas get to and are understood by the transfer targets. It does not necessarily mean that they are accepted or incorporated into official policy and at this point there is no way of measuring JOCI's impact on official thinking and positions.

The role of the founders/facilitators

The role of the founders and/or facilitators is an important factor in determining the possible success of a Track Two initiative in getting its ideas to stakeholders, including, crucially, to Track One audiences. The credibility that the founders carry with the conflicting parties, as well as their ability to attract key participants, often through a personal connection, is seen as essential.

Indeed, the role played by the founders of the Jerusalem Old City Initiative – John Bell, Michael Bell and Mike Molloy – created the necessary dynamic which led not only to a successful Track Two initiative, but also, ultimately, to the transfer of the Special Regime proposals to key constituents. In short, success was based, at least initially, on two fundamentals: 1) the founders' high degree of credibility with, and direct access to, decision makers in Israel, Palestine and the United States; and 2) the founders' ability to attract first rate participants from these three countries, who were both influential and also had access (in some cases unfettered) to decision makers.

The founders derived their credibility and personal connections with the major parties largely from their extensive diplomatic experience in the Middle East, which preceded their involvement in JOCI. Michael Bell, for example, was the Canadian Ambassador to Israel on two separate occasions and was widely known and respected by the Israeli establishment. He also served as Ambassador to Egypt and Jordan. Mike Molloy served as Canada's Ambassador to Jordan, and had long-standing relationships with senior officials in the Arab world and Israel. Perhaps even more significant, in the context of the Israeli–Palestinian conflict, Molloy was an advisor to the Canadian team that established the Multilateral Refugee Working Group (RWG) following the Madrid Conference in the 1990s and was Canada's Middle East Peace Process Coordinator and Chair of the RWG from 2000–2003. In these capacities he worked very closely with Palestinians, Israelis and members of the international community on the sensitive Palestinian refugee issue. He is remembered positively within Washington's establishment regarding the work he did on the Palestinian refugee file, and this certainly helped when meetings were being arranged in Washington over the course of the Initiative.[6]

The extensive contacts that Mike Molloy and Michael Bell had in Canada, as well as the United States, Europe, and with various international organizations, were to prove very useful in aiding the entire JOCI process, including transfer.

With respect to the Canadian context, Michael Bell and Molloy were able to leverage their knowledge of Canadian institutions, and their links to people in positions of power within these institutions. Their networks in the then named Department of Foreign Affairs and International Trade (DFAIT), along with the Canadian International Development Agency (CIDA) and the International Development Research Centre (IDRC) were important in securing support for JOCI. This included resources to fund the work of the Initiative as well as help with facilitating meetings in Israel, Palestine, and the US. This was no small feat given the shift in Canadian foreign policy under the Harper government to a decidedly pro-Israeli position, and the obvious political complexities this created within the foreign policy bureaucracy. Michael Bell's tenacity ensured success in securing funds from a sometimes reluctant DFAIT, without which, JOCI would not have been able to operate.

The Canadian government link, at least within the first few years of the Con-servative government, when the shift in policy was still relatively subtle, was important in other ways as well. The fact that three former Canadian diplomats started JOCI and were financed by the Canadian government, which also sent officials to attend some of the critical meetings, elevated regional interest in the Initiative. Canada was seen positively by Arabs and Israelis at the time because of its enduring support of peace initiatives in the region, so the link was a useful one in reinforcing JOCI's credibility and demonstrating to regional players the seriousness of the Initiative.

Their long-standing careers in international diplomacy gave Mike Molloy and Michael Bell strong connections to fellow diplomats in other countries and in key institutions including in the United Nations and the European Union. As we will highlight later in this chapter, these contacts became very useful when the time came for advocating JOCI proposals within these key countries and institutions.

The third director of JOCI, John Bell, also served as a Canadian and then United Nations diplomat in the region prior to starting the Initiative. Critically, however, it was the role he played during the JOCI process that is particularly important in the context of transfer. John Bell lived in the region (in Jerusalem itself) throughout most of the lifespan of the Initiative, working for the international NGO Search for Common Ground. Fluent in Arabic, he developed strong personal links with Israeli and Palestinian partners. Being located in Jerusalem allowed him to meet with partners on a regular basis and, on occasion, with political leadership when situations required that he do so. His presence on the ground proved an important component of the Initiative, sustaining the dialogue between visits of the larger JOCI team and helping to cement the goodwill and credibility that JOCI had initially developed in the region, especially with its partners.

The reputation of the three directors and the connections they enjoyed in the region and elsewhere played a distinct role in their ability to recruit to JOCI influential regional and international partners. These partners – Palestinian, Israeli, and American – had very strong links, and, in many cases, direct access to the highest levels of decision makers in their respective countries. The partners recruited by the JOCI founders played a defining role in helping to transfer JOCI ideas to Track One participants. And the fact that many of them were recruited at the outset and stayed actively involved throughout the duration of the Initiative spoke volumes about their commitment to the JOCI enterprise and the ideas developed over the course of a decade, a point we return to later in the chapter.

Regional and international participants

The literature on transfer identifies a rather interesting predicament for Track Two practitioners when deciding on the type of partners to recruit to participate in their initiative.

On the one hand, in order to maximize change, participants need to be removed from the formal governmental decision-making process. They must have the autonomy to participate in a Track Two process, not feel constrained by political or personal considerations and be able to develop ideas that may fall well outside of official policy frameworks. These types of Track Two processes may develop some interesting and perhaps even innovative ideas. But they are unlikely to gain much traction with the political establishment, at least not initially. Thus, the chances of transfer to Track One audiences or other key constituents are likely to be negligible.

On the other hand, in order to maximize transfer, participants need to be close to, or have some kind of access to the political leadership and the wider establishment. In such circumstances, ideas emanating from Track Two processes have a far better chance of being transferred to officials through participants; the shorter the line-of-access to the leadership, the greater the chances for transfer occurring.

One of the leading practitioners of Track Two processes, Herbert Kelman of Harvard University, identifies the characteristics of the ideal kind of participant for transfer, which are: 1) politically involved and influential (though not official); 2) actively interested in finding a negotiated solution; 3) part of the mainstream of their communities; 4) close to the centre of the political spectrum; 5) credible within their communities; and critically 6) have access to decision makers, including having personal linkages to the leadership.[7]

Closeness to the political establishment does, however, raise a host of interesting issues; predominant amongst them is what the literature refers to as the 'autonomy dilemma'.[8] That is, the extent to which participants of this type are willing, or perhaps, even able to work on developing proposals at variance with the official positions of their respective political leaderships or, at the very least, mainstream opinion in their societies. Whether or not the autonomy dilemma figured into the JOCI process is a point we return to shortly.

With respect to JOCI and its recruitment of partners, there is an interesting and perhaps necessary mix of both types of participants, with diverse expertise and experiences. All contributed in their own way to making the JOCI process a success, including in the design of the product and in advocacy. One of several possible examples of the first type of participant, two young Israeli architects, Yehuda Greenfield-Gilat and Karen Lee Bar-Sinai, produced a highly original and innovative study which addressed the physical and geographical challenges to entry and exit points in and out of the Old City. Using the Jaffa Gate as a case study, they developed a unique model which, they argued, met the needs of security for a Special Regime while maintaining the urban and architectural fabric of the historic Old City.[9]

Nevertheless, it should be stressed that the JOCI founders were determined to forge a product that could be delivered to key constituents, in the hopes of influencing negotiations whenever they were to resume. This, therefore, necessitated also attracting to the Initiative participants described by Kelman as individuals who would be in a strong position to advocate on behalf of the Special Regime model, thus maximizing the prospects for transfer. It is participants such as these that we will focus on in the context of this chapter.

Early on, JOCI attracted what one participant characterized as the Jerusalem A Team. Later when the ideas for the Special Regime were sufficiently developed and the drafting of the document on governance was about to commence, senior Israeli and Palestinian partners requested meetings with the directors in London, to debate, test and refine the underlying principles of the Initiative. This rigorous process was critical to ensuring that the fundamentals of the JOCI proposals were both ready and acceptable for dissemination and transfer to key constituents.

Palestinian partners

Our Palestinian partners had considerable access to the leadership, but their relationship with decision makers differed from the Israeli one. The distance between Palestinian civil society actors and the Palestinian Authority is often minimal. Our

Palestinian partners were either part of the government apparatus, or, at the very least, participated with the knowledge that to do so was politically acceptable.

Four of our key partners are very public about their participation in the Initiative. Issa Kassissieh was at that time Deputy Chief of Staff to the Prime Minister of the Palestinian Authority, and once a policy analyst in the PLO's Negotiation Affairs Department, Head of the Palestinian team for multilateral talks, and the official responsible for the Jerusalem portfolio when he was the Director of the International Relations Department at Orient House in Jerusalem. Hiba Husseini is a leading lawyer, chair of the Al-Mustakbal Foundation, and served as legal advisor to the Palestinian Negotiations Team in the Oslo, Stockholm, Camp David and Annapolis processes. Manuel Hassassian was Executive Vice President of Bethlehem University who also served as the Palestinian Ambassador to the UK. Nazmi al-Jubeh, a professor at Beir Zeit University is a leading specialist in the archaeology of the Old City of Jerusalem and a delegate at various peace negotiations. We also had the participation of other high-ranking Palestinian political figures who preferred to remain anonymous.

The autonomy dilemma, which we introduced earlier, certainly figured in the context of our relationship with Palestinian partners in at least two ways. First, in times of increased political and security tensions in the region, the willingness of Palestinians to continue to participate in the process was severely tested. Second, the degree to which they were able to work on ideas that varied considerably from official lines was a continually underlying issue.

Despite these limitations, the advantage of securing partners at the level described are many. Most significant was the fact that the Palestinian leadership was aware of this Canadian-led Track Two process on Jerusalem and was willing to allow people close to it to participate. Because the Palestinian leadership was kept informed about the contents of the discussions with the Initiative both by the Palestinian participants and through frequent briefings from the JOCI team, the transfer of the final JOCI products would be relatively straightforward.

Israeli partners

A number of influential Israelis participated from the outset in the Jerusalem Old City Initiative, and became its key advocates within Israel. They were from the security and legal establishment, as well as from academia. Gilead Sher, who was the former Head of Bureau and Policy Coordinator for Israel's Prime Minister Ehud Barak, had served as co-Chief Negotiator in the 1999–2001 Camp David summit and Taba talks. Pini Meidan-Shani who served as the Foreign Policy Advisor to Ehud Barak was a member of Israel's peace negotiations team during the Oslo process. Daniel Seidemann participated in numerous unofficial talks between Israelis and Palestinians since 1994 and served in 2000–2001 as a member of the committee of experts authorized by Barak's office to implement the emerging political understandings with the Palestinians. Moty Cristal, who was Deputy Head of the Negotiation Management Centre at Barak's office, participated in both the Camp David and Taba summits. Many members of the Jerusalem Institute for Israel Studies, a highly influential independent think tank that conducts research and tests ideas on Jerusalem, and has strong links to Israeli government ministries were involved. In addition, while not directly involved with the Initiative, other key Israelis attended various JOCI meetings. Those included former Israeli Foreign Minister Shlomo Ben Ami, who was also Israel's top negotiator at the 2000 Camp David talks, and Tal Becker, an advisor to then-foreign minister Tzipi Livni and a lead member of the Israeli negotiating team in the Annapolis process.

It is important to point out that all of our Israeli partners participated in the JOCI process as private citizens, active members of the country's robust civil society, and were, therefore, not directly part of government at the time of their involvement. This offered many advantages, as they were able to participate without the normal constraints associated with being in government, particularly as it relates to a subject as sensitive as Jerusalem. Moreover our partners remained closely connected to the political and security apparatus in Israel, and often had direct and regular access to the highest ranking officials up to and including the Prime Minister and Defense Minister levels.

However, to some degree, these participants were not immune to the autonomy dilemma. Potential political and/or other career ambitions, as well as their general positions in Israeli society mitigated or perhaps constrained their willingness to participate in or at least to sign off on proposals that were dramatically outside of what was politically viable within their society. Seidemann for example, made an enormous contribution to the Initiative despite doubts about some aspects of the final product. Nevertheless Israeli participants found the process and the ideas that emerged from it sufficiently interesting to remain engaged throughout.

International participants

International participants were an essential component of the JOCI Initiative, contributing to process, product and transfer. Our international partners were recruited by JOCI directors to provide critical technical expertise in the areas of security, governance and law, as well as in property and archaeology. They led JOCI's working groups, alongside our Palestinian and Israeli partners, and they authored some of our main proposals. In many cases international participants also had strong connections and credibility with important constituencies, and thus proved particularly helpful on advocacy campaigns within those respective constituencies.

With respect to aiding the transfer process, international participants added significant credibility to the Initiative, helping to raise its profile and reinforce the seriousness to which JOCI was taken by Israelis, Palestinians and international actors like the United States and the European Union. To cite but one of many examples of high profile internationals who participated in JOCI, one can point to General John de Chastelain, the twice former Chief of the Defense Staff of the Canadian Armed Forces, former Canadian Ambassador to the US, and Chair of the Independent International Commission on Decommissioning of Arms in Northern

Ireland. The fact that he led our Security Working Group and co-authored the security elements of the Special Regime model, reinforced the seriousness of the JOCI product and raised its stature with all key players including the US, which certainly helped when briefing actors in Washington. Former Royal Canadian Mounted Police Deputy Commissioner Roy Berlinquette brought to the Initiative a broad understanding of corporate, administrative and operational aspects of policing and security and deep expertise on policing in post-conflict situations.

Two former American ambassadors, Dan Kurtzer and Art Hughes, played significant roles in aiding the transfer of JOCI proposals, especially in the United States, the essential third party in the Palestinian–Israeli peace process with the greatest capacity to help bring about a resolution to the long-standing conflict.

Dan Kurtzer, the guiding hand behind the multilateral peace process established after the Madrid Peace Conference, served as the US Ambassador to Israel from 2001 to 2005, a period that overlapped with Michael Bell's term in Israel. The two knew each other and when Kurtzer finished his term in Israel, and left the diplomatic world to assume an academic position at Princeton University, Bell eagerly recruited him to the Initiative. Bringing Kurtzer to JOCI was considered a real coup, as his deep connections in Israel, the United States government, in Washington's important think tank community, and in the influential American Jewish community brought JOCI additional credibility with these constituencies.

Kurtzer served as a trusted advisor, attended critical meetings throughout the decade-long process, and offered advice on both product and the process of transfer and dissemination of JOCI ideas. Indeed, Kurtzer lent his name to JOCI in a major way beginning in 2007 when he co-authored a piece in the influential American public affairs journal *Foreign Affairs* introducing JOCI ideas to the public for the first time.[10] Kurtzer was to continue to promote JOCI throughout Washington, particularly within the Obama administration. There are recurring references in media outlets in both the West and in the Middle East where Kurtzer refers to JOCI proposals as a viable option for the Old City.[11]

While Kurtzer was indispensable to JOCI it was US Ambassador Art Hughes who played the most influential role in aiding JOCI's transfer process in Washington. Hughes had a long and distinguished career in the American foreign service, holding several important positions in the Middle East including: United Nations Director General in the Egypt–Israel Multinational Force and Observers (1998–2004), US Ambassador to Yemen (1991–1994), Deputy Chief of Mission in Tel Aviv (1986–1989), Deputy Assistant Secretary of Defense for Near East and South Asia (1989–1991) and Deputy Assistant Secretary of State for Near Eastern Affairs (1994–1997).

At the suggestion of the Washington-based Middle East Institute, Hughes attended the November 2005 Istanbul meeting. Given his expertise in security matters with particular reference to the Middle East, Hughes was asked to join the SWG to work alongside John de Chastelain and Roy Berlinquette, as they co-authored the JOCI security paper for the Special Regime. From then, Hughes proved an integral part of the JOCI team. He played an active role on the GWG, and co-wrote the mandate document outlining the basic tenets of the Special Regime proposals.

In so many ways, therefore, Hughes was heavily invested in the Initiative, and came to be publicly associated with it. While his contributions to the development of the Special Regime concept were in themselves worthy of note, in the context of this chapter, it is his rather significant role in helping to transfer JOCI ideas to key stakeholders in Washington that concerns us.

In the early stages of the Jerusalem Old City Initiative, Hughes assisted JOCI directors with arranging meetings with various Washington stakeholders to brief them on JOCI product and activities. However, it was not long before Hughes' role was formalized and he assumed the title, Washington Coordinator for the Jerusalem Old City Initiative. He became responsible for coordinating JOCI activities in Washington, including advocacy with government and non-government institutions. Given Washington's essential role in the peace process, the position was a key one.

Indeed, in Hughes, JOCI had a consummate Washington insider, a man whose nearly half-a-century career gave him an exceptional understanding of the workings of the most senior levels in government agencies and bureaucracies (particularly in the State and Defense Departments), as well as in the various public affairs organizations and think tanks that make up the core of Washington's political elite.

JOCI's success in transferring its ideas in Washington was facilitated primarily through the work of Hughes. JOCI briefed senior personnel from the Department of State, Department of Defense, the Congress, the George Mitchell and John Kerry peace teams, as well as key players from the numerous public policy and political affairs organizations that influence American Middle East policy. With Hughes' assistance JOCI regularly reached out to over 60 influential Washington insiders. A more detailed discussion of those briefings is provided below.

Timing

Timing is the third factor worth considering when explaining JOCI's ability to transfer its ideas to stakeholders. While influential leadership and partners are essential in facilitating transfer, at the end of the day, transferring ideas to Track One actors (policymakers, negotiators, foreign ministries) can really only occur with a degree of effectiveness under the right political and diplomatic circumstances, at a time, for example, when a peace process is formally in place. The conflicting parties must be receptive to receiving such ideas.

We were introduced to the importance of timing to Track Two processes in Chapter 1 of this volume, where Peter Jones delved into the question of determining the optimal moment for a third party to initiate a Track Two process. He addressed the question within the context of the ripeness vs. readiness continuum. To recap, ripeness addresses the optimal moment to intervene in a conflict cycle, while readiness refers to the time when 'credible people are ready to begin informal discussions aimed at exploring ways to reframe the dispute'.

With respect to the question of timing, ripeness as understood in the literature did not immediately figure into why JOCI was founded when it was. Feelings in the region were still very raw with the failure of the Camp David and Taba talks and the violence that followed during the Second Intifada, so it was unlikely that Israelis and Palestinians would engage again for the foreseeable future in formal peace negotiations.

However, as one of the founders noted, it would be more accurate to state that anti-ripeness was at play at the beginning of the process, and that this reality actually worked in favour of JOCI undertaking its work. If Jerusalem was just too sensitive to be discussed at the formal level, then an opportunity existed for it to be discussed at an informal level, especially one that was low-key, under the political radar, but run by people with credibility. After all, the peace talks had largely faltered over the status of Jerusalem, and there was some degree of acknowledgement that more preparatory work on the subject was needed. In a sense then, in 2003, serious people from both sides of the conflict were ready to engage in some kind of informal process on Jerusalem, to research and explore possibilities without the pressures of a fixed time limit and away from the political microscope. The fact that no other significant informal process focusing exclusively on Jerusalem was taking place at the time made JOCI doubly attractive.

While the lack of a formal peace process and the need to conduct more work on Jerusalem played an important role in explaining JOCI's early traction, it was the very long duration of the initiative (2003–2013) that actually contributed positively to the relationship between timeliness and transfer.

In short, the political environment in the Middle East and in Washington over the course of the decade in which the process took place was highly fluid and was at various junctures receptive to JOCI ideas. A number of opportunities arose in which JOCI could advocate its ideas to the major Track One actors. Ultimately, this included the Annapolis Process (2007–2008) and the 2013–2014 US-mediated Palestinian–Israeli peace process, where JOCI was well positioned and able to feed its ideas (i.e. the Special Regime model) into formal consultations.

Advocacy

So far this chapter offered an explanation of the role of the founders and facilitators on the one hand, and regional and international partners on the other, played in the transfer of JOCI proposals to Track One audiences. We have argued that JOCI's success was largely due to the efforts of this group of experienced, well-connected and committed individuals, who were able to advocate on behalf of JOCI especially during opportune political and diplomatic events and processes. However, it is important to understand that the promotion of JOCI ideas was not done in an *ad hoc* manner; quite the contrary. A well-orchestrated, tightly controlled advocacy strategy figured greatly in JOCI's plan for developing and promoting its proposals. What follows is a discussion of advocacy, the fourth factor we identify in explaining the success of JOCI in transferring its ideas to key stakeholders.

The founders of JOCI understood that tackling the highly contentious and emotive issue of Jerusalem was not without risk. It required the Initiative's work to unfold with the utmost of care and sensitivity so as not to raise concerns, if not outright opposition, particularly from various constituents in Palestine, Israel, the US and Canada. To do so would greatly curtail the effectiveness of the Initiative, if not kill it outright.

The Jerusalem Old City Initiative developed at the outset an advocacy strategy to deal with this complex reality, and to prepare the groundwork for transferring the ideas developed by the Initiative to Track One actors and other stakeholders when an appropriate time presented itself. The strategy consisted of three inter-related dynamics: 1) a policy of informing stakeholders on the work of the Initiative on a regular basis; 2) a tightly controlled public relations campaign; and 3) the holding of meetings and briefings with Track One audiences at key moments in the initiative such as the release of the JOCI proposals, or when the political climate was open to receiving such proposals.

Informing stakeholders

Given the highly sensitive nature of Jerusalem, an advocacy strategy that consisted of keeping the major stakeholders informed of the intent and progress of the Initiative was deemed to be highly prudent. Two related reasons informed this strategy. On the one hand, it was a way to begin to test and build support for the Initiative's ideas, to inculcate or get buy-in from key constituents, thus contributing to the overall transfer process. On the other hand, the strategy of keeping interested parties regularly informed had the possible advantage of alleviating concerns about the work and intent of the Initiative, thus neutralizing potential opposition.

Thus, it is within this context that during the decade-long project JOCI directors, and at times our international partners, traveled to Israel and Palestine frequently to meet with stakeholders to brief them on the progress of the Initiative, to seek advice, etc. Within Israel for example, JOCI met directly with members of Israel's government, members of the Knesset, as well as people in key ministries. The same degree of interaction took place within the Palestinian territories, and included consultations and briefings with senior negotiators and PLO officials, the office of the presidency of the Palestinian Authority, the Negotiations Affairs Department, the Negotiations Support Unit and a variety of Palestinian thinkers. Of course, none of this suggests that the people JOCI met necessarily supported the ideas; just that they agreed to receive the JOCI team. Indeed in some cases it was made clear that they did not like the ideas or, at the very least, thought that they would not work. On the other hand senior Palestinian officials told the JOCI team that ours was the only Track Two exercise that went out of its way to keep them informed and that this was very much appreciated.

The strategy of regularly informing key stakeholders was also very much at play elsewhere, including in Washington and Ottawa. The directors found it helpful to bring the Initiative's major regional partners to Washington and Ottawa on various occasions to reiterate the importance of the work, helping counter potential criticism from domestic lobby groups for example. Ironically, in the case of Washington and Ottawa, it was our regional partners, people like Pini Meidan-Shani and Gilead Sher, Nazmi al-Jubeh and Dani Seidemann, whose briefings helped to reconfirm the importance of continuing support for the project. With respect to Washington, this meant talking to people in a myriad of government agencies and public affairs organizations and other special interest groups as diverse as the American Israel Public Affairs Committee and Americans for Peace Now.

Controlling the public message

One of the major appeals of engaging in Track Two diplomacy is that it provides a low-key forum to tackle issues too sensitive to be addressed at the formal political level. In fact, the entire process is normally conducted in a manner that allows participants the anonymity desired to carry out their work, far away from the political and public limelight.

Continuing to maintain this level of anonymity requires a clear public relations strategy, a high priority for the JOCI team from the outset. The sensitivity of dealing with an issue like Jerusalem, combined with the high calibre of regional participants engaged in the process, meant that initially at least, publicity of any sort was avoided and outreach was restricted to the minimum necessary to reassure interested parties. Indeed, locating the Initiative within a university context, and publicly identifying it as a long-term university research project allowed the team to downplay the more sensitive diplomatic and political aspects of the work.

As the process evolved, a low-key public relations campaign was launched. It involved the creation of a website which contained: 1) literature explaining the broad parameters of the Initiative, 2) newsletters providing general information about activities, and 3) a list of commissioned research papers. This ensured a degree of transparency, until the time was right to fully reveal our ideas in a public forum.

Eventually the directors concluded that the time was ripe for a more robust strategy which included controlled engagement with media, and participation in academic and policy workshops to bring the Initiative gradually into the public arena, thus preparing the ground for the process of transfer. It began in earnest in 2007 when, as we stated elsewhere, a succinct article outlining JOCI proposals for the Old City appeared in *Foreign Affairs*, a staple for the Washington establishment. The article brought the Initiative considerable public attention, especially in influential media circles, including a front-page story in Canada's leading national paper, *The Globe and Mail*. At this stage in the process, JOCI directors and some of the Initiative's partners also participated in relatively low-key workshops or roundtables at various think tanks, especially in Washington. The first public presentation on JOCI took place in Jerusalem in April 2007 when Michael Bell addressed an event hosted by the Jerusalem Institute for Israel Affairs.

By the spring of 2010, the proposals for the Old City were completed, and in May of that year, the team formally unveiled the JOCI proposals at the Mayflower

Hotel in Washington in an event hosted by the prestigious Middle East Institute. The event attracted hundreds of people including many from Washington's policy and think tank community. Significantly, it also drew the attention of the global media which covered the 'new Canadian peace plan for Jerusalem', confirming the high level of seriousness paid to the Initiative. JOCI proposals were widely reported on in the American press and also in the Israeli, Canadian and wider global press. The stories were largely positive or neutral in tone.[12]

Meetings and briefings with Track One and related audiences

The third element of the JOCI advocacy campaign included meetings and briefings of Track One audiences and closely related influential policy groups. As explained earlier in this chapter, the meetings and briefings were facilitated by the Initiative's network of influential partners, and were held at opportune moments when key players were receptive to receiving the JOCI team. We will highlight some of the more significant examples to demonstrate the high degree of transfer that occurred beginning with the United States, key members of the international community, and Israelis and Palestinians.

Examples of transfer in the United States

The 2013–2014 peace process

The Jerusalem Old City Initiative began its work in 2003, shortly after the last major peace talks between Israel and the Palestinians failed. Although there were attempts to restart the peace process in the early 2000s, they were unsuccessful. In July of 2013, and under the auspices of the US Secretary of State John Kerry, Palestinians and Israelis entered into direct peace talks with an ambitious nine-month timeline to come up with a framework for peace. Significantly, a Track One peace process was now underway to which ideas emanating from Track Two could be informally channeled. JOCI was well positioned to feed its ideas into this process.

Martin Indyk was named as the US Special Envoy for Israeli–Palestinian negotiations. By the first week of September 2013, Indyk's office had invited the JOCI team to Washington to discuss its proposals for resolving the conflict over Jerusalem's Old City. In the lead up to the meeting JOCI sent its formal proposals to the State Department as well as a total of 17 supporting documents on a range of issues dealing with the Old City from property and archaeology to security. Then, in mid-October, JOCI's three directors, along with Washington Coordinator Art Hughes provided a day-long briefing session to Indyk's team.

The above presents perhaps the clearest example to date that JOCI ideas were fed into official diplomacy. As one colleague noted, 'We handed over our proposals, our work is now done'. Of course, whether or not these proposals, or even elements of them, influence official proposals or will be adopted at some future stage is another matter. The point being made here is that there was strong, demonstrated interest in JOCI ideas from those that led the most recent official peace process.

US government and political leadership in Washington prior to 2014

It is also important to reiterate that rather than seeing the briefings to US officials in October 2013 as a single event, it is better to understand them as the culmination of advocacy efforts in Washington over the 10-year life of the project. Over those years a range of US government officials, political leaders in Congress, and influential figures in public policy and lobby organizations based in Washington were briefed about the work on the Old City. Examples of these briefings follow.

The Jerusalem Old City Initiative team met with and discussed the Special Regime model with dozens of US government personnel in the Department of State, the Department of Defense, and in Congress. They met, in particular, with individuals who held key positions on the Middle East.

The Obama peace team, 2009–2011

In January 2009, the Obama Administration appointed George Mitchell as the US Special Envoy for Middle East peace, with the aim of restarting negotiations between Palestinians and Israelis. The Jerusalem Old City Initiative briefed several members of Mitchell's team on the Special Regime model, then again when David Hale replaced Mitchell in 2011 as Special Envoy.

Department of State

In addition to the Mitchell/Hale peace team, JOCI met with and briefed several members of the Near East Affairs bureau of the State Department including the Assistant Secretary of Near East Affairs. A number of other State Department officials with responsibilities for the Middle East were briefed including the Ambassador to Israel, as well as the Director, Israel and Palestinian Affairs.

Department of Defense

Several members of the Office of the Secretary of Defense were briefed during various years of the Initiative including, for example, the Deputy Assistant Secretary for the Middle East, the Director for Middle East Affairs, the Officer in Charge Israel Affairs and the Assistant to the President for the Middle East.

The US Congress

The Jerusalem Old City Initiative team met with several influential congressional representatives and senior congressional staffers over the years of the Initiative. This included, significantly, the Chair of the Foreign Affairs Committee.

Influential public policy and political affairs organizations in the US

Although not officially Track One actors, an almost equally important set of players in the United States is the myriad of public policy and political affairs organizations including think tanks, academic research centres, and lobby groups such as the American Israeli Public Affairs Committee (AIPAC). These groups are important because they are able to influence public opinion and government policy on the Israeli–Palestinian conflict. The revolving door of personnel that alternates between government positions and these organizations is an important dynamic that makes these organizations and their leadership important players in US policymaking circles.

JOCI briefed the leadership or key individuals in over 25 organizations, including the Brookings Institution, the Washington Institute for Near East Policy, the Wilson Center, the Council on Foreign Relations, and the Atlantic Council. Those briefed received copies of our proposals, helping to promote our ideas on the Old City within the Washington establishment. Ultimately our efforts paid off on the question of transfer as many of those briefed subsequently joined the government, especially members of the Kerry-led Middle East peace team.

Examples of transfer in the international community

While recognizing the pre-eminence of the US in the peace process other members of the international community also matter including the United Nations and the European Union, and the JOCI team took care to extend its advocacy to both. The directors presented JOCI proposals to the European Union Middle East Peace Process Committee in Brussels in 2009.

The following year there were presentations to interested United Nations delegations in New York. The invitation to present at the UN came only a few weeks after the formal unveiling of JOCI proposals in Washington. Further, JOCI proposals and the ideas they generated became known to a diverse range of international diplomats and global leaders. In May of 2010, in a speech given at the Chateau Laurier hotel in Ottawa praising Canada's commitment to the UN, Secretary-General Ban Ki-Moon explicitly mentioned the work of the Jerusalem Old City Initiative, possibly even conflating the project with formal government policy, though it was, of course, completely at arm's length for the government.[13]

Examples of transfer: Israel and the Palestinian Authority

Transferring ideas to key Palestinians and Israelis differed significantly from our Washington approach. From the beginning it was part of JOCI's advocacy strategy to keep the Israeli and Palestinian political elite up to date with what it was doing. Frequent briefing of influential Israelis and Palestinians included those who were part of the government apparatus. This insured familiarity if not buy-in regarding JOCI ideas.

Transferring the Special Regime concept in the region was complex and sensitive. Consequently the task of transferring ideas was left to the discretion of JOCI's capable Palestinian and Israeli partners, whose links to their respective governments were described above. They were able to engage their political elite when the timing was right. In short, they knew their society and the norms in which officials operate, and thus could more easily determine whether or not the time was ripe to discuss our ideas.

Product

Finally, we address the fifth and, perhaps, the most obvious factor that contributed to successful transfer – the attractiveness of the Special Regime idea to key constituents, including Track One actors. As we have seen, credible founders and influential participants backed by an effective advocacy strategy can facilitate transfer, and if the timing aligns with an opening in the peace process, this could mean feeding ideas into official diplomacy. However, at the end of the day, successful transfer and impact largely depend on how well the proposals themselves are received by key stakeholders.

The relative ease with which the JOCI directors and their regional and international partners secured access to senior officials in the US, Europe and the Middle East reflects the significant interest garnered by the ideas about the future of the Old City developed during the life of the Initiative. Indeed JOCI's Israeli and Palestinian partners expressed a great deal of reluctance to bringing the project to a completion at the final meeting.

Earlier in this chapter, we raised the issue of the participation of influential Palestinians and Israelis with strong links to government. To what degree would they be willing to engage in a process that could potentially develop a product that sits outside of their respective government positions on the Old City (i.e. each claiming sovereignty)? We referred to this as the autonomy dilemma.

The idea of developing some kind of special arrangements[14] for the governance of Jerusalem's Old City as a way to resolve competing claims was not a new idea. Indeed, academic and long-time participant in Track Two and Track One processes on Jerusalem, Menachem Klein, makes a convincing argument to this effect in Chapters 4 and 5. He argues that special arrangements for the Old City which moved beyond the sovereignty dilemma were actually raised in negotiations during the Camp David process.[15] They had not been well defined or developed in any significant way, and perhaps because of this, did not gain much traction. However, the crucial point here is that the concept of some sort of special arrangement for Jerusalem was not unknown to Palestinians and Israelis, that the concept entered into prior official negotiations, and thus that any taboos over the subject were broken, raising it as a possible option for future negotiators.

With this background in mind, the interest of high-level regional partners in participating in a Track Two process working on developing a model for special governance arrangements for the Old City was understandable. Many of the Israeli partners had been actively involved in the negotiations at Camp David, so it would not be difficult to understand why they were especially interested in working with JOCI on developing in greater detail the Special Regime concept.

It is important to stress here that the JOCI Special Regime model was independent of anything raised before and was entirely conceptualized by the founders, and developed in greater detail in partnership with international and regional partners. The point is that the concept, however vaguely conceptualized was not entirely alien to key stakeholders, and this contributed to interest in it, and of course, to the overall transfer process.

Further, JOCI's Special Regime concept was attractive because it offered Track One actors a highly detailed and developed model of governance (found in three documents totalling more than 36,000 words) and a possible alternative to resolving what appears to be the most intractable of issues facing Israelis and Palestinians. It dealt with the thorny issues of governance, security and borders, and of contested holy spaces. There was recognition of the enormous amount of work that went into developing the ideas and of the high level of expertise found in the international and regional participants.

In many ways, therefore, JOCI did exactly what Track Two initiatives are intended to do. It allowed the parties to work quietly in an unofficial capacity, away from political or time pressure, to develop detailed proposals that could assist Track One actors in finding viable solutions for the conflict over Jerusalem's Old City.

Conclusion

From the beginning, one of JOCI's central goals was to transfer its ideas to official policymakers, in hopes of contributing to the resolution of the conflict over the Old City of Jerusalem. We believe JOCI was successful in transferring its main ideas contained in the Special Regime model to key stakeholders engaged in the Palestinian–Israeli conflict. The evidence supporting this is ample. What is less clear, however, at least for now, is the extent to which JOCI has impacted the key actors engaged in the conflict.

We recognize the distinction between transferring ideas to stakeholders and influencing their views in a significant way. At the end of the day, it is still too early to measure our impact. What we can say is this: JOCI's ideas have reached key stakeholders in Israel, the Palestinian territories, the United States, Canada, the European Union, the United Nations, and other vested interests, and these ideas have been disseminated to the public. We believe that what these ideas have achieved with the Israelis is the acceptance of the idea that something special needs to be done for the Old City. For the Palestinians, on the other hand, the Special Regime offers a potentially viable option should their desired position not be attainable. JOCI's ideas have been recognized by influential media outlets, such as *The Atlantic*,[16] as well as key NGOs like the International Crisis Group[17] and those associated with the Geneva Accords.

Moreover, our participants have both shaped and, to varying degrees, bought into the process for over a decade and continue to promote our ideas.[18] For example, we are aware of at least one influential Palestinian–Israeli group that has taken JOCI's ideas and are working together to expand upon them; while a recently initiated Track Two process based out of Spain and spearheaded by JOCI alumni uses elements of the Special Regime to tackle the specificities of Jerusalem's Holy Esplanade. Although the timing may not be ripe for official negotiations at the time of writing, when the peace process does resume, our ideas are there for the taking. In the meantime, we hope that by publishing these three volumes, JOCI ideas will continue to be circulated and discussed and ultimately, offer a contribution to finding a long-lasting solution to the conflict over Jerusalem.

Notes

* Dr. Najem would like to acknowledge the support of the Humanities Research Group at the University of Windsor, which through its Fellowship programme, gave him the resources to complete this work.

1 See, for example, J. Burton, *Conflict and Communication: The Use of Controlled Communication in International Relations* (London: Macmillan and New York: Free Press, 1969); H. C. Kelman, 'The Problem Solving Workshop in Conflict Resolution', in *Communication in International Politics,* ed. R.L. Merritt (Urbana, IL: University of Illinois Press, 1972); R. J. Fisher, *Interactive Conflict Resolution* (Syracuse, NY: Syracuse University Press, 1997); R. J. Fisher (ed.), *Paving the Way: Contributions of Interactive Conflict Resolution to Peacemaking* (Lanham, MD: Lexington Books, 2005).

2 Unless otherwise stated, the material and evidence for this chapter originates from first hand participation in the process, interviews with JOCI participants, as well as from the wealth of archival material amassed by JOCI.

3 In addition to Peter Jones's excellent and succinct account of the transfer issue found in Chapter 1 of this book, see, for example, C. Chataway, 'The Problem of Transfer From Confidential Interactive Problem-Solving: What is the Role of the Facilitator?' *Political Psychology* 23, no. 1 (2002): 165–189; Fisher, *Paving the Way*; and E. Cuhadar, 'Assessing Transfer from Track Two Diplomacy: The Cases of Water and Jerusalem', *Journal of Peace Research* 46, no. 5 (2009): 641–658.

4 T. P. Najem, and G. Roma, 'On the Track to Officialdom: Transferring the Idea of the Jerusalem Old City Initiative to Key Decision Makers' (forthcoming, 2017).

5 These variables include setting, culture, personalities involved, the role of a facilitator, timing, and others.

6 Interview with A. Hughes conducted by T. Najem, May 2013.

7 Kelman, 'The Problem Solving Workshop in Conflict Resolution'.

8 B. Job, 'Track 2 Diplomacy: Ideational Contribution to the Evolving Asian Security Order', in *Asian Security Order: Instrumental and Normative Features,* ed. M. Alagappa, 241–279 (Stanford, CA: Stanford University Press, 2003): 243.

9 The study is found in Volume Two, Chapter 14 of this series: Y. Greenfield-Gilat and K. L. Bar-Sinai, 'Jaffa Gate Crossing Facilities: Spatial Study', in *Governance and Security in Jerusalem: The Jerusalem Old City Initiative*, eds. T. Najem *et al.* (Routledge, 2017).

10 M. Bell and D. Kurtzer, 'The Missing Peaces', *Foreign Affairs*, March/April 2009.

11 R. Khouri, 'Daniel Kurtzer Offers a Valuable Plan', 5 April 2015, *The Daily Star.*

12 See, for example, H.L. Krieger, 'Special Regime for Sharing J'lem', *The Jerusalem Post,* 6 May 2010; R. Boswell, '"Special regime" Proposed for Jerusalem's Old City', *CanWest*

News, 8 May 2010; M. Buel, 'Jerusalem Old City Initiative Release New Peace Plan', *Voice of America News,* 11 May 2010.

13 A. Gavai, 'Ban Ki-Moon Speech Throws Light on Canada-UN Relationship', *Embassy Magazine,* 19 May 2010.

14 The concept of a 'Special Regime' (or *lex specialis* in legalise) is increasingly used in international law to describe a secondary system of governance within the framework of general principles of international law and state responsibility. Special regimes – or, special systems, models, and/or arrangements, as they are sometimes also called – allow for unique dispute settlement methods that were not previously envisioned in international law. See 'Regime Interaction in International Law: Theoretical and Practical Challenges', Lauterpacht Centre for International Law, University of Cambridge, Conference, 26 June 2009, http://www.lcil.cam.ac.uk/events/regime-interaction-interna tional-law-theoretical-and-practical-challenges; B. Simma and D. Pulkowski, 'Of Planets and the Universe: Self-Contained Regimes in International Law', *The European Journal of International Law,* 17, no. 3 (2006): 483–529.

15 See also A. Hanieh, 'The Camp David Papers', *Journal of Palestine Studies* 30, no. 2 (2001): 75–97.

16 *The Atlantic* and the S. Daniel Abraham Center for Middle East Peace, 'Is Peace Possible', last modified 14 November 2011, http://www.theatlantic.com/special-report/is-p eace-possible.

17 International Crisis Group, *Extreme Makeover: Israel's Politics of Land and Faith in East Jerusalem,* (Middle East Report no 134, 20 December 2012), 31.

18 For example, D. Kurtzer continues to promote the ideas of the Jerusalem Old City Initiative. See, D. Kurtzer (ed.), *Pathways to Peace: America and the Arab-Israeli Conflict* (New York: Palgrave Macmillan, 2012), 209–214.

References

Bell, M. and D. Kurtzer. 'The Missing Peaces'. *Foreign Affairs* 88, no. 2(2009): 131–139.

Boswell, R. '"Special regime" Proposed for Jerusalem's Old City'. *CanWest News,* 8 May 2010.

Buel, M. 'Jerusalem Old City Initiative Release New Peace Plan'. *Voice of America News,* 11 May 2010.

Burton, J. *Conflict and Communication: The Use of Controlled Communication in International Relations.* London: Macmillan and New York Free Press, 1969.

Chataway, C. 'The Problem of Transfer From Confidential Interactive Problem-Solving: What is the Role of the Facilitator?' *Political Psychology* 23, no. 1(2002): 165–189.

Cuhadar, E. 'Assessing Transfer from Track Two Diplomacy: The Cases of Water and Jerusalem'. *Journal of Peace Research* 46, no. 5(2009): 641–658.

Fisher, R.J. *Interactive Conflict Resolution.* Syracuse, NY: Syracuse University Press, 1997.

Fisher, R.J. (ed.) *Paving the Way: Contributions of Interactive Conflict Resolution to Peacemaking.* Lanham, MD: Lexington Books, 2005.

Gavai, A. 'Ban Ki-Moon Speech Throws Light on Canada-UN Relationship'. *Embassy Magazine,* 19 May 2010.

Hanieh, A. 'The Camp David Papers'. *Journal of Palestine Studies* 30, no. 2(2001): 75–97.

Hughes, Art. Interview by Tom Najem, May 2013.

International Crisis Group. *Extreme Makeover: Israel's Politics of Land and Faith in East Jerusalem.* Middle East Report 134, 20 December 2012.

Job, B. 'Track 2 Diplomacy: Ideational Contribution to the Evolving Asian Security Order'. In *Asian Security Order: Instrumental and Normative Features,* edited by M. Alagappa, 241–279. Stanford, CA: Stanford University Press, 2003.

Kelman, H.C. 'The Problem Solving Workshop in Conflict Resolution'. In *Communication in International Politics*, edited by R.L. Merritt. Urbana, IL: University of Illinois Press, 1972.

Khouri, R. 'Daniel Kurtzer Offers a Valuable Plan'. *The Daily Star*, 5 April 2015.

Krieger, H.L. 'Special Regime for Sharing J'lem'. *The Jerusalem Post*, 6 May 2010.

Kurtzer, D. (ed.) *Pathways to Peace: America and the Arab-Israeli Conflict*. New York: Palgrave Macmillan, 2012.

'Regime Interaction in International Law: Theoretical and Practical Challenges'. Paper presented at conference held at the Lauterpacht Centre for International Law, University of Cambridge. Last modified 26 June 2009. http://www.lcil.cam.ac.uk/events/regime-interaction-international-law-theoretical-and-practical-challenges. (Last accessed: 26 April 2016.)

Simma, B. and D. Pulkowski. 'Of Planets and the Universe: Self-Contained Regimes in International Law'. *The European Journal of International Law* 17, no. 3(2006): 483–529.

The Atlantic and the S. Daniel Abraham Center for Middle East Peace. 'Is Peace Possible?' Last modified November 14, 2011. http://www.theatlantic.com/special-report/is-peace-possible. (Last accessed: 26 April 2016.)

4

NEGOTIATING JERUSALEM

The impact of Track Two on Track One[1]

Menachem Klein

Background

East Jerusalem was the jewel of the territories that Israel captured in less than a week of war in June 1967. The eastern part of the city, containing Judaism's holiest sites – the Western Wall and the Temple Mount – had been inaccessible to Israelis during 19 years of Jordanian rule. With the fighting just ended, the Israeli government annexed Jordanian East Jerusalem and adjoining territories, creating a single large municipality with a large population of Palestinian Arabs. Israel unilaterally declared this new entity to be 'United Jerusalem, the Eternal Capital of Israel'. Following the annexation, Israel began what has been its national project since 1967: settling Jews in the territories it won control of in the war of that year. In no other populated Palestinian territory has Israel reached the same level of achievement – annexation and the creation of near demographic parity with the original population.

The facts that Israel created on the ground shaped her mind. Negotiating Jerusalem was a taboo for Israel, any questioning of the Israeli act was illegitimate. The results for Israel were, first, that Jerusalem was not seen as an actual urban living space but rather as a symbolic and metaphysical entity. These conditions opened the door for civil society organizations. First and foremost were Jerusalem-based ones, to follow the local developments and later to establish Track Two negotiations. Second, it prevented the Israeli officials from preparing for negotiations. When Israel committed itself in Oslo agreements (1993, 1995) to include Jerusalem in the negotiations on the final status of the territories it occupied in 1967, the hands of Israeli politicians were tied by their commitments not to compromise the 'eternal unification' of their capital. It was too sensitive politically. Therefore the bureaucracy neither allowed nor initiated developing negotiation strategies and alternatives on Jerusalem.

Thus, since 1993, the way for Track Two was open. The initiators of Track Two could act without interfering in Track One that at that time did not exist. Moreover, they based their talks on studying the situation on the ground at a level of expertise that official branches did not achieve. Their professionalism on the one hand and the need to prepare the final status talks on the other hand protected them from being blamed by the politicians. In addition, the heads of the Israeli and the Palestinian Track Two teams reported to senior decision makers respectively.

A careful reading of the Track Two studies on the Palestinian–Israeli case shows that they deal mainly with one dimension of Track Two activities: changing public opinion through advocacy and consciousness-raising, with the aim of getting Israelis to accept the PLO as a legitimate partner for peace talks. Apart from the Oslo case, no research exists on the direct impact of Track Two on the official level or on the services it provided to official negotiators. The lacuna can be explained by the fact that these types of activity were impossible before the Oslo agreement of 1993. Only then were Israelis permitted by law to meet with PLO members.[2]

Introduction

Since 1994 Jerusalem was addressed in more than 30 Israeli and Palestinian Track Two forums. These contacts created a common professional discourse and a program based on a more or less agreed-upon database. In some cases the participants stopped at that point but, at times, they went beyond it in an attempt to find a political structure that would encompass and give direction to the points on which the experts reached consensus. Some of the groups dealt with the city and the metropolitan region only, while others included Jerusalem within a wider framework and addressed all the issues of a permanent status agreement. Hereafter is a short summary of some of the main Track Two channels.[3]

In May 2000, the Jerusalem Institute for Israel Studies published 'Peace Arrangements in Jerusalem', a paper that summarized this think tank's work on the issue from its creation in 1994.[4] The team presented three principal and several secondary alternative solutions (see below). Although the publication was directed at an Israeli audience, at least one alternative was based directly on the discussions held in Track Two talks involving Institute scholars. Furthermore, the other two options included concepts that were formulated during these discussions.

The Beilin–Abu Mazen understandings were shaped during secret negotiations conducted in 1994–1995. The Palestinian and Israeli teams formulated an unofficial statement of understanding on the parameters of the permanent agreement. Their goal was to finish the job by May 1996, the time set for the opening of the permanent status talks. The intention was that this unofficial understanding would be presented jointly by both sides when official talks began. Israel would hold national elections that would also serve as a plebiscite on the framework agreement, making it possible to reach a full agreement within a short time. Most of the discussions were conducted between the Israeli team that had originally been involved in the

Oslo initiative – on the Israeli side, Dr. Ron Pundik and Dr. Yair Hirschfeld, under the direction of Yossi Beilin and on the Palestinian side, two Palestinian-British scholars, Dr. Ahmed Khalidi and Hussein Agha, under the direction of Abu Mazen. Drs. Khalidi and Agha, Fatah members since the 1960s, had been on the advisory team to the Palestinian delegation to the Madrid conference. Khalidi had also participated in the negotiations at Taba that led to the Oslo II agreement. The concluding session of the discussions on the document took place on 30 October, 1995. It was not an official agreement, but rather a non-binding understanding formulated by academic negotiators with the knowledge and under the direction of Beilin and Abu Mazen. The intention was that the political leadership on each side would take it as a starting point for their negotiations.

Prime Minister Yitzhak Rabin was assassinated on November 1995, just a day before the paper was to be presented to him. As a result, the initiative never attained formal status and remained a Track Two product.

The Beilin–Abu Mazen document could not stand for long in its original form. It required updates. Since 1996, academic figures on both sides have conducted unofficial talks on a revised version of the Beilin–Abu Mazen plan and have reported their discussions to their respective political leaderships.

The London track (not to be confused with JOCI's London Caucus) meetings took place in the late 1990s and early 2000s and were managed by Orient House, an Arab think tank directed by Faisal al-Husseini, on the Palestinian side and the Economic Cooperation Foundation (ECF, an NGO founded by Yossi Beilin) on the Israeli side. These NGOs allowed Beilin and Husseini to feel out negotiation options without committing their respective leaderships.

Although the Beilin–Abu Mazen document was not officially presented as a framework for the London track, the fundamental assumptions on which the document was based were in the air during discussions of municipal management in the Jerusalem area, the Jerusalem economy, inter-police cooperation, the meaning of the term 'open city' and the price that would have to be paid for openness in various areas.

The Madrid channel was established in 1996. The Israeli team was led by Professor Shlomo Ben-Ami, a member of the Knesset for the Labor party, and the Palestinian, by Faisal Husseini, the director of Orient House and the PLO minister for Jerusalem Affairs. The channel was directed by Miguel Morratinos, the European Union's special envoy to the Middle East and representatives of the Spanish government. It addressed all the issues of the permanent status agreement. The Madrid channel also collected ideas raised in parallel channels. Because the participants were frank with each other and developed relations of mutual trust, and because they took an inclusive approach, they were able, in March 1999, to agree on a paper. However, this document remains classified.

The Madrid channel was one of the more successful of these informal discussion frameworks. The paper it produced was aimed at the political elite. The Palestinian Authority and Israeli political leadership found it difficult to accept the Madrid paper because of its comprehensiveness. Moreover, the paper was ahead of its time – there was no public or institutional legitimization for the positions it took. As a result, the political leaders who were the patrons of the Madrid channel did not fully adopt its conclusions. They were not willing to be identified with the paper, nor were they willing to bring it into the public discourse or put it on the political agenda.

The Oklahoma paper, a joint statement on the principles that were to guide the negotiations on Jerusalem, was published in January 2000. This publication followed discussions held under the auspices of the University of Oklahoma and the Rockefeller Foundation. Israelis, Egyptians, Jordanians, Palestinians and Americans who had met several times over the previous two years signed the statement. This channel was unique in seeking to influence Arab and Jewish public opinion no less than decision makers. Before 2000 this was the only one of the informal channels whose participants went public, announced their position and submitted their paper to the heads of the relevant states. However, when the media's interest in the initiative waned, the Oklahoma paper lost most of its influence. In the end, it helped shape public opinion, but not policy.

Notably, current unofficial negotiating efforts have made shaping public opinion one of their main goals, as can be seen in the Ayalon-Nusseibah initiative (www.mifkad.org.il) and the Geneva model agreement (www.heskem.org.il).

As far as is known, most of the groups met under Western European auspices (Sweden, Denmark, Norway, Great Britain, France, Holland, Italy, Portugal, Greece, Cyprus, Spain, Belgium and the European Union), sometimes under the sponsorship of governmental institutions, sometimes at the initiative of non-governmental organizations (NGOs). A Palestinian participant in many Track Two meetings summed them up as follows: 'The Dutch and Swedish track sponsored issues related to planning, zoning and infrastructure for the whole city in times of peace, while the British track focused more on the political dimension of the conflict in Jerusalem. The Spanish track sponsored the religious dimension of the Holy City and the Greek track focused on the discussion of general issues in preparation of the final talks.'[5] The United States government was influenced by the Israeli taboo that forbade any discussion of the future of Jerusalem. Washington did not initiate informal channels for talks on a subject that could have impinged on US domestic politics through the Jewish vote and the Jewish lobbies.

It would be difficult to exaggerate the importance of the informal channels and their contribution to the negotiations. They constructed the professional and political infrastructure and created a common language between the two sides. Track Two negotiators made several breakthroughs and formulated creative ideas that were later brought to the negotiating table. These ideas included new concepts of sovereignty – suspended, joint and divine; a common economic regime for Jerusalem and Al-Quds; territorial exchange by mutual agreement; a Jewish–Muslim–Christian religious council that would coordinate management of the holy places; cooperation between the Palestinian and Israeli police and the creation of a joint police force for the seam zone between East and West Jerusalem; and the concept of the Holy Basin.[6]

However, Track Two channels had their own shortcomings. They were conducted almost exclusively between professionals. Insufficient effort was made to bring together community leaders representing the two peoples who will have to live side by side under the terms of a peace accord. Second, government officials and bureaucrats rarely participated. True, a few highly placed decision makers on each side were briefed about the issues discussed, but they preferred not to participate in Track Two meetings. Their attitudes varied. Some of them underestimated the potential of Track Two talks for creating understanding, let alone an acceptable agreement. Others were indifferent. And some used the channels to float experimental balloons without incurring political costs.

Thus, when the formal track was about to commence, and as it proceeded, officials and professionals found themselves dependent upon each other and this interdependence gave rise to relationships among them. Since political constraints prevented official negotiators from adequately preparing their brief for negotiations over Jerusalem, they had no choice but to open their minds to understandings reached and ideas exchanged in the Track Two talks over the capital city.

Impact of Track Two ideas

A comparison of the creative ideas and understandings produced in Track Two with the positions taken by the decision makers during the official discussions shows what parameters shaped the official talks and limited the influence of Track Two.

The Track Two products examined in this work are those on which there is substantial written documentation: the publications of the Jerusalem Institute for Israel Studies, the Beilin–Abu Mazen understandings, papers presented in the Track Two meetings known as the London track, as well as the products of the Madrid channel and the Oklahoma channel. Nevertheless, it should be noted that the same players often attended different Track Two encounters, both on the Israeli and Palestinian side, which created a diffusion of ideas between the different informal channels. Therefore, the reader should bear in mind that the Track Two products presented here benefited also from the outputs of less documented Track Two channels and reflect ideas and approaches raised in these other channels.

A comparison of the issues raised during the informal negotiations with those addressed during the formal negotiations shows the substantial impact of the Track Two talks. This paper seeks to identify the methods and players that linked the two types of negotiation and to show how Track Two ideas were transmitted to the official forum.

To facilitate such a comparison, I have organized the content of the proposals and ideas raised during the negotiations along four axes: time, space, subject and side.

The time axis differs between the two negotiations. For the official negotiations, the time axis plots meetings that took place during the year 2000. This year-long period can be divided into three phases, with the pivot being the seminal negotiating event of the year, the Camp David summit. The pre-Camp David period includes negotiations from early 2000 up to Camp David. The Camp David phase consists of the official discussions during the summit (11–24 July 2000). The third phase stretches from the end of the summit up to the Taba talks of January 2001, where official negotiations terminated.

Track Two negotiations were conducted over a much longer period. The meetings between the years 1994 and 2000 divide into five main channels; different ideas were proposed and discussed in each of these forums.

The ideas and proposals raised during the official and unofficial negotiations addressed six geographical units within East Jerusalem. These form concentric circles, starting from the largest, most inclusive geographical zone and zooming in towards the smallest: metropolitan Jerusalem, the external Arab neighbourhoods that lie a distance from the Old City, the internal Arab neighbourhoods that lie adjacent to the Old City, the Holy Basin, the Old City (the area inside the city walls) and the Temple Mount/al Haram al-Sharif.

The proposals regarding these spaces addressed three subjects: sovereignty, administration and cultural and religious rights. The first two are relevant to all spaces, while the latter refers to the holy places only. In Chapter 5 the interested reader can find a more detailed summary of ideas raised in Track Two and Track One. Arranging the material according to the four axes of time, space, subject and side answers three basic questions essential for this study. What were the issues under discussion? When were they discussed and by whom? Once these questions are answered, it is possible to address the third: the impact of Track Two negotiations on formal channels.

The official negotiations were conducted mainly by politicians and diplomats, who were most concerned with the issues of sovereignty and borders. The participants in the unofficial tracks were, in contrast, urban planning specialists and lay citizens of Jerusalem. As such, these latter talks tended to focus on administrative aspects of the problems.

Three sides took an active part in the official negotiations: Palestinians, Israelis, and Americans. The Israelis and Palestinians were the two sides to the conflict, while the Americans acted as mediators who offered proposals and ideas of their own. No Americans participated in Track Two talks. Instead, the third party in most cases was a European facilitator. Since Palestinian and Israeli Track Two participants established dialogue among professionals and managed successful discussions, the European third party acted as a facilitator rather than as a mediator.

The rich reservoir of Track Two ideas, concepts and suggested solutions regarding Jerusalem makes it impossible to draw a map that shows what was not brought to the attention of the official negotiators or was rejected by them.[7] This study will instead adopt an inclusive rather than an exclusive approach. In other words, I will trace back to their Track Two origins concepts – such as 'open city', 'Holy Basin', 'special regime', different types of sovereignty, 'umbrella municipality' – that figured in the official negotiations.

A few preliminary remarks: first, there are two different contexts in which one can address post-1967 East Jerusalem. There is a legal one: the Israeli annexation of the Jordanian area, the geographic scope of the region and its legal status. From this perspective, the pre-1967 war border is the formative line. The second context is the urban reality on the ground. Since 1967, East Jerusalem has been a provider of services and utilities to a population that extends beyond the inhabitants of the city itself. Metropolitan Jerusalem spreads beyond the annexation line and makes that boundary artificial. 'Metropolitan' is a functional concept, relating to the influence of the urban centre over the periphery, regardless of the city's official jurisdiction. Metropolitan areas have no boundaries, only a variety of soft borders. In their search to find a realistic compromise on Jerusalem, Israeli and Palestinian negotiators preferred to build on this proposition.

Second, during the negotiations Israeli politicians often used the geographical term 'Metropolitan Jerusalem' to serve their own interests. They wanted to include in it settlements located outside the jurisdiction of the Jerusalem municipality. As they planned to divide the metropolitan area into two municipalities, they wanted to expand the Israeli share by including in it a large area that extends from Jerusalem to the settlements of Ma'aleh Adumim to the east of the city, to Gush Etzion on its south and to Givat Ze'ev to the north. The Palestinian capital of Al-Quds would, in this scheme, include also the suburbs of Abu-Dis, al-'Azariya and parts of Dahiat al-Barid and al-Ram that are currently outside the Israeli municipality. However, according to this Israeli concept, the Palestinian capital would be smaller and weaker than the Israeli capital and be surrounded by the metropolitan area of Jewish Jerusalem.

Third, it should be emphasized that, during the official negotiations, proposals with regard to Jerusalem were often raised as part of package deals that also included proposals relating to other permanent status issues, such as refugees, borders and settlements. In the official talks it is impossible to know exactly what role the Jerusalem issue played in the package deal negotiations – that is, how difficulties or breakthroughs in addressing those other issues affected the talks on Jerusalem and vice-versa. In contrast, during most Track Two negotiations, the Jerusalem issue was addressed on its own, and in some cases the negotiators even avoided the political aspects of the issue. As a result, the official proposals are presented for the most part outside of their context in the broader give and take.

Fourth, negotiators have often used symbolic and metaphorical language when discussing Jerusalem. Such rhetorical devices enabled the actors to avoid dealing with the actual items on the agenda. However, in this study I track the actual ideas and the method used here makes it possible to analyze these ideas on their own. The reader should bear in mind that this is not an account of the actual negotiations. In practice, Jerusalem was discussed with other subjects, and coolly rational negotiations blended with heated emotional rhetoric.

Substance – ideas going from Track Two to Track One

Below I sum up the main issues that were raised in Track Two negotiations and then brought to the formal negotiating table. After describing these issues, I examine how officials modified them while introducing and integrating them in Track One talks. The detailed discussion with full references is in Chapter 5.

The concept of a Jerusalem municipality expanded to encompass the city's metropolitan area is a Track Two product. It derived both from facts on the ground – Israel's construction of settlements near Jerusalem and twelve Jewish neighbourhoods on former Jordanian territory; and from the assumption that sharing an expanded Jerusalem would be easier than dividing the existing city. Another factor in the creation of the metropolitan concept was the reality and ideal of Jerusalem as an open city.

Track Two negotiators suggested dividing the expanded municipal area into two sub-municipalities, Jerusalem and Al-Quds. Some unofficial channels avoided referring specifically to the issue of sovereignty and addressed administrative arrangements only, while some Israeli proposals at Track Two talks suggested that the two sub-municipalities would remain under supreme Israeli sovereignty, while the Palestinians received functional autonomy over all its territory or full sovereignty over most of it. Two Israeli approaches were presented on where exclusive Palestinian sovereignty should end: at the Israeli annexation boundaries or at the entrance of the Old City or the Holy Basin. The Palestinian side demanded full sovereignty over its populated area, and in some Track Two talks this was accepted by the Israelis. However when the sides formulated their joint text they hid this understanding between the lines.

The Jerusalem metropolitan concept was adopted by the official negotiators and supported by the Americans. In contrast to some of the unofficial channels, the formal negotiators did not avoid dealing with the issue of sovereignty. On the contrary, sovereignty was the main theme of the negotiation in light of the political nature of these encounters. Thus most of the debates on Jerusalem were on Palestinian sovereignty over different areas, the metropolitan area included. The Palestinians were willing to accept Israel's definition of settlements in the Jerusalem area as part of metropolitan Jerusalem so long as the Palestinians themselves received sovereignty over all lands between the settlements and Jewish Jerusalem.

Most Track Two talks on metropolitan Jerusalem introduced the idea of establishing an umbrella municipality that would reflect Jewish demographic superiority in the region. Another idea was to create a metropolitan council with equal representation, but these ideas did not make it past the gate to the official negotiating table. Some suggestions were to establish only a coordinating committee between the two municipalities, thus leaving each municipality with its full administrative powers. The later concept was endorsed by the official track and discussed during the Taba talks.

On the issue of Jerusalem neighbourhoods, Track Two discussions were limited to the eastern city only. West Jerusalem's current status as sovereign Israeli territory was unquestioned and outside the negotiations. East Jerusalem was divided to the external and the internal Arab neighbourhoods surrounding the Old City. Some Israeli Track Two proposals suggested granting Palestine sovereignty over the external neighbourhoods only, while limiting its powers in the internal ones to neighbourhood-municipal government. Track Two Israeli participants developed a wide range of modular functional autonomy options. Fewer Track Two proposals involved granting full sovereignty to Palestine over internal neighbourhoods. Indeed, the Israeli position in the official talks moved from the first model in the middle of the Camp David summit to the second one in Taba. The Palestinians in both Track Two and Track One adhered to their principle of having full sovereignty over the Arab neighbourhoods of the city. It should be noted that in some Track Two talks this principle was mutually agreed on. Thus one can find in those Track Two discussions the roots of the divided sovereignty formula that was included in President Clinton's ideas – 'what is Jewish should be Israeli, and what is Arab – Palestinian'. This formula guided the sides negotiating at Taba at the last stage of their formal discussions.

Ideas raised during the official negotiations regarding Palestinian civil status were similar to ideas expressed in most of the Track Two proposals. Both suggest that current Arab residents of Jerusalem would go from being East Jerusalemites holding Jordanian passports to being full citizens of the State of Palestine living in Jerusalem and enjoying the right to vote in Palestinian general elections.

In the official negotiations, the Palestinians' fallback position on the line separating areas of full sovereignty was identical to their Track Two fallback position: to share sovereignty on the basis of UN Security Council resolution 242 in a physically undivided city. The Israeli fallback position was to manoeuvre between different levels of Palestinian state sovereignty and neighbourhood authorities. This was not a fallback position of any substance. Therefore, in the course of the talks the Israelis changed their position and were ready to give more sovereignty to the Palestinians than they had been willing to grant at the beginning of the negotiations. The Palestinians, for their part, stood their ground on what was for them a matter of principle.

Another Palestinian fallback position that they presented at Taba was the idea of re-establishing a fixed and closed boundary between the Palestinian and the Israeli cities in Jerusalem. They raised it in response to Israel's unwillingness to accept the idea that Jerusalem would remain fully open and physically undivided with international borders around and outside. Following their willingness to expand Palestinian sovereignty in Jerusalem, the Israelis introduced in the Taba talks the idea of a semi-open city with 'soft' borders dividing sovereign territories. For them it was a strategic change. Neither this concept nor the full division that the Palestinian side tabled in reaction to it were Track Two products. Track Two discussions were all governed by the Israeli concept of a fully open city.

The Holy Basin concept of putting the religious and historical core of Jerusalem under a special regime was developed in Track Two meetings and endorsed by Track One negotiators. The concept defines the Holy Basin's geographical and administrative boundaries under its special regime. Unlike other parts of Jerusalem, where administrative powers would be divided between the sides, the Holy Basin would operate under joint Israeli–Palestinian control. The basic principles were freedom of movement and worship, freedom of access, jurisdiction determined by the individual's nationality rather by territory, a joint Palestinian–Israeli unarmed police patrol and a grant of administrative powers to representatives of the three monotheistic religions. It was the Israelis who introduced this concept both in Track Two and in the official talks. As a result, when they declared the need to preserve the basin as an undivided unit, the Israeli side reserved for itself supreme sovereignty and overall security authority. This concept appeared explicitly in the official negotiations.

Alternatively, both sides could agree to suspend sovereignty claims on the Holy Basin and jointly administer the area. However, it should be noted that in this alternative too, the Israeli side has a superior status to the Palestinian side. The proposal suspends sovereignty only for Arab neighbourhoods in the Holy Basin and for the al Haram al-Sharif, not for the Jewish Quarter and the Western Wall, which would fall under Israeli sovereignty. The same principle guided the other Israeli offer to transfer sovereignty over the Holy Basin to an outside entity. Israel never suggested putting the Jewish Quarter and the Jewish holy sites under a third party's sovereignty. Since this option addressed territories on the Palestinian side, Israel suggested that the third party would be one or more of the following: the UN, the Organization of Islamic States or a committee of a few Arab states. The option of third party sovereignty was not a Track Two product but one of the two Israeli compromise responses made during the official negotiations to the Palestinian rejection of the Israeli concepts. The Palestinian side was consistent in demanding its full sovereignty over the Arab-populated areas. The second idea was to defer a decision on sovereignty in the Holy Basin for three to five years, during which Israel and the Palestinians would jointly administer the area. This offer resembles a Track Two suggestion to suspend all rights, claims and positions regarding the Holy Basin for the duration of the agreement or until otherwise decided. But the Palestinian side had already rejected this alternative prior to the Camp David summit.

Israeli negotiators presented two options for joint administration under an Israeli umbrella. One option was that a joint administrative committee would oversee daily life and manage the civilian affairs of the Holy Basin as a whole. According to the second option this committee would coordinate and supervise the operations of Palestinian and Israeli territorial, neighbourhood-based divisions.

The Israelis presented the Holy Basin concept in a modular form that made it easy to retreat to fallback positions, to discuss the Old City only and, with a few adjustments, also to negotiate over the Temple Mount/al Haram al-Sharif. Indeed all the above-mentioned options on the Holy Basin were presented also in the discussions on the Old City and Temple Mount/al Haram al-Sharif official talks. The modularity of the Israeli proposals and the Israeli negotiators' easy movement among them created a perception of flexibility and moderation that covered the tactical profile of the Israeli offers and its strategic hard core of preserving Israeli superiority. It stood in contrast to the Palestinian stand, which was firm and stuck to their fundamental principle without tactical manoeuvrability. At Camp David, the American mediators were highly impressed by the Israeli tactics and echoed them in their own proposals. Later, in his proposals, President Clinton distanced himself from the Israeli positions, but not in regard to the Old City and the Temple Mount.

On the subject of the Temple Mount, most ideas the Israelis presented in the official negotiations were compatible with what they offered in Track Two negotiations. In regard to sovereignty, Israel's positions in both Track Two and Track One were that the site would remain under Israel's supreme sovereignty and under its security supervision, while the Palestinians would exercise certain administrative responsibilities and maintain law and order there. Religious administration of the compound would be entrusted to the Palestinian Muslim Waqf, in the role of guardian or custodian of the al-Aqsa mosque. Another proposal was that the Palestinians be granted sovereignty either over all of the al Haram al-Sharif, or over the edifices of the al-Aqsa Mosque and the Church of Holy Sepulchre only, while Israel would maintain residual sovereignty over the areas not transferred to the Palestinians. The option of suspending claims of sovereignty over a period of several years was also first raised in Track Two. It goes without saying that the Western Wall was excluded by Israel from the joint administration arrangements, even though its religious significance derives from it being part of the compound.

A few ideas discussed in the official talks had no precedent in Track Two ideas. The most important of these was the Israeli demand to establish a Jewish prayer compound on the Temple Mount. Only one Israeli Track Two paper suggested accepting the principle of a right of Jewish worship there, but even that paper specified that implementation of this right would be suspended because of the likelihood that such prayer would be detrimental to public security and order. No other Track Two documents addressed this issue, which led to a highly charged debate at Camp David. The idea of granting the Palestinians a sovereign corridor through the Muslim Quarter between Al-Quds and al Haram al-Sharif was put forward by Israel's official negotiators at Camp David as a way of ensuring free Palestinian access to what would remain under Israeli supreme sovereignty, and to bridge over the different sovereign claims on the Old City.

Both in Track Two and official negotiations the Palestinian side rejected any solution less than full and exclusive sovereignty on the Temple Mount, leaving Israel with sovereignty over the Western Wall. Sovereignty was the Palestinians' main concern; once that was guaranteed, they were prepared to guarantee freedom of access for non-Muslim visitors, as well as to coordinate with Israel excavations or construction that could cause damage to the subterranean area of the Temple Mount.

Several offers that were raised during the Track Two negotiation did not make it past the gate into the official talks. Nevertheless, they included some interesting ideas that deserve discussion here.

The concept of an umbrella municipality that would unite under it the separate Israeli and Palestinian capitals was discussed on a number of occasions in Track Two frameworks. This would consist of Palestinian and Israeli representatives and would coordinate the Israeli and Palestinian sub-municipalities. Official negotiators, however, preferred the idea of a joint coordinating committee between two separate municipalities. This different approach derives from the differences between the participants in the unofficial and official talks. Many of the participants in the unofficial channels were professionals and scholars who specialize in issues of urban planning, in addition to citizens of Jerusalem who understand the complexities and needs of the city. The members of the official negotiating teams, on the other hand, were usually politicians who put a greater emphasis on issues such as sovereignty and borders rather than on the practical problems of governing two urban entities that must serve as a capital for two countries.

The Madrid non-paper presented a totally different concept of sovereignty and administration in the Jerusalem metropolitan area, which also received no attention during the official negotiations. The participants in this channel chose to undertake a different line of thought: the basic unit for city management would be neighbourhoods, not municipalities. In keeping with this approach, the two sides agreed orally that the Palestinian state would receive sovereignty over neighbourhoods in which 90 per cent or more of the population was Palestinian, while Israel would retain sovereignty in neighbourhoods where 90 per cent or more of the population was Jewish. The Israeli and Palestinian neighbourhoods would each elect a municipal council, and these two councils would administer daily life through empowerment of the neighbourhoods. All citizens of the Jerusalem metropolitan area would be entitled to elect an assembly, based on parity between the two nations, which would symbolically represent the two parts of Jerusalem. Both national states would agree to cede central powers to this elected assembly. The assembly would operate a metropolitan police force and would possess planning and zoning powers. The assembly would also serve as a metropolitan council that would empower its two executive branches – the two municipalities. These municipalities would govern a decentralized system with neighbourhoods and citizen-consumers at the centre. An umbrella coordinating body would be established, composed of Palestinian and Israeli representatives. In short, this structure would keep the states out of the metropolitan municipal government and bring local institutions to the fore.

In regard to the holy sites, the Madrid track suggested that a council representing the three monotheistic religions would govern the holy places. However, each religious authority would enjoy jurisdiction over its own holy sites. In other words, the sovereignty dilemma would be defused via religious administration of holy sites and metropolitan institutions. Finally, both sides would acknowledge the aspirations and collective rights of Israelis and Palestinians in metropolitan Jerusalem. Neither side would negate the other's attachment to the part of Jerusalem under its rule.

This concept of metropolitan Jerusalem was apparently too revolutionary for the official negotiating teams. Composed as they were of people who held power in central governing institutions, they had no interest in ceding power to local agencies and institutions. This was all the more true with regard to Jerusalem, both a holy city and the capital of their respective states. The two central governments both wanted the power and legitimacy that control of Jerusalem implied.

During the London track, the Palestinians presented two proposals on Jerusalem that were never discussed in the official negotiations. The first was the idea of establishing a condominium – meaning that there would be joint, undivided sovereignty over the city as a whole. According to this offer, the city would be administered by a single umbrella municipality comprised of equal numbers of Palestinian and Israeli representatives. In other words metropolitan Jerusalem would be a binational city, the capital of two states. Such a proposal ran counter to the Palestinian goal of self-determination in a nation-state, and to the Israeli goal of guaranteeing the Jewish character of Israel and Jerusalem in any final status agreement.

Official negotiators had the same reasons for not bringing the second offer to the formal negotiating table – that of internationalizing Jerusalem. According to this line of thought, metropolitan Jerusalem would be defined on the basis of UN resolution 181 and governed by a neutral international body. Neither Israel nor Palestine would have sovereignty in the city.

Sovereignty over the Temple Mount was at the heart of the official negotiations at Camp David and thereafter and became the 'make or break' issue of the negotiations. However, two types of sovereignty raised in Track Two were not addressed in the official talks. The first was the idea of null sovereignty – meaning that neither party, nor a third party, would be given sovereignty over the Mount. The second type was that of divine sovereignty, by which sovereignty on the Temple Mount/al Haram al-Sharif would be vested in God. In both cases, as in the case of suspended sovereignty that Israel put on the table, the sides would have to divide administrative powers between them and find practical arrangements in the context of having no symbolic sovereign over the site. But the official negotiators were busy competing over symbolic sovereignty and its physical manifestations, so these ideas never attracted their attention.

Other criteria by which we can examine Track Two and official negotiations are that of strategic offers versus the fallback and tactical proposals raised to test the waters. Among the strategic offers put forth by Israel and the US, for example, were: the idea of expanding the Jerusalem metropolitan municipality in order to divide it into two sub-municipalities; the idea of an open, undivided city; the suggestion to transfer sovereignty over the external neighbourhoods to the Palestinians; and the idea of Palestinian functional sovereignty over the internal neighbourhoods. The ideas of reserving the Holy Basin as one sovereign whole and placing it under a special regime and the idea of dividing the Old City according to a 2.5:1.5 or 2:2 formula, under supreme Israeli sovereignty, can also be seen as strategic offers. In regard to the Temple Mount, a few strategic offers were made: reserving supreme Israeli sovereignty over the Temple Mount while granting the Palestinians custodianship there, divided sovereignty (horizontally or vertically), and third-party sovereignty by the UN Security Council. The Palestinian delegation took two strategic positions: receiving full sovereignty over all Arab neighbourhoods, and full sovereignty over Haram al-Sharif/the Temple Mount. The Palestinian rejection of all the Israeli and American proposals that fell short of this red line were of a strategic nature, since Israel was utterly opposed to redividing the city along the pre-June 1967 lines or to not recognizing Israeli sovereignty over the Jewish neighbourhoods built beyond that line or over the Western Wall.

As tactical and fallback Israeli offers, it is possible to mention ideas such as postponing the resolution of the sovereignty dispute for a given period, or leaving it undecided and open, and granting Arafat a sovereign compound in the Muslim Quarter with a safe passage to the Palestinian capital. Tactical offers regarding sovereignty over the Temple Mount were: divine sovereignty, no sovereignty or deferring the decision over the matter of sovereignty over the Temple Mount.

It is worth mentioning that, in the formal talks, it was the Israeli side followed by the American mediator that raised most of the ideas to which the Palestinians responded with red-line positions. Most of these ideas were based on Track Two discussions, as we have just seen. The next section discusses the way that the Israelis brought these proposals to the official negotiation table and the reason behind the forms that the decision makers gave them.

How they get there – communication channels and division of labour between Track Two participants and formal negotiators

From 1993 onwards, Israeli Track Two negotiators enjoyed high access to decision makers and maintained open channels of communication with them, especially under governments led by the Labor Party. Track Two negotiators were also able to conduct a public discourse on the Jerusalem problem, an issue that the Israeli establishment was unwilling to address even though the Oslo accords committed Israel to negotiate the city's final status. Public opinion and decision makers' minds were dominated by the taboo over dividing 'united Jerusalem, the eternal capital of Israel'. Politicians gave their staff no guidance on how to deal with the subject, nor did they let ministerial professionals prepare alternatives for the negotiations. Politicians found it convenient to let extra-governmental bodies like the Jerusalem Institute for Israel Studies and the Economic Cooperation Foundation take the responsibility and initiative for informally exploring political alternatives with the Palestinians. These two organizations paved the way for formal negotiations and placed the issue of Jerusalem before the public. Once formal negotiations commenced they had a great impact on the shaping of the Israeli position.

Founded and headed by the architects of the Oslo accords, the ECF had a stronger relationship with the establishment than did the JIIS. The ECF was politically oriented, explicitly seeking to influence Israeli political leaders. Its findings were forwarded to high-ranking decision makers. The Beilin–Abu Mazen document, for example, was submitted to Foreign Minister Shimon Peres and was about to be presented to Prime Minister Rabin. The public, however, received only an unauthorized report on the document, when it was leaked to a journalist several months later.

The JIIS was not as politically well-connected as the ECF but enjoyed close cooperation with Jerusalem's municipal establishment on local issues. The JIIS operated through more versatile and diversified communication channels. Since its establishment in 1994, this think tank held secret meetings with sitting prime ministers and members of the Knesset and organized closed-door seminars for the establishment's elite. In these meetings, JIIS fellows and staff presented the results of their research to the directors-general of cabinet ministries and heads of security organizations. It also conducted seminars with Orient House and reported on these orally to Mayor Ehud Olmert. Israeli leaders listened carefully to the Track Two experts but remained noncommittal. Alongside this, during the years 1994–2000, Jerusalem Institute fellows initiated public discussion of Jerusalem's future by publishing research books and articles, conducting seminars and lectures and giving interviews to local and foreign media correspondents.

In these ways, both the Israeli establishment and the public learned about the Jerusalem problem. They heard experts present, from an Israeli viewpoint, the reasons why the longstanding taboo against negotiating over Jerusalem had to be broken – so that a viable agreement could be reached with the Palestinians. The first group to change views on the issue was educated middle-class professionals. From there it radiated to a wider public and from there to the political elite. This created an environment conducive to new thinking and, in time, facilitated the Barak government's change of position. From 1999 onwards, as the subject became a central issue on the national agenda, the public began attending to the experts more and more. These specialists, who did not belong to the establishment, became accessible to the public, and enjoyed the advantage of not having any competition from the establishment itself. As is often the case, the last people to grasp that old beliefs had to change were the politicians. They would never have reached this understanding had the environment in which they operated not changed.

Ironically, right-wing parties and politicians also contributed to the process of changing Israeli public opinion on Jerusalem. Beginning in 1994, right-wing figures publicly accused Israeli governments (including the Likud government led by Binyamin Netanyahu) of permitting PLO institutions and personnel to operate in East Jerusalem, of failing to establish Israeli governmental institutions there and of not enforcing Israeli law in the Arab part of the city. Ironically, these calls to strengthen Israel's hold in East Jerusalem signalled to the public that Israel's control there was in fact weakening. Furthermore, they highlighted the gap between the rhetoric about a united city and the reality on the ground. In voicing this criticism, the right helped show the public that, in fact, Jerusalem was not united.

In June 2000, on the eve of the Camp David Summit, the JIIS assessed that both the public and the negotiating process were ripe for putting Jerusalem up for discussion. It disseminated the alternatives for Jerusalem that its fellows and staff had formulated. Even prior to this, when final status negotiations commenced at the end of 1999, the Institute made its database available to the Israeli negotiating team headed by Ambassador Oded Eran. It also assembled a small team of five people to supply the peace and negotiation staff in the prime minister's office and the Ministry of Foreign Affairs with ideas and alternatives. Reuven Merhav, a former director-general of the foreign ministry, coordinated this team, which consisted mostly of former members of the establishment. They also forwarded its material directly to the negotiating team through Gidi Greenstein, personal assistant to Gilad Sher, who handled the negotiations on behalf of Prime Minister Barak in the secret and open final status talks.

Parallel channels opened based on personal know-how rather than membership in an organization or research institute. This author served in 1999–2001 as an advisor to Shlomo Ben-Ami, minister of public security and foreign affairs, who together with Gilad Sher negotiated the final status agreement on behalf of the Barak administration. After the Camp David Summit of July 2000, two informal advisory forums were established to submit fresh ideas to the Israeli establishment. The first was a political consulting team that operated from the end of Camp David to the end of the Taba negotiations (October 2000–January 2001). Gilad Sher coordinated this small body of academic experts and former high officials, which met each Tuesday in Prime Minister Barak's office. The second was a team of Jerusalem experts, which included scholars, architects and urban planners, coordinated by Dr. Moshe Amirav. In contrast to the former team, which discussed a long list of issues on the Palestinian–Israeli agenda, the latter dealt solely with the difficulties that arose during the negotiations over Jerusalem. A summary of their discussions was forwarded by Amirav to Dani Yatom, head of the political-security desk in Prime Minster Barak's office. The author was a member of both these teams.

Track Two practitioners succeeded in getting decision makers in Israel to look at Jerusalem in terms of the reality on the street rather than ideology. The official team needed creative ideas, maps and data. For the most part, Track Two negotiators were successful in presenting Israeli decision makers with Jerusalem's demographic reality and its implications for Israel. Demography has a special status in Israeli and Zionist consciousness because the Israeli public and its leaders are afraid that the country's Jews will become a minority. Demography has been at the heart of the public debate on the future of the occupied territories ever since June 1967. Indeed, demography was always a central issue in Israeli thought. During the period of the British Mandate, the Zionists in Israel were acutely aware that the Jews were a minority in Palestine and an even smaller minority in the Middle East as a whole. The mainstream Zionist leadership realized that the Jewish state they sought to establish would have to rest on a large Jewish majority within its borders. This led them to accept partition of Palestine, to ban the return of Arab refugees after the war of 1948, and to encourage the immigration of those defined Jewish by Israeli law. Concern for maintaining and strengthening the Jewish majority was a major factor in determining Israel's economic, agricultural and physical planning, and other policies during the country's first half century. In other words, Track Two participants managed to influence the official negotiators and the Israeli public by making use of the predominant discourse.

Track Two negotiators succeeded in marketing a number of ideas and concepts that shaped the agenda of the Palestinian–Israeli negotiations during the year 2000: the Holy Basin; different sovereignty models on the Temple Mount; expanding East Jerusalem along its functional and metropolitan boundaries in order to allot sovereignty to both sides; a special regime to govern holy sites and the Holy Basin; and finally, granting the Palestinian municipality functional authority over the Old City and its adjacent neighbourhoods.

Among these issues, Israeli Track Two practitioners had limited impact on their negotiators when it came to alterative models of sovereignty different from the classic definition (sovereignty for one side denies all sovereign rights of the other side). They were much more successful in introducing decision makers to concepts such as a special regime and the Holy Basin. Throughout the final status talks the Israeli establishment held fast to a sovereignty model that granted Israel sovereignty over the Palestinians in the Old City and, in most versions, also in its adjoining neighbourhoods, while demanding residual sovereignty on the Temple Mount. The establishment rejected the principle of equivalence that lies at the basis of concepts such as divine and null sovereignty. The Israelis tried to attain, through administrative arrangements, powers not included in these models.

In conclusion, Israeli Track Two practitioners were able to have an impact on their country's official negotiating team because of the latter's shortcomings. A. Kleiman portrays the Israeli official negotiator as being dominated by security ethos and security subculture. Senior retired or serving security officers over-shadowed professional civilian diplomats. They possessed formal and informal powers and were over-represented in the Israeli negotiation teams. The security subculture so prominent in Israeli life was expressed both in Israeli negotiation style and in substance. Inclusive in nature, Israeli security thinking covers topics such as how to enter negotiations and conduct them and how to perceive the Palestinian side and read its hidden agenda. Thus the dominant security subculture helped to create a group dynamic within the Israeli negotiating teams, and in civilian–military relations. The Israeli negotiator typically views diplomatic negotiation as a war of attrition. He either sets an ambush for his opponent and defends every inch of his territory in a battle of will in which details became principles; or he launches an offensive aimed at breaking the other side's resistance. This latter strategy involves presenting maximum demands that will allow the negotiator to back down and make concessions later on, pressuring the Palestinian side by tabling fresh counterproposals, using divide and rule tactics, and playing off the other side's ambitions, power struggles and emotions. Due to its professional bureaucracy, the Israeli tough negotiator is always armed with the proper tools – charts, data, maps, final status drafts, legal documents and precedents.[8] Israeli official negotiators were unprepared for negotiating Jerusalem due to the Israeli annexation of East Jerusalem in June 1967. It created a taboo that governed the minds of decision makers, the bureaucracy and the public. The IDF planning department and the security establishment treated East Jerusalem as a civilian issue lying beyond its terms of reference. Track Two practitioners entered into the vacuum that the Israeli establishment created. When final status talks opened, the Israeli administration called Track Two actors to assist. They opened their door to ideas, an exchange of views, and data on East Jerusalem.

On the Palestinian side, the key player involved in Track Two negotiations over Jerusalem was Orient House, headed by Faisal Husseini, a member of the PLO

Executive Committee. The PLO's negotiations department (through the NSU, the Negotiations Support Unit) did not deal directly with the issue of Jerusalem, which left Orient House to function as the professional-technical branch by preparing working papers and a database. This written material included reports on the ideas which were presented to them during their contacts with the Israelis. The reports sent to the leadership on Track Two negotiations were written in Arabic, since there was no demand for material in English. These papers were presented to Faisal Husseini, who in turn forwarded them to the leadership, a procedure that prevented the authors of the papers from knowing who read them and how they were used. Some Track Two team members would give private reports to senior members of the Palestinian establishment with whom they maintained personal relations; at times these reports contradicted each other. The Track Two negotiations team met with Faisal Husseini before and after every meeting with the Israelis in order to receive instructions and present their report. Unlike their Israeli counterparts, the Palestinian Track Two practitioners did not take an active part in shaping the leadership's stands, and did not attend face-to-face meetings with Arafat or with the Palestinian delegation. Throughout the secret negotiations that preceded the Camp David Summit (the Stockholm negotiations) there was no contact between the head of the Palestinian team, Abu-Ala'a, and the Orient House experts. One of these experts had sporadic contact with Yasser abd-Rabbo when the latter led the Palestinian team that negotiated with Oded Eran at the beginning of 2000, and with Abu Mazen shortly before the start of the Camp David summit.

Faisal Husseini rarely participated in person in Orient House Track Two meetings, so his reports on them to the Palestinian leadership were generally second-hand reports. He enjoyed a long history of open channels with Israelis but, from 1993 onward, he used this channel to launch official talks with Israeli and foreign politicians and officials while leaving Track Two for his professional staff. Furthermore, the Orient House experts were usually requested to report to Faisal Husseini and, more rarely, to others, on Israeli activities in Jerusalem dating from the 1967 war, rather than on Track Two ideas. They were not asked to present any recommendations on strategies and tactics for the negotiations, and only rarely were they asked to report Israeli proposals and discuss Palestinian alternatives. Up to the last stage of the talks in Taba, none of the experts were included in the Palestinian delegation. A specialist was invited to attend the Camp David summit but his participation was cancelled as a result of internal political intrigues and battles over prestige. The Palestinian delegation to Camp David occasionally contacted experts who remained in Jerusalem, asking for maps and answers to technical questions. In short, before and during the Camp David Summit the Palestinian Track Two professionals had a very limited impact on the Palestinian leadership.[9]

The Palestinians saw JIIS and ECF not only as enjoying a free channel of communication with the establishment but also as representing the views of the Israeli leadership. The Palestinians therefore believed it would be worthwhile to connect with these organizations as it would enable them to learn about Israeli tendencies, exchange messages between the two sides and even influence the Israeli establishment. The fact that during Camp David negotiations the Palestinian leadership was presented with the same ideas that Orient House experts had heard during Track Two negotiations was, for the Palestinians, proof of this perception. Furthermore, they also viewed the Israeli side as having better organized working procedures and a higher level of internal coordination between team members.[10]

Two main concepts, the Holy Basin and the special regime, were formulated by the JIIS and ECF teams and presented by them during Track Two negotiations. The Orient House professionals were willing to address these ideas for four reasons. First, they saw them as being part of the open city concept that they sought to agree on with their Israeli counterparts. Second, the Orient House team hoped to expand the Holy Basin area governed by the special regime to include sites located in the western part of the city such as the Monastery of the Cross (in the Valley of the Cross) and the Muslim Cemetery in Mamilla. In their view, including Muslim and Christian sites in West Jerusalem in the special regime would produce a more equitable agreement. This also motivated the Orient House delegation to demand territorial compensation in Lifta and al-Maliha, two Palestinian villages which were destroyed in the 1948 war and which have since then been part of West Jerusalem, in exchange for the Jewish neighbourhoods built beyond the 1967 borders. Furthermore, the Palestinians thought that the special regime could also include the internal neighbourhoods and the church of al-Azariyah, enabling a more balanced agreement. The third reason for which the Orient House delegation expressed its willingness to discuss these concepts was that they considered the Holy Basin and special regime ideas to be attractive to religious leaders and to believers who feel attached to Jerusalem holy places. The fourth reason was that by accepting ideas of a special regime mostly over East Jerusalem territory it would be easier for the Palestinians to come to terms with Israeli sovereignty in the neighbourhoods built beyond the 1967 lines.

In fact, the Palestinian reaction to the Holy Basin and special regime concepts was twofold. On the one hand, as mentioned above, their approach was to expand the area governed by the special regime, including in it also a large part of East Jerusalem and a few areas in the western part of the city. On the other hand, the Palestinians also felt that these concepts, conceived by the Israelis, neglected Palestinian rights in East Jerusalem. Therefore, their fallback position was that the special regime would apply only to the Old City. However, they did not present a viable solution for the need to include, under the special regime, sites outside the Old City, such as the Mount of Olives and the holy places in the Jehosephat Valley. In the end, the Palestinian delegation accepted the Israeli idea of joint sovereignty in the Old City, on condition they receive full sovereignty over the Temple Mount/al Haram al-Sharif, with Israel receiving sovereignty over the Western Wall.[11]

Orient House professionals did seriously consider Israeli models of divine, null, or joint sovereignty over Haram al-Sharif/the Temple Mount, and regarded them as an intellectual exercise. They decided to go along with these ideas, challenging the Israeli negotiators with questions about their practical implementation. According to the Palestinians, at first the Israelis were able to present only a general, unstructured concept rather than concrete answers. Later on, when the Israelis did present structured ideas, the Palestinians concluded that the compromises worked to the detriment of Palestinian interests (this was also the case later, when the same ideas were raised during the formal negotiations). The Palestinian Track Two practitioners were not willing to give up their claim to full sovereignty on al Haram al-Sharif, so the debate never got beyond a preliminary stage of clarifying stands and testing the waters. In response to these Israeli ideas, the Palestinians suggested dividing sovereignty in the Old City, with the Jewish Quarter remaining under Israeli sovereignty and the other three quarters falling under Palestinian sovereignty. They promised to guarantee freedom of access to the Jewish holy places and especially the Jewish cemetery on the Mount of Olives.[12]

Unlike Track Two negotiators, who were open to consider Israeli ideas, if only for tactical reasons, the Palestinian leadership displayed no similar flexibility or interest. There were two main reasons for their reluctance. First, the political leadership in Jerusalem (Faisal Husseini) and the central leadership (Abu Mazen) wanted to know exactly what each side would get. They had almost no interest in abstract concepts and lacked legal training. As such, they understood only full sovereignty and were interested only in operative issues about how power would be parcelled out. The answers they received from the Israelis on these arrangements did not satisfy the Palestinian leadership, at first because the discussions were ambiguous (the sides did not address the special regime details nor the exact powers granted to each side), and later because they sensed that the special regime would negate Palestinian sovereign rights in East Jerusalem.

Moreover, the Palestinian leadership's principal concerns were to base the negotiations on United Nations Security Council Resolution 242 and to obtain full sovereignty over the Temple Mount/al Haram al-Sharif. The leadership was not attentive to religious matters or other aspects of the agreement on Jerusalem. Indeed, the Israeli leadership's major strategic concern was also sovereignty, but it succeeded in using Track Two ideas as tactical tools. The Palestinians did not.[13]

In sum, the Orient House negotiators worked in accordance with the same norms and procedures used by the PLO and Palestinian Authority, even though both were weak in Jerusalem and the Palestinian establishment remained outside the city. Socially, politically and culturally, East Jerusalem is part of the West Bank. According to Omar Dajani, the Palestinian negotiation teams have high expectations but displayed little ability to translate these expectations into working plans and achievements. Palestinian experience was marked by statelessness, occupation and fragmentation; it is hardly surprising that in the peace process the Palestinian political system was dysfunctional. Their strategies were based on introducing principles of international law and third party intervention to help the weaker Palestinian side reach a just solution with Israel. In practice, the Palestinian modus operandi is dominated by disorganization, a high level of political competition between weak institutions organized into parallel agencies, and between different negotiators with overlapping responsibilities and limited coordination. The Palestinian system was dogged by Arafat's personal intervention, centralism and micro-management methods. He exerted power through a patronage system and his style of leadership was based on deliberate chaos and deinstitutionalization. The PLO has never had a strong and influential political planning department, nor has it sufficiently integrated professionals into its bureaucracy and decision-making process. The leadership did not provide the support units with guidelines for their data collection and held few preparation sessions to define detailed goals, tactics and fallback positions prior to rounds of negotiation with Israel. Rules set by the PLO Negotiation Affairs Department about the inclusion of its professional support staff in the delegation were often ignored or incompletely implemented. As a result, Palestinian negotiators developed a high degree of mutual distrust. A dynamic of competition for funding and political power discouraged unorthodox thinking and open debate, produced mixed messages, and resulted in Palestinian decision-making and negotiating strategy being determined to a large part by the personal interests of the negotiators. This state of affairs improved after Camp David 2000. The level of preparation increased significantly, in particular with regard to technical issues, thanks to the Palestinian leadership's exposure to Israeli working standards and proposals, and thanks to American pressure.[14] At this last stage of the official negotiations, Track Two professionals enjoyed a greater impact on the Palestinian negotiators than before. In conclusion, while the Israeli Track Two practitioners communicated with their leadership throughout the peace process, their Palestinian colleagues did so only towards the end of the formal talks. Palestinian and Israeli Track Two negotiators also differed in their impact.

The missing perspectives

Three combined subjects characterize the Jerusalem dispute: border setting, reaffirming collective identity and respecting the religious holiness. Jerusalem is the spiritual identity centre for millions of people worldwide. The Holy City represents for them God's eternity. For others, Jerusalem is the focus of their national identity and aspiration.

Borders and collective identity

In contrast to anthropologists who stress the decline of nationality via hybridization, sociologists suggest the persisting salience of national boundaries. Symbolic boundaries are often used to enforce, maintain, normalize or rationalize social boundaries. Social boundaries are also employed to contest and reframe the meaning of social boundaries. Cultural sociologists centre their attention on how boundaries are shaped by context, by the cultural repertoires, traditions and narratives, as well as how group boundaries are shaped by institutionalized definitions of cultural membership.[15]

The negotiations on Jerusalem in both official and unofficial tracks did not deal equally and simultaneously with all the aspects of this subject. More attention was given to setting borders than to other related issues. The negotiators did not acknowledge that boundaries are both made by identity and create it. Integrating boundary and territory in its wider socialization narrative was absent in both Track Two and the official talks. Track Two professionals preferred to stick to the technical and practical aspects of their profession and not touch the symbolic perspectives of Jerusalem. They gained accessibility to the decision makers by thinking differently and preparing alternatives that excluded the symbolic aspects of the land. This approach would create a crisis in the talks – as indeed happened in Camp David 2000.

Most Israeli Track Two practitioners played a major role in preserving sociospatial Israeli Jewish identity by expressing models of power relations aimed to secure Israeli hegemony on East Jerusalem and its holy Muslim and Christian shrines.

In spite of globalization, Passi[16] concludes that boundaries still function as territorial limits for state sovereignty. Contemporary boundaries are complicated social processes and discourses rather than fixed lines. Yet Track One and Track Two focused on line fixing more than on border regime and boundaries as institutions. Passi suggests two important conclusions on border construction that are relevant to Jerusalem. First he sees a link between boundary construction and ontological identity narrative. The construction of meaning occurs through narratives connected to the nation, state and territory as well as media, education, memorials, ceremonies and everyday life customs. Second, he sees a link between boundaries both as symbols and as a specific form of institution and state power. By excluding the 'other' through a border the powerful state can institutionalize identities. In other words, border construction is an expression of both physical and normative power relations. Similarly Duncan[17] argues that in order to understand how sites are constructed socially, it is necessary to study the discourse of the Other. The binary opposition of us against them serves the dual purpose of reinforcing and defining group identity and hegemony. Placing and representing the Other is an act of power, part of symbolizing the site in time and space. Track Two failed to have an impact in changing the Israeli aim to reflect in the final status agreement the asymmetry between the powerful Israelis and their subjected Palestinians. Indeed not a few Track Two talks went along this line too.

Newman and Passi[18] further developed the conclusion that boundaries are connected to national identity and the constitution of nation state. They are constructed by social, political and discursive forces, not just as objectives. Boundaries have deep symbolic, historical, cultural and religious meanings for different communities. Boundaries are perceived as the embodiment of implicit and explicit norms, values, moral and legal codes. They manifest themselves in numerous social practices.

Similar to Newman and Passi is the Lamont and Molnar[19] perspective on social identity. They discuss group boundaries, collective identity, generation shared definitions of us/them, and constitution of social actors through boundaries as a central process in contentious politics. The nation state is a producer of differences and acts as internal homogenizer through ethnic classifications. Symbolic and social boundaries put clear distinctions between the pure and the impure in defining appropriative citizens. In contrast to studies treating boundaries as markers of differences, Lamont and Molner show that others deal with boundaries as interfaces facilitating knowledge production and enabling communication across communities. Boundaries are conditions not only for separation and exclusion but also for communication, exchange, bridging and inclusion. Border societies have produced a range of multiplex and translational identities moving beyond the more monolithic categories. Borders became not sites of division and opposing identities but sites of interaction, hybridization and negotiation. Beyond simple separation, boundaries have two elements – checkpoints and mental maps – argues Migdal.[20] Checkpoints refer to the sites and practices that groups use to differentiate members from others, and enforce separation and categorization. They can be physical or virtual (dress/language). Mental maps incorporate elements of meaning people attach to spatial configurations; the loyalties they hold, the emotions that a grouping evokes and their cognitive world order. Beyond state borders, multiple sets of boundaries can exist. While state borders create single units, mental boundaries can have differential and discontinued spatial experiences, different divisions of space, and monitoring of boundaries. Most times multiple maps coexist but at other times they clash. This variety of perspectives and functions was absent in Track One and were not presented to the official negotiators by Track Two participants. They did not offer a catalogue of the key boundary mechanisms – activation, maintenance, transportation, bridging, crossing, dissolution, expansion, expulsion, protection of autonomy, or accumulation.

The religious aspect

David Smock[21] summed up some of the best publications in the developing field of religion and peacemaking. These publications do not argue that religion does not have a major role in evoking wars, maintaining conflicts and preventing peace; they argue that peace cannot be achieved if religious issues and groups are excluded from the process. Religious principals must be reinterpreted, especially in conflicts where religious values are part of the dispute; they transcend the disputed area; and religious authorities and institutions enjoy high social status. In cases where religious identities play a key role in the conflict, traditional diplomacy may not work well or gain legitimacy without bringing in the religious factor.

The involvement of religious leaders and the establishment of interfaith dialogue to resolve religious conflicts are crucial in facilitating the peacemaking process. Done in a classic Track Two negotiation it complements the diplomatic peacemaking. These publications suggest focusing religious peace building on apology and forgiveness as well as on building social justice. Smock refers to the African peacemaker Hizkias Assefa who argues that religious leaders can be an inspiration to their societies in general and to their political elites in particular once they explore common values such as justice and compassion and practice them in public life. Peacemaking calls for going beyond finding practical arrangements, making rational choices and cognitive commitments. The sides must reach the deep-seated base of their behaviour. Rational peacemaking and conventional negotiation process are not enough; they cannot change people's conflict behaviour. Those who are involved in the conflict should go through a process of mental therapy: examine critically their attitude and actions, look deeply into their emotions and work to change them. Religious authorities can help in promoting reconciliation with the 'other', re-humanizing the enemy and legitimizing the concessions. Thus religious leaders translate peace beliefs to rituals, practices and experiences creating a peace community.

Roger Friedland and Richard Hecht[22] deal with the same argument but from the territorial perspective. They state that urban space cannot be separated from culture, and all kinds of meanings existed before the planner began working. The meaning given to a place is not static. Sacredness is always open to interpretations and reinterpretations that locate the holy site in the community mind, rituals and historical memory.

Studies on the sacred places, they argue, position them as opposite to 'normal', immaterial and, consequently strip the sacred of its central property – its power. 'Authority to speak the word, to visit the place, to control its rites all involves questions of power....yet power and the adjudication of access is absolutely essential to the organization and constitution of sacred sites. This is particularly the case where, as often happens, divergent communities or groups contest control and interpretation of sacred sites... it is no wonder that states have sought to control them and indeed often to base their legitimacy upon that control.'[23]

Freidland and Hecht understand the holy place as multifaceted. They profile it as both outside the ordinary and as concrete places with histories, politics and deep connection to sovereignty. The histories and politics of the holy site are dynamic, thus the place is fluid, always being built and re-built in order to mark an identity and give meaning to the time line. A holy place is both a physical compound and the territory of collective imagination and memory.

Track Two rarely touched Temple Mount. Before Camp David 2000, only two Track Two meetings were held on religious issues, both in July 2000.[24] Track One talks on Temple Mount focused only on state sovereignty.

Another shortcoming of Track One is revealed by Hassner.[25] He uses a phenomenological approach to conclude that conflict over sacred space cannot be resolved by dividing, sharing or replacing the sacred space as suggested by Clinton (and accepted by Israel) in Track One. Sacred spaces are indivisible – meaning perfectly cohesive; they have unambiguous and inflexible boundaries and cannot be exchanged or substituted for another good. A dispute over holy place involves religious ideas, divine presence and absolute values – there is no room for compromise unless the compromise or the division is forced. But a forced arrangement leads to an unstable and fragile situation by the unsatisfied side. A better and balanced approach addressing the dispute must combine political pragmatism with the symbolic weight of the holy place. However, this was not done. Flexibility was not introduced into the sacred and the charismatic and did not prevent the religious elements from escalating the conflict.

Track Two teams failed to include religious experts or leaders. The Israeli team consulted with lawyers, political scientists, engineers, architects and only a few religious leaders. The absence of religious experts and leaders from the preparation for the negotiation had two direct consequences: both parties were caught off guard by the demands raised by their opponents, and the excluded religious leaders succeeded to influence the negotiation from outside. Religious leaders hold the power, authority and knowledge about the boundaries of meaning of the holy place – but they were not included in the talks. Instead of seeking insights into religious dimensions of the conflict, negotiators treated the issue either as a purely political problem to be addressed by standard political tools or as an instrumental obstacle.

Built-in shortcomings of Track Two

Some Track Two shortcomings are the direct consequence of the different nature of the channels themselves: while the formal negotiations were an authorized panel, in which decision makers participated for the purpose of decision making, Track Two negotiations were a laboratory for experimenting with ideas, building up a reservoir of different proposals, gathering information, helping to prepare for the official talks, or trying to prevent oncoming crises in the formal negotiations. Track Two suffered from the following shortcomings and inability to bring the official track to succeed.

First, Track Two meetings were conducted almost exclusively between professionals. Insufficient effort was made to bring together community leaders representing the two peoples who would have to live side by side under the terms of a peace accord.

Second, major Track Two teams dealing with the Jerusalem question (JIIS and London track) shared a professional approach and personal attachment to the city, a benefit that most of the official team members lacked. Many of the participants in the unofficial channels were professionals and academic specialists in urban planning, as well as citizens of Jerusalem who understood the complexities and needs of Jerusalem the city. As a consequence, they frequently discussed administrative issues and made efforts to answer local municipal needs. The participants in the official negotiations, on the other hand, were usually politicians who put a greater emphasis on issues such as sovereignty and borders, while tending to disregard the practical issues of urban life.

Third, Palestinian–Israeli talks were between unequal partners. A regional power negotiated with a poor know-how organization representing occupied people. In the official talks Israel tried to exploit this gap and preserve its superiority. However, successful Track Two meetings were based on equality and win-win gains. Track Two participants failed to transfer to the official negotiators their way of creating mutual trust and partnership equality.

Fourth, Track Two impact was limited to fields of practical and functional compromises, the fields in which its experts could exercise their professionalism. Track Two on Jerusalem did not include negotiations on religious issues, symbols and identities because it fell out of the participants' expertise, personal qualifications and beliefs. Almost all were secular academics lacking religious knowledge and empathy to religious beliefs, organizations and leaders. Many of them belong to educated upper middle classes disconnected from both religious communities and lower classes that oppose the peace process.

It is therefore suggested that negotiation teams include religious and secular participants, experts in politics and urban planning next to people from the fine arts, security officers sitting with welfare experts, economists and social workers. The more Track Two operates and the more inclusive it is – the better. Although the number of each side's experts and optional participants is limited and in many cases the same delegates re-meet under different hats, the intense exchange of ideas, the many chances to meet and build personal relations and mutual trust are important gains. When the time comes and the sides are ripe, these peace process veterans will discover new ideas and move ahead based on what they have achieved up to that point.

Impact assessment

Like many Track Two activists and scholars, Herbert Kelman of Harvard University tried to find criteria by which the success of Track Two negotiations in changing the political systems and values could be measured. Professor Kelman is not only a Track Two theoretician but a practitioner as well. He developed and uses his Working Group Model as an unofficial third-party effort to promote resolution of the Israeli–Palestinian conflict in Track Two meetings based on interactive problem solving.[26] Kelman's method is to bring together politically engaged and highly influential Palestinians and Israelis for private confidential discussions facilitated by a panel of social scientists that are knowledgeable about international and inter-communal conflict, group process and the Middle East. These discussions take place in an intensive workshop designed to enable the parties to explore each other's perspective and understand each other's concerns, needs, fears, priorities and constraints. On the basis of this analysis, participants are encouraged to engage in a process of creative, joint problem solving in order to generate new ideas that are responsive to both sets of needs and fears, and so to resolve their conflicts. The ultimate goal is to transfer the insights and ideas gained from these interactions into the public debate and the decision-making processes in the two communities.[27] These meetings were productive on the subjects of a future Palestinian state, Jerusalem and the Palestinian refugees.[28]

According to Kelman, Track Two is successful insofar as it contributes to changes in the political culture on each side in ways that make the parties more receptive to negotiation. Such outcomes include 'the emergence of a sense of possibility'; 'belief that at least some elements on the other side are interested in a peaceful solution'; 'greater awareness of the other's perspective'; 'initiation of mutually reassuring actions'; 'a shared vision of a desirable future'; 'exploration of ideas for the overall shape of a solution to the conflict'; 'exploration of ideas for moving the negotiations forward'; and 'developing "cadres" with direct experience in communication with the other side'.[29] Like Kelman, Benjamin Gidron *et al.* note that 'recent literature on international conflict resolution emphasizes Track Two diplomacy, which focuses on the roles actors outside the government play in resolving conflicts'.[30]

Kelman and Kidron show how Israeli and Palestinian Track Two groups contributed to the official talks by trying to bring the two peoples to change their historical course from bloody conflicts to permanent peace and to prefer diplomacy to military solutions. In different venues, described in detail in this study, Track Two members had a great impact on setting the negotiation agenda, vocabulary and substance. Track Two ideas were often tabled at the official talks, at times in their original form but in many other cases transformed to fit the negotiation strategies and styles of the two political leaderships.

For their part, the Track Two professionals were eager to inject their insights, ideas and proposals (whether fully thought out or tentative) into the official talks. On both the Palestinian and Israeli sides, however, official-professional dialogue was shaped by the decision makers' selectivity, preferences and limited availability. Each official chose the professional voice he would listen to and placed time limits on professional involvement. The outsider professional was called in either intermittently or when the talks faced a deadlock and a serious crisis. The leader also decided which level of political official the professional would meet with, and was able to limit access to senior decision makers and to the negotiating team. The officials' decision about which professionals to heed did not depend solely on the professionals' skills and expertise. The officials tended to prefer mainstream, level-headed voices, as well as people that the political leader sensed were loyal to him, to his negotiating goals or to his administration. Former civil servants and experts who maintained open channels with the administration also had a great advantage. Furthermore, the decision makers' selection was influenced by 'packaging' considerations. A professional's influence increased to the extent that his ideas were consistent with other components of the deal the political leader had prepared or already offered.

Finally, in choosing his negotiating strategy and tactics, the leader's approach was shaped also by political and public relations considerations. The decision maker did not share these considerations with the ex-establishment professionals and confided only in his own close and loyal assistants. Consequently, ideas created or understandings reached in Track Two were rarely adopted by the official negotiators in their original form. They were either rejected outright or revised or placed in a different context. It goes without saying that they were presented in a style very different from that used by the Track Two professionals, which had smoothed their acceptance by the opposing side on Track Two. This is neither to say that the decision maker went beyond his authority and responsibility, nor to conclude that the Israeli–Palestinian case is unique. Quite the opposite is true.[31] A good example is that of the 'umbrella municipality', an idea that was repeatedly brought up during Track Two negotiations but never discussed in formal negotiations. The dissimilar nature of the participants is a direct consequence of the different nature of the channels themselves.

Track Two meetings are also less intense than official negotiations (as can be seen in the different time axis in this research – one year of official negotiations in comparison to six years of Track Two negotiations). The longer time scale of Track Two negotiations allows for a process of rethinking and maturation. The impact of the different nature of the channels can be clearly seen in the different ways of addressing the question of the Temple Mount/al Haram al-Sharif. While in the Track Two negotiations the approach was relatively open and different types of sovereignty were offered, in the official negotiations there was difficulty in presenting innovative ideas regarding sovereignty, and it was usually dealt with in its traditional, zero-sum form. Moreover, during the official negotiations, the question of sovereignty in regard to all of the spaces addressed in this work was more extensively dealt with in comparison to Track Two negotiations, because of the political nature of this subject. Track Two negotiations, as mentioned above, tended to focus more on administrative and urban issues.

Points of limited success

Track Two limits

Cuhadar[32] concludes that Track Two had an impact on process only, as against having an impact also on negotiation results. As this study shows, political competition within each side (between Track Two channels and team members as well as between official negotiators) limited the impact of Track Two even on the process. Not all data and Track Two work were transferred to relevant official teams. In addition, Track Two access to decision makers and negotiators was limited. Research publications by Israeli Track Two members, including by the author of this study, helped to change public opinion thereby indirectly influencing the political elite. Through Track Two the weak Palestinian side was able to improve its capacity and close some gaps with Israel, in particular in data gathering. However, this achievement had almost no impact on the Camp David summit of 2000.

Track Two actors benefitted from deficiencies

The architects of Track Two on Jerusalem were able to have an impact on the official talks because a certain void existed both in the minds and in the operations of the official actors while the political clock of the official track was ticking. In Israel a taboo against discussing any possibility of dividing Jerusalem was overruled by officials.

On the other side, the PLO and the Palestinian Authority officials' knowledge on the urban reality in Jerusalem was very limited. With few exceptions, the PLO seniors came from 'outside' Palestine in 1994 – but then Israel did not let the Palestinian Authority operate in Arab Jerusalem. The Palestinian negotiators lacked essential data on Jerusalem and the methods of translating it into political options. Ever since the end of the 1967 war they demanded that Israel withdraw to 4 June 1967 lines in Jerusalem but the Israeli annexation project and its massive building in the former Jordanian area made this impossible. Israel succeeded in moving half of the city's Jewish population to the annexed area, creating an almost equal demographic balance between Israeli Jews and Palestinian Arabs in the Eastern City. Thus Israel unilaterally created an irreversible situation. The data on the Israeli settlements and annexation project in Jerusalem was provided to the PLO and Palestinian Authority establishment by Palestinian Track Two participants. They collected data first hand because they were Jerusalemites; what they missed they got from their Israeli counterparts at Track Two meetings. Based on that information the PLO and Palestinian Authority negotiators could revise their stands and develop alternatives. However, this effort was not enough. Lack of coordination between Palestinian headquarters in Jerusalem and the national negotiating institutions located in Ramallah and Gaza, as well as sharp political competition between the local and national leaderships, limited the impact of Palestinian Track Two actors on their officials. The space that the officials created enabled Track Two operators to survive. Their impact on Track One depended on their distance from the officials: the greater the distance, the lesser their impact.

But Track Two also has had major achievements. Track Two contacts created a common professional discourse and a program based on a more or less agreed-upon base of data. Thus Track Two paved the way for formal negotiations, initiated terms of reference and placed the issue of Jerusalem before the public. Once formal negotiations commenced, they had a great impact on the shaping of the Israeli position.

Mutual perceptions and misperceptions

Both Palestinian and Israeli main Track Two forums saw each other not only as enjoying a free channel of communication with the establishment but also as representing the views of their leadership. Each side therefore believed it would be worthwhile to connect with its counterpart as it would enable it to learn about the others' tendencies, exchange messages and even influence the other's establishment. Eventually, each Track Two actor's communication with its leadership was more problematic than perceived by the other side.

Acting as agents of change

Track Two negotiators made several breakthroughs and formulated creative ideas that were later brought to the negotiating table mainly by the Israeli side. Both the

Israeli establishment and the public heard experts present reasons, from the point of view of Israel, why the longstanding taboo against negotiating over Jerusalem had to be broken in order to reach a viable agreement with the Palestinians. In this regard Track Two did not have a direct impact on the politicians. Track Two participants were mostly professionals who preferred not to confront the decision makers and not to be perceived as intervening in politics. As is often the case, the last people to grasp that old beliefs had to change were the politicians from both sides. Had the environment in which they operate not changed, they would never have reached this understanding.

Public education

Israeli and Palestinian experience shows that parties interested in promoting negotiations should raise public awareness and manage public debate on negotiation issues. Prior to the official negotiations there was only one case in which the participants in the informal channels went public, announced their position and submitted their paper to the heads of the relevant states. At that stage few Israeli experts (including the author of this research) went public and published ideas and data showing the many lines already dividing Jerusalem socially, religiously, politically, geographically and economically. They also showed the peace benefits coming from negotiating and redividing Jerusalem. Although they did not speak on behalf of Track Two, these publications were agents of change that helped public opinion and decision makers to review their stands. When the official talks terminated with no results, two Track Two initiatives went public and asked the public to support their models.

Track Two participants that go public while officials hesitate act with great civil courage and social responsibility since they challenge the conventional wisdom and the national consensus. They are ready to face the politicians' response. The political establishment can lose its tolerance and deny these actors access, status and material benefits.

Interaction between decision makers and Track Two actors

When the formal track was about to commence, and as it proceeded, officials and professionals found themselves dependent upon each other, and this inter-dependence gave rise to relationships among them. Since political constraints prevented official negotiators from adequately preparing their brief for negotiations over Jerusalem, they had no choice but to open their minds to understandings reached and ideas exchanged in the Track Two talks over the capital city.

In Track Two conducted by professionals, the division of labour between politicians and experts is preserved. The danger is that the two will become disengaged. The framework of the political arrangement may be determined without or indeed in contradiction to professional input. Political considerations may override professional necessities, and the absence of experts from the principal discussions would cause trouble for the statesmen later, when they have to find solutions to the problems raised by the political framework. Similarly, professional recommendations may be made without any political input or overview. The statesman and the expert may not understand each other's language.

Acknowledging that professional dialogue by itself was not enough, some Track Two managers decided to include a political framework in order to achieve political breakthroughs and provide the decision makers with tools if and when the negotiations on Jerusalem commenced. These participants also agreed that without a political framework for their Track Two talks, the professional dialogue could not go very far. Naturally, most of the attention in these channels was devoted to political principles and very little to distinctly professional questions.

Track Two ideas were often tabled at the official talks, at times in their original form but in many other cases transformed to fit the negotiation strategies and styles of the two political leaderships. The politicians neither incorporated Track Two experts into their inner circle nor shared with them their strategic goals and negotiation tactics.

Notes

1 Although Track Two is well researched, the case of the impact of Track Two on Israeli–Palestinian official talks is still lacking. Only in late 2009 did Esra Cuhadar publish the first research on the subject (Cuhadar 2009). I was among those Cuhadar interviewed, based on my experience and this study. Much of her conclusions are based on this study and my book *The Jerusalem Problem* [Klein 2003]. Hence there are similarities between her findings and this chapter. Yet the premise of her study prevented her from describing in detail the impact that Track Two discussions on Jerusalem made on official diplomacy, which is what I do below. Finally, I incorporated in this research knowledge and conclusions that I gained by participating in many Track Two meetings and advising the Israeli Track One team. Without being a practitioner I would not be able to write this study. The reader is invited to judge if my participation misled my observation and judgement.

2 M. Klein, *The Jerusalem Problem: The Struggle for Permanent Status* (Gainesville: University Press of Florida, 2003): 23–42.

3 Unless referred otherwise this section is based on Klein, *The Jerusalem Problem*, 23–42.

4 JIIS, *Peacemaking in Jerusalem – A Task Team Report* (Jerusalem: The Jerusalem Institute for Israel Studies, 2000).

5 I. Kassassieh, 'Second Track Negotiations: The Jerusalem File', *Jerusalem Quarterly* 15 (2002). www.jqf-jerusalem.org.

6 M. Hassassian, 'Final Status Negotiations on Jerusalem: An Inside Look', Presentation at PASSIA, 13 March 2001. www.passia.org; Kassassieh, 'Second Track Negotiations'.

7 The output of some of the informal channels may be found in the following sources: Y. Hirschfeld, *Oslo, a Formula for Peace* (Hebrew) (Tel Aviv: Yitzhak Rabin Center for Israel Studies and Am Oved, 2000): 212–217; M. Maoz and S. Nusseibeh (eds), *Jerusalem: Points of Friction and Beyond* (Dordrecht: Kluwer, 2000); N. Chazan, 'Negotiating the Non-Negotiable: Jerusalem in the Framework of an Israeli-Palestinian Settlement', *Occasional Papers of the American Academy of Arts and Sciences* 7 (March, 1991); M. Shatayyeh (ed.), *Scenarios on the Future of Jerusalem* (Jerusalem: Palestinian Center for Regional Studies, 1998); M. Abdul Hadi (ed.), *Dialogue on Jerusalem* (Jerusalem: PASSIA, 1998); Y. Hirschfeld, 'Keeping Oslo Alive: Developing a Non-Governmental Peace Strategy', in *Is Oslo Alive?* (London: The Konrad Adenauer Foundation, 1998): 68–114; IPCRI, *Jerusalem Maps* (Jerusalem: IPCRI, May, 1999); Hassassian, 'Final Status Negotiations on Jerusalem'; Kassassieh, 'Second Track Negotiations'; A. Friedman and R. Nasarallah (eds),

Jerusalem Berlin Forum: Divided Cities in Transition (Jerusalem: The International Peace and Cooperation Center and the Jerusalem Institute for Israel Studies, 2003).

8 A. Kleiman, 'Israeli Negotiating Culture', in *How Israelis and Palestinians Negotiate – A Cross-Cultural Analysis of the Oslo Peace Process*, ed. T. Cofman Wittes (Washington, DC: United States Institute of Peace Press, 2005): 81–132.

9 N. al-Jubeh, interviewed by the author, 24 January 2005; M. Hassassian, interviewed by the author, 20 April 2005.

10 M. Hassassian, interviewed by the author.

11 N. al-Jubeh, interviewed by the author; M. Hassassian, interviewed by the author.

12 N. al-Jubeh, interviewed by the author; M. Hassassian, interviewed by the author.

13 N. al-Jubeh, interviewed by the author; M. Hassassian, interviewed by the author.

14 O. Dajani, 'Surviving Opportunities: Palestinian Negotiating Patterns in Peace Talks with Israel', in *How Israelis and Palestinians Negotiate – A Cross-Cultural Analysis of the Oslo Peace Process*, ed. T. Cofman Wittes (Washington, DC: United States Institute of Peace Press, 2005): 39–80.

15 M. Lamont and V. Molnar, 'The Study of Boundaries in the Social Sciences', *Annual Review of Sociology* 28 (2002): 167–195.

16 A. Passi, 'Boundaries as Social Processes – Territoriality in the World of Flows', in *Boundaries, Territory and Post-modernity*, ed. D. Newman (London: Frank Cass, 1999): 69–88.

17 J. Duncan, 'Sites of Representation – Place, Time and Discourse of the Other', in *Place, Culture, Representation,* ed. J. Duncan and D. Leg (London: Routledge, 1993): 39–56.

18 Passi, 'Boundaries as Social Processes'.

19 Lamont and Molnar, 'The Study of Boundaries in the Social Sciences'.

20 J.S. Migdal, 'Mental Maps and Virtual Checkpoints – Struggles to Construct and Maintain State and Social Boundaries', in *Boundaries and Belonging – State and Societies in the Struggle to Shape Identities and Local Practices*, ed. J. Migdal (Cambridge: Cambridge University Press, 2004): 3–23.

21 D. Smock, 'Introduction', in *Religious Contributions to Peacemaking – When Religion Brings Peace Not War*, ed. D. Smock (Washington, DC: United States Institute for Peace, 2006): 1–5.

22 R. Friedland and R. Hecht, 'Sacred Urbanism: Jerusalem's Sacrality, Urban Sociology and the History of Religion', paper presented in the conference on Jerusalem Across the Disciplines (Phoenix: Arizona State University, February 2007).

23 Friedland and Hecht, 'Sacred Urbanism'.

24 Klein, *The Jerusalem Problem*.

25 R. Hassner, 'To Halve and to Hold – Conflicts over Sacred Space and the Problem of Indivisibility', *Security Studies* 12, no. 4 (Summer, 2003): 1–33.

26 H.C. Kelman, 'Informal Mediation by the Scholar/Practitioner', in *Mediation in International Relations: Multiple Approaches to Conflict Management*, eds. J. Bercovitch and J. Z. Rubin (New York: St. Martin's Press, 1992): 64–69. H.C. Kelman, 'Interactive Problem Solving: An Approach to Conflict Resolution and its Application in the Middle East', *PS: Political Science and Politics*, 31 (1998): 190–198. H.C. Kelman, 'Negotiations as Interactive Problem Solving', *International Negotiation* 1, no. 1 (1996): 99–123.

27 H.C. Kelman, 'Promoting Joint Thinking in International Conflicts: An Israeli-Palestinian Continuing Workshop', *Journal of Social Issues* 50 (1994): 157–178. M. Maoz *et al.*, 'The Future of Israeli-Palestinian Relations', *Middle East Policy* 7, no. 2 (2000).

28 Maoz *et al.*, "The Future of Israeli-Palestinian Relations; Chazan, 'Negotiating the Non-Negotiable'".

29 D. Lieberfeld, 'Evaluating the Contribution of Track Two Diplomacy to Conflict Termination in South Africa 1984–90', *Journal of Peace Research* 39, no. 3 (2002): 370.

30 B. Gidron, S.N. Katz, and Y. Hasenfeld, 'Introduction, Theoretical Approach and Methodology', in *Mobilizing for Peace: Conflict Resolution in Northern Ireland, Israel/Palestine and South Africa*, eds. B. Gidron, S.N. Katz and Y. Hasenfeld (Oxford: Oxford University Press, 2002): 6.

31 Klein, *The Jerusalem Problem*, 24–25.

32 E. Cuhadar, 'Assessing Transfer from Track Two Diplomacy: The Case of Water and Jerusalem', *Journal of Peace Research* 46 (2009): 641–658.

References

Abdul Hadi, M. (ed.) *Dialogue on Jerusalem.* Jerusalem: PASSIA, 1998.

Agha, H.S., A. Feldman and Z. Schiff. *Track II Diplomacy Lessons from the Middle East.* Cambridge, MA: MIT Press, 2003.

Arthur, P. 'Some Thoughts on Transition: A Comparative View of the Peace Process in South Africa and Northern Ireland'. *Government and Opposition* 30, no. 1(1995): 46–59.

Arthur, P. 'Time, Territory, Tradition and the Anglo-Irish "Peace" Process'. *Government and Opposition* 31, no. 4(1996): 426–440.

Arthur, P. 'Quiet Diplomacy and Personal Conversation: Track Two Diplomacy and the Search for a Settlement in Northern Ireland'. In *Democracy is a Discussion – The Challenges and Promise of a New Democratic Era,* edited by S. Myers, 70–95. New London, CT, 1998.

Ben-Ami, S. *A Front Without a Rearguard: A Voyage to the Boundaries of the Peace Process.* Tel Aviv: Miskal-Yedioth Ahronoth Books and Chemed Books, 2004.

Chazan, N. 'Negotiating the Non-Negotiable: Jerusalem in the Framework of an Israeli-Palestinian Settlement'. *Occasional Papers of the American Academy of Arts and Sciences,* no. 7: (March 1991).

Chigas, D.V. 'Unofficial Intervention with Official Actors: Parallel Negotiation Training in Violent Intrastate Conflicts'. *International Negotiation* 2, no. 3(1997): 409–436.

Cingoli, J. (ed.) *Israelis, Palestinians Coexisting in Jerusalem.* Milano: Centro Italiano per la Pace in Medio Oriente, 2001.

Chufrin, G.I. and H.H. Saunders. 'A Public Peace Process'. *Negotiation Journal* 9, no. 2 (1993): 155–177.

CIPMO (Italian Center for Peace in the Middle East) and The Orient House – Arab Studies Society Jerusalem and the Economic Cooperation Foundation. *Israelis, Palestinians Coexisiting in Jerusalem.* Milano: Centro Italiano per la Pace in Medio Oriente, 2001.

Cochrane, F. 'Beyond the Political Elites: A Comparative Analysis of the Roles and Impacts of Community-Based NGOs in Conflict Resolution Activity'. *Civil Wars* 3, no. 2(2002): 1–22.

Cuhadar, E. 'Assessing Transfer from Track Two Diplomacy: The Case of Water and Jerusalem'. *Journal of Peace Research* 46, no. 5(2009): 641–658.

Dajani, O. 'Surviving Opportunities: Palestinian Negotiating Patterns in Peace Talks with Israel'. In *How Israelis and Palestinians Negotiate – A Cross-Cultural Analysis of the Oslo Peace Process,* edited by T. Cofman Wittes, 39–80. Washington, DC: United States Institute of Peace Press, 2005.

Davies, J. and E. Kaufman (eds) 'Second Track/Citizen's Diplomacy: An Overview'. In *Second Track/Citizens' Diplomacy – Concepts and Techniques for Conflict Transformation,* edited by J. Davies and E. Kaufman, 1–12. Lanham, MD: Rowman and Littlefield, 2002.

Duncan, J. 'Sites of Representation – Place, Time and Discourse of the Other'. In *Place, Culture, Representation,* edited by J. Duncan and D. Leg, 39–56. London and New York: Routledge, 1993.

Fisher, R J. 'The Potential Contribution of Training to Resolving International Conflict'. *International Negotiation* 2, no. 3(1997): 471–486.

Fisher, R.J. *Interactive Conflict Resolution.* Syracuse, NY: Syracuse University Press, 1997.

Friedland, R. and R. Hecht. 'Sacred Urbanism: Jerusalem's Sacrality, Urban Sociology and the History of Religion'. Paper presented in the conference on Jerusalem Across the Disciplines, Arizona State University, February 2007.

Friedman, A. and R. Nasarallah (eds) *Jerusalem Berlin Forum: Divided Cities in Transition.* Jerusalem: The International Peace and Cooperation Center and the Jerusalem Institute for Israel Studies, 2003.

Gidron, B., S.N. Katz and Y. Hasenfeld. 'Introduction, Theoretical Approach and Methodology'. In *Mobilizing for Peace: Conflict Resolution in Northern Ireland, Israel/Palestine and South Africa*, edited by B. Gidron, S.N. Katz and Y. Hasenfeld, 3–38. Oxford: Oxford University Press, 2002.

Hanieh, A. 'The Camp David Diaries'. *Journal of Palestine Studies* 31(2001): 75–97.

Hassner, R.E. 'To Halve and to Hold – Conflicts over Sacred Space and the Problem of Indivisibility'. *Security Studies* 12, no. 4(2003): 1–33.

Hassassian, M. 'Final Status Negotiations on Jerusalem: An Inside Look'. Presented at PASSIA, 13 March 2001.

Hirschfeld, Y. 'Keeping Oslo Alive: Developing a Non-Governmental Peace Strategy'. In *Is Oslo Alive?* 68–114. Jerusalem: The Konrad Adenauer Foundation, The Harry S. Truman Research Institute at the Hebrew University and the Palestine Consultancy Group, 1998.

Hirschfeld, Y. *Oslo, a Formula for Peace* (Hebrew). Tel Aviv: Yitzhak Rabin Center for Israel Studies and Am Oved, 2000.

IPCRI. *Jerusalem Maps*. Jerusalem: IPCRI, May 1999.

JIIS. *Peacemaking in Jerusalem – A Task Team Report*. Jerusalem: The Jerusalem Institute for Israel Studies, 2000.

Kassassieh, I. 'Second Track Negotiations: The Jerusalem File'. *Jerusalem Quarterly* 15(2002): 49–53.

Kelman, H.C. 'Informal Mediation by the Scholar/Practitioner'. In *Mediation in International Relations: Multiple Approaches to Conflict Management*, edited by J. Bercovitch and J.Z. Rubin, 64–96. New York: St. Martin's Press, 1992.

Kelman, H.C. 'Negotiations as Interactive Problem Solving'. *International Negotiation* 1, no. 1 (1996): 99–124.

Kelman, H.C. 'The Contributions of Non-Governmental Organizations to the Resolution of Ethno-national Conflicts: An Approach to Evaluation'. Paper Presented at the Carnegie Corporation Conference on the Role of International NGOs in Ethnic and Nationalist Conflicts, New York, 1996.

Kelman, H.C. 'Promoting Joint Thinking in International Conflicts: An Israeli-Palestinian Continuing Workshop'. *Journal of Social Issues* 50, no. 1(1994): 157–178.

Kelman, H.C. 'Interactive Problem Solving: An Approach to Conflict Resolution and its Application in the Middle East'. *PS: Political Science and Politics* 31, no. 2(1998): 190–198.

Kelman, H.C. 'Interactive Problem Solving as a Tool for Second Track Diplomacy'. In *Second Track/Citizens' Diplomacy – Concepts and Techniques for Conflict Transformation*, edited by J. Davis and E. Kaufman, 81–106. Lanham, MD: Rowman and Littlefield, 2002.

Kimmerling, B. and J.S. Migdal. *The Palestinian People, A History*. Cambridge, MA: Harvard University Press, 2003.

Kleiman, Aharon. 'Israeli Negotiating Culture'. In *How Israelis and Palestinians Negotiate – A Cross-Cultural Analysis of the Oslo Peace Process*, edited by T. Cofman Wittes, 81–132. Washington, DC: United States Institute of Peace Press, 2005.

Klein, M. *The Jerusalem Problem: The Struggle for Permanent Status*. Gainesville, FL: University Press of Florida, 2003.

Lamont, M. and V. Molnar. 'The Study of Boundaries in the Social Sciences'. *Annual Review of Sociology* 28(2002): 167–195.

Lieberfeld, D. 'Evaluating the Contribution of Track Two Diplomacy to Conflict Termination in South Africa 1984–90'. *Journal of Peace Research* 39, no. 3(2002): 355–372.

Macmillan, M. *Peacemakers – Six Months that Changed the World*. London: John Murray, 2003.

Maoz, M., G. Khattib, I. Dakak, Y. Katz., Y. Sayigh, Z. Schiff, S. Shamir, K. Shikaki. 'The Future of Israeli-Palestinian Relations'. *Middle East Policy* 7, no. 2(2000): 90–112.

Maoz, M. and S. Nusseibeh (eds) *Jerusalem: Points of Friction and Beyond*. London: Kluwer, 2000.

McDonald, J.W. 'Further Exploration of Track Two Diplomacy'. In *Timing the De-escalation of International Conflicts*, edited by L. Kriesberg and S.J. Thorson, 201–220. Syracuse, NY: Syracuse University Press, 1991.

MacDonald, J.W. 'The Need for Multi-Track Diplomacy'. In *Second Track/Citizens' Diplomacy – Concepts and Techniques for Conflict Transformation*, edited by J. Davis and E. Kaufman, 49–60. Lanham, MD: Rowman and Littlefield, 2002.

Migdal, J.S. 'Mental Maps and Virtual Checkpoints - Struggles to Construct and Maintain State and Social Boundaries'. In *Boundaries and Belonging -State and Societies in the Struggle to Shape Identities and Local Practices*, edited by J.S. Migdal, 3–23. Cambridge: Cambridge University Press, 2004.

Montville, J. 'The Arrow and the Olive Branch: A Case for Track Two Diplomacy'. *Conflict Resolution: Track Two Diplomacy*, edited by J. McDonald and D. Bendahmane, 5–20. Washington, DC: Foreign Service Institute, Department of State, 1987.

Newman, D. and A. Passi. 'Fences and Neighbors in the Postmodern World – Boundary Narratives in Political Geography'. *Progress in Human Geography* 22(1998): 186–207.

Ginat, J. 'Temple Mount–al Haram al-Sharif: A Proposal for Solution'. *Middle East Peace Process Vision Versus Reality*, edited by J. Ginat, E.J. Perkins and E.G. Corr, 372–374. (Oklahoma Paper). Brighton: Sussex Academic Press, 2002.

Passi, Anssi. 'Boundaries as Social Processes – Territoriality in the World of Flows'. In *Boundaries, Territory and Post-modernity*, edited by D. Newman, 69–88. London: Frank Cass, 1999.

Ross, D. *The Missing Peace – The Inside Story of the Fight for Middle East Peace*. New York: Farrar, Straus and Giroux, 2004.

Rouhana, N.N. 'Unofficial Third-Party Intervention in International Conflict: Between Legitimacy and Disarray'. *Negotiation Journal* 11, no. 3(1995): 255–270.

Rouhana, N.N. 'Interactive Conflict Resolution: Issues in Theory, Methodology, and Evaluation'. In *International Conflict Resolution after the Cold War*, edited by D. Druckman and P.C. Stern, 294–337. Washington, DC: National Academy Press, 2000.

Saunders, H.H. 'Possibilities and Change: Another Way to Consider Unofficial Third Party Intervention'. *Negotiation Journal* 11, no. 3(1995): 271–275.

Saunders, H.H. 'We Need a Later Theory of Negotiation: The Impact of Pre-Negotiation Phases'. *Negotiation Journal* 1, no. 3(1985): 249–262.

Shatayyeh, M. (ed.) *Scenarios on the Future of Jerusalem*. Al-Bireh: Palestinian Center for Regional Studies, 1998.

Sher, G. *Just Beyond Reach: The Israeli-Palestinian Peace Negotiations 1999–2001*. Tel Aviv: Miskal-Yedioth Ahronoth Books and Chemed Books, 2001.

Smock, D.R. 'Introduction'. In *Religious Contributions to Peacemaking – When Religion Brings Peace Not War*, edited by D. R. Smock, 1–5. Washington, DC: US Institute of Peace, 2006.

Susskind, L.E., A. Chayes and J. Martinez. 'Parallel Informal Negotiation: A New Kind of International Dialogue'. *Negotiation Journal* 12, no. 1(1996): 19–29.

Swisher, C. E. *The Truth About Camp David: The Untold Story About the Collapse of the Middle East Peace Process*. New York: Nation Books, 2004.

The Italian Center for Peace in the Middle East. *Israelis, Palestinians Coexisting in Jerusalem*, 2001.

The Madrid Non-Paper.

Waage-Henriksen, H. *Peacemaking is a Risky Business – Norway's Role in the Peace Process in the Middle East 1993–96*. Oslo: PRIO – International Peace Research Institute, 2004.

Wanis-St. John, A. 'Back Channel Diplomacy –The Strategic Use of Multiple Channels of Negotiation in Middle East Peacemaking'. Ph.D. diss., Fletcher School of Law and Diplomacy: Tufts University, 2001.

5

NEGOTIATING JERUSALEM

Detailed summary of ideas raised in Track Two

Menachem Klein

Following the premise of my study, metropolitan Jerusalem does not include the internal and external Arab neighbourhoods currently under Israeli sovereignty. For the sake of the negotiation analysis these neighbourhoods will be examined separately, although from a geographical point of view they are part of the metropolitan area. The external ring of Arab neighbourhoods includes to the north, the neighbourhoods of Semiramis, Kufr 'Aqeb, part of the Qalandiya airport, that part of al-Ram and Dahiat al-Barid that lies within Jerusalem's current municipal borders, Bait Hanina, Sho'afat, Sho'afat refugee camp, Anata, Ras Hamis, al-Tur and Ras al-'Amud. The southern territory includes the neighbourhoods of Jabel Mukabar, Sawahra al-Gharbiyya, Sur Baher, Um Tuba, Bait Safafa, Sharafat, al-Walajeh and Isawiyeh. The internal ring of Arab neighbourhoods includes Wadi Joz, Silwan (with the exception of that part called 'the City of David'), Sheikh Jarah, Salah al-Din and Sultan Suleiman streets, Sawwaneh and Abu-Tur. Israel built 13 Jewish neighbourhoods, such as Gilo, East Talpiyot, Ramot and Pisgat Ze'ev, in close proximity to the Palestinian internal and external rings.

The Holy Basin, as defined in the London Track Two meetings, includes Mount Zion and the nearby Christian cemetery, the archaeological park along the Old City's southern wall and in the City of David, the Ofel (the excavations just to the south of the Temple Mount), Jehosephat Valley, the Muslim cemetery along the eastern wall and the Jewish cemetery and Christian churches on the Mount of Olives. The walled area of the Old City with its four quarters – Jewish, Muslim, Armenian and Christian – was, in some negotiations, discussed as part of the Holy Basin while, in others, it was regarded as a separate unit. Therefore, some of the proposals presented below address the larger Holy Basin area while others deal specifically with the Old City.

The Temple Mount, which the Palestinians call al Haram al-Sharif, includes the zone and buildings on the mount's surface as well as the area below the surface. It also includes the Western Wall – that part of the Temple Mount/al Haram al-Sharif western retaining wall that has traditionally been a site of Jewish prayer, sometimes called the Wailing Wall – and its adjoining plaza.

Ideas raised during Track Two negotiations

As stated in the introduction to Chapter 4, the aim of this study is to trace concepts used in official negotiations back to their Track Two origins. Therefore, I will first present the original ideas and concepts raised during the Track Two channels mentioned in the aforementioned chapter. This chapter is organized according to the geographical spaces discussed in Chapter 4. In each geographical space, the ideas are presented according to their relevant track, and organized according to the three subjects: sovereignty, administration and cultural and religious rights.

Metropolitan area

The Jerusalem Institute of Israel Studies

The Jerusalem Institute of Israel Studies (JIIS) presented three principal and several secondary alternative solutions for the Jerusalem problem.[1]

The first proposed solution concerning the metropolitan area (bearing in mind its different meanings, as noted above) suggested that all of Jerusalem remain under Israeli sovereignty. The second proposed that Jerusalem remain under Israeli sovereignty, but that functional sovereignty would be granted to the Palestinians in different parts of the city. The third recommended that the city be divided, granting the Palestinians full sovereignty over part of East Jerusalem.

According to the first two proposals, the boundaries of the Jerusalem municipality would be revised for pragmatic reasons. For example, they suggested expanding it to include two large Jewish settlements in the West Bank, Giva't Ze'ev and Ma'aleh Adumim. These two Jerusalem Institute proposals also stipulated the annexation to the Jerusalem municipality of Palestinian suburbs of the city that now lie in the West Bank, outside the Israeli-defined Jerusalem (Abu Dis, al-'Azariya, Sawahara al-Sharqiyeh, Dahiat al-Barid and al-Ram).

On the administrative level, the first proposal suggested that ultimate authority would be in Israel's hands, apart from specific functions and activities which require mutual dependency between the Israeli and Palestinian parts of the city and therefore would be under joint metropolitan administration.

According to the second proposal, administration would be organized in a framework of sub-municipalities. Joint committees would be established in order to coordinate the activities of the different municipalities. The Palestinian municipality would be granted municipal powers, excluding security activities which would remain under Israel control.

The third proposal offered several alternatives regarding the municipal areas over which the Palestinians would be given sovereignty. One suggestion was to limit this area to the external ring of Arab neighbourhoods; another was to add to these several internal neighbourhoods. This latter idea meant granting the Palestinians sovereignty over all the Arab neighbourhoods, excluding the Holy Basin and the neighbourhood of Bayt Safafa.

From a civil status perspective, all three proposals suggested that the residents of Jerusalem, of all religions, would be free to choose whichever citizenship they wished. Palestinians would be allowed to choose Israeli, Palestinian or Jordanian citizenship. Palestinian citizens could participate in the elections for the Palestinian Authority council, unless they chose to be Israeli citizens.[2]

The Beilin–Abu Mazen paper

This approach suggested expanding the territory of the Jerusalem municipality by annexing Ma'aleh Adumim and Givat Ze'ev to the Israeli part, and al-'Azariya and Abu Dis, as well as distant suburbs of East Jerusalem, to the Palestinian part.

On administration, it suggested the establishment of an umbrella municipality, administrated by a Jewish majority and headed by a mayor. Two sub-municipalities would function under the umbrella: a Jewish sub-municipality called Jerusalem that would provide services to and be responsible for all the Jewish neighbourhoods in the west and east of the city, including the Old City, and an Arab sub-municipality called Al-Quds that would provide identical services to the Arab residents in the new and expanded parts of Jerusalem. The umbrella municipality would assume authority over matters affecting both the sub-municipalities, such as master development plans, main roads, sewage and so on.[3]

London track

According to Israeli suggestions there would be two municipalities in Jerusalem, one that would administer Israeli and another, the Palestinian neighbourhoods. Israel proposed a different arrangement in the Holy Basin. In addition, it was suggested that a joint coordination body would be established for issues of mutual interest.[4]

In the wake of the Israeli side's initiative in discussing models of sovereignty, the Palestinians responded, in the London Track, with their own suggestions. Their first proposal was to share sovereignty, on the basis of United Nations Security Council Resolution 242, in an open city. It envisioned that the pre-1967 lines would delineate the western limit of Palestinian sovereignty and the eastern limit of Israeli sovereignty. Each side would have absolute authority and enjoy the full benefits of sovereignty in their respective halves of the city. As for the Jewish neighbourhoods ('settlements') to the east of the 1967 line, they would be either fully evacuated or there would be an agreement by which Israelis would remain under Palestinian sovereignty. This was conditional on Israeli consent to allow the re-establishment of Palestinian neighbourhoods in the west.

Alternatively, the Palestinians suggested the possibility that, in case of Israeli rejection of their first proposal, a fixed and closed boundary would be re-established along the 4 June 1967 lines.[5]

It is important to note that all of the above proposals, as well as the Madrid non-paper suggestion that was not tabled at the official negotiations, emphasized the idea that Jerusalem should remain open and physically undivided. The only exception was the Palestinian suggestion in the London track talks to re-establish a closed boundary. They also agreed that the city's municipal boundaries needed to be redrawn to allow the city to be shared, while taking into account that it serve as a dual metropolitan centre. The proposals differed, however, in the limitations they placed on Israeli rule beyond the 1967 lines and the structure of the municipality.

Neighbourhoods

The Jerusalem Institute for Israel Studies Policy Paper of 2000 specifically addressed the issue of sovereignty over the external ring of Arab neighbourhoods was specifically addressed in JIIS's policy paper of 2000. The first and second proposals included the idea that there would be territorial exchanges in the West Bank that would grant the Palestinians sovereignty over southeastern Jerusalem neighbourhoods such as Sawahreh al-Gharbyeh, Sur Baher and Um Tuba, in exchange for Israel's annexation of the suburbs of Ma'aleh Adumim, Givat Ze'ev, Gush Etzion and Efrat, all of which lie in the West Bank. The third proposal suggested that Israel recognize Palestinian sovereignty over part of the eastern city, including the above-mentioned external neighbourhoods at its southern end, with the addition of Kufr 'Aqeb, Bayt Hanina plus Sho'afat at the northern end. The neighbourhoods on the eastern slope of the Mount of Olives, such as Ras al-'Amud, al-Tur and al-Shayakh, were also considered external neighbourhoods that should be transferred to Palestinian sovereignty. Furthermore, the third proposal also provided for the transfer of sovereignty over internal Arab neighbourhoods and presented three alternatives. The first suggestion was to transfer sovereignty over the main business area of East Jerusalem, such as Salah al-Din Street, Bab al-Zahara, Shaykh Jarah and Wadi Joz. The second was to transfer sovereignty over all Arab neighbourhoods in Jerusalem except for Bayt Safafa and the Holy Basin area, which the Jerusalem Institute thought could not be removed from Israeli sovereignty for geographical or historical reasons. The third offer was similar to the second, but with the provision that the Holy Basin, minus the Jewish Quarter of the Old City, be placed under a special regime. Or, instead of a special regime, the three non-Jewish Quarters in the Old City would fall under Palestinian sovereignty, as would all neighbourhoods in Palestinian Jerusalem except for Bait Safafa and Sho'afat.[6]

The Beilin–Abu Mazen understandings addressed the issue of sovereignty over the internal neighbourhoods as well, suggesting that those like Shaykh Jarah and Wadi Joz would be administered as a borough of the Al-Quds sub-municipality, even if they would not be under Palestinian sovereignty.[7]

The Oklahoma Paper suggested that the western/Jewish part of Jerusalem would be under Israeli sovereignty and recognized as the capital of Israel, while the eastern/Arab part would be under Palestinian sovereignty and recognized as the capital of Palestine.

Holy sites

The Jerusalem Institute for Israel Studies proposed preserving the Holy Basin's unique character as a physically undivided whole. It would be given a special status and remain under Israeli sovereignty. In keeping with the special status of places holy to more than one faith, such as the Temple Mount/al Haram al-Sharif, religious administration would be shared. The Jerusalem Institute also suggested that overall security in the Holy Basin would be Israel's overarching responsibility, but that it would be accomplished through a joint Palestinian–Israeli patrol.[8]

The Beilin–Abu Mazen understandings also emphasized that the Holy Basin should be given a unique status. In practice, sovereignty would remain Israeli, but daily life would be managed jointly with the Palestinians.[9]

The London Track put forward the proposal that the Holy Basin, including the Old City, would be regarded as one physical unit, placed under the sovereignty of one party (Israel) or the two parties jointly. From an administrative point of view, matters such as education, religion, social welfare and public services would be jointly run in the Holy Basin.

This group also discussed the issue of jurisdiction in the Holy Basin. The negotiators there proposed that jurisdiction be linked to individuals rather than territory. Palestinian criminal jurisdiction would apply to Palestinians, Israeli criminal jurisdiction to Israelis while tourists would be subject to the law of the country they entered originally, Israel or Palestine.

According to the London Track understanding, movement throughout the Holy Basin would be free to all citizens and residents of Israel and Palestine. Israelis or Palestinians would be able to enter and exit freely from any gate under their country's sovereignty. Special policing arrangements would be implemented, consisting of joint unarmed Israeli–Palestinian police patrols.

Alternatively, the London Track talks suggested that all considerations of rights in and claims to the Holy Basin be suspended for the duration of the agreement or until otherwise decided. In this case, the administration of a specific area of policy or government would be performed by one party alone, or jointly, or divided between the parties on the basis of territorial or personal criteria.[10]

The Madrid non-paper contrasted with the Beilin–Abu Mazen document and related only generally to all holy places and stated that free access, order and security should be guaranteed by both sides, in accordance with special arrangements to be made by mutual consent.

The Oklahoma paper. The issue of the Old City itself was usually addressed during Track Two negotiations within the framework of the Holy Basin. However the Oklahoma paper refers specifically to the walled area of the Old City. Due to its religious, cultural and historical importance, this paper recommended that the parties jointly agree to special arrangements.

The Temple Mount/al Haram al-Sharif

The Jerusalem Institute Israel Studies proposed that Israel would maintain its sovereignty over the Temple Mount, but the Palestinians would be able to fly their flag there. All three of the Institute's proposals mandated that the Western Wall, as well as those parts of the western and southern retaining wall of the Temple Mount that border on the archaeological garden, remain under Israel's sovereignty, creating a territorial continuity between these walls and the Jewish Quarter, which would be under Israeli sovereignty.

All three JIIS proposals emphasized that freedom of access be respected. In order to ensure freedom of access to the Islamic and Christian holy sites in the Old City, they suggested that the Palestinians be granted a corridor between the Palestinian capital in Jerusalem, Al-Quds, and al Haram al-Sharif.[11]

On an administrative level, the papers suggested that believers would undertake the administration of the sites, but Israel would retain security authority on the Temple Mount.[12] To this the second proposal added the idea that Israel grant functional autonomy to the Muslim religious institutions that administer the mosques in the Temple Mount/al Haram al-Sharif compound. The third proposal suggested, as an alternative, that Palestine grant controlling and management authority to a religious Muslim body while maintaining the status quo in regard to freedom of worship and access for Jewish believers.

The London Track offered several alternative proposals regarding sovereignty over the Temple Mount, some of which were adopted during the official negotiations. In the official talks the Israelis sought to bypass the classic interpretation of the concept of sovereignty by offering any number of alternative suggestions for different types of sovereignty over the Temple Mount.

The first of these was joint sovereignty, in which each side would be considered the sole sovereign over the same piece of land, except under a different name. Al Haram al-Sharif would be placed under Palestinian sovereignty while Israel would retain sovereignty over the Temple Mount.

The second proposal was to suspend claims of *de jure* sovereignty for an agreed period.

A third was that the state of Palestine would exercise full sovereign rights over the edifice of al-Aqsa Mosque and over the Church of the Holy Sepulchre. Israel, in turn, would maintain its claim of sovereignty over the compound, excluding the area referred to as Palestinian.

Alternatively, *the London Track* suggested that Palestine also exercise full sovereign rights over the entrance passageway to the mosque. It also recommended that the Palestinian Ministry of Religious Affairs, in conjunction with other Palestinian government agencies, guarantee freedom of worship at al Haram al-Sharif at all times and to all believers. However, a joint administration would establish arrangements aimed at allowing both Muslims and Jews to worship in the compound. In other words, there might be restrictions on Jewish prayer in order to protect public order and safety. The Jewish right to worship there would be acknowledged but not realized. (Israel raised the issues of freedom of access and worship during the official negotiations, in order to allow Jewish worship on the Temple Mount.)

According to the London Track, the religious administration of the compound would be entrusted to the Waqf, the Muslim religious trusteeship in Jerusalem. The Waqf would also be responsible for carrying out all actions necessary for the maintenance and preservation of the site. Palestine would be the designated guardian of the al-Aqsa Mosque, meaning that the president of Palestine would be the al-Aqsa Mosque's official custodian.

Under this proposal, any physical change to the compound, or to any of its buildings, would be allowed only after prior authorization of the Joint Planning Committee of the Joint Administration. In addition, the parties would establish a supervisory force composed of observers representing states and international organizations.

Like the JIIS proposals, the London Track suggested that freedom of access to the compound be guaranteed, so that pilgrims and visitors would enjoy safe and convenient passage between the compound and the territories controlled by Palestine. To this end, special transit routes would be established in Israel and the Palestinian territories.[13]

The Oklahoma paper referred only in a general manner to the issue of the holy places in Jerusalem. According to this paper, the special religious needs of all three religions would be ensured, as would freedom of worship and free access to holy places. The paper suggested maintaining the status quo in the holy places and establishing a coordinating committee between the different religions.

Ideas raised during the official negotiations

I would like to call the reader's attention to some ideas that demonstrated the innovative character of the *Track Two negotiations*. The first of these, raised for the first time during those negotiations, was the proposal to expand Jerusalem's municipal territory. This would enable the city to be treated as a metropolitan area that could encompass two sub-municipalities, the Israeli capital of Jerusalem and the Palestinian capital of Al-Quds. The idea of a Jerusalem metropolitan city was useful to negotiators both on the administrative level and in dealing with the issue of sovereignty. It should be noted that there were also other administrative structures that were shaped and conceived during Track Two meetings, but did not reach the table in the formal negotiations.

The Holy Basin geographical space was another concept that was first brought up during Track Two negotiations. It followed from the Israeli wish to maintain sovereignty not only over the Old City but also over other parts of the city around it that have a religious and cultural meaning for Jews. However, since the Holy

Basin area also encompasses sites that are holy to the other two monotheistic religions, the Israelis offered to place this area under a special regime. The idea was that Israel would keep its sovereignty over the area, while the Palestinians would receive limited powers there.

The concept that a different kind of sovereignty might apply to the Temple Mount/al Haram al-Sharif – such as suspended, divided, or joint sovereignty Palestinian custodianship – was also a Track Two outcome. The intention of the negotiators was to give different interpretations to the concept of sovereignty in order to bypass the zero-sum character of classic sovereignty. Other types of sovereignty were also proposed; although they were not used by the formal negotiators.

This section analyzes the ideas and proposals raised during official negotiations, with the purpose of discerning their origins in Track Two.

Pre-Camp David

During the months that preceded the Camp David negotiations (January–July 2000), the Israeli and Palestinian official negotiators exchanged several suggestions regarding the size and character of the Jerusalem metropolitan area, focusing on the question of each side's sovereignty.

The initial Israeli offer, though presented as unofficial, was that the neighbourhoods of Abu-Dis, al-'Azariya, Sawahreh al-Sharqiyya, Dahiat al-Barid and al-Ram be transferred to Palestinian sovereignty and that the Palestinians would establish their capital, Al-Quds, in Abu Dis. The Israeli municipality would consist of the current municipal area together with Jewish-populated territory that would be annexed from the West Bank, extending from Ma'aleh Adumim in the east to Gush Etzion in the south and Givat Ze'ev in the north.[14]

The Palestinians' starting point was the pre-1967 cease-fire line, by which the western part of the city is Israeli, while the eastern part would be transferred in whole to Palestinian sovereignty.[15] Consistent with this demand, they suggested granting special status to Jewish neighbourhoods east of the 1967 lines.[16] The Israelis, however, on their part, were unwilling to go back to the old border.

Knowing that Israel would demand that its annexation of East Jerusalem be recognized and grounded in the permanent settlement, Faisal Husseini, who held the Jerusalem portfolio in the PLO Executive Committee, countered that the Palestinians would demand that Palestinian property in West Jerusalem be returned to them. He claimed that 70 per cent of the land in West Jerusalem was Palestinian property.

Husseini's gambit was a product of internal disagreements within the Palestinian team over the question of land compensation. It was also aimed ultimately at reaching a point at which Israel would concede all or most of its claims in Arab East Jerusalem, while the Palestinians would abrogate claims in the west side of the city.[17]

In May–June 2000, the Israelis fleshed out their initial proposal on expanding Jerusalem's municipal territory and dividing it into two capitals.[18] They proposed defining the Jerusalem metropolitan city as the ZOJ (Zone of Jerusalem). According to this offer, the ZOJ would extend from Ma'aleh Adumim in the east to Gush Etzion in the south and Givat Ze'ev in the north. The ZOJ would include two capitals: Jerusalem and Al-Quds.[19]

The Palestinians, at this stage, were willing to discuss Israel's offer to divide the Jerusalem metropolitan area into two capitals, thus displaying more flexibility than previously. Their condition was that they receive sovereignty over all Arab neighbourhoods in East Jerusalem, in both the external and internal rings, while Israel would maintain sovereignty only in Jewish neighbourhoods.[20] Dennis Ross, the American chief mediator and special peace envoy to the Middle East, favoured this concept of separation in Jerusalem in principle. Prior to the Camp David summit, he tried unsuccessfully to convince Prime Minister Ehud Barak to accept it.[21] At Camp David, however, the Americans did not pursue this proposal and instead fell into step with Barak's negotiating strategy. They therefore rejected Abu Ala's request to push Israel on the Jerusalem issue.[22] Subsequent to the failure of the summit, the Americans adopted the principle of separation in Jerusalem, but not in full (see below). According to Swisher, even before the summit, the Palestinians' main condition for this line of discussion was that Israel forego its insistence on sovereignty over al Haram al-Sharif/the Temple Mount.[23]

A Palestinian source states that during negotiations that took place in Nablus, in June 2000, the Israelis proposed that the issue of Jerusalem be postponed for two years. To this Arafat responded: 'not even two hours'.[24] This response corresponded with the Palestinians' general demand that no subject related to the permanent status agreement, including Jerusalem, be deferred or removed from the agenda.[25]

However, it should be noted that, at the end of 1999, Abu-Abu Mazen and some other Palestinian leaders supported the idea of deferring negotiations over Jerusalem. They reasoned that this would give them time to change the facts on the ground in East Jerusalem, enabling Palestinians to enter future negotiations from a stronger position.[26]

The Israelis suggested handing over to Palestinian administration those neighbourhoods in the external ring in northeastern Jerusalem that were within the current municipal boundaries. Within the internal ring of Arab neighbourhoods, they offered the Palestinians functional autonomy, under Israeli sovereignty.[27]

During negotiations that took place in early June 2000, Hassan Asfur, a Palestinian negotiator and cabinet minister, held a private talk with Israel's foreign minister, Shlomo Ben-Ami. Asfur displayed a willingness to discuss the idea of Palestinian functional autonomy over the internal neighbourhoods, on the condition that Al-Quds, the Palestinian section of Jerusalem, be expanded to include northern Palestinian neighbourhoods that lay under Israeli sovereignty.[28] Alternatively, he proposed Palestinian sovereignty over the internal neighbourhoods in exchange for including Givat Ze'ev and Ma'aleh Adumim in the Jewish sovereign territory of Jerusalem.[29] However, Asfur retreated from this position later that same month and demanded full Palestinian sovereignty over the internal neighbourhoods.

The idea of the Holy Basin seems not to have been raised prior to the Camp David negotiations. The negotiations over the holy places in Jerusalem concentrated at this stage on the issue of the Old City. The Israeli proposal during May 2000 was to establish a special regime there.[30] The Palestinians, at the beginning of June, presented their opening offer: special arrangements regarding the holy places within the Old City would be jointly formulated, while sovereignty over the Old City would be Palestinian. These sovereign areas would include the Jewish Quarter, which the Palestinians promised to treat with respect. Later on that month, the Palestinians presented a more pragmatic stand. They were ready to accept Israeli sovereignty over the Jewish Quarter, and there alone.[31]

Apparently, while participating in the Stockholm Track Two talks, Ben-Ami suggested that the Temple Mount and the Church of the Holy Sepulchre be given extraterritorial status.[32] The idea was raised again during negotiations that took place in Nablus in June 2000. At this meeting the Israelis suggested granting special status to all holy places in Jerusalem,[33] while the Palestinians demanded full sovereignty over the Temple Mount with the exception of Israeli sovereignty over the Western Wall.[34]

Negotiations at Camp David

At Camp David the Israelis tried to create a new, informal, international consensus whereby Resolution 242 would not apply to Jerusalem – meaning that Jerusalem's permanent border would not be the 4 June 1967 lines.[35] The Palestinians, for their part, viewed Resolution 242 as the basis of any peace accord. They stood by the prevailing Arab and international interpretation of the resolution, that East Jerusalem be separated from West Jerusalem along the pre-war line. However, they demanded sovereignty only over the Arab neighbourhoods in the eastern city, leaving the new Jewish neighbourhoods in East Jerusalem under Israeli sovereignty. In other words, the Palestinians accepted the principle that the dividing line would run through the eastern city between the Jewish and Arab neighbourhoods.[36] Nonetheless, they demanded that Jerusalem's Jewish neighbourhoods be counted as territory for which they would receive equal territorial compensation elsewhere. The Israelis, who considered these areas to be urban neighbourhoods and not settlements, rejected this demand.[37]

During the summit the Americans expressed their support for the idea of expanding the city's borders, with each side supplying municipal services to its citizens.[38] They pressured the Palestinians to agree to the annexation to Israel of two settlement blocs in the Jerusalem metropolitan area. In return, Palestine would receive territory that had been under Israeli sovereignty before 1967, but much less than in a 1:1 ratio.[39]

As for the external ring of Arab neighbourhoods, from the early stages of the summit the Israelis proposed to transfer them to Palestinian sovereignty as part of the municipality of Al-Quds. The Americans offered Arafat the same.[40]

Israel was not, however, prepared to grant the Palestinians sovereignty over the internal ring of Arab neighbourhoods. The Israeli negotiators proposed instead that the Palestinians in these neighbourhoods remain under supreme Israeli sovereignty, while receiving municipal autonomy. Overall responsibility for security would remain in Israel's hands.[41] According to this offer, the existing sovereign status would remain basically unchanged. In addition, the Israelis demanded that buildings in Arab neighbourhoods inhabited by Jews and under Jewish ownership remain under Israeli sovereignty.[42] From an administrative point of view, the Israeli proposal would have upgraded the status of Palestinians living under Israeli supreme sovereignty, in which the state of Palestine would have limited powers but overriding security authority would remain in Israeli hands. Instead of being residents of East Jerusalem bearing Jordanian passports and having the right to vote for the Palestinian Authority's national political institutions, they would become full citizens of the state of Palestine living in Jerusalem.[43]

The Palestinians rejected this idea and demanded sovereignty over all of the neighbourhoods in East Jerusalem. They were willing to discuss their municipal responsibilities in these neighbourhoods, but only if this fundamental demand was met.[44] In other words, each side was willing to negotiate the issue of Palestinian administration of the neighbourhoods, but only if the other side accepted its demands for sovereignty.[45]

In an attempt to get around this impasse, the Israelis suggested discussing municipal responsibilities independent of the issue of sovereignty, while each side continued to maintain its demand for sovereignty. However, the Israelis were not willing to state precisely which neighbourhoods would be encompassed by the discussion, so the Palestinians refused to continue negotiations.[46]

At the beginning of the Camp David summit, the Americans supported Israel's demand for supreme sovereignty in the internal neighbourhoods. In keeping with this, they proposed that the Palestinians receive functional sovereignty in these areas. They offered the Palestinians responsibilities such as planning and zoning, jurisdiction and law and order.[47] According to Akram Hanieh, editor of the semi-official daily newspaper *al-Ayyam*, the Americans regarded this state of affairs as a 'special regime' applying to the internal neighbourhoods.[48]

Ben-Ami wrote that, towards the end of the summit, the Israelis were willing to discuss the idea of granting the Palestinians limited sovereignty over some of the internal neighbourhoods in return for concessions on the issues of the Temple Mount and the Old City.[49]

The Palestinians rejected the Israeli proposals. They insisted on receiving full sovereignty over all Arab neighbourhoods, external and internal.[50] Nonetheless, Ben-Ami wrote, by the end of the conference Sa'eb Erekat, the Palestinian minister of local government and municipal affairs, broached the idea of limited Palestinian sovereignty over the internal neighbourhoods. The limitations he referred to were in areas such as security, planning and zoning and the legal status of the Israelis in such neighbourhoods.[51]

This Israeli idea, that Israel retain supreme sovereignty while the Palestinians would receive extensive functional sovereignty, was raised again in regard to the Holy Basin. The Israeli negotiators suggested that the entire Holy Basin constitute one sovereign unit. Sovereignty, according to this proposal, would remain with Israel while most operational powers would be in Palestinian hands. This could be seen as a special kind of arrangement or regime.[52] As with the external and internal neighbourhoods, the Palestinians demanded full territorial sovereignty over the Holy Basin.[53]

With regard to the Old City, Israel's initial suggestion was to establish a special regime there, while maintaining Israeli supreme sovereignty. Israel suggested that the characteristics and details of the special regime be jointly discussed.[54]

The Palestinians' initial idea was to divide sovereignty over the Old City. At the beginning of the negotiations, Muhammad Rashid, Arafat's economic advisor and confidant, privately suggested dividing sovereignty according to a 2.5:1.5 formula, meaning that the Muslim and Christian Quarters would be under Palestinian sovereignty; the Jewish Quarter, under Israeli sovereignty and the Armenian Quarter, under joint sovereignty.[55]

The idea of dividing the Old City was raised also by the Americans who offered a 2:2 formula, meaning that sovereignty over the Muslim and Christian Quarters would be transferred to the Palestinians, while Israel would maintain its sovereignty over the Jewish and Armenian Quarters.[56]

At first, this American formula was not to the Israelis' liking, but at a later stage they agreed to it. Although it was proposed time and again throughout the summit, the Palestinians did not agree to the 2:2 formula because Arafat rejected the idea of Israeli sovereignty over the Armenian Quarter.[57]

At a later stage of the summit the Americans put together a formula that linked sovereignty in the Old City to sovereignty in the internal neighbourhoods. One possibility was to fully divide sovereignty in the Old City between Israel and the Palestinians, according to the 2:2 formula. In that case the Palestinians would receive functional autonomy in the inner circle of Palestinian neighbourhoods. Alternatively a special regime would be established in the Old City (the details of which would be agreed on) and the Palestinians would receive full sovereignty in the internal neighbourhoods.[58]

The Israelis demonstrated their readiness to accept the second of these alternatives, offering the Palestinians full sovereignty over the internal neighbourhoods in return for a special regime in the Old City.[59]

The Palestinians did not approve of establishing a special regime, claiming that it presupposed Israeli sovereignty over the Old City. The Israelis, however, claimed that a special regime would in fact limit Israel's supreme sovereignty, thus allowing both sides decreased sovereignty over the Old City, instead of dividing it.[60] Despite the Israeli and American offers, the Palestinians held to their demand for sovereignty over the whole Old City, except for the Jewish Quarter.[61]

Beyond these disagreements, both sides realized that al Haram al-Sharif/the Temple Mount was the make-or-break issue.[62]

Israel's negotiators offered several proposals. The first was to leave the question of sovereignty over the Temple Mount undecided, whether for a specified period of time or indefinitely.[63]

Their second proposal was to maintain the status quo, but give it legal grounding by declaring that the administration of the Mount's surface and mosques would be transferred to the Palestinians. The Israelis would maintain their supreme sovereignty there.[64]

As their third option, the Israelis offered the Palestinians custodianship over the Temple Mount, using the term 'sovereign custody'. This, they explained, would be similar to religious custody over the Temple Mount, while Israeli sovereignty would be maintained. Arafat would be designated the guardian or 'servant' of the Islamic holy places in Jerusalem. Custody would be granted by the members of the Security Council of the UN, together with Morocco as representative of the Organization of the Islamic Conference. This idea would translate in practical terms into official Palestinian administration of the site, similar to that proposed in the second offer.[65]

Israel also suggested the construction of an access road from Palestinian Al-Quds to al Haram al-Sharif through the Muslim Quarter. The road would be under Palestinian sovereignty, thus ensuring Palestinian sovereignty over a defined area of the Muslim Quarter. There would be no barriers or checkpoints on this road and thus all would be ensured access to the Muslim holy places, as the Palestinian delegation demanded. Israel also offered Arafat the establishment of a presidential area, a sovereign compound, in the Muslim Quarter, which would be included in the corridor under Palestinian sovereignty.[66]

The Americans' position was close to that of the Israelis. They advocated the preservation of formal Israeli sovereignty in the holy places while granting the Palestinians all actual administrative powers there. In connection with the Israeli scheme of granting the Palestinians custodianship over the Temple Mount, they suggested that the UN Security Council and Morocco be authorized to give the Palestinian state sovereign custody or religious sovereignty over al Haram al-Sharif, while Israel retained residual sovereignty over the Temple Mount.[67] Residual sovereignty is a type of joint sovereignty in which one side enjoys more powers; the other side retains the residual powers not assigned to the first side. The American proposal suggested that the UN be given the responsibility of nominating the Palestinian guardian. According to this formula, the UN would also determine the parameters of the guardian's performance, taking into consideration Israeli needs such as praying on the mount and prohibiting underground construction, recognizing Israel's control over the Western Wall and its demand for international supervision of the Palestinian guardian. In the areas that would not be under Israeli control, Palestinian law would apply. There would be a Palestinian office on the mount as well as a secure access road to al Haram al-Sharif.[68]

In general, it can be said that the American approach towards the issue of the Temple Mount was to divide the disputed areas into 'slices' of sovereignty. At a certain stage the Americans proposed dividing it into four areas of sovereignty: the main buildings (al-Aqsa Mosque and Dome of the Rock); the plaza area; the Western Wall; and the subterranean spaces. The two sides would have a different mix of powers over each of these areas.[69]

The Palestinians, for their part, would accept nothing less than full Palestinian sovereignty over al Haram al-Sharif/the Temple Mount.[70] In regard to the Western Wall, publicly and officially they demanded that it be under autonomous Israeli administration, but not Israeli sovereignty. With this, they took a more rigid stand than they had prior to the summit. Unofficially, however, the Palestinians demonstrated their readiness to accept Israeli sovereignty over the Wall.[71] It should be noted that in Hebrew, the term 'Western Wall' refers specifically to that section of the Temple Mount's western retaining wall that has traditionally served as a place of Jewish prayer, but more generally to the entire western retaining wall, including unexposed parts in the Muslim Quarter. These differing definitions were not addressed in this part of the negotiations; nevertheless, at a later stage they became points of severe contention. The Israelis rejected the idea of transferring sovereignty over the Temple Mount to the Palestinians. Their precondition for reaching an agreement over the Temple Mount was that Israel would maintain sovereignty there, even if it were limited.[72]

A different idea, raised by the Americans, was to divide sovereignty over the Temple Mount vertically, by giving the Palestinians supreme sovereignty over the zone and buildings on the surface of the Mount and the Israelis sovereignty beneath the surface and in the Western Wall and adjoining plaza, which are located at a lower level than the Islamic holy sites.[73] This offer corresponded to Israel's demand for sovereignty over the subterranean portion, which according to their claim contains ruins from the Jewish Temples.[74] According to Hanieh, the Israelis were actually the authors of this American proposal.[75] The Israelis deny this – but were willing to accept it on condition that the Palestinians also agree. The Palestinians rejected it, however, and continued to demand full sovereignty over the subterranean area as well.[76]

Towards the end of the summit, the Israelis suggested that in return for a higher amount of flexibility on the part of the Palestinians in regard to the Temple Mount, they would divide sovereignty in the Old City according to the 2:2 formula, transfer sovereignty over the external Arab neighbourhoods to the Palestinians and grant them limited sovereignty over the internal neighbourhoods.[77] The Palestinians rejected this offer. Alternatively they suggested that both sides relinquish their demand for sovereignty. The Israelis were not willing to address this suggestion seriously as they suspected that it was raised without Arafat's official approval.[78]

In addition to the issue of sovereignty, the two sides discussed administrative arrangements on the Temple Mount/al Haram al-Sharif. The Israelis consistently stressed their commitment to ensuring free access to the site to members of all religions.[79] They stressed the importance of security and prohibiting excavation of the site and insisted that a defined and agreed upon space on the Mount be set aside for Jewish prayer.[80] This Israeli demand was repeated several times during the negotiations and was supported by the Americans.[81]

A more complicated version of the Israeli proposal was that Morocco, as representative of the Islamic states, would construct a building that would have the status of a diplomatic legation, part of which would serve as a synagogue. The Palestinians firmly rejected Israel's demand and agreed to continue under their current sovereignty arrangements allowing freedom of access to visitors of all religions, including Jews.[82]

When the negotiations at Camp David reached a dead end, the Americans offered to defer decisions regarding the entire Jerusalem area, or specifically the issues of sovereignty over the Temple Mount, the Old City and the Holy Basin, for a period of five years.[83] They suggested that during this moratorium, Arafat be given a sovereign office in the Old City[84] and that the Palestinians would receive temporal custodianship over al Haram al-Sharif.[85] Regarding the internal neighbourhoods, the Americans posited that during this period the Palestinians would enjoy the special autonomous status proposed by Israel.[86] The Israelis were willing to defer negotiations over several issues;[87] however, the Palestinians rejected this idea entirely.[88]

Post-Camp David discussions

After the Camp David summit, during negotiations that took place at Bolling Air Base in December 2000, the Israelis suggested that the Jerusalem metropolitan area be divided according to the principle of 'what is Jewish will be Israeli and what is Arab will be Palestinian'. In contrast, the Palestinians reverted to talking about dividing Jerusalem into two capitals according to the pre-1967 lines.[89] The Palestinians also opposed Israel's demand to include Ma'aleh Adumim and Givat Ze'ev in the extended Jewish capital, although they were willing to agree to Israeli sovereignty over the Jewish neighbourhoods in eastern Jerusalem. According to Ben-Ami, the Palestinian thinking was to give up the division of the city along the pre-June war lines in exchange for an Israeli willingness to give up its demand for sovereignty over the Temple Mount.[90]

Nevertheless, at a later stage of the negotiations, the Palestinians agreed that Israel could retain sovereignty over the Jewish neighbourhood in East Jerusalem and even presented a map showing the connections between these settlements to the western city.[91] This map became the subject of a further dispute when the Israelis claimed that the connections proposed by the Palestinians were unreasonably narrow and devoid of urban logic. Instead they suggested that both parties go over the maps together in order to delineate reasonable urban links within the extended Jewish capital, as well as in the Palestinian capital of Al-Quds.[92]

The Clinton parameters

On 23 December, U.S. President Bill Clinton presented his ideas regarding a possible solution to the conflict. On the division of Jerusalem, he proposed to follow the rule that the Arab areas be under Palestinian sovereignty and the Jewish areas under Israeli sovereignty; in other words, he adopted the Israeli stand on this issue.[93]

The Israelis, for their part, wanted to further expand their share of the metropolitan city by annexing a very extensive block of territory in the Ma'aleh Adumim area, comprising the area from the Kedar settlement to the south all the way to Nofei Prat and Kfar Adumim settlements to the northeast of Mishor Adumim and from there west to Jerusalem. They also demanded that the Givat Ze'ev, Giv'on and Beit Horon settlements northwest of Jerusalem be annexed to the Jerusalem municipality and that they be connected by a wide corridor to the Ramot neighbourhood.

The Palestinians rejected this demand. They argued that Israel's annexation of the large Ma'aleh Adumim area would allow the settlements to swell at the expense of the Palestinian neighbourhoods of 'Anata, 'Isawiyah, al-Za'im, al-'Azariya and Hizme.[94] A similar debate was conducted regarding Givat Ze'ev. The Palestinians claimed that the annexation of this area would come at the expense of the development of the city of Ramallah and of north Jerusalem neighbourhoods Bayt Iksa and Bayt Hanina. Because of these reservations, the Palestinians withdrew their agreement to include Ma'aleh Adumim and Givat Ze'ev in the settlement blocs to be annexed by Israel and removed them from the Palestinian map.[95]

Negotiations at Taba

The Palestinians raised the issue of territorial compensation once more during the Taba negotiations. They demanded equivalent territorial compensation in West Jerusalem in exchange for the annexation to Israel of the Jewish neighbourhoods in the eastern city. They made a similar demand concerning Palestinian property that had remained in West Jerusalem after the 1948 war. Some Palestinian negotiators insisted that Israel establish arrangements for paying compensation or restoring this Palestinian property.[96]

At Taba negotiators raised a number of administrative issues regarding the metropolitan area. The two sides discussed the formation of a coordinating committee to address security, planning and construction, economics and general coordination between the particular interests of each municipality. The Palestinian condition was that no umbrella administrative structure or special arrangement would limit their independent activity in any way.

The issue of the external Arab neighbourhoods was raised again in the negotiations after Camp David, when the Israelis demanded that the Sho'afat refugee camp and the village of al-Za'im, suburbs of East Jerusalem, be moved in order to create a broad contiguous area of Israeli sovereignty that would include Ma'aleh Adumim and the road to the Dead Sea littoral. The Palestinians rejected this completely and demanded full sovereignty over all the external Arab neighbourhoods and over all of Bayt Safafa – both the formerly Jordanian part and the section that had been in Israeli territory between 1948 and 1967, whose residents are Israeli citizens. Furthermore, they demanded territorial contiguity between Bayt Safafa and Bethlehem.[97] In general, the message the Palestinians conveyed after the Camp David summit was that they wanted sovereignty over all of Jerusalem's Arab neighbourhoods. In regard to the internal ring of Arab neighbourhoods, however, American chief negotiator Dennis Ross assumed that the Palestinians would be ready to accept some limitations on their sovereignty.[98] The Israelis made some concessions regarding this issue as well and, at Taba, in keeping with President Clinton's principle that Arab neighbourhoods would be Palestinian and Jewish ones Israeli, they agreed to place the neighbourhoods close to the Old City, such as Silwan, Ras al-'Amud and Shaykh Jarah, under Palestinian sovereignty.[99]

The issue of the Holy Basin was discussed after the Camp David negotiations more extensively than ever before. In August 2000 the Israelis presented an official proposal to transfer sovereignty over the Holy Basin to an outside entity. On the administrative level this proposal included administration of the Holy Basin by a joint committee, which would also be responsible for security and public order. The location of government institutions in the Holy Basin would be prohibited, with the exception of religious-management bodies. National institutions would be located at an equal distance from the Holy Basin. (A direct line drawn from the Temple Mount to the Knesset building is the same length as a line drawn from the Temple Mount to the building designated for the Palestinian parliament in Abu-Dis.)

According to this Israeli proposal, Muslims and Arabs would enter the Holy Basin at points different from those used by Israeli citizens. Within the Holy Basin there would be freedom of movement, in keeping with the principle of an open city, with the exception of restrictions that would be instituted to ensure that opening the area to all would not adversely affect the daily life of its inhabitants. How the designated entrances and movement restrictions would be reconciled with the concept of an open city was not discussed. Jurisdiction, according to this proposal, would be linked to the individual, with Israelis subject to Israeli law and Palestinians subject to Palestinian law.

The Palestinians were not entirely pleased with the idea of the Holy Basin or with its access arrangements as they wanted the open city concept to apply to the whole of Jerusalem. If Jerusalem were not to be an open city, they said, it might as well be completely divided – the Holy Basin included.[100]

In order to ensure their sovereignty over the Holy Basin, the Palestinians stated that they respected the Jewish bond to the Mount Olives, the City of David and Mount Zion (a message similar to that conveyed by them after Camp David through the American mediators). They were therefore prepared to provide for all Israel's needs in this area, as long as it remained under Palestinian sovereignty.[101]

Later that December, at Bolling Air Force Base, the Palestinians softened their demands and demonstrated their readiness to discuss the concept of the Holy Basin, so long as the arrangement did not include full Israeli sovereignty there. But the Israeli offer to establish a special regime in the Holy Basin did not apply to the Western Wall or the areas within the Holy Basin, which they said must remain under Israeli sovereignty (the Jewish Quarter, Mount Zion, the City of David, the tombs of the kings and the Mount of Olives).[102]

During the Taba negotiations, the Israelis proposed dividing sovereignty in the Holy Basin, with Israel retaining sovereignty in the Jewish and Armenian Quarters, the Western Wall, Mount Zion and the archaeological park next to the southern wall, the City of David and the Ofel, Jehosephat Valley and the Jewish cemetery on the Mount of Olives, the churches at Gethsemane and the Muslim cemetery along the eastern wall. In addition, they demanded sovereignty over Jewish-owned houses in Arab neighbourhoods. This offer would have given the Palestinians sovereignty over the Christian and Muslim Quarters, not including Jewish-owned houses there or the Armenian Quarter. By the end of the bargaining over this proposal, Israel had agreed to cede the Muslim cemetery and the Gethsemane churches, but not the Jewish cemetery and the road leading there.[103]

Another option put forth by the Israelis was to defer the decision on the Holy Basin for three to five years, during which Israel and the Palestinians would jointly administer it. During this intermediate period, the existing arrangements would continue in the areas of sovereignty, law and justice. A fourth option, suggested by them even before Taba (during August 2000), was to transfer sovereignty to an outside entity – the UN Security Council and representatives of the Jerusalem committee of the Conference of Islamic States. This option also stipulated joint administration, since the third party would grant each side administrative powers in accordance with the principles established by President Clinton.[104] These proposals reminded the Palestinians of the proposals they had rejected at Camp David, as their structure was similar to the Israeli and American proposals on the Temple Mount. Consequently, they backtracked and officially demanded sovereignty over the entire Old City. According to the Palestinian proposal, special arrangements would apply to the Jews living in the quarters under Palestinian sovereignty, with assurances that their daily life would not be negatively affected by Palestinian sovereignty. Special arrangements would also apply to the places sacred to Judaism in sovereign Palestinian areas (such as the Jewish cemetery on the Mount of Olives), which would be administered by Israel. Unofficially, the Palestinians were willing to recognize Israeli sovereignty in the Jewish Quarter and the adjacent houses occupied by Jews in the Armenian Quarter.[105]

At this stage, there were also negotiations that focused specifically on the Old City, without treating it only as part of the Holy Basin. The Israelis demanded a special regime in the Old City. They claimed that the area was so small that a physical partition would be absurd and even impossible. Consequentially, they offered to declare the Jewish Quarter Israeli and the Muslim one Palestinian, with both of them being under the 'umbrella' of a special regime.[106] Later, Israel proposed that the entire Old City be placed under a special regime. Instead of dividing sovereignty, the two sides would divide between them powers and authorities, while agreeing to defer the issue of sovereignty or declare divine sovereignty over the area.[107]

The Palestinians continued to demand that sovereignty over the Old City be divided geographically. They suggested a 2.75:1.25 formula, meaning that the Jewish Quarter and about a quarter of the Armenian Quarter would be under Israeli sovereignty; the Muslim and Christian Quarters as well as the rest of the

Armenian Quarter, under Palestinian sovereignty.[108] Nevertheless, shortly afterwards, the Palestinians acknowledged the need for an overall special regime and also revised their proposed sovereignty separation arrangements to a 1.5:2.5 formula, by which half of the Armenian Quarter, that part of it bordering the Jewish Quarter, would be under Israelis sovereignty and the other half, under Palestinian sovereignty.[109]

The negotiations over a special regime in the Old City focused also on the administrative characteristics of such a regime. During a meeting that took place in September 2000, both sides reviewed these characteristics. The Israelis cited the need for planning and zoning rules to ensure historical preservation. They further noted the need for a special identification card for the residents of the Old City. They also called for the establishment of a special police force that would be responsible for tourism and securing freedom of worship. The Israelis proposed that the police personnel be unarmed. They also suggested that the holy places within the Old City be registered as official UNESCO World Heritage sites. The Palestinians did not make any proposals of their own, but noted the Israeli ideas.[110]

During negotiations that took place at Taba, Egypt in January 2001, both sides eventually accepted the World Heritage site designation. This status automatically imposes limits on construction and physical changes and requires conservation. The Palestinians reconfirmed that neighbourhoods such as Gilo, East Talpiot, French Hill and Ramot would be part of Israel, although they did not include Har Homa/Jabel Abu Ghneim and Har Gilo in their map, as the Israelis did.[111] Unlike the Israeli map, the Palestinian one included all of Bayt Safafa, which up to the June 1967 war was divided between Israel and Jordan.

Negotiators at Taba also discussed the 'open city' concept at length. The Israelis proposed a 'soft' border between the two capitals, running mainly along Road No. 1, a north–south artery that separates East from West Jerusalem. This would enable a degree of control and supervision of passage from one city to the other. Traffic would be regulated at a number of transit points and passage would be free only to the residents of Israeli or Palestinian Jerusalem. The two cities' residents would be required to present a special certificate of residence in order to enjoy this right of free passage. All other entrants into West or East Jerusalem would need to go through passport control.

The Israelis proposed creating three degrees of openness in Jerusalem. There would be total freedom within the Holy Basin or the Old City. There would be minimal control for Jerusalemites holding a Jerusalem residence certificate who wished to pass between the two capital cities. And there would be maximal control for non-Jerusalemites wishing to cross the sovereign line separating the two cities and the two states in Jerusalem. In other words, Israel proposed a complex arrangement instituting a variable level of openness according to geographical and personal criteria. Thus entry into West Jerusalem would be considered entry into Israel – though without limiting the freedom of movement currently enjoyed by the Arab Palestinian residents of East Jerusalem. On the other hand, the myth of a Jerusalem open to all would not be completely destroyed. The Palestinians saw

Israel's proposal as a hybrid whose implementation would complicate life in the city. They claimed that only complete freedom of movement, access and internal passage between the two cities would ensure Jerusalem's development. A half-closed area that could be crossed only at certain points would harm the city's natural fabric of life as well as its development.[112]

The Palestinians, in contrast to the Israeli model of 'soft' physical separation, took the position that the entire area of Jerusalem and Al-Quds must be open. They did not define the boundaries of the open area – that is, where Jerusalem would end. They presented Israel with two alternatives. The first was to set up border control around both cities. These external control arrangements would be in the form of an international border for Israelis wishing to enter Palestine and for Palestinians and other Arabs wishing to enter Israel. Traffic within this area would be free and controlled at the exits. The 'other' citizen's passage from one capital to the other within Jerusalem would not be considered as a passage from one state – Israel or Palestine – to the other. However, the control points would create the symbols of separation between the two capitals and the hinterland of each state. Alternatively, the Palestinians proposed establishing a 'hard' border between Jerusalem and Al-Quds against the 'soft' ones that Israel proposed.

As in Camp David, during the negotiations that took place later on, the Temple Mount remained the critical issue that prevented agreement. The Israelis and the Americans repeated their proposal to invest sovereignty over the Temple Mount in a third party – the UN Security Council or the Organization of Islamic Conference.[113] According to their offer, the council would then transfer sovereignty to the representatives of the Islamic states, which in turn would entrust Arafat with administrative and judicial authority on al Haram al-Sharif. A joint agreement would set out which governmental powers would be granted to the Palestinians and the nature of the residual powers that Israel would enjoy on the Temple Mount.[114]

Another option was that the two sides would ask the UN Security Council to recognize them as claiming sovereignty over the Temple Mount/al Haram al-Sharif and recognize the division of sovereign powers between them, as set out in a joint agreement.[115] It should be noted that Israel wanted to receive powers and standing equal to that of Palestine, including a statement that Palestinian custodianship applied to the al-Aqsa mosque and the Dome of the Rock and Jewish custodianship to the Temple Mount.[116]

However, the Palestinians declared that full sovereignty over the Temple Mount should be included in their sovereignty over East Jerusalem and the Old City. They insisted on possessing full sovereignty, according to conservative nineteenth- and early twentieth-century definitions of the term. Their motivation was not negative, that is to negate Israeli sovereignty, but rather positive – to attain Palestinian sovereignty over the site, either exclusively or through Islamic sovereignty.[117]

During the negotiations that took place at Bolling Air Force Base, the Israelis suggested sharing sovereignty over the site, or even disregarding it completely, on condition of Arab recognition of the Jewish bond to the Temple Mount.[118] The

Palestinians again insisted that they be granted full sovereignty over the Temple Mount.[119]

Israel's minister of foreign affairs, Ben-Ami, suggested, on his own initiative, transferring sovereignty over the Temple Mount to the Palestinians, as they requested. In exchange, he proposed, the Palestinians would undertake not to excavate under al Haram al-Sharif, because of its holiness and centrality to the Jews and to allocate space on the Temple Mount for Jewish prayer.[120] In other words he was ready to give up sovereignty in name but not some of its manifestations and powers. This was consistent with Barak's general principle of achieving authority on the Temple Mount and changing the status in favour of Israel.

Israel and the U.S. offered further ideas, in an attempt to reach a compromise between the egalitarian model they favoured and Arafat's exclusivist model. There was discussion of combining horizontal and vertical divisions of the site. Al-Aqsa and the Dome of the Rock would be under Islamic sovereignty and the surrounding plaza under that of the Security Council, either alone or with representatives of the Conference of Islamic States. A different proposal suggested that the plaza would be under Islamic sovereignty, the half-meter of ground just under the surface would be under Security Council sovereignty and the rest of the subterranean area under Israeli sovereignty.[121] But the Palestinians continued to insist on receiving full and sole sovereignty on al Haram al-Sharif. This was unacceptable to the American president.

According to the ideas that President Clinton presented on 23 December 2000, the Palestinians would be given sovereignty over the al-Sharif plaza and the Western Wall compound would be under Israeli sovereignty. As for the subterranean area of the Temple Mount, Clinton suggested two options for joint sovereignty. The first option was that there would be a firm commitment by both sides not to dig or excavate beneath al Haram al-Sharif or behind the Wall. The second suggestion was that there would be shared functional sovereignty over the issue of excavation. In other words, mutual consent would be required before any digging or excavation could take place. The guiding idea was to find a solution that upgraded the status quo, in Clinton's words 'guaranteeing Palestinian effective control while respecting the conviction of the Jewish people'.[122]

At the Taba talks of January 2001, the issue of sovereignty over the Temple Mount came up via discussion of the Holy Basin and its special regime – each side held fast to its previous position.[123] In addition to the proposals mentioned above, Israel offered an alternative that combined two of the proposals it had raised so far, suggesting that, for an agreed period, such as three years, al Haram al-Sharif/ the Temple Mount would be under international sovereignty of the five permanent UN Security Council members and a representative of the Jerusalem committee of the Conference of Islamic States. The Palestinians would be the guardian/custodian of the Muslim shrine. At the end of that period either the parties would agree to a new solution or agree to extend the existing arrangements. In the absence of an agreement, the parties would go back to implementing the Clinton formulation.[124]

The Palestinians were not willing to accept the division presented in the Israeli offers and maintained their demand for full sovereignty over the Temple Mount. They also rejected Israel's sovereignty all along the western retaining wall and asked that Israel make do with sovereignty over the Western Wall only.[125]

During the course of the official talks, a few administrative aspects of the site were also discussed. The first was the issue of excavations and construction, within and under the Temple Mount/al Haram al-Sharif compound. The Israelis asked that the Waqf prohibit such excavations. The Palestinians showed readiness to accept this demand, agreeing not to dig beneath the Temple Mount plaza once they held full sovereignty. They also approved of establishing an international regulatory body that would ensure the preservation of the site and, in addition, were willing to sign a declaration saying that the Palestinian side would not excavate the site because of its sensitivity to all believers (although they were not willing to mention the Jews specifically). The Israelis, on their part, stated that they would be willing not to conduct excavations beneath the Temple Mount plaza under Israeli sovereignty, in the event that Arafat accepted that the subterranean zone beneath the Temple Mount plaza would be under Israeli sovereignty.[126]

With regard to flying flags in the holy places, the Israeli negotiators asked that flags be placed only at the entry point to the Temple Mount or the Holy Basin and not anywhere else.[127]

From a symbolic perspective, it was very important for the Israelis that any solution regarding the Temple Mount reflect the Jewish religious and cultural bond to the site.[128] This became even more significant to the Israelis after Camp David, during which Palestinian negotiators publicly denied any Jewish historical or religious attachment to the Temple Mount.[129]

Notes

1   JIIS, *Peacemaking in Jerusalem – A Task Team Report* (Jerusalem: The Jerusalem Institute for Israel Studies, 2000).
2   JIIS, *Peacemaking in Jerusalem*, 39–56.
3   M. Klein, *The Jerusalem Problem: The Struggle for Permanent Status* (Gainesville: University Press of Florida, 2003): 33–34.
4   CIPMO (Italian Center for Peace in the Middle East), The Orient House – Arab Studies Society Jerusalem, and the Economic Cooperation Foundation, *Israelis, Palestinians Coexisiting in Jerusalem* (Milan: Centro Italiano per la Pace in Medio Oriente, 2001), 259–330.
5   CIPMO, *Israelis, Palestinians Coexisiting in Jerusalem*, 209–239.
6   JIIS, *Peacemaking in Jerusalem*, 39–56.
7   Klein, *The Jerusalem Problem*, 36.
8   JIIS, *Peacemaking in Jerusalem*, 39–50.
9   Klein, *The Jerusalem Problem*, 35.
10   CIPMO, *Israelis, Palestinians Coexisiting in Jerusalem*, 259–330.
11   JIIS, *Peacemaking in Jerusalem*, 39–56.
12   JIIS, *Peacemaking in Jerusalem*, 39–56.
13   CIPMO, *Israelis, Palestinians Coexisiting in Jerusalem*, 209–239.

14   Klein, *The Jerusalem Problem*, 44; C.E. Swisher, *The Truth About Camp David: The Untold Story About the Collapse of the Middle East Peace Process* (New York: Nation Books, 2004): 267–268.

15   S. Ben-Ami, *A Front Without a Rearguard: A Voyage to the Boundaries of the Peace Process* (Tel Aviv: Miskal-Yedioth Ahronoth Books and Chemed Books, 2004), 39; Klein, *The Jerusalem Problem*, 45 and 58–59.

16   G. Sher, *Just Beyond Reach: The Israeli-Palestinian Peace Negotiations 1999–2001* (Tel Aviv: Miskal-Yedioth Ahronoth Books and Chemed Books, 2001), 114.

17   Klein, *The Jerusalem Problem*, 58.

18   Ben-Ami, *A Front Without a Rearguard*, 39; Klein, *The Jerusalem Problem*, 42.

19   Sher, *Just Beyond Reach*, 114.

20   Ben-Ami, *A Front Without a Rearguard*, 78; D. Ross, *The Missing Peace – The Inside Story of the Fight for Middle East Peace* (New York: Farrar, Straus and Giroux, 2004), 635.

21   Ross, *The Missing Peace*, 639–40.

22   Ross, *The Missing Peace*, 659.

23   Swisher, *The Truth About Camp David*, 273.

24   A. Hanieh, 'The Camp David Diaries', *Journal of Palestine Studies* 31 (Winter, 2001): 81.

25   Klein, *The Jerusalem Problem*, 46.

26   Klein, *The Jerusalem Problem*, 48.

27   Klein, *The Jerusalem Problem*, 44–45; Ben-Ami, *A Front Without a Rearguard*, 115.

28   Ben-Ami, *A Front Without a Rearguard*, 78.

29   Ben-Ami, *A Front Without a Rearguard*, 78.

30   Ben-Ami, *A Front Without a Rearguard*, 39.

31   Sher, *Just Beyond Reach*, 114; Ben-Ami, *A Front Without a Rearguard*, 115; Swisher, *The Truth About Camp David*, 273.

32   Klein, *The Jerusalem Problem*, 45.

33   Ben-Ami, *A Front Without a Rearguard*, 117.

34   Ben-Ami, *A Front Without a Rearguard*, 115; Klein, *The Jerusalem Problem*, 44.

35   Klein, *The Jerusalem Problem*, 74–75.

36   Klein, *The Jerusalem Problem*, 77; Swisher, *The Truth About Camp David*, 273.

37   Klein, *The Jerusalem Problem*, 75.

38   Ben-Ami, *A Front Without a Rearguard*, 143.

39   Klein, *The Jerusalem Problem*, 75.

40   Sher, *Just Beyond Reach*, 186, 191 and 230; Ben-Ami, *A Front Without a Rearguard*, 185; Ross, *The Missing Peace*, 674 and 681.

41   Ben-Ami, *A Front Without a Rearguard*, 168; Klein, *The Jerusalem Problem*, 71; Hanieh, 'The Camp David Diaries', 84; Swisher, *The Truth About Camp David*, 295; Ross, *The Missing Peace*, 674 and 681.

42   Klein, *The Jerusalem Problem*, 71.

43   Klein, *The Jerusalem Problem*, 81.

44   Ben-Ami, *A Front Without a Rearguard*, 204; Hanieh, 'The Camp David Diaries', 86.

45   Ben-Ami, *A Front Without a Rearguard*, 204.

46   Sher, *Just Beyond Reach*, 204; Ben-Ami, *A Front Without a Rearguard*, 204.

47   Sher, *Just Beyond Reach*, 186; Ben-Ami, *A Front Without a Rearguard*, 185; Hanieh, 'The Camp David Diaries', 96; Ross, *The Missing Peace,* 671, 681 and 687.

48   Hanieh, 'The Camp David Diaries', 88.

49   Ben-Ami, *A Front Without a Rearguard*, 218.

50   Klein, *The Jerusalem Problem*, 76; Hanieh, 'The Camp David Diaries', 96, Ross, *The Missing Peace*, 673 and 679.

51   Ben-Ami, *A Front Without a Rearguard*, 208–209.

52   Klein, *The Jerusalem Problem*, 72–74; Hanieh, 'The Camp David Diaries', 84 and 95; Sher, *Just Beyond Reach*, 204; Ross, *The Missing Peace*, 674 and 681.

53   Klein, *The Jerusalem Problem*, 74; Ross, *The Missing Peace*, 679.

54   Ben-Ami, *A Front Without a Rearguard*, 168; Sher, *Just Beyond Reach*, 173 and 188; Hanieh, 'The Camp David Diaries', 84.

55   Ben-Ami, *A Front Without a Rearguard*, 156; Klein, *The Jerusalem Problem*, 78.

56   Sher, *Just Beyond Reach*, 187; Ben-Ami, *A Front Without a Rearguard*, 185; Klein, *The Jerusalem Problem*, 74; Hanieh, 'The Camp David Diaries', 83, 87 and 96; Ross, *The Missing Peace*, 687–689.

57   Ben-Ami, *A Front Without a Rearguard*, 207; Hanieh, 'The Camp David Diaries', 86.

58   Klein, *The Jerusalem Problem*, 74; Sher, *Just Beyond Reach*, 230; Ben-Ami, *A Front Without a Rearguard*, 221; Hanieh, 'The Camp David Diaries', 96; Ross, *The Missing Peace*, 705–707.

59   Ben-Ami, *A Front Without a Rearguard*, 218.

60   Ben-Ami, *A Front Without a Rearguard*, 219.

61   Sher, *Just Beyond Reach*, 229.

62   Swisher, *The Truth About Camp David*, 321.

63   Klein, *The Jerusalem Problem*, 72.

64   Sher, *Just Beyond Reach*, 186–187 and 230; Ben-Ami, *A Front Without a Rearguard*, 183, 185 and 219; Hanieh, 'The Camp David Diaries', 88, 96.

65   Ben-Ami, *A Front Without a Rearguard*, 207 and 218; Klein, *The Jerusalem Problem*, 72; Hanieh, 'The Camp David Diaries', 83 and 88; Swisher, *The Truth About Camp David*, 284.

66   Ben-Ami, *A Front Without a Rearguard*, 210; Klein, *The Jerusalem Problem*, 72; Hanieh, 'The Camp David Diaries', 84, 95.

67   Sher, *Just Beyond Reach*, 186–187 and 230; Ben-Ami, *A Front Without a Rearguard*, 183, 185 and 219; Hanieh, 'The Camp David Diaries', 88 and 96; Ross, *The Missing Peace*, 682–683 and 704–705.

68   Ben-Ami, *A Front Without a Rearguard*, 204.

69   Klein, *The Jerusalem Problem*, 92.

70   Sher, *Just Beyond Reach*, 173; Ben-Ami, *A Front Without a Rearguard*, 156; Klein, *The Jerusalem Problem*, 81; Hanieh, 'The Camp David Diaries', 96; Ross, *The Missing Peace*, 688 and 699.

71   Klein, *The Jerusalem Problem*, 77.

72   Ben-Ami, *A Front Without a Rearguard*, 205.

73   Klein, *The Jerusalem Problem*, 73.

74   Klein, *The Jerusalem Problem*, 73 and 76.

75   Hanieh, 'The Camp David Diaries', 83.

76   Klein, *The Jerusalem Problem*, 73.

77   Ben-Ami, *A Front Without a Rearguard*, 218.

78   Ben-Ami, *A Front Without a Rearguard*, 219.

79   Klein, *The Jerusalem Problem*, 72.

80   Ben-Ami, *A Front Without a Rearguard*, 205.

81   Klein, *The Jerusalem Problem*, 73; Ben-Ami, *A Front Without a Rearguard*, 204; Hanieh, 'The Camp David Diaries', 80, 83.

82   Klein, *The Jerusalem Problem*, 76.

83   Sher, *Just Beyond Reach*, 230; Ben-Ami, *A Front Without a Rearguard*, 221; Klein, *The Jerusalem Problem*, 77–78; Hanieh, 'The Camp David Diaries', 96.

84   Ben-Ami, *A Front Without a Rearguard*, 186.

85   Ben-Ami, *A Front Without a Rearguard*, 186 and 221–222; Klein, *The Jerusalem Problem*, 77–78; Hanieh, 'The Camp David Diaries', 87, 96.

86   Klein, *The Jerusalem Problem*, 77–78; Hanieh, 'The Camp David Diaries', 95.

87   Klein, *The Jerusalem Problem*, 78.

88   Klein, *The Jerusalem Problem*, 77–78; Hanieh, 'The Camp David Diaries', 87, 95–96.

89   Ben-Ami, *A Front Without a Rearguard*, 366.

90   Ben-Ami, *A Front Without a Rearguard*, 367.

91   Ben-Ami, *A Front Without a Rearguard*, 367.

92   Ben-Ami, *A Front Without a Rearguard*, 367.

93   Sher, *Just Beyond Reach*, 361; Ben-Ami, *A Front Without a Rearguard*, 369, 381 and 459.

94   Klein, *The Jerusalem Problem*, 114–115; Ben-Ami, *A Front Without a Rearguard*, 424.

95 Klein, *The Jerusalem Problem*, 114–115; Ben-Ami, *A Front Without a Rearguard*, 424.
96 Klein, *The Jerusalem Problem*, 120; Sher, *Just Beyond Reach*, 410.
97 Klein, *The Jerusalem Problem*, 91 and 115; Sher, *Just Beyond Reach*, 254.
98 Sher, *Just Beyond Reach*, 267; Ben-Ami, *A Front Without a Rearguard*, 279.
99 Klein, *The Jerusalem Problem*, 115; Sher, *Just Beyond Reach*, 36; Ben-Ami, *A Front Without a Rearguard*, 369, 381 and 459.
100 Klein, *The Jerusalem Problem*, 119–122.
101 Sher, *Just Beyond Reach*, 345; Ben-Ami, *A Front Without a Rearguard*, 280.
102 Sher, *Just Beyond Reach*, 275 and 285; Ben-Ami, *A Front Without a Rearguard*, 366.
103 Klein, *The Jerusalem Problem*, 116–118.
104 Sher, *Just Beyond Reach*, 248; Klein, *The Jerusalem Problem*, 119.
105 Sher, *Just Beyond Reach*, 410; Klein, *The Jerusalem Problem*, 119–122.
106 Sher, *Just Beyond Reach*, 275.
107 Klein, *The Jerusalem Problem*, 93.
108 Sher, *Just Beyond Reach*, 257.
109 Sher, *Just Beyond Reach*, 267, 273, 361 and 410; Ben-Ami, *A Front Without a Rearguard*, 280, 366, 369, 381 and 459; Klein, *The Jerusalem Problem*, 94 and 119–120.
110 Sher, *Just Beyond Reach*, 275.
111 Klein, *The Jerusalem Problem*, 115.
112 Klein, *The Jerusalem Problem*, 120–122.
113 Ross, *The Missing Peace*, 721.
114 Sher, *Just Beyond Reach:*, 247; Klein, *The Jerusalem Problem*, 95.
115 Klein, *The Jerusalem Problem*, 93–94; Sher, *Just Beyond Reach*, 267.
116 Sher, *Just Beyond Reach*, 248; Klein, *The Jerusalem Problem*, 95.
117 Sher, *Just Beyond Reach*, 344–349; Klein, *The Jerusalem Problem*, 97.
118 Sher, *Just Beyond Reach*, 355; Ben-Ami, *A Front Without a Rearguard*, 366.
119 Ben-Ami, *A Front Without a Rearguard*, 366.
120 Sher, *Just Beyond Reach*, 357; Ben-Ami, *A Front Without a Rearguard*, 375–377.
121 Klein, *The Jerusalem Problem*, 95.
122 Sher, *Just Beyond Reach*, 361; Ben-Ami, *A Front Without a Rearguard*, 369, 381 and 459; Klein, *The Jerusalem Problem*, 103.
123 Klein, *The Jerusalem Problem*, 122.
124 Klein, *The Jerusalem Problem*, 119.
125 Ben-Ami, *A Front Without a Rearguard*, 414; Sher, *Just Beyond Reach*, 349 and 388.
126 Sher, *Just Beyond Reach*, 344–349; Klein, *The Jerusalem Problem*, 97.
127 Sher, *Just Beyond Reach*, 248; Klein, *The Jerusalem Problem*, 94.
128 Sher, *Just Beyond Reach*, 338, 345 and 355; Ben-Ami, *A Front Without a Rearguard*, 366; Klein, *The Jerusalem Problem*, 80.
129 Klein, *The Jerusalem Problem*, 81.

References

Abdul Hadi, M. (ed.) *Dialogue on Jerusalem*. Jerusalem: PASSIA, 1998.
Agha, H.S., A. Feldman and Z. Schiff. *Track II Diplomacy Lessons from the Middle East*. Cambridge, MA: MIT Press, 2003.
Arthur, P. 'Some Thoughts on Transition: A Comparative View of the Peace Process in South Africa and Northern Ireland'. *Government and Opposition* 30, no. 1(1995): 46–59.
Arthur, P. 'Time, Territory, Tradition and the Anglo-Irish "Peace" Process'. *Government and Opposition* 31, no. 4(1996): 426–440.
Arthur, P. 'Quiet Diplomacy and Personal Conversation: Track Two Diplomacy and the Search for a Settlement in Northern Ireland'. In *Democracy is a Discussion – The Challenges and Promise of a New Democratic Era*, edited by S. Myers, 70–95. New London, CT, 1998.

Ben-Ami, S. *A Front Without a Rearguard: A Voyage to the Boundaries of the Peace Process*. Tel Aviv: Miskal-Yedioth Ahronoth Books and Chemed Books, 2004.

Chazan, N. 'Negotiating the Non-Negotiable: Jerusalem in the Framework of an Israeli-Palestinian Settlement'. *Occasional Papers of the American Academy of Arts and Sciences*, no. 7: (March 1991).

Chigas, D.V. 'Unofficial Intervention with Official Actors: Parallel Negotiation Training in Violent Intrastate Conflicts'. *International Negotiation* 2, no. 3(1997): 409–436.

Cingoli, J (ed.) *Israelis, Palestinians Coexisting in Jerusalem*. Milano: Centro Italiano per la Pace in Medio Oriente, 2001.

Chufrin, G.I. and H.H. Saunders. 'A Public Peace Process'. *Negotiation Journal* 9, no. 2 (1993): 155–177.

CIPMO (Italian Center for Peace in the Middle East) and The Orient House – Arab Studies Society Jerusalem and the Economic Cooperation Foundation. *Israelis, Palestinians Coexisiting in Jerusalem*. Milano: Centro Italiano per la Pace in Medio Oriente, 2001.

Cochrane, F. 'Beyond the Political Elites: A Comparative Analysis of the Roles and Impacts of Community-Based NGOs in Conflict Resolution Activity'. *Civil Wars* 3, no. 2(2002): 1–22.

Cuhadar, E. 'Assessing Transfer from Track Two Diplomacy: The Case of Water and Jerusalem'. *Journal of Peace Research* 46, no. 5(2009): 641–658.

Dajani, O. 'Surviving Opportunities: Palestinian Negotiating Patterns in Peace Talks with Israel'. In *How Israelis and Palestinians Negotiate – A Cross-Cultural Analysis of the Oslo Peace Process*, edited by T. Cofman Wittes, 39–80. Washington, DC: United States Institute of Peace Press, 2005.

Davies, J. and E. Kaufman (eds) 'Second Track/Citizen's Diplomacy: An Overview'. In *Second Track/Citizens' Diplomacy – Concepts and Techniques for Conflict Transformation*, edited by J. Davies and E. Kaufman, 1–12. Lanham, MD: Rowman and Littlefield, 2002.

Duncan, J. 'Sites of Representation–Place, Time and Discourse of the Other'. In *Place, Culture, Representation*, edited by J. Duncan and D. Leg, 39–56. London and New York: Routledge, 1993.

Fisher, R.J. 'The Potential Contribution of Training to Resolving International Conflict'. *International Negotiation* 2, no. 3(1997): 471–486.

Fisher, R.J. *Interactive Conflict Resolution*. Syracuse, NY: Syracuse University Press, 1997.

Friedland, R. and R. Hecht. 'Sacred Urbanism: Jerusalem's Sacrality, Urban Sociology and the History of Religion'. Paper presented in the conference on Jerusalem Across the Disciplines, Arizona State University, February 2007.

Friedman, A. and R. Nasarallah (eds) *Jerusalem Berlin Forum: Divided Cities in Transition*. Jerusalem: The International Peace and Cooperation Center and the Jerusalem Institute for Israel Studies, 2003.

Gidron, B., S.N. Katz and Y. Hasenfeld. 'Introduction, Theoretical Approach and Methodology'. In *Mobilizing for Peace: Conflict Resolution in Northern Ireland, Israel/Palestine and South Africa*, edited by B. Gidron, S.N. Katz and Y. Hasenfeld, 3-38. Oxford: Oxford University Press, 2002.

Hanieh, A. 'The Camp David Diaries'. *Journal of Palestine Studies* 31(2001): 75–97.

Hassner, R.E. 'To Halve and to Hold – Conflicts over Sacred Space and the Problem of Indivisibility'. *Security Studies* 12, no. 4(2003): 1–33.

Hassassian, M. 'Final Status Negotiations on Jerusalem: An Inside Look'. Presented at PASSIA, 13 March 2001.

Hirschfeld, Y. 'Keeping Oslo Alive: Developing a Non-Governmental Peace Strategy'. In *Is Oslo Alive?* 68–114. Jerusalem: The Konrad Adenauer Foundation, The Harry S. Truman Research Institute at the Hebrew University and the Palestine Consultancy Group, 1998.

Hirschfeld, Y. *Oslo, a Formula for Peace* (Hebrew). Tel Aviv: Yitzhak Rabin Center for Israel Studies and Am Oved, 2000.

IPCRI. *Jerusalem Maps*. Jerusalem: IPCRI, May 1999.

JIIS. *Peacemaking in Jerusalem – A Task Team Report*. Jerusalem: The Jerusalem Institute for Israel Studies, 2000.

Kassassieh, I. 'Second Track Negotiations: The Jerusalem File'. *Jerusalem Quarterly* 15(2002): 49–53.

Kelman, H.C. 'Informal Mediation by the Scholar/Practitioner'. In *Mediation in International Relations: Multiple Approaches to Conflict Management*, edited by J. Bercovitch and J.Z. Rubin, 64–96. New York: St. Martin's Press, 1992.

Kelman, H.C. 'Negotiations as Interactive Problem Solving'. *International Negotiation* 1, no. 1 (1996): 99–124.

Kelman, H.C. 'The Contributions of Non-Governmental Organizations to the Resolution of Ethno-national Conflicts: An Approach to Evaluation'. Paper Presented at the Carnegie Corporation Conference on the Role of International NGOs in Ethnic and Nationalist Conflicts, New York, 1996.

Kelman, H.C. 'Promoting Joint Thinking in International Conflicts: An Israeli-Palestinian Continuing Workshop'. *Journal of Social Issues* 50, no. 1(1994): 157–178.

Kelman, H.C. 'Interactive Problem Solving: An Approach to Conflict Resolution and its Application in the Middle East'. *PS: Political Science and Politics* 31, no. 2(1998): 190–198.

Kelman, H.C. 'Interactive Problem Solving as a Tool for Second Track Diplomacy'. In *Second Track/Citizens' Diplomacy – Concepts and Techniques for Conflict Transformation*, edited by J. Davis and E. Kaufman, 81–106. Lanham, MD: Rowman and Littlefield, 2002.

Kimmerling, B. and J.S. Migdal. *The Palestinian People, A History*. Cambridge, MA: Harvard University Press, 2003.

Kleiman, Aharon. 'Israeli Negotiating Culture'. In *How Israelis and Palestinians Negotiate – A Cross-Cultural Analysis of the Oslo Peace Process*, edited by T. Cofman Wittes, 81–132. Washington, DC: United States Institute of Peace Press, 2005.

Klein, M. *The Jerusalem Problem: The Struggle for Permanent Status*. Gainesville, FL: University Press of Florida, 2003.

Lamont, M. and V. Molnar. 'The Study of Boundaries in the Social Sciences'. *Annual Review of Sociology* 28(2002): 167–195.

Lieberfeld, D. 'Evaluating the Contribution of Track Two Diplomacy to Conflict Termination in South Africa 1984–90'. *Journal of Peace Research* 39, no. 3(2002): 355–372.

Macmillan, M. *Peacemakers – Six Months that Changed the World*. London: John Murray, 2003.

Maoz, M., G. Khattib, I. Dakak, Y. Katz., Y. Sayigh, Z. Schiff, S. Shamir, K. Shikaki. 'The Future of Israeli-Palestinian Relations'. *Middle East Policy* 7, no. 2(2000): 90–112.

Maoz, M. and S. Nusseibeh (eds) *Jerusalem: Points of Friction and Beyond*. London: Kluwer, 2000.

McDonald, J.W. 'Further Exploration of Track Two Diplomacy'. In *Timing the De-escalation of International Conflicts*, edited by L. Kriesberg and S.J. Thorson, 201–220. Syracuse, NY: Syracuse University Press, 1991.

MacDonald, J.W. 'The Need for Multi-Track Diplomacy'. In *Second Track/Citizens' Diplomacy – Concepts and Techniques for Conflict Transformation*, edited by J. Davis and E. Kaufman, 49–60. Lanham, MD: Rowman and Littlefield, 2002.

Migdal, J. S. 'Mental Maps and Virtual Checkpoints – Struggles to Construct and Maintain State and Social Boundaries'. In *Boundaries and Belonging – State and Societies in the Struggle to Shape Identities and Local Practices*, edited by J.S. Migdal, 3–23. Cambridge: Cambridge University Press, 2004.

Montville, J. 'The Arrow and the Olive Branch: A Case for Track Two Diplomacy'. *Conflict Resolution: Track Two Diplomacy*, edited by J. McDonald and D. Bendahmane, 5–20. Washington, DC: Foreign Service Institute, Department of State, 1987.

Newman, D. and A. Passi. 'Fences and Neighbors in the Postmodern World – Boundary Narratives in Political Geography'. *Progress in Human Geography* 22(1998): 186–207.

Ginat, J. 'Temple Mount–al Haram al-Sharif: A Proposal for Solution'. *Middle East Peace Process Vision Versus Reality*, edited by J. Ginat, E.J. Perkins and E.G. Corr, 372–374. (Oklahoma Paper). Brighton: Sussex Academic Press, 2002.

Passi, Anssi. 'Boundaries as Social Processes – Territoriality in the World of Flows'. In *Boundaries, Territory and Post-modernity*, edited by D. Newman, 69–88. London: Frank Cass, 1999.

Ross, D. *The Missing Peace – The Inside Story of the Fight for Middle East Peace*. New York: Farrar, Straus and Giroux, 2004.

Rouhana, N.N. 'Unofficial Third-Party Intervention in International Conflict: Between Legitimacy and Disarray'. *Negotiation Journal* 11, no. 3(1995): 255–270.

Rouhana, N.N. 'Interactive Conflict Resolution: Issues in Theory, Methodology, and Evaluation'. In *International Conflict Resolution after the Cold War*, edited by D. Druckman and P.C. Stern, 294–337. Washington, DC: National Academy Press, 2000.

Saunders, H.H. 'Possibilities and Change: Another Way to Consider Unofficial Third Party Intervention'. *Negotiation Journal* 11, no. 3(1995): 271–275.

Saunders, H.H. 'We Need a Later Theory of Negotiation: The Impact of Pre-Negotiation Phases'. *Negotiation Journal* 1, no. 3(1985): 249–262.

Shatayyeh, M. (ed.) *Scenarios on the Future of Jerusalem*. Al-Bireh: Palestinian Center for Regional Studies, 1998.

Sher, G. *Just Beyond Reach: The Israeli-Palestinian Peace Negotiations 1999–2001*. Tel Aviv: Miskal-Yedioth Ahronoth Books and Chemed Books, 2001.

Smock, D.R. 'Introduction'. In *Religious Contributions to Peacemaking – When Religion Brings Peace Not War*, edited by D.R. Smock, 1–5. Washington, DC: US Institute of Peace, 2006.

Susskind, L E., A. Chayes and J. Martinez. 'Parallel Informal Negotiation: A New Kind of International Dialogue'. *Negotiation Journal* 12, no. 1(1996): 19–29.

Swisher, C.E. *The Truth About Camp David: The Untold Story About the Collapse of the Middle East Peace Process*. New York: Nation Books, 2004.

The Italian Center for Peace in the Middle East. *Israelis, Palestinians Coexisting in Jerusalem*, 2001.

The Madrid Non-Paper.

Waage-Henriksen, H. *Peacemaking is a Risky Business – Norway's Role in the Peace Process in the Middle East 1993–96*. Oslo: PRIO – International Peace Research Institute, 2004.

Wanis-St. John, A. 'Back Channel Diplomacy – The Strategic Use of Multiple Channels of Negotiation in Middle East Peacemaking'. Ph.D. diss., Fletcher School of Law and Diplomacy: Tufts University, 2001.

PART II

JOCI proposals to resolve the conflict over Jerusalem – The Special Regime model

6

THE JERUSALEM OLD CITY INITIATIVE DISCUSSION DOCUMENT

New directions for deliberation and dialogue

Michael Bell, Michael J. Molloy, John Bell and Marketa Evans

Executive summary

The Old City of Jerusalem is perhaps the most contentious issue in the Arab–Israeli conflict. Its sovereignty, administration and control are questions of great dispute, and its Holy Sites resonate powerfully in the hearts and minds of Muslims, Jews and Christians everywhere. The Old City cannot be divorced from its political, social and economic links to Jerusalem as a whole, nor from its Israeli or Palestinian hinterlands. This includes the issues of security, barriers, settlements and freedom of movement. However, if questions respecting the Old City remain unresolved, a durable peace between Israelis and Palestinians will be impossible.

Over the past half-century, there has been no shortage of proposals regarding the status of Jerusalem and the Holy Sites, but none has been successful. Many begin with a focus on the political imperatives of sovereignty, framing the problem as a case of traditional conflict management – a dispute over territory or political control. We believe that such frameworks lead to proposals that perpetuate exclusivism.

The Jerusalem Old City Initiative adopts a different approach. Its core building block is the needs of Jerusalem's stakeholders, for if those needs are not addressed, continued conflict is certain. Understanding and addressing deeply rooted and authentic needs – both spiritual and practical – is a potentially powerful avenue to building workable solutions. Essential as well is the preparation of publics and policy makers through advocacy and public education.

Within this context, the Jerusalem Old City Initiative proposes a range of creative approaches for moving forward on the Old City. Specifically, it aims to:

- stimulate a wide-ranging research agenda, investigating the religious, social, economic, political, symbolic, security and legal needs of all stakeholders;

- advance practical cooperation and improve conditions on the ground through a needs-based approach that ensures equity and dignity, and that builds durable civil society networks to tackle practical projects;
- provoke rigorous discussion about future governance options for the Old City among Israelis, Palestinians, and fair-minded members of the international community; and
- generate new possibilities and ways of thinking regarding the Old City, through public education and advocacy.

This document is not designed to be an exhaustive final word on the Jerusalem issue; indeed, it deliberately steers away from advocating off-the-shelf 'solutions'. A focus on needs and local engagement led us to adopt a 'bottom-up' approach, including in-depth, locally commissioned research.

Our intention is to follow this discussion document with a work plan focusing on the essentials of Old City life and governance. With Israelis and Palestinians in the forefront, members of civil society, academic institutions, think tanks and other non-governmental organizations can work together to identify and pursue arrangements that are integrated and sustainable. The engagement process we propose is a modular one – building on identified needs to promote practical projects, research, discussion and advocacy aimed at addressing those requirements.

In our view, a single governance approach for the Old City is necessary to address key practical and symbolic needs, and the linkages between issues. We are therefore proposing an institutional framework aimed at creating conditions that support equity, security and predictability in day-to-day life. Our intent is also to maintain the integrity of the Old City; the area is too small, densely populated and architecturally linked to be divided and managed by a series of authorities and police forces. Given the level of mistrust between the parties, such complex arrangements are virtually certain to break down, threatening new crises and more violence.

We are therefore suggesting consideration be given to:

- establishing an interim Special Regime that meets the needs of stakeholders, within the framework of a two-state solution for Israel and Palestine, with Yerushalayim and Al-Quds as their capitals;
- appointing an administrator with executive powers; the administrator would be an internationally respected individual, possibly nominated by the Quartet, but agreed to by the parties;
- forming a Governing Council, composed of Israelis, Palestinians, and possibly outside representatives drawn from countries acceptable to the parties;
- vesting in the administrator and council responsibility for security, law enforcement, public services, infrastructure, residency, property ownership, the legal regime, zoning and building, and other relevant regulations;
- giving Israeli and Palestinian authorities responsibility for a wide range of issues respecting their nationals, including health, education, family law and religious observance; and

- establishing a single Old City police force composed of internationals, Israelis and Palestinians.

Any arrangement for the Old City must also take into account the Holy Sites as profound symbols of identity. If access to these sites is endangered, or there is no agreement on control, the very identity of one or the other stakeholders is likely to appear threatened, leading to breakdown. In our proposal, the Special Regime would be responsible for ensuring and maintaining the religious status quo. Existing practices and traditions would be fully respected, including freedom of access.

Agreement between the parties may well be possible by satisfying many critical needs, without prejudice to sovereignty claims. Israelis and Palestinians could agree *a priori* on the assignment of sovereignty between them, the main point of contention being the Haram al-Sharif/Temple Mount area. They could thereafter assign to the Special Regime interim responsibility for specific functions necessary for security and governance. Alternatively, they might decide to postpone the sovereignty issue until conditions of peace permit more productive deliberation.

In our view, the international community must be prepared to underwrite development of the Old City and Jerusalem as a major world focal point, once a peace is signed. International agencies could also play a key role by transferring offices to the Jerusalem area to provide economic stabilization and encourage political stability. Such action would also serve as a material and symbolic commitment to a comprehensive peace.

The Old City has a spiritual and economic potential that can only be realized when it is governed in a manner affording security, equity and dignity. In times of relative stability, its attraction to pilgrims and tourists has made it a central economic engine for both Israel and Palestine. With a just, lasting and secure peace, the Old City's capacity could be expanded enormously. For this process to begin, there is a compelling need for sustained, constructive dialogue and understanding between the peoples of the three great Abrahamic religions. Above all, success will depend on the ability of the Israelis and Palestinians to develop conditions that permit agreement and coexistence in this most symbolic and sacred of cities.

I An old conflict, a new approach

After more than a century, the Israeli–Palestinian conflict continues to have profound and frightening consequences. The wounds of violence and injustice are deep. The occupation challenges the collective dignity of Palestinians and creates a humanitarian tragedy. Israelis suffer from widespread terror attacks that create massive insecurity and reinforce a firm belief that tough security measures are a *sine qua non* for survival, and that a Jewish state will never truly be accepted in the Middle East.

Over the years, there have been many attempts to find accommodation, most recently the Camp David negotiations of 2000 and the Oslo Accords that preceded them. But attempts to reach agreement on the core issues of Jerusalem, refugees,

MAP 6.1 Israel, The West Bank and map of Jerusalem
© Shaul Arieli

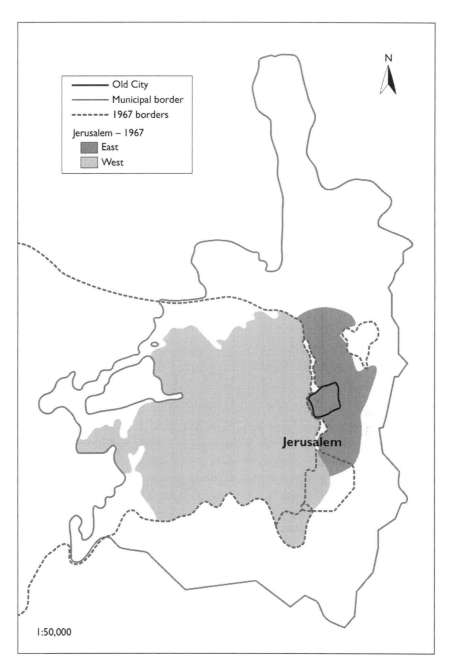

MAP 6.2 Old City borders
© Shaul Arieli

settlements and borders have been unsuccessful. In January 2001, the parties came close to agreement at Taba, but suspicion, distrust and mutual demonization had already become pervasive as violence replaced negotiation.

Many of those we spoke to in developing this document described past negotiators as poorly equipped to deal with questions concerning final status. Yet these questions are the grit and sinew of the conflict, and to approach them without comprehensive preparation threatens any possible future peace. Some we interviewed said negotiators did not give sufficient weight to spiritual and emotional dimensions, focusing instead on ownership and sovereign control. Many of those involved at the time accept they could have benefited from more extensive preparation.

With these lessons in mind, we are proposing an approach for agreement on the Old City of Jerusalem that recognizes sovereignty as a fundamental goal, but that takes into account the full range of factors that make progress towards conflict resolution so challenging. Jerusalem, particularly the Old City, is a microcosm of the greater struggle. Conceptual progress on how, within a two-state solution, Israelis and Palestinians can live in their respective capitals of Yerushalayim and Al-Quds, with workable and sustainable arrangements for the Old City and the Holy Sites, could demonstrate the level of mutual compromise, acceptance and confidence essential for a broader peace.

We propose to begin not with political givens, but by identifying the needs of all sides regarding the Holy Sites, as well as the Old City. We believe that this needs-based approach can facilitate broad community, national and international buy-in and, ultimately, provide a way out of the Jerusalem conundrum by inviting creative approaches to otherwise restrictive sovereignty paradigms. Our aim is to initiate a process whereby stakeholders themselves analyze and clarify the practical and symbolic needs for the Old City.

This 'bottom-up' approach begins with identifying the basic needs of Israelis and Palestinians, and moves towards options for governance, security, economic development, human rights, heritage preservation, education, legal frameworks, property ownership, international involvement and through them to the issue of sovereignty. This initial focus on practical issues and political and symbolic needs, rather than sovereignty per se, may assist in 'unpacking' the complex attachments to the Old City.

We are not suggesting that negotiations on Jerusalem should begin quickly or that political answers can or even need to be found immediately. But we do believe the concerned parties cannot afford to ignore the need to develop and explore sustainable options that could serve as reference points for eventual negotiations. Because of the complex nature of these issues, the development of methodologies and alternative scenarios should begin sooner rather than later.

The time is ripe. A new, still fragile environment is emerging in the Holy Land. The four years of the Al Aqsa Intifada have recently yielded to the prospect of renewed dialogue and the possibility of meaningful negotiations. Despite violent incidents, as the situation continues to stabilize there is a growing openness to discussion. Yasser Arafat's successor, the Palestinian President Mahmoud Abbas, has a constructive and determined reform program. Israeli Prime Minister Sharon has effected withdrawal from Gaza and northern parts of the West Bank. For their part, most Israelis and Palestinians appear heartily sick of violence and may be prepared to accommodate each other if trust can be re-established. Many on both sides recognize that the status quo is unacceptable.

Positive movement on the Israeli–Palestinian conflict requires bolstering political will. Now more than ever, the preparation and education of publics, opinion makers and leaders seems imperative if the Camp David and Oslo miscalculations are not to be repeated. We are therefore proposing a process of academic, think tank and civil society engagement. This discussion document is the first step in what we hope will be a larger initiative involving fair-minded international actors as supporting partners, with the key players, Israelis and Palestinians, in examining options for a special status for the Old City. Its intent is to identify, for further research and discussion, issues essential to the wellbeing of the Old City, and to develop workable options for collaborative action and advocacy. We hope that with the concerted effort and good will of all parties, the issue of Jerusalem may ultimately be resolved.

II Why Jerusalem, why the Old City?

One of the major stumbling blocks to peace in the Middle East is the status of Jerusalem. In negotiations to date, Jerusalem has been left until last because of its seeming intractability. This was the case at Camp David where many directly involved in the discussions have told us the lack of preparation was corrosive. Yet it is this city, holy to the three great monotheistic faiths, that cries out for a fresh approach.

Jerusalem is the pivot for any agreement precisely because so many regard it as a symbol of their identity. The history of Jews, Muslims and Christians is written in its streets, architecture and Holy Sites. For millennia, believers from all three faiths have sought meaning in its stones. Saint Jerome preached that Christians must: 'adore where His feet have stood'. The Prophet Mohammed said that: 'He who performs the pilgrimage to Mecca, visits my grave [in Medina] … and prays for me in Jerusalem – God will not ask him where he failed.' For Jews, the Old City remains the most vibrant focus of identity and pilgrimage. Many Jews believe that the spirit of God has never left the site of the Temple. Over the millennia, they have expressed their yearning with a prayer proclaiming: 'Next year in Jerusalem.' With strong attachments like these, it is not surprising that an undercurrent of intolerance regarding Jerusalem has arisen in each of these faiths throughout history. Clashes of identity and heritage have led to uncompromising exclusivity.

Virtually everyone we spoke to agrees that the Old City and its Holy Sites, particularly the Temple Mount/Haram al-Sharif, represent the core of the conflict because no one can feel satisfied unless his or her issues of relation and identity to this site are fulfilled. It is to this site, representing one-sixth of the 0.9 square kilometers of the walled city, that both Muslims and Jews have their deepest religious and territorial attachments. The Western Wall, as part of the original Herodian enclosure of the Temple Mount site, is the most powerful locus of Jewish prayer and pilgrimage. For Muslims, the Haram al-Sharif is the site from which Mohammed ascended to heaven. This begs the question: why not limit ourselves to developing special arrangements for the Haram al-Sharif/Temple Mount, leaving the rest of the Old City for negotiations between Israelis and Palestinians on the basis of territorial division?

The Haram al-Sharif/Temple Mount is geographically and emotionally linked to its symbolic, political and economic surroundings in the Old City. For this reason, we believe it is incumbent on decision makers to treat the area within the walls as one unit for governance. Singling out the Haram al-Sharif/Temple Mount, for separate agreement, with an actual division of the site by barbed wire and guard posts, would meet neither the physical nor the emotional needs of worshippers, and would damage the soul of the city. To many we spoke with, the other Holy Sites in the Old City, especially the Church of the Holy Sepulcher, and the intertwined and dense nature of life within the walls, make it an inseparable whole.

We believe that the walled city may provide a natural contiguous space within which to develop new arrangements. Practical measures that would work within the confines of the Old City may become unmanageable if extended beyond the walls, especially if under the exclusive national control of one or the other parties. The clear definition of the walled city could facilitate security, governance and the development of arrangements involving a third party presence. It could provide both sides with clear boundaries for developing mutual interests and new processes within a circumscribed space.

Some maintain that looking at the Old City alone and not the broader Jerusalem conurbation is artificial. They say the walled city cannot be dissociated from the rest, economically, socially or politically. They refer to the many crucial heritage sites outside the city walls, most prominently the Jewish cemetery on the Mount of Olives and the Muslim cemetery outside the Lion's Gate, as well as the many churches, such as those adjoining the Garden of Gethsemane. They also argue that there can be no advances respecting the Old City outside of a comprehensive peace agreement that includes the status of the rest of Jerusalem, because trade-offs within and among core issues will have to be made in the course of negotiations.

We agree that context matters. The important Holy Sites outside the Old City cannot be ignored, and we want to encourage new ideas for managing them, without infringing national sovereignty over Yerushalayim or Al-Quds. Neither can analysis and ideas regarding the future of the Old City be divorced from the current security-based climate, other critical political compromises, or from the larger city of Jerusalem. Very few live their lives strictly within the confines of the Old City; most have family and social relations beyond the Old City and often venture through the gates to the modern city. Jerusalem's symbolism, as well as its infrastructure, transportation, water, education, health, social services, economic and social ties, and the legions of tourists eager to visit their Holy Sites within and outside the walls, make it inseparable from the rest of the conurbation.

Our focus within the walls is not to separate the issue from its landscape, but to draw attention to sustainable arrangements for this most delicate area. We believe that without agreement on the Old City, the most sensitive religious sites will continue to serve as flashpoints for violence, especially with the rise of militant religious expression around the globe. Progress might well be made on many fronts in the Israeli–Palestinian conflict, including security and settlements, only to be upended by an otherwise small yet volatile event in the Old City.

III Sovereignty: the heart of the matter?

Moving ahead without first tackling the issue of sovereignty seems naïve or galling to many Israelis and Palestinians, the former because they control the city, the latter because they want control. Most often for both parties, all other questions seem secondary.

Many of the Palestinians we spoke to were fearful of processes that appear to solidify gains made by Israelis with little concrete result for their community. We heard repeatedly that sovereignty over the Haram al-Sharif and the Old City, possibly excluding the Western Wall and the Jewish Quarter, is fundamental to Palestinian needs: the end, not the starting point of discussion. Any attempt to weaken such sovereignty will fail, we were told, because the notion is linked to the losses of Palestinians since 1948, founded in international law and, above all, tied to their dignity.

On the other hand, we heard that Israelis could well view any process introducing an international presence to assist in the governance of Jerusalem and the Old City as an unacceptable attempt to dilute control over their vital interests. Some we spoke to were not willing to consider, after millennia of exile, any change in the status quo. We believe that out of historical habit, Muslims and Jews have tended to conflate religious and political exclusivity, which exacerbates the problem of practical and psychological control – for who can give up the Divine?

These opposing opinions, while resonant within their specific communities are, in fact, the basis of the conflict. While they describe clearly the perceived needs of many on each side, they also define failure at resolution because they are exclusionary. Insisting one side or the other have full sovereignty in the Old City, including a monopoly on the use of force, is saying there will be no agreement, stability, predictability, or shared justice.

In theory, a range of other sovereignty arrangements seems possible, including joint, shared or cooperative sovereignty over certain areas, functional sovereignty, or suspension of claims – simply agreement not to agree while establishing a practical division of powers. Past approaches have often proposed a division of sovereignty for the Old City and a patchwork of responsibilities divided up by site or neighbourhood. We believe the resulting fragmented arrangements, while perhaps having some theoretical logic, would fuel existing divisions and leave the city prone to serious inter-communal instability. This, in turn, would jeopardize any comprehensive solution reached between Palestinians and Israelis. In fact, there have been second thoughts on this precise issue among some of those who authored the Geneva Accord, even though these texts advocate precisely such measures.

In a sense, the citizens of the Middle East are victims of the nation–state concepts developed in the West. Some feel trapped and agree that the Old City requires a special arrangement to break the deadlock of exclusionism. It may be that the complexities of the region's history, heritage and politics do not lend themselves to a wholesale adoption of such ideas, and that to insist on them at the outset would lead to certain failure. We believe that formal sovereignty can only be tackled effectively when needs, emotions and the requirements for dignity and equity have been met, and both parties are participating actively in their city's governance. A needs-based approach that is comprehensive and concrete may pave the way to new political directions, find openings currently ignored, and assure the security and control to which both sides are entitled.

IV Needs: the starting point

It is our firm view that Jerusalem will remain a source of conflict until its status is resolved to meet the emotional, psychological and material needs of those whose identity is etched into it. Although efforts have been made in this direction, little consideration has been given to the essential role of cultural and symbolic factors in peace building and governance.

With this in mind, we have identified the following needs as a starting point to unpacking the complex issues that currently limit sustainable progress on the Old City:

Social: Consideration must be given to the social needs of the estimated 35,000 residents of the Old City. Critical as well are the Old City's links to the remainder of Jerusalem, particularly with respect to basic infrastructure and municipal regulation.
Property ownership: With no systematic form of ownership in the Old City, the question of 'rights' becomes problematic, as does the potential for development.
Economic: The Old City is the focus for pilgrimages and tourism in Jerusalem, as well as for Israel and a future Palestinian state. The continuing conflict has had a serious negative impact on its economic wellbeing.
Political: As both peoples consider Jerusalem to be their capital, there are critical political issues to be resolved.
Religious, symbolic and heritage: The question of heritage and identity, links to the Holy Sites, and the ensuing needs for preservation, access, security and respect are fundamental concerns for both sides.

Clearly, any discussion of needs must take into account the Old City's diverse stakeholders and their varied levels of attachment, and political and religious commitment. These stakeholders include:

- residents of the Old City;
- Jerusalemites with access to, and an interest in, the Old City;
- Palestinians and Israelis who view the Old City's Holy Sites as fundamental to their identity, or who wish secure access to and control of them;
- leaders on both sides, who view the Old City as a key policy and negotiation issue;
- Jews and Arabs outside of Israel and Palestine who view the Old City as a crucial part of their religious and cultural identity, as well as the core of the ongoing conflict;
- Jews, Muslims and Christians around the world who view the Old City's religious sites as having meaning in their own spiritual lives;
- international actors with an interest in stability in the Middle East and, therefore, in resolving the conflict over Jerusalem in an equitable and sustainable manner.

Needs vary considerably according to stakeholder. Some, for example an Armenian resident of the Old City, will be concerned with a wide variety of needs, from living conditions, to access to the Holy Sepulcher. On the other end of the spectrum, a citizen of Denmark may have an undefined symbolic interest in the Old City, but is much less likely to be interested in the conditions of residents. The overriding interest of international actors will likely be in the stability of the city's governance arrangements.

Too often in the past, the focus has been on the deemed political requirements of the national protagonists to the detriment of other key needs and stakeholders, whether the wants of residents or global interest in the Holy Sites. Indeed, negotiations have floundered partly because they ignored the needs and interests of greater communities until it was too late, for example, the larger Muslim interest in the city.

On the pages that follow, we review each of the needs identified above, often suggesting possible avenues for moving forward.[1] This analysis is intended as a beginning, not an exhaustive assessment of such needs. We are convinced that with further deliberation and input from all parties concerned, supported by a series of well-considered changes on the ground, the stage will be set for continuing progress.

A Social needs

Despite its small size and population, conditions in the 0.9 square kilometers of the walled Old City are complex. A host of factors contribute, including demographic and spatial challenges, inadequate municipal services and governance structures, a lack of economic opportunity, and a poverty rate as high as 40 per cent. Complicating the situation are high rates of drug use, a breakdown of traditional social mechanisms and networks, and feelings of social and political inequity.

The population of the Old City has grown rapidly over the past three decades. In 2002, it had an estimated 35,000 residents, of which 11.3 per cent were Jewish and 88.7 per cent were Arab and Armenian. The Old City has about the same population density overall as Manhattan, and in some parts of the Muslim quarter, density is equivalent to that of the Calcutta slums. This can be attributed to a larger than average family size, a fixed number of available housing units, and difficulty in obtaining building permits, a problem that Palestinians believe is due to political motives. We were also told that some Palestinians are reluctant to leave the Old City for fear of losing their property.

As well, since 1995 the city has witnessed an influx of Palestinians with Israeli-issued Jerusalem identity cards returning to live in Jerusalem, so as not to lose these cards and the social services that come with them. This rapid population increase has resulted in housing shortages for lower income groups who cannot afford the high rents and taxes of more affluent areas in East Jerusalem. This, in turn, has intensified demand for accommodation and basic services in the Old City, and resulted in residents making unplanned expansions and additions to existing buildings, without technical guidance or supervision. In many cases, these changes to the physical shape and condition of the buildings have inflicted irreparable damage on their historic and cultural value. As the architecture of the Old City, especially in the Muslim Quarter, was not designed for current densities, there is little privacy or natural light, and open public space for children is limited. The high noise levels from overcrowding cause stress and exacerbate domestic problems.

The recent construction of a barrier around Jerusalem has also triggered a population movement. Thousands of Palestinians who once lived in East Jerusalem and reside today outside the complex of walls and barriers being built to the north, south and east of the city are moving back within the municipal boundaries. They are also driven by the fear of losing the social and economic benefits that come with residency. An estimated 60,000 to 90,000 Palestinians living outside Jerusalem's municipal borders, and outside the wall, carry Israeli identity cards, thus making them eligible for permanent residence in Israel. Their expected migration towards the city centre will undoubtedly make the housing shortage in East Jerusalem and the Old City even more severe and prohibitively expensive.

While the Muslim population continues to grow in the Old City, there is a continuous outflow from the already small Christian community because of overcrowding, lack of economic opportunity and complex inter-religious tensions. Many people attribute the Jewish Quarter's shrinking population to a lack of facilities and amenities. As well, a growing number of secular Israelis are leaving because of the increasingly ultra-orthodox community that dominates the Jewish Quarter. According to our sources, this emigration is numerically offset by the influx of ideologically committed Israelis who seek the 'Judaization' of the Old City as a whole. The result has been a small net inflow of Jews into the Old City.

Until a few years ago, basic public services did not exist in many parts of the Old City. Today, even after intensified efforts towards improvements in that direction, the standard and extent of such services is still markedly inferior to other sectors of Jerusalem. Garbage disposal, water and sewage systems, electricity and telephone lines are comparative luxuries. Improvements have been slow, and in some places ineffective, due to economic and political factors.

Full answers to the Old City's social plight must await wide-ranging political changes that provide residents with a sense of dignity, ownership and security regarding their future. Nonetheless, specific issues can be addressed immediately, such as the urgent need for better housing conditions and municipal services, and equity in issuing building permits. Steps like these, in conjunction with improved economic conditions, may bring about positive social change and begin the process of improving community relations and initiating mutual trust, which many argue is essential if the Old City is to be resurrected. Modest gains now can help create the confidence and momentum for further progress.

For consideration

Based on our discussions with stakeholders, we have identified the following as practical initiatives that could be undertaken in the near term.

- *A comprehensive survey of housing stock and structure* in the Old City for the purpose of renovation and rehabilitation. Although groups such as the Welfare Association have conducted similar studies in the Arab Quarters, a more comprehensive study of the Old City could be undertaken, with results linked to municipal planning projects. This would promote confidence and trust among Palestinians, and provide much needed data on their needs and concerns. It is likely that any expansion of the current housing stock would have to be carefully controlled in order to conform to the Old City's morphology and heritage.
- *Restoration and rehabilitation* of the Old City through a series of projects designed to improve city life, including enhancement of the city's architectural heritage, giving due respect to all the communities concerned. While many such projects are currently under way (for example, the Palestinian Housing Council's 'Project for Restoration and Maintenance of Buildings in the Old City', and the Welfare Association's 'Old City Revitalization Plan') they would benefit greatly from enhanced coordination and funding. An international fund may be useful in this regard.
- *Loans and grants* to Old City residents to help them upgrade existing structures in accordance with international standards, and under a credible professional supervision and inspection regime.
- *An increased number of, and ease of access to, housing permits* for Palestinians outside the Old City, thereby reducing overcrowding within the Old City by giving residents choices in where they will live.
- *The facilitation of micro projects* through improved credit facilities, 'soft' loans for business, and training for female entrepreneurs. These projects might include, for example, cottage-type industries, better childcare facilities, youth clubs, libraries and playgrounds.

- *Key infrastructure projects.* For example, the introduction of cable television throughout the Old City could minimize the number of antennae on historic rooftops, thereby helping to meet World Heritage Site requirements. As well, central heating systems would improve conditions in homes that are damp, cold and unhealthy.
- *A services survey* of the entire Old City could establish where services such as garbage disposal, water, sewage, electricity and telephone lines are lacking.
- *A pilot project by a joint team of Israelis and Palestinians to establish principles to underpin joint planning.* These principles would recognize the needs of both sides, as well as the Old City as a whole, and could serve as the template for further municipal planning. Some work of this sort has been undertaken by the Jerusalem municipality and can be built on; however, there is a need to develop processes that allow Palestinian participation. Given the current level of distrust between Palestinians and the Israeli-dominated municipal government and administration, it may be useful to employ an external party that enjoys the confidence of both communities to facilitate efforts to improve urban planning, enhance public space, and meet the Old City's urgent housing needs.
- *Development of community-level institutions.* The establishment of cultural and social institutions at the community level would assist in social development. For instance, numerous educational programmes have been put in place to ameliorate the social and public health conditions of the Old City's Arab population. These programmes have begun to make modest improvements, but require ongoing efforts and continued financial support. Many of those we spoke to believe community empowerment is essential in ending the cycle of mistrust, exclusion and poverty.
- *A 'clean-up' campaign*, possibly with the support of agreed upon members of the international community, backed by a sustained, community-based educational programme to modify behaviour, instil community pride, and ensure that clean-up activities are maintained over the long term. Such a step could have a powerful impact on the attitudes of residents and their sense of self-worth.

B Property ownership needs

Property ownership may well be one of the Old City's most complex issues, as land laws are based on an array of Ottoman, British, Jordanian and Israeli legislation, tradition and practice. Unlike other parts of the Jerusalem conurbation, the Old City has no systematic form of ownership registration. Some 'owners' have the right to use and bequeath land through a judicial ruling, key money or a mortgage, without the property being registered in their name. With no clear proof of ownership for many properties, protracted legal disagreements are common.

Divisions and estimates are often disputed, but most agree that over half of Old City property – more than 450 dunams out of a total of 900 – is owned either by the Islamic *waqf* or the churches. Most of the remainder held by either individual

Palestinians or the Israeli government. Many see the high proportion of ownership by religious institutions as a complicating factor in issues of residency, participation and taxation. Transactions between the religious institutions, the Israeli state and private individuals have been fraught with ambiguities and friction.

PROPERTY COMPLICATIONS

The Greek Orthodox Patriarchate is the largest single landowner in the Old City and among the largest 10 landowners in Israel and Palestine. Its properties include the West Jerusalem site of the Knesset and the Church of the Holy Sepulcher in the Old City. Although transactions between Israel and the Patriarchate on property within the pre-1967 borders have been more cordial recently, transactions in the Old City pose a continuing threat to the demographic, commercial and sectarian status quo.

One example of the fractious nature of property ownership in the Old City is the recent controversy over the sale of church-owned property by the Patriarchate. According to media reports, Patriarch Irineos leased two hotels – the Petra and the Imperial – to Israeli-backed Jewish investors for a period of 200 years. Located just inside Jaffa Gate, the Imperial Hotel was a frequent meeting place for Palestinian moderates and members of Israel's 'peace camp' during the 1990s. There were allegations that Irineos leased the hotels to demonstrate to the Israeli government that he was not sympathetic to Palestinian interests.

In late April 2005, some 500 protestors carrying Palestinian flags scuffled with Israeli police near the Church of the Holy Sepulcher while Irineos was conducting Good Friday mass. Fifteen people were injured. In response, the governments of Greece, Jordan and the Palestinian Authority launched separate investigations into the Patriarchate's actions; all subsequently called for Irineos's removal. In August 2005, the Holy Synod of Greek Orthodox clergy replaced Irineos with Theophilos, the current Patriarch.

Emotionally, the situation is equally complex. A key issue for Palestinians is restitution of, or compensation for, lost property. In 1948, all Jews were expelled when the Jordanians took control of the city. Following the 1967 war, the Israelis expropriated 116 dunams for redevelopment of the Jewish Quarter. The most sensitive aspect of the expropriation was the demolition of the Mughrabi area and the expulsion of its residents to create a plaza facing the Western Wall.

These issues are important, not only as symbols or because of 'rights' questions, but also because they are a major hindrance to the carefully planned development that must take place if the Old City is to realize its religious, historic, economic, archaeological and human potential. As well, any changes in land ownership, particularly transactions that bring non-Israeli properties into Israeli hands, are likely to result in strong emotional reactions among Palestinians. For these reasons, the question of land ownership is key to conflict management in the Old City.

For consideration

We have identified the following as property ownership options that could usefully be explored:

- A cooperative effort by universities, think tanks and policy experts to explore possible solutions to ownership issues.
- A process to identify claims, facilitated by an impartial third party that has the confidence of both Israelis and Palestinians. While this would undoubtedly be a complicated exercise, reconciliation of claims – including issues related to recent settlements in the Old City – is essential for fair and stable land management.
- Development of compensation schemes for land lost within the Old City.
- Development – with Palestinian input – of a new tenancy law permitting more flexible use of properties, and supporting an urban plan for the Old City that balances the housing needs of residents with economic goals and the need to preserve heritage sites.
- Evaluation of property disputes, and development of a dispute resolution mechanism that sets a standard for future activity, including how parties deal with claims for restitution and restoration – for example, the mosques in the Maghrabi area and the Hurva and other synagogues in the Jewish Quarter.

C Economic needs

In considering the economics of the Old City, it becomes readily apparent that there is a strong connection between its potential as the core of the Israeli and Palestinian tourism industry, and issues of security and equity. Tourism will thrive when tourists and residents feel secure. But security will not be attainable or sustainable unless Israelis and Palestinians believe their interests, their economic opportunities, and their ability to access services and influence developments are themselves secured.

As the focus of religious pilgrimages and tourism, the Holy Sites and archaeological features of the Old City are its economic base. Yet it is difficult to determine their precise economic impact, as neither Israeli nor Palestinian sources provide comprehensive information on economic activities within the Old City. For example, while Israeli authorities maintain statistics on hotel stays, employment and car rentals, they do not keep records of apartment rentals, restaurant sales, or sales of souvenirs, handicrafts and antiques. As well, statistics that are available are often regarded with suspicion, due to the high degree of mistrust between Israelis and Palestinians.

That said, tourism is generally acknowledged as Israel's second largest industry. According to Israeli statistics, pilgrimages and tourism employ 280,000 people within the territory Israel claims as its sovereign jurisdiction, either directly or indirectly as guides, drivers, site managers, hotel employees and shopkeepers.

Israeli tourism statistics do not provide information on the number of people visiting the Old City. It is clear, however, that most tourism itineraries include several nights in Jerusalem and at least one day visiting the Old City. According to statistics on foreign tourists, 51 per cent visit the Western Wall, 41 per cent the Jewish Quarter, 23 per cent the Mount of Olives, 21 per cent the Church of the Holy Sepulcher, and 14 per cent the Via Dolorosa. The industry caters to Europeans and North Americans who come as Christian and Jewish pilgrims. Today, few tourists enter the Old City from the West Bank; those who do come overland from Jordan. Muslim tourism to the Old City is negligible because of political and security concerns.

Jerusalem was once a major destination for domestic tourists. Many Israelis spent hours strolling the streets of the bazaars, not only in the Jewish Quarter, but throughout the other Quarters as well. For years, visits were incorporated into educational enrichment programmes for Israeli students. Although much of this activity was curtailed by the outbreak of violence, the Jewish Quarter and the Western Wall remain the focal point of Jewish pilgrimage and prayer, as well as a gathering place for Jewish holidays, celebrations and events of national importance.

According to statistics our research associates were able to gather, Palestinian domestic tourism to Jerusalem has also declined enormously. East Jerusalem, including the Old City, was once the hub of West Bank economic and social life. However, Israeli restrictions on Palestinian movement have drastically reduced these activities, including attendance at Muslim prayer at the Haram al-Sharif. Palestinians believe these restrictions to be largely politically motivated – increasingly so with the construction of a physical barrier around the Jerusalem conurbation.

TOURISM IN THE OLD CITY

With the continuing violence since the beginning of the second Intifada, tourism in the Old City has plummeted, and dependent industries have suffered greatly. One practice in particular affecting Old City merchants involves the cruise ships that stop at the ports of Eilat, Haifa and Ashdod for one-day stopovers. Tourists are bussed to Jerusalem, where they are taken on a hurried tour that most often begins at the Dung Gate in the Jewish Quarter and includes the Western Wall, the Cardo, the Church of the Holy Sepulcher and, sometimes, the Via Dolorosa. Little or no time is allocated for purchasing souvenirs and artifacts, eating in restaurants or taking in the ambience of historic streets and neighbourhoods. Most tours avoid the market areas of the Muslim and Christian Quarters, and any small purchases made are by the occasional tourist who strays from the main tour. Jewish tourists on 'solidarity missions' or cultural tours such as 'Birthright' are taken directly to the Old City and the Jewish Quarter, without time or permission to visit the Muslim, Christian or Armenian Quarters. This was understandable when the Intifada was at its height, although violence seldom penetrated inside the Old City.

Old City bazaars declined strikingly during both Intifadas, with about 200 shops closing during the Al Aqsa disturbances. Some shopkeepers estimate that 50 per cent of colleagues lost their businesses because of the decline in visitors; albeit some are now reopening. Many Old City merchants suggested that the municipality favours their downtown competitors in West Jerusalem, through tax discounts, for example. According to merchants, Israeli tour guides often discourage visitors from making purchases in the Old City. Palestinians complained that Christian and Muslim sites are largely ignored in Israeli public relations efforts, and that Palestinians find it difficult to register as tour guides. At the same time, however, others have observed that many Palestinian websites ignore Jewish sites in an attempt to de-legitimize Jewish connections to the Old City.

In addition to political tensions, the increasing popularity of low-end, foreign-produced goods for the growing Arab population has lessened the romantic appeal of the Old City as a Middle Eastern souk. Ancient crafts, old copper, carpets, and antique and spice shops have largely given way to modern, mass-produced items. Low-end boutiques and restaurants have also helped to erode the city's exotic appeal, although such shops do meet the needs of the residents.

With peace, the Old City could again become a major economic engine, with tourism and pilgrimage as the fuel for economic revitalization. Certainly, progress is difficult in the face of current political tensions. However, while it may not be possible to achieve significant gains immediately, we believe that recognition of common interests can be the impetus for practical steps in this direction.

For consideration

The economic welfare and future of the Old City is very much dependent on resolution of the conflict and the full return of tourism. However, there are possible areas of work that can address the needs of residents, commercial actors on both sides, and national interests with a stake in the area's development, such as:

- increased coordination between Palestinians and Israelis, and greater understanding of the needs of shop owners, to achieve a more equitable approach to competition for tourism;
- comprehensive and balanced information on Old City sites for tourists;
- joint planning on improving visitor services and minimizing inequities. Studies could be conducted for developing a professionally based and representative Old City Board of Tourism;
- establishment of the Old City as a tax free zone;
- reconfiguration of tourist routes for the benefit of all commercial enterprises; and
- an increase in tourist facilities in East Jerusalem, to ensure equity between Palestinians and Israelis.

D Political needs

The status of Jerusalem, with the Old City at its centre, has been the subject of intense political and legal debate. The official Israeli position is that the entirety of Jerusalem is the united, eternal capital of Israel. Officially, Palestinians assert that according to international law, Israel has no right to any part of East Jerusalem, including the Old City, that the occupation itself is illegal, and that East Jerusalem should be their capital. As deeply held as these positions are by many, the vast majority of Palestinians and Israelis we spoke to recognize that such views are likely to perpetuate the conflict. In either scenario, there would be a winner and a loser, fostering irredentism and the seeds of future conflict.

ACCESS TO RELIGIOUS SITES

During Jordan's 1948–1967 rule over East Jerusalem, Jewish access was barred. Although the 1948 armistice stipulated freedom of access to the Holy Sites in East Jerusalem, in practice it was given only to Christians and Muslims. The restriction on Jews may have been a response to them as a perceived security threat in the aftermath of the 1948 war, when members of the Irgun and other irregulars fought Jordanian troops for control of the Jewish Quarter in one of the war's bloodiest confrontations. We were told that Jordanians feared the Jewish Quarter would be used as a staging ground for Jewish terrorist activities, and for infiltrating through the Old City into East Jerusalem. Jordanians were also concerned about the political ramifications of access – specifically, that the area would fall under Israeli control. Whatever perceptions existed, Jordanians razed much of the Jewish Quarter, destroying some 50 synagogues and seminaries. The denial of access to the Western Wall during this period does much to explain the emotional impact of the Israeli victory in 1967, and the subsequent discomfort Israelis feel with Palestinian assertions of exclusive sovereignty over the Old City and the Haram al-Sharif/Temple Mount.

Today, Israeli institutions of state exercise control over the Old City, satisfying the majority of Jewish citizens, who feel their interests are well protected. Palestinians, on the other hand, feel bitter and disenfranchised. Our consultations in the Arab world also revealed that even the most moderate of Muslims believe the Israeli monopoly on decision making and control is humiliating. Some we spoke to, both Israeli and Palestinian, maintained that the political importance of the Haram al-Sharif in the Muslim narrative has increased significantly in recent years, precisely because the Old City is under Israeli rule.

Christians and their churches also have a major stake in Old City governance – specifically, the ability to access and maintain the Christian Holy Sites unimpeded. However, Christian opinion is divided and divisive, we were told, with many evangelical believers satisfied with the status quo. The more established denominations are either passive or committed to the realization of Palestinian political objectives because of the human rights appeal of such goals. Although less outspoken, some Palestinian Christians have said they fear the pressure that a more purely Islamic environment would create for them. Some cited this as the reason Christians are emigrating from the Holy Land, Jerusalem in particular.

There are other sources of contention as well. The Israeli barrier wall around Jerusalem has created a new dimension regarding control of the city. Although the barrier is not directed at the Old City alone, many Palestinians and Israelis view it as a new and concrete definition of Jerusalem space, further consolidating Israeli control. As discussed earlier, the barrier also creates significant problems for West Bank Palestinians wishing to access the Old City and its Holy Sites, weakens the economic, social and political linkages between those inside and outside the barrier, and has contributed to overcrowding as those living in Jerusalem's periphery move to the Old City to avoid being caught outside the barrier. Settlement growth in the Muslim and Christian Quarters populated by Israeli religious nationalists is an additional source of tension. According to figures provided by our research associates, settlers have acquired some 80 properties in Arab Quarters, facilitated by Israeli state subsidies and administrative support. Many believe that if the Jewish presence continues to increase in areas of serious Arab poverty and high density, there is a significant threat of violence. The Aqabat Khalidi area of the Old City, for example, has the highest Palestinian population density, yet our researchers say it is the target for takeovers by radical settlers.

In a poll on peace issues conducted in December 2004, Khalil Shikaki found that both Israelis and Palestinians had softened on the difficult issues of refugees and borders, but had toughened their stance on the future of Jerusalem and the Old City. These 'hardened' positions seem less problematic regarding the rest of Jerusalem, where there appears to be an increasing readiness to give what is 'Jewish to Jews and what is Arab to Arabs', as was discussed at Camp David and Taba. For the first time, some leaders of the Israeli religious nationalist movement have suggested that Arab neighbourhoods in East Jerusalem outside the Old City may need some kind of special status outside Israeli control. However, this does not take into account Israel's continuing expansion in East Jerusalem.

The situation in the Old City and its Holy Sites is much more complex. Israeli negotiators of the Geneva Accord received much criticism for agreeing to the principle of Palestinian sovereignty over the Haram al-Sharif/Temple Mount, and for daring to consider negotiating away such an important symbol of heritage without reference to any public and political process. We encountered widespread and vociferous opposition among Israelis and in the Diaspora respecting such an option. Conversely, the gap between current Israeli control over the Old City and the need for other forms of authority by Palestinians and other stakeholders, such as Muslims around the world, is a source of friction and conflict, especially regarding the Holy Sites. The Old City Tunnel demonstrates what can occur when these interests and needs collide.

THE OLD CITY TUNNEL

During the 1970s, Israeli authorities dug a viewing tunnel under Arab-owned property along the northern sections of the western wall of the Haram al-Sharif/ Temple Mount. Designed to expose more of the ancient Jewish Temple's enclosure walls, the construction sparked considerable controversy. The tunnel consists of a long passageway, averaging 1 meter wide and more than 2 meters high, that extends from the established Western Wall pilgrimage site. At its far end, the tunnel cuts across an underground canal leading to cisterns from the Roman period, most of which are located beneath Muslim *waqf* property, the Via Dolorosa, and a wing of the Sisters of Zion Convent in the Muslim Quarter.

In the 1990s, the Israelis created a northern exit to the tunnel complex to simplify the visiting process, and allow more pilgrims and tourists access to Jewish historical sites. The *waqf* protested these plans on the basis that construction would compromise historic buildings from the Mameluk period, and the Al Aqsa mosque platform. As well, many Palestinians saw the construction as part of a continuing Israeli plan to dispossess them. When the new exit opened in September 1996, five days of rioting resulted in the deaths of 56 Palestinians and 14 Israelis.

Based on our research, we have summarized the perceived political needs of the Old City as follows:

Palestinian needs

- control, authority and title over the Old City, particularly the Haram al-Sharif, and recognition of their legitimacy by other parties;
- among some, a willingness to modify the above requirements to permit Israeli control over the Jewish Quarter and the Western Wall; and
- restitution for lost properties in the Jewish Quarter and Jewish settlements elsewhere in the Old City.

Israeli needs

- control, authority and title over the Old City and its surrounds, because of its essential role in Jewish history, heritage and tradition;
- for many, recognition of the long-established Israeli position of Jerusalem as a single entity under their sovereignty; and
- among some, a willingness to ascribe sovereignty in specific instances to the Palestinians, because of demographics and the importance of specific locales in religious narratives.

Common needs

- personal safety and security;
- a legitimate and effective security regime;
- an effective governing authority that enjoys broad-based legitimacy;
- governance mechanisms capable of withstanding the challenges imposed by strongly contending interests;
- participation of the respective states in decision making;
- equitable distribution of services based on needs;
- national markers, such as flags or security personnel, near or on the Holy Sites, in order to demonstrate the status of ownership and establish the security of worshippers, specifically the Western Wall for Israelis and the Haram al-Sharif for Palestinians;
- recognition from other communities, nations and institutions of the legitimate attachment to their respective Holy Sites; and
- free and unimpeded access and dignity in worship, without incitement or interference.

Political needs beyond national aspirations

The Old City is a unique case internationally because of the number and importance of its Holy Sites, and the attachments of competing sides. As well, its religious and symbolic attachments reach out beyond the national goals of Israelis and Palestinians to believers around the globe. In times of difficulty, these views cause the Old City to become a flashpoint for extremism and violence. As indicated below, there are a wide range of interests in the Old City:

- *Muslims* who view the city as the third holiest site of Islam after Mecca and Medina and, for this reason, believe the Islamic Holy Sites must be under legitimate Muslim control – or, at the very least, not under the control of an occupying power such as Israel. This group also wants free access to its Holy Sites and security guarantees.
- *Jews* who view the city as an essential and central part of their heritage, and for whom the Temple Mount is emblematic of their faith. Many Jews in the Diaspora view Jerusalem, the Old City and the Temple Mount as representing their 'soul', and therefore beyond political compromise.
- *Christians* who view the city as the site of their Saviour's passion and resurrection, and who want freedom of access and worship with respect to their Holy Sites.
- *Arabs* who view the city as a symbol of their struggle against Israel. Its relevance to their Christian or Muslim heritage, combined with its occupation by Israel, lead them to believe the Old City should be under Palestinian control.
- *Governments, policy makers and citizens around the world* who believe the city is a critical piece in resolving the Middle East conflict, and who consequently look to a just and comprehensive resolution of the city's status.

These wider circles of interest in the Old City underscore the need for creative answers beyond classic territorial sovereignty.

Based on the foregoing, it is clear that an effective governing structure for the Old City must meet complex requirements, including:

- legitimacy;
- the ability to, in the eyes of residents and stakeholders, meet multiple needs;
- security and stability within its boundaries;
- both Israeli and Palestinian influence over governance and status;
- the ability to withstand tensions generated from outside.

E Religious, symbolic and heritage needs

The Old City and its Holy Sites are central to the identities of Jews, Muslims and Christians, both individually and collectively. They are at the core of how individuals define themselves, reflecting their concept of self, including their heritage, culture, belief and value systems. In the context of the Israeli–Arab conflict, the result has been an explosive fusion of religious identity, nationalist ambitions and a struggle for power and control. Many of those we interviewed suggested the Camp David peace negotiations broke down because both sides wanted sovereignty over the one Holy Site – the Haram al-Sharif/Temple Mount – which each view as exclusively their own, but which is physically indivisible. This kind of attachment makes Jerusalem immune to United Nations resolutions, legislative dictates or anything suggesting coerced agreement.

Belief systems often overlie practical needs. With this in mind, and recognizing that symbolic issues are often intertwined with political control, we have tried to isolate key elements of what we heard concerning religious symbols. These factors explain to some degree why Palestinians and Israelis, and believers around the world have developed such powerful attachments to the Holy Sites, and conflate them with national and political aspirations and needs.

Symbols

- Religious symbols galvanize national and tribal sentiments, gathering the committed into impermeable groups.
- They become a litmus test in the face of threats, provide stability in the face of change, and become barometers of success, achievement and power.
- Their loss creates a profound sense of insecurity for individuals and groups, threatens the certainty of faith, and fosters resentment and rejection.
- Fear of loss, threat or tragedy heightens attachment to symbols and structures.

A COMMON CHARTER

Neither the Palestinians nor the Israelis can solve their problems and reach peace in isolation, but denial of their interdependence makes real progress impossible. Even with the best of ideas, understanding the other's needs is a prerequisite to success.

Given this logic, it seems critical to begin an early process aimed at developing mutual understanding, before negotiations begin. A 'common charter' could highlight shared needs that transcend ideological and historical narratives. Not limited to high-minded principles, the charter would also include concrete needs regarding security, status, legitimacy, economics, and a healthy environment. Most current approaches incorporate these needs into questions of governance and symbolism, rarely examining them on their own. The charter could also address the Old City's physical and social conditions, as well as provide a 'code of ethics' on human rights, collective rights and religious needs.

For consideration

These dynamics play out most dramatically with respect to the Haram al-Sharif/ Temple Mount. Control over the site is a talisman for success; lost control signifies failure and humiliation. For this reason, there is a need for processes and arrangements aimed at creating a win–win situation that will address the strong symbolic attachment of both parties to the Old City's Holy Sites, and to the Haram al-Sharif/Temple Mount in particular. These might include, for example:

- a charter respecting the needs of both sides, including religious needs;
- a parallel study of both sides' historical connections to the Haram al-Sharif/ Temple Mount;
- proposals setting out new perceptions of inclusion related to religious traditions; and
- public advocacy and education strategies.

It is important as well to examine how arrangements on the ground at the Haram al-Sharif/Temple Mount can provide sufficient control, without exclusivity, to each of the parties regarding their interests. Several areas of practical effort have been identified as key, including:

- examining the possible role of Muslim guards around the compound to ensure respect for heritage and tradition, or placing security solely in the hands of a single integrated Old City police force;
- examining how unambiguous recognition of the site's importance to Jews can be provided, as it is more likely they will accept Muslim prerogatives if their own narrative is recognized. The reverse is true as well;

- providing options for visits by non-Muslims, conceivably under UNESCO supervision; and
- exploring the possible role of third-party arbitration of disputes over archaeological digs, construction and access, while fully respecting the status quo regarding *waqf* responsibilities.

V The institutional framework for peace

Although needs can be met through a series of independent measures, we believe that a single governance approach is likely the only vehicle that can meet them effectively. We are therefore proposing an institutional framework aimed at creating conditions for trust, equity, security and predictability in day-to-day life. Our intent has also been to maintain the integrity of the Old City; the area is too small, densely populated and architecturally linked to be divided and managed by a series of authorities and police forces, as proposed in the Geneva Accord, for example.

A Governance

We contend that an effective and equitable governing authority is a *sine qua non* of a peaceful and sustainable solution that strives for fair treatment of individuals and communities, and the application of sound governance principles. For this reason, we urge that consideration be given to an administrative structure for the Old City that would exist under international law, possibly for a specified interim period of 15 years. Governance by this 'Special Regime', a significant element of which would consist of international staff funded by international resources, could allow time for trust to mature before Palestinians and Israelis assume their full responsibilities and develop the necessary mechanisms to replace it.

Some of the Palestinians we spoke to were concerned that a Special Regime might turn out to be simply a formula to legitimize Israeli control. Conversely, some of our Israeli contacts felt it might result in their loss of control and ownership of the Old City. However, we believe that the current relationship between the two groups will not support a strictly bilateral arrangement, unless the Old City is divided by barriers. Not only is this option undesirable, it is physically impossible, particularly given the competing claims and attachments of both national groups to the Haram al-Sharif/Temple Mount complex.

Barring a meaningful third party presence, domination of the Old City by one party or the other, as is currently the case, is inevitable, as is a continuation of the conflict. Many we spoke to share our view that an arrangement styled on the Geneva Accord, with a variety of interacting security forces and a complex dispute settlement mechanism, might satisfy the requirement for fairness in principle, but would be unworkable in practice. Should governance mechanisms break down in the Old City, as we think they would without a system equipped with the tools to ensure peace, order and good government, the sustainability of any agreement would be seriously threatened. The history of Israeli and Palestinian non-compliance respecting their commitments serves as a strong incentive to require no less.

An arrangement such as the one we propose for consideration could form part of a comprehensive settlement based on the Clinton parameters, establishing two sovereign states with Yerushalayim and Al-Quds as their capitals, but going beyond these parameters respecting the Old City. The Special Regime we envisage would require a Governing Council, perhaps composed equally of Israelis and Palestinians, possibly reinforced by international representatives. Israeli and Palestinian members would be chosen by national governments in a manner that each would determine.

We recognize that, given the overriding national, communitarian and strategic imperatives, and the small size and populations of the area, government by the residents of the Old City alone would be impractical. The head of the Governing Council, the administrator, would be an internationally reputed individual, nominated and endorsed by the Quartet (composed of Russia, the European Union, the United Nations and the United States), and acceptable to both parties. The administrator would exercise executive authority within the Old City. The administrator would maintain close working relationships with the religious leadership. In our view, a single, comprehensive mechanism is necessary to ensure effective governance over such a highly contested area.

Ideally, Israelis and Palestinians would have already come to agreement on the eventual assignment of sovereignty and could then delegate to the Special Regime interim responsibility for specific security and governance functions. However, even if unable to agree on sovereignty for the long term, they could assign the exercise of such functions to the Special Regime, thereby reserving their claims while allowing other elements of a comprehensive peace to be implemented.

We recognize that it would be difficult now for many on either side to accept a far-reaching paradigm shift to a Special Regime. However, a process that begins with refining options, followed by vigorous discussion at the level of academics and think tanks, and subsequently broadening to include the public and leaders, could facilitate the required changes.

For consideration

Based on our research and discussions to date, we suggest that further consideration be given to the following governance scenarios:

- The Governing Council's legislative and oversight functions would include responsibility for security, law enforcement, specific public services, infrastructure, residency, property ownership, zoning and building, commercial and other relevant regulations, and the legal regime.
- A Religious Council would play a critical role, giving due recognition to the sanctity of the Old City and promoting religious harmony and fair-minded intercourse on religious issues.

- The Old City administrator would be responsible for governance and enforcement, while a court system would ensure adherence to the rule of law.
- A single Old City police force composed of internationals, Israelis and Palestinians would be responsible for security.
- Israeli and Palestinian national authorities could exercise functions such as health, education, family law and religious observance for their own populations.
- Inhabitants of the Old City would have residence status, but carry the nationality that the Israeli and Palestinian national governments choose to accord.
- Whatever sovereignty provisions are agreed, it is likely the Special Regime would have responsibility for ensuring and maintaining the religious status quo during the interim period.
- Established practices and traditions would be fully respected, including access to, and worship at, religious sites.
- The closest possible working relationship would need to be maintained between the leadership of the various denominations and the Old City administrator and Governing Council.
- There could be a moratorium on any excavations within the Old City area because of their sensitivity.
- Any excavations could be conducted under the supervision of an archaeological services branch of the Special Regime, using UNESCO criteria, under the direction of the administrator and with the consent of both Israeli and Palestinian authorities.

Consideration should also be given to one of the imaginative ideas presented to us by Michael Turner, Chairman of the Israel World Heritage Committee. In this scenario, the boundaries of the Jerusalem World Heritage Site would go beyond the Old City walls to encompass the area defined by the furthest extent of the ancient necropolis, which extends into both East and West Jerusalem. As we interpret it, this would mean that UNESCO provisions for the administration of this single world heritage site would potentially extend through three jurisdictions (Israeli, Palestinian and Special Regime), providing a common planning basis for maintaining and developing the areas composing ancient Jerusalem in and beyond the Old City. At the same time, each jurisdiction would administer the areas for which it is responsible.

Rationale: meeting the needs

This basic framework is intended to meet the needs of stakeholders by providing them with input into decision making, in tandem with equity and the advantages offered by a third party presence.

- The Governing Council would meet the needs of both sides for control, title and authority, without exclusivity.

- It would provide legitimacy in the eyes of communities worldwide.
- The third party role would provide both a facilitator and coordinator able to exercise authority.
- The Special Regime would maintain the integrity of the Old City, permitting it to be a useful economic engine for all sides.
- The need for security, and freedom of access to Holy Sites, would be met through a single Old City police force, thereby avoiding fragmentation under tension.
- The Governing Council would provide a special focus on the social and other needs of residents currently less attended to, and work to improve their living conditions.

B A legal framework

The Old City is currently under Israeli jurisdiction. On 28 June 1967, Israel applied Israeli law and jurisdiction over East Jerusalem and the Old City. In 1980, the *Basic Law: Jerusalem as the Capital of Israel*, a mostly symbolic step, was also applied defining Jerusalem as the 'complete ... united ... capital of Israel'. The question of whether these steps amounted to annexation has been one of debate. Until 1999, a simple majority of the Knesset would have been sufficient to annul or amend these laws.

In 1999 and 2000, the Knesset passed laws stipulating that 'no authority relating to the Jerusalem region ... may be transferred to a foreign political body, whether permanently or for a set period'. This can only be changed if a majority of Knesset passes a new *Basic Law*.

Although Israeli law is applied most often, the legal situation in the Old City remains very complex, as the following examples illustrate:

- Jordanian law is relevant for issues related to the Islamic *waqf*. 'Customary law' based on larger family order, including 'Sulha', mediation by Elders and customary religious practices, is used for resolving disputes among Palestinians, who often reject the applicability of Israeli law and the jurisdiction of Israeli courts.
- In 1967, residents of the Old City were offered the option of applying for Israeli citizenship. Although most residents have not exercised this option, they have been given permanent residency status and an Israeli identification card. However, they can lose their status if they depart Israeli jurisdiction and can no longer demonstrate that Israel is the 'centre of their life'.
- The steps Israel has taken since 1967 to expropriate land for public use have left much room for ambiguity, resulting in mismanagement and the questionable appropriation of property. According to some we spoke to, the situation is explosive and cannot wait for longer-term solutions.
- Planning and zoning of building construction is chaotic and often unregulated.

- The Holy Sites in the Old City are protected from desecration under a special Israeli law passed in 1967, which also preserves freedom of access and worship. However, two prior legal frameworks are also relevant: the Palestine Order in Council (Holy Places) of 1924 that excludes court jurisdiction over the Sites and the Ottoman firman of 1852 that affirmed the 'status quo' of four key Christian Sites, including the Church of the Holy Sepulcher.

Changes in law under special status

Special status will require that applicable criminal and civil laws be re-examined. Although we have argued that an *ab initio* focus on sovereignty should be avoided, some maintain that law enforcement requires an issuing authority that in turn makes resolution of the sovereignty issue imperative. It has also been suggested that if special status relies on existing law, as may be the case, these laws rely for their enforcement on the very sovereign jurisdiction that this document argues may best be postponed. For example, some legal experts argue that certain laws related to health, environment and taxation could only be implemented through specific Israeli government ministries. We are not convinced that Israeli sovereignty is necessary for implementing or enforcing laws. If the two parties formally agree to a new authority for the Old City, new mechanisms could be developed that facilitate the amendment, transfer and adoption of specific legal provisions.

Organizations other than the Israeli Government or the Jerusalem municipality currently provide several services for the Old City. These include electricity for all quarters except the Jewish Quarter, a significant number of educational institutions, and some social services provided by Palestinian organizations and religious groups. Further complicating the situation are the widely diverse groups living in a small area, the numerous visitors, and the range of external organizations already established in the Old City. There are also complex legal questions regarding Israeli and Palestinian residents who would not be living in their sovereign territory if control of the Old City were under a Special Regime. The requirement for closer commercial cooperation that peace and security would bring also raises the question of what commercial law would apply to joint transactions in the Old City.

The Old City's complexity, the current application of several national laws, and the presence of other important stakeholders such as the churches, suggest strongly that carefully developed legal arrangements will be needed to ensure smooth functioning. This applies not only to civil and criminal law, but to matters such as health and safety regulations as well. What law or regulations will apply in the Old City? Will they be uniform or vary depending on the area or person served? For some, the Old City's small size also puts into question the feasibility of creating a full array of institutions to provide services and authority. In our view, however, this may be the price of a viable peace.

We believe that changes to legal status or the provision of services should be made only when necessary to meet the needs of stakeholders. On the other hand, efficacy may well require a single body of legislation, whatever its origins, which is administered by a single legislative and legal system, both of which are integral parts of the Special Regime. Without the simplicity of one legal framework applicable to the Old City, including all residents and visitors, any governance scenario may be very difficult to administer.

However, it is for discussion and debate whether services such as health and education could conceivably remain under the authority of the national governments. For example, could a Palestinian resident choose to remain under Israeli health coverage? A complicating issue is that many benefits the Israeli state currently provides to Old City residents are sufficiently attractive that residents could react negatively to any proposed changes. Similarly, the question of whether taxation would be applied according to nationality is fraught with difficulties and must be addressed thoroughly.

It appears to us that clear and simple lines of authority are a prerequisite for success. For this reason, the most practical starting place may be the interim adoption of existing Israeli law to be administered by the Special Regime. A process of legal evolution would then have to take place under the Special Regime's Governing Council. That said, some changes would seem to be required immediately to address specific needs – for example, changes to the *Absentee Law* of 1951 that permits the seizure of absentee property.

For consideration

The issue of legal status for a Special Regime is complex and will require extensive study. The questions, options and needs described below are only some of the broad spectrum that can help guide this process.

- **Source of authority:** The Source of Authority, power and legal basis for any administration in the Old City other than Israeli or Palestinian rule will have to be defined. A resolution by the United Nations Security Council is one possibility. A charter or constitution for the Old City may also be created to set out the governing structure and form the basis of legal decisions, principles and rights. What is the role of international law in establishing legitimacy and a Source of Authority in the Old City?
- **Special status:** Is there a need for a charter or 'constitution' that can give expression to the 'universal meaning' of the Old City and ensure the creation of an administrative regime that guarantees equity and security?
- **Palestinian customary and Sharia law:** The continued use of customary law by Palestinians suggests the possibility of developing 'mediation arbitration institutes' to regularize such activities. The question of the links between Sharia law and other systems should also be examined, i.e. how will Sharia recognize another legal system?
- **Residency:** The issue of residency is complex. One approach could be to declare as residents all those registered under Israeli regulations, as well as anyone who

becomes a resident according to future laws and regulations as implemented by the Special Regime. The issue of Old City residents who are not currently registered with Israeli authorities will have to be examined carefully and sympathetically.

C Security options

The Old City is small, overcrowded and poor, with differing religions, nationalities, ethnicities, cultures and politics. As a result, law enforcement and ensuring public order and safety are enormous challenges. Any security mechanism must also take full account of Jerusalem as the focal point of individual and group identities, and the sensitivities and mistrust this engenders. Taken together, these physical and symbolic factors make the Old City a soft target, as well as a desirable one, for those seeking to disrupt Muslim–Jewish and Israeli–Palestinian co-existence. Disruptions could range from provocative political action to outright terrorism, which would not only cause death and suffering, but would also threaten existing political agreements and enrage the region's inhabitants, as well as communities worldwide. The great majority of Israelis and Palestinians we spoke to share the view that, without guarantees of a fair-minded security mechanism, no agreement respecting the Old City would be sustainable.

Within the parameters described above, a variety of options exist for the organization and mandate of a security force. Our Israeli and Palestinian colleagues have developed a number of scenarios, each with its attendant advantages and risks. With further study and development, we are convinced these options will stimulate discussion among experts, instil public confidence that effective alternatives are available, and provide decision makers with solid choices in eventual negotiations.

One option that we believe warrants full consideration is the creation of a police and security force composed of internationals, Israelis and Palestinians. A viable force with officers from countries that enjoy the confidence of both Palestinians and Israelis may be the only vehicle that compensates for the lack of trust between the parties. Incidents involving inter-communal problems will require a fair-minded party to take the necessary action, be it arrest, trial or incarceration, to meet the expectations of both sides. An international police force could also serve as a disincentive for the parties to turn national mechanisms into instruments for territorial gain or struggles for power, as occurred, we are told, with the joint Palestinian–Israeli security procedures developed within the failed Oslo framework.

The security force we envisage would almost certainly require the following elements:

- a clear and simple mandate;
- a Chief of Police[2] appointed by the administrator, with the agreement of Palestinian and Israeli authorities;

- an adequate personnel base;
- monitoring and access control of people and goods at the Old City's gates and walls;
- a ban on weapons within the walls, except those required by the security forces themselves;
- effective, technologically advanced security aids, such as biometric identification systems and other mechanisms;
- community policing, supported by local community liaison officers, to deal with law and order issues among permanent residents;
- a special intervention force, to ensure public order during possible emergencies resulting from the fragile political environment;
- a recruitment process based on specific and internationally recognized policing criteria, with emphasis on experience in peacekeeping, peace enforcement, investigations, intelligence, counter-terrorism and conflict resolution;
- a force based on citizens from countries that have the confidence of both Israelis and Palestinians;
- at its inception, an international contingent based mainly on nationals from a single country, to ensure common and accepted operational procedures, and command and control mechanisms;
- a willingness on the part of force members to commit for a minimum number of years, to ensure familiarity with the environment and build trust among residents;
- an extensive training period involving, at minimum, basic Hebrew and Arabic language skills, cultural studies, stress management, and intensive training in the working environment, including relations with Palestinian and Israeli liaison officers;
- coordination with Israeli and Palestinian police and security organizations on issues such as intelligence; and
- development of working relationships with counterpart Israeli and Palestinian authorities to ensure effective interface between the Old City, Al-Quds and Yerushalayim.

We have given considerable thought to the question of movement into and out of the Old City that is efficient, yet secure. Such a system would seem to require the most sophisticated possible technology to minimize any disruption to the efficient flow of goods and peoples, whether they be Old City residents, Israelis or Palestinians, pilgrims, tourists, religious figures, business persons, practitioners or officials. Enforcement mechanisms would have to meet the highest possible standards. Different entry–exit criteria would likely be necessary for the Old City's various gates, depending on their uses. Certainly, nationals of one country would only be permitted to move to the other, via the Old City, when equipped with the necessary travel documents.

We have had discussions with two local architects respecting the physical configuration of transit points, the Old City gates, that would also ensure respect for

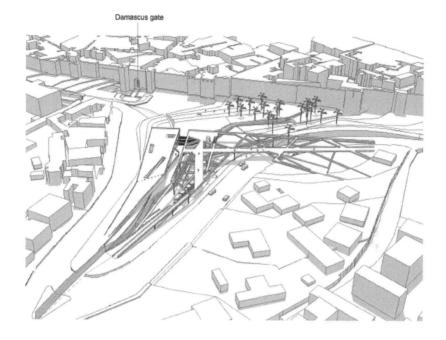

FIGURE 6.1 A transportation border zone in Jerusalem
Source: Faculty of Architecture and Town Planning, Technion, Israel.

the area's historic fabric. They had recently completed a project on a border zone facing the Damascus gate in the former 'no man's land' that was designed to ensure physical separation, combined with ease of movement and workable security mechanisms. Their construction blends naturally into the open landscape and urban space of Jerusalem, thereby maintaining the visual perception of the conurbation as a whole, albeit with a border dividing it. In our view, this represents a positive view of separation that deserves much further attention in operationalizing the Special Regime concept.

D Role of the international community

We believe members of the international community have a critical role to play in determining outcomes for the Old City. Non-politicized international facilitation will not only be important in administration, but international attention and engagement will be pivotal in breaking the current deadlock and securing a commitment to improve conditions in the Old City.

Global interest in the Holy Sites will be the international community's motive to engage. The citizens of many countries, particularly the diasporas of the peoples of the Holy Land and believers of the three monotheistic faiths worldwide, are keenly interested in the future of the Old City. Responsible governments and international organizations also have a stake in its future, and may play an important role in the peace-building process. For example, engagement of the Organization of the Islamic Conference may be necessary to legitimize the future status of Jerusalem, support Palestinian decisions respecting the city, and enable new relationships between Israel and the Muslim world. However, nothing should threaten the primary role of the peoples of the Holy Land in determining the future of the Old City.

For consideration

The international community must be prepared to underwrite any agreement reached between the parties, and provide substantial moral and material support. For example, Arab East Jerusalem currently receives little international aid in comparison to other territories occupied in 1967. As described below, there are many other possibilities for international engagement that would support and help revitalize the Old City and the Jerusalem conurbation:

- Within the context of peace, an international agency or agencies could be transferred to an area of Jerusalem that would benefit Yerushalayim, Al-Quds and the Old City. This could provide economic sustainability for all three, enabling public buy-in by both Israel and Palestine. It would also serve as a material and symbolic commitment to the sustainability of a comprehensive peace. One possibility would be to move the cultural arm of UNESCO to Jerusalem as a reflection of the city's cultural importance, similar to the relocation of other UN agencies to Vienna following the Second World War. Given the likely fragility of post-conflict Jerusalem, there is great merit in considering such stabilizing steps.
- The transfer of foreign embassies from Tel Aviv to Yerushalayim following a peace agreement, and the creation of embassies accredited to the Palestinian state in Al-Quds would provide unambiguous endorsement of a peace agreement.
- An international conference could be held on the economic revitalization of Jerusalem, to reinforce a peace agreement and solidify the status of the Old City within the framework of two states, two capitals and the international presence.
- A sizeable fund could usefully be created to develop the Old City and its surroundings as an even greater historic, religious, archaeological and symbolic focal point. As well, the fund could initiate projects aimed at improving inhabitants' quality of life and building bridges between faiths and ethnicities.
- Members of the international community who enjoy the trust of both Palestinians and Israelis could financially assist the existing landscape of civil society concerned with Jerusalem and the Old City.

THE POWER OF CREATIVE THINKING

Without creative thinking, this Initiative will get nowhere. Many tend to doubt there are any ideas that go beyond accepted conventions; as a result, they either resentfully or reluctantly accept the status quo or, depending on their politics, rejoice in it. Demonstrating the power of creative thinking, Danny Seidemann, a Jerusalem lawyer, has proposed an idea that should satisfy those who believe in a viable two-state solution, with two capitals in Jerusalem.

In this scenario, which responds to the specific physical needs of Palestinians and Israelis, as well as to their religious, symbolic and heritage requirements, the Palestinian Embassy in Israel could be housed on the premises of the former Palace Hotel in West Jerusalem. The building currently serves as the headquarters of the Israeli Ministry of Trade and Industry. During the British Mandate, the Palace Hotel was erected in the centre of the new city to serve as the Palestinian equivalent of the Jewish-favoured King David. It is an impressive structure with a distinct Palestinian provenance, which may symbolically respond to the Palestinian need for a presence in the west of the city, where many of the Palestinian elite lived before Israeli independence.

The Israeli Embassy would be located in the building currently housing the Seven Arches Hotel on the Mount of Olives in the eastern part of the city. This is a prestigious location, even though it lacks the architectural sophistication of the old Palace Hotel building. It is adjacent to the Jewish cemetery on the Mount, which has particular relevance in Jewish ritual and observance. If the cemetery were under the jurisdiction of the Israeli Embassy, Jews worldwide would be reassured it would be protected and maintained. At the same time, the Mamilla Muslim cemetery, which is directly opposite the Palace Hotel, could be restored from its current neglect and the Palestinian Embassy property expanded to embrace it, thereby creating a fair-minded balance.

VI The economics of peace

Peace would have significant economic implications, not just for the Old City, but for the entire Jerusalem conurbation as well. In fact, when considering the economics of peace, no one we spoke with advocated looking at the Old City in isolation – and we have not attempted to do so here. Our research associates believe that a sustainable peace would have both positive and negative economic impacts on the Old City, and throughout the Jerusalem conurbation and beyond. As described below, the proposals made in this discussion document would have a number of important economic implications.

Job creation in the Jerusalem conurbation

General estimates indicate that if our suggestions for engaging the international community were adopted, more than 9,000 jobs would be created. Approximately

TABLE 6.1 Estimated direct and indirect impact on employment

Sources of new jobs	Increase in foreign workers	Direct increase in local workers	Increase in local service workers	Total number of local jobs created	Total number of jobs created
		A. International involvement			
New and relocated embassies	3,000	5,000	18,000	23,000	26,000
Old City administration	350	1,500	3,700	5,550	5,900
International organizations	100	150	500	650	750
Subtotal	*3,450*	*6,650*	*22,200*	*29,200*	*32,650*
		B. Stability in Jerusalem			
Increased tourism		13,500	27,000	40,500	40,500
Total new jobs	**3,450**	**20,150**	**49,200**	**69,700**	**73,150**

two-thirds of these jobs would go to local residents, with each new job, in turn, fuelling the local economy through the consumption of goods and services. Using a multiplier of two, more than 18,000 jobs would be created in the service sector. Under this scenario, the total number of new jobs for the local population would be close to 24,000, an approximate 10 per cent increase in employment. New jobs as a result of construction have not been factored into these estimates, as such a boom could be less predictable in duration.

Without taking into account specific actions to increase international financial support for Jerusalem, we believe that a stable situation in the conurbation would greatly increase tourism, creating an estimated 13,500 new jobs directly and 27,000 new jobs indirectly (again, using a multiplier of two). This represents a 12 to 14 per cent increase over the number of people currently employed in Jerusalem. Table 6.1 shows the impact on employment of both increased international involvement and a stable environment in Jerusalem.

Diplomatic representation

Currently, some 85 countries have diplomatic representation in Israel, Palestine, or both. With peace, foreign governments would likely replicate their missions in the two capitals in Jerusalem because of the political sensitivities involved, as is the case in Rome with the Vatican and the Quirinale Palace. A solution to the present conflict would also lead the way for other countries to establish representation in either or both countries, including members of the Arab League, other Muslim countries, and perhaps additional countries in Africa, Asia and the Americas. Based on a conservative estimate of about 150 embassies in the Jerusalem conurbation, we anticipate more than 3,000 jobs would be created for foreigners posted there (assuming an average of 20 persons per embassy), which would then result in an additional 5,000 jobs (an average of 33 persons per embassy) for local inhabitants.

Old City administration

With the creation of special status, the Old City would require a separate labour force, both local and foreign, to support its administration. The size of the governance structure would depend on the functions taken up by the administration, which could range from providing all services to the Old City, to somewhat more limited functions, with the municipalities of Yerushalayim and Al-Quds providing specific services to their own nationals, such as health care and education.

Our researchers estimated the size of the administration's work force, based on the assumption that certain services would be outsourced (for example, health and education), while the Old City administration itself would be responsible for others (for example, security, planning, supervision and inspection). In this estimate, a total of 1,750 persons would be employed in the administration – accounting for 20 per cent of all public employment. Some 250 foreign workers would work there, either permanently or for an interim period, depending on the terms of their agreement. The remaining 1,500 employees would be local, with 1,000 in existing jobs in the Old City or the Jerusalem municipality, and 500 in jobs newly created as a result of special status arrangements.

International organization bureau

One scenario suggests the relocation of an international organization to greater Jerusalem as an expression of the international community's support. The cultural bureau of UNESCO is one organization that seems appropriate for such a role. Under this 'minimalist' scenario, 250 employees, consisting of 100 foreign and 150 local workers, would live in Jerusalem. The bureau would be a magnet for activity; with meetings, committee gatherings and conferences held regularly, it is likely that thousands would visit Jerusalem each year, providing further economic spin-offs.

Tourism

According to our researchers, tourism in the Holy Land could increase by between three and four million people each year under peaceful conditions. The Israeli Ministry of Tourism calculates that every additional million tourists create 45,000 jobs. Using 20 per cent as a measure of Jerusalem's share of the tourism labour force, and assuming the number of tourists increased from 1.5 million in 2004 to three million, that would mean a total of 13,500 new jobs for the greater Jerusalem area. If the number of tourists were to increase to four million, 22,500 jobs would be created. For the purposes of this discussion document, we have used the more conservative estimate of three million tourists annually, and the corresponding number of 13,500 new jobs.

Land and real estate

The transfer of embassies and international organizations would create demands on the reservoir of land in Jerusalem and the surrounding area. At present, there is a limited amount of open land available for development within the Israeli-defined municipal boundaries. As well, environmental and local community groups have been engaged in efforts to preserve green space within the city. With the entry of embassies and international organizations there would be even more competition for space. One option for addressing this issue is the creation of embassy areas located within the boundaries of Yerushalayim and Al-Quds.

As Jerusalem is unable to meet the requirements of its population even now, the increased demand for housing in Jerusalem would be felt throughout the market. Property is more expensive than in Tel Aviv, and Jerusalem residents are already moving to less expensive towns and villages on the edges of the conurbation. A combination of higher wages and increased demand would inevitably contribute to inflated housing prices in the city. Planning efforts to address housing issues would require a great deal of work, as well as imagination, determination, and sensitivity to cultural heritage.

Infrastructure

Although Jerusalem's infrastructure has undergone rapid development, the changes described above would require additional investment, including in the Old City. It is likely that much of the existing infrastructure would need to be redesigned – including, for example:

- *The existing and planned road and rail system*. Currently under development, the system is intended to serve a united city under Israeli rule, and provide Jewish sections of the conurbation with greater access. However, benefits to Arab sections will be limited, and many we spoke with strongly believe these shortcomings have to be addressed. Many also anticipate the need to develop longitudinal highways or freeways that would link Al-Quds with Ramallah in the north, and Bethlehem in the south and beyond.
- *The city's airport*. Closed in 2000 due to tensions in Jerusalem, the airport is located in the Atarot/Kalandia area in the north of the city. Although the challenges of ownership, control and security would have to be resolved first, its reopening could provide healthy competition for the Ben-Gurion International Airport in Israel and Amman's Queen Alia International Airport, further benefiting the Old City, Yerushalayim and Al-Quds.
- *Management of effluents*. Poor water management – exacerbated by population growth and increased consumption – has already created a serious

sanitation and environmental hazard. As these pressures would increase in the scenarios we have outlined, Israel and Palestine would need to cooperate on the development of new systems, including for the Old City.

- *Electric grid and water distribution system*. Increased demands would require changes to both of these systems.
- *Security barrier*. Almost everyone we interviewed felt that the Israeli security barrier currently under construction would have to be substantially modified or dismantled entirely, regardless of what arrangements are made respecting the border between the two capitals. At the same time, however, any control mechanisms that are eventually put in place between the two capitals would need to reflect the obligations of the peace agreement between the two parties.

Planning and development frameworks

Obviously, considerable advance planning is required to deal with work force and other changes that peace would bring. Following are some of the issues to be addressed in the process:

- The local population would need to be prepared – culturally, psychologically and technically – for changes in roles and activities.
- Mechanisms must be found to ensure fair and equitable Palestinian participation in the economy.
- Existing detailed plans were developed by the Israelis and are therefore unilateral.
- Current plans are not based on assumptions of the increased population a Special Regime would bring, the type of population increase expected, or the division of the Jerusalem conurbation between Israel, Palestine and the Old City.
- Planning tools and ordinances would be needed to deal with the numerous complex and interrelated issues affecting the Old City and beyond.
- Infrastructure development, including water supply and sewage, electricity, communication and transportation, would require immediate attention.

VII Sovereignty revisited

A sovereignty 'first and only' approach will make agreement between Palestinians and Israelis more, not less, difficult, as it will focus on power and control. We have attempted to demonstrate that the needs of stakeholders can be better addressed through a process of desegregation, examination and creativity. We have also described an overarching framework, a Special Regime designed to ensure that these needs are managed equitably, effectively and comprehensively.

Our goal has been to expand discussion beyond political and symbolic needs, to address the social, economic, security and cultural requirements of all key stakeholders; including residents, Israelis and Palestinians living outside the Old

City; Jews, Muslims and Christians outside of Israel and Palestine; and members of the international community. We believe this type of comprehensive and inclusive approach will greatly increase the likelihood of agreement on the Old City.

If stakeholders' needs can indeed be met through a Special Regime, where does that leave the question of sovereignty? We believe that if the parties ultimately wish to pursue a durable agreement on the Old City, the arrangements they hope to establish through sovereignty will in the end be met by many of the needs-based findings, without precluding sovereignty arrangements when paradigms have changed. Our view is that an exclusionary focus on sovereignty now could have serious negative consequences for the governance of the Old City, and therefore for Israelis, Palestinians, the region and beyond. Exclusion precludes legitimacy, equity and stability.

There will be many who will disagree, however. For some Israelis, 'sovereignty' – in the sense of full control – remains non-negotiable. For their part, many Palestinians believe they must assert sovereignty; some may still be at a stage where full authority is a *sine qua non* for agreement because their own lack of such control means Israeli control. We believe the situation to be even more complex. We have been told that the involvement of other Arab and Muslim states in the Haram al-Sharif solution is necessary for the parties to move ahead, especially the Palestinians. The strong links between sovereignty in the Old City and the status of the Haram al-Sharif/Temple Mount cannot be overstated.

In fact, a sovereignty-first approach may be the most practical and straightforward option for a broader peace agreement because it picks up where Camp David and Taba left off, and where the Geneva Accord has gone. It has the virtue of being more comfortable ground for the two negotiating authorities because it is familiar. Indeed, this approach is necessary for many matters in contention under a two-state paradigm. However, the Old City is the exception because of the parties' mutual attachment to the Haram al-Sharif and the Temple Mount, which comprise one and the same entity, and are physically inseparable.

Although we strongly advocate a needs-based approach to resolving the dilemma of the Old City, it is incumbent to define what we believe to be the most workable sovereignty arrangement, including for the implementation of a Special Regime. We propose that the parties either agree on sovereignty for the Quarters and Holy Sites, or reserve their decision for future negotiation. If sovereignty is agreed *ab initio*, specific functional elements could then be entrusted to a Special Regime on an interim basis, after which the sovereign parties would fully undertake sovereign responsibilities, having come to agreement between themselves on the mechanisms for doing so.

With the agreement of Israel and a Palestinian state, the ideas presented above relating to governance and security can be applied to this scenario. They may also be applied in a circumstance where sovereignty is less defined, but interim authority is clearly delegated to the Special Regime by Israel and a Palestinian state. In this context, we suggest that the Special Regime temporarily exercise specific functions that would otherwise accrue to Israel and Palestine.

For consideration

If sovereignty requires resolution a priori, we present the following questions and ideas for consideration:

- Would Palestinians recognize Jewish attachments regarding the Holy Sites under their sovereignty? This may be the key to turning Palestinian sovereignty over the Haram al-Sharif/Temple Mount into a starting point for understanding, cooperation and stability.
- Would some Israelis find it acceptable to have Muslim sovereignty over the Haram al-Sharif, together with a Religious Council for managing religious affairs? At Taba, it was proposed that the Haram al-Sharif be put under interim international sovereignty of the Security Council Permanent Five, plus Morocco, with the Palestinians as custodians under an overriding Israeli regime.
- Would forgoing a sovereignty agreement on the Haram al-Sharif/Temple Mount permit its management as a Holy Site without direct political links or the provision of extra-territoriality for all Holy Sites in the Old City?

VIII Moving forward

The strategies set out in this paper identify possible new directions to meet the needs of Palestinians, Israelis and other concerned parties. Achieving these goals, particularly agreement by the two sides to special arrangements for the Old City, will be a very difficult task. But the core issues will not simply go away; they are too deeply ingrained in individual and collective mindsets. It is our view that policy makers have a responsibility to explore creative options for addressing them. To do otherwise will condemn entire populations and future generations to violence, and social and economic hardship.

We acknowledge that governance structures alone are not sufficient to ground perceptions about the Old City and its Holy Sites. A Special Regime does not mean the end of fear. Even under peace accords, it is likely that an atmosphere of tension and distrust will continue, at least initially. Strong emotions like these will take decades to reconcile, but we must begin the difficult process of changing mindsets now. How else will it be possible to reach agreement?

A Guiding the way

We believe that the ultimate success of the approach outlined in this discussion document depends on the commitment of Israelis, Palestinians and the international community to a process that:

- *Is needs-based and sensitive to the current situation*, in that it:
  - reflects sensitivity to historical and religious narratives;

- aims to preserve current practices and arrangements that work – in particular, the religious status quo; and
- attempts to address the needs of stakeholders, thus diminishing the likelihood of conflict due to unmet individual and collective needs, especially political and symbolic needs.

- *values partnerships, engagement and public education,* with emphasis on:

  - local partnerships that address the unique needs of both Israeli and Palestinian communities;
  - involvement of civil society, academic and educational communities;
  - engagement of key external policy makers acceptable to both sides; and
  - pursuit of sustained public education about the role of Jerusalem, Jerusalemites, Israelis and Palestinians as custodians of the Old City.

- *is comprehensive, forward-looking, integrated* and:

  - works to improve conditions on the ground, while ensuring the principles of equity and dignity are respected;
  - works to ensure that worthwhile approaches become templates for future negotiators;
  - considers the role of international law and the legal consequences of any options developed;
  - devotes due attention to the interests of external stakeholders; and
  - diminishes the culture of demonization by recognizing the needs of all sides.

B A modular process

Working within the broad guidelines set out above, our aim is to launch processes in identified sectors or 'modules', in which both Israelis and Palestinians participate, with international facilitators, in an effort to resolve some of the pressing issues currently facing the Old City.

These modules would address a range of identified needs, including governance, economic, social, educational, symbolic, security, legal and commercial needs. At minimum, they must involve both political and heritage narratives, the core issue of sharing sacred space, and the 'unpacking' of religious and symbolic needs. Success will depend on whether both sides believe they can live out their heritage and traditions, and ensure a promising future for themselves, without the tight box of absolute territorial sovereignty.

Research is one avenue for moving forward, but it is not enough. Indeed, many previous proposals concerning Jerusalem have foundered because they lacked realistic strategies for putting recommendations into effect. We envision a flexible and comprehensive process that weaves together in-depth studies, active projects on the ground, advocacy and communication to disseminate findings and perspectives, and an over-arching framework to coordinate and guide the process. Each module could proceed at a different speed so that no single module need arrest progress in others. Although each would operate independently, they would often be tied to and influence each other. Work could advance where and when circumstances permit, depending on political sensitivities, resources, interest and the situation on the ground. This kind of flexibility will be particularly important in the early stages of the process, to encourage a sustainable atmosphere of engagement and cooperation.

A critical element of the modules would be the development of 'facilitation groups', initially composed of representatives from international, non-governmental and academic institutions, as well as the private sector. Weighted in favour of Palestinians and Israelis, these groups would undertake research and pursue joint Israeli–Palestinian projects to meet identified needs, support the development of special arrangements for the Old City, and open minds to a variety of non-threatening options. The pragmatic engagement of fair-minded external partners, acceptable to Israelis and Palestinians, who can act as catalysts in developing conceptual frameworks, workable alternatives, and on-the-ground assistance could be critical for success.

We propose development of a work plan based on this discussion document. Once the work plan is agreed to, the initiative could be managed by a secretariat responsible for identifying and coordinating research and projects, activating modules in direct partnership with and between Israelis and Palestinians, fund-raising, maintaining and enlarging networks, and pursuing ongoing advocacy of policy options with publics and decision makers. Often missing in Track Two efforts, an information and advocacy process is essential for building critical mass and influence.

For consideration

That said, a number of dilemmas and tensions present themselves and should be considered in further developing and refining the process:

- *Division or integration?* Is it better to proceed towards hard divisions (as the Geneva Accord suggests) before attempting any integration or joint activities because the parties are such hardened enemies? Some believe that too much goodwill has been assumed in the past, with dire results, as during the Oslo process.
- *Status quo or a new arrangement?* What projects and studies can be pursued without prejudicing future negotiations? This is a double-edged sword: Palestinians will not wish to legitimize the status quo of Israeli control; Israelis will not agree to steps that assume diminishing authority. Finding the right space and timing for projects will be a complex task. In the tough politics of the Middle East, many will be suspicious about the motives and biases of international engagement, and both sides will likely attempt to sway intervention to their advantage.

Our Palestinian contacts were concerned to avoid another open-ended process like Oslo that, in their view, facilitated Israeli settlement expansion and control over Jerusalem. To mitigate these concerns – and those of the Israelis – the parameters of the Old City initiative proposed here, including its guiding principles, would have to be clearly set out and agreed to.

- *Local versus international?* The issue of which needs are best met by local action and which require degrees of international engagement will have to be clarified as work proceeds.
- *Where to begin?* Which areas should be engaged immediately and which are best left for the longer term? Some argue that it is best to agree first on the end point, for example sovereignty, before beginning the education process on more intangible issues such as narrative. Others will argue as forcefully that there can be no agreement before the appetite for exclusivity is diminished through, for example, developing codes of conduct. The proper balance and effectiveness between these approaches will necessarily come from experience and experimentation.
- *Influencing the public debate?* Leaders on both sides use the symbols of Jerusalem to rally their people and gain public legitimacy. They may be loath to give that up, even with the prospect of greater rewards at hand. Affecting the public debate on the Old City may require engaging international actors to weigh in, increasing public awareness to sway leaders' positions, lobbying, or even educating leaders directly. The advocacy portion of this initiative must be developed with great care, as agreement and implementation will require much political will, courage and personal strength.
- *How to address two societies?* Any process must take into account that Israeli and Palestinian societies are different and will not respond identically to challenges, proceeding to their answers at differing speeds. Flexibility will be required.

C Public education

Educational institutions and the media can be important pipelines for effecting change and bringing forward new ideas. Many on both sides are mired in mythologies about the other, and lacking in knowledge about Jerusalem, and its inhabitants and symbolism. This affects the positions that political leaders on each side can take, resulting in unbridgeable gulfs between them. If these myths and assumptions are not addressed, leaders and negotiators may once again come to the brink of compromise and step back, or be rebuffed by surges of public opinion.

Many concluded that an active education process about Jerusalem – its history, current urban reality, and meaning to both sides – is essential in ensuring that Palestinians and Israelis will be ready to accept the compromises required for agreement on final status. This requires direct exposure of Israelis to Palestinian Jerusalem, of Palestinians to Jewish religious history and heritage in the Old City, and of Israelis to their own national feelings about the city and its heritage, as well as to the overlapping claims of Muslims and Christians.

International interest in the Old City, including Western and Christian perspectives, is often subsumed within the polarized Israeli–Palestinian debate. The importance of Jerusalem to Christians and to Western civilization may be an issue that both Palestinians and Israelis need to better understand. As well, a process aimed at enhancing awareness of tribalism, which underlies much of the broader conflict and influences decision making and public reaction to events in Jerusalem, may help all parties involved achieve greater mutual understanding.

D A first step

Our research over the past two years has acquainted us with the extensive body of high-quality work by academics and experts on the question of Jerusalem, its Holy Sites and its Old City. What is lacking is adequate dissemination of this material, a common understanding of the issues, and a framing of needs that can support action.

The experience of Camp David and Taba underscores the price to be paid when negotiations are undertaken without sufficient preparation and without serious efforts to understand the real needs of 'the other' when issues central to religious and national identity are at stake. That experience also demonstrates the cardinal importance of education and preparation of the public prior to negotiations – complex, fraught and difficult though this may be.

The Camp David and Taba experiences also demonstrate the difficulty that Track Two exercises have had in influencing policy outcomes given the absence of mechanisms to ensure that the insights generated in unofficial circles reach the desks of, and are absorbed by, policy makers, potential negotiators and leaders.

Sooner or later it will be necessary for Israeli and Palestinian negotiators to return to the table in an attempt to resolve final status issues: unilateral action, even so-called 'coordinated unilateral action' can move us in the direction of peace, but the hard issues, including the future of the Old City, can only be resolved through negotiation and agreement.

We hope to encourage movement to the negotiating table by creating a network involving Israelis, Palestinians and serious third parties to:

- contribute to the creation and dissemination of knowledge about the Old City of Jerusalem and the issues that need to be addressed if negotiations are to succeed;
- 'push the envelope' in proposing creative solutions to the issues that have eluded resolution to date;
- promote public education and engagement designed to advance a more empathetic understanding of the legitimate needs and aspirations of both sides; and
- promote practical projects aimed at improving living conditions within the Old City, and enhancing its potential as a major contributor to Israeli and Palestinian wellbeing.

The intent of this document is to encourage and facilitate this process. If it provokes both debate and action towards these ends, then the first step in the process will have been taken.

Notes

1 Statistics cited in this section are based on a study by Joseph Glass and Rassem Khameisi that was commissioned for this project.
2 Within the Jerusalem Old City Initiative Chief of Police, Police Chief and Chief of Police services are used interchangably.

References

Abu Odeh, A. 'Two Capitals in an Undivided Jerusalem'. *Foreign Affairs* 71, no. 2(1992): 183–188.

The Agreement on Jerusalem and its Price. Jerusalem: Israel-Palestine Center for Research and Information, May 2000.

Albin, C. 'Negotiating Indivisible Goods: The Case of Jerusalem'. *Jerusalem Journal of International Relations* 13, no. 1(1991): 45–76.

Amirav, M. and S. Hanna. 'Jerusalem: Resolving the Unresolvable'. *International Spectator* 27, no. 3(1992): 3–24.

Arab Studies Society. *Multi-Sector Review Project of East Jerusalem: Multi Sector Strategy for East Jerusalem*. February 2003. http://www.multi-sector.org. (Last accessed: September 2005.)

Armstrong, K. *Jerusalem: One City, Three Faiths*. New York: Knopf, 1996.

Bahat, D. *The Illustrated Atlas of Jerusalem*. Jerusalem: Carta, 1996.

Baskin, G. 'Jerusalem Should Be Shared'. *Washington Post*, 26 June 1994.

Baskin, G. (ed.) *New Thinking on the Future of Jerusalem: A Model for the Future of Jerusalem: Scattered Sovereignty*. Jerusalem: Israel-Palestine Center for Research and Information, 1994.

Baskin, G. and R. Twite (eds) *The Future of Jerusalem: Proceedings of the First Israeli/Palestinian International Academic Seminar on the Future of Jerusalem*. Jerusalem: Israel-Palestine Center for Research and Information, 1993.

Ben-Dov, M. *Historical Atlas of Jerusalem*. New York: Continuum, 2002.

Benvenisti, M. *City of Stone: The Hidden History of Jerusalem*. Berkeley: University of California Press, 1996.

Berkovitz, S. *The Battle for the Holy Places: The Struggle Over Jerusalem and the Holy Sites in Israel, Judea, Samara and the Gaza District*. Jerusalem: Jerusalem Institute for Israel Studies, 2000.

Breger, M.J. and O. Ahimeir (eds) *Jerusalem: A City and Its Future*. Syracuse, NY: Syracuse University Press, 2002.

'Briefing on the Blueprint for Israeli-Palestinian Peace'. In *The Geneva Initiative: A Blueprint for Israeli-Palestinian Peace*. Washington: Brookings Institute. Last modified 3 December 2003. www.brookings.edu/comm/events/20031203.pdf. (Last accessed: September 2005.)

'Building Interreligious Trust in a Climate of Fear: An Abrahamic Trialogue'. United States Institute of Peace. February 2003. http://www.usip.org/pubs/specialreports/sr99.html. (Last accessed 26 April 2016.)

Central Bureau of Statistics (Israel). *Jerusalem: Facts and Trends*. Jerusalem: Jerusalem Institute for Israel Studies, 1999.

Chesin, A., B. Hutman and A. Melamed. *Separate and Unequal: The Inside Story of Israeli Rule in East Jerusalem.* Cambridge, MA: Harvard University Press, 1999.

Cingoli, J. (ed.) *Israelis, Palestinians Coexisting in Jerusalem.* Milan: Italian Centre for Peace in the Middle East, 2001.

Cust, L.G.A. *The Status Quo and the Holy Places.* Jerusalem: Ariel Publishing House, 1980.

Dumper, M. 'Israeli Settlement in the Old City of Jerusalem'. *Journal of Palestine Studies* 21, no. 4(1992): 32–53.

Dumper, M. 'Jerusalem's Infrastructure: Is Annexation Irreversible?' *Journal of Palestine Studies* 23, no. 3(1993): 78–95.

Dumper, M. *Islam and Israel: Muslim Religious Endowments and the Jewish State.* Washington, DC: Institute for Palestine Studies, 1994.

Dumper, M. *The Politics of Jerusalem Since 1967.* New York: Columbia University Press, 1997.

Dumper, M. *The Politics of Sacred Space: The Old City of Jerusalem in the Middle East Conflict.* Boulder, CO: Lynne Rienner, 2002.

Eliade, M. *The Sacred and the Profane: The Nature of Religion.* Translated by Willard R. Trask. New York: Harper & Row, 1961.

Ferrari, S. 'The Vatican, Israel and the Jerusalem Question (1943–1984)'. *The Middle East Journal* 39, no. 2(1984): 316–347.

Friedland, R. and R. Hecht. 'The Politics of Sacred Place: Jerusalem's Temple Mount'. In *Sacred Places and Profane Spaces: Essays in the Geographics of Judaism, Christianity and Islam,* edited by J. Scott and P. Simpson-Housley, 21–61. New York: Greenwood, 1991.

Friedland, R. and R. Hecht. *To Rule Jerusalem.* New York: Cambridge University Press, 1996.

Glass, J. and R. Khameisi. *The Socio-Economic Conditions in the Old City of Jerusalem.* unpublished, 2004.

Gold, D. *Jerusalem.* Tel Aviv: Jaffee Centre for Strategic Studies, 1995.

Gonen, R. *Contested Holiness: Jewish, Muslim and Christian Perspectives on the Temple Mount in Jerusalem.* Jersey City, NJ: Ktav, 2003.

Gopin, M. *Holy War, Holy Peace: How Religion Can Bring Peace to the Middle East.* New York: Oxford University Press, 2002.

Gorenberg, G. *The End of Days: Fundamentalism and the Struggle for the Temple Mount.* New York: Free Press, 2000.

Halabi, O. *Jerusalem: The Effects of Israel's Annexation of Jerusalem on the Rights and Position of its Arab Population.* Jerusalem: Palestinian Academic Society for the Study of International Affairs, 1990.

Heller, M. and S. Nusseibeh. *No Trumpets, No Drums.* New York: Hill and Wang, 1991.

Hirsch, M., B. Housen-Couriel and R. Lapidoth (eds) *Whither Jerusalem: Proposals and Positions Concerning the Future of Jerusalem.* The Hague: Martinus Nijhoff Publishers, 1995.

Hodgkins, A. B. *Israeli Settlement Policy in Jerusalem: Creating Facts on the Ground.* Jerusalem: Palestinian Academic Society for the Study of International Affairs, 1998.

Israeli and Palestinian Public Opinion on the Future of Jerusalem. Jerusalem: Israel-Palestine Center for Research and Information, June 1996. http://www.ipcri.org. (Last accessed September 2005.)

Jerusalem: Religious Aspects. Jerusalem: Palestinian Academic Society for the Study of International Affairs, 1995.

A Jerusalem Road Map. Jerusalem: Israel-Palestine Center for Research and Information, May 2003. http://www.ipcri.org. (Last accessed September 2005.)

Johnston, D. and C. Sampson (eds) *Religion, the Missing Dimension of Statecraft.* New York: Oxford University Press, 1994.

Jospe, R. 'The Significance of Jerusalem: A Jewish Perspective: Jewish Religion is National, and Jewish Nationhood is Religious'. *Palestine-Israel Journal of Politics, Economics and Culture* 2, no. 2(1995): 32–40.

al-Jubeh, N. 'The Palestinian Attachment to Jerusalem: Jerusalem is a Symbol of Palestinian Religious, Political and National Identity'. *Palestine-Israel Journal of Politics, Economics and Culture* 2, no. 2(1995): 77–80.

Klein, M. 'The Islamic Holy Places as a Political Bargaining Card (1993–1995)'. *Catholic University Law Review* 45, no. 3(1996): 747–750.

Klein, M. *Jerusalem: The Contested City*. New York: New York University Press, 2001.

Klein, M. *The Jerusalem Problem: The Struggle for Permanent Status*. Gainesville, FL: University Press of Florida, 2003.

Landau, Y. 'Healing the Holy Land: Inter-religious Peacemaking in Israel/Palestine'. *Peaceworks* 51(2003). http://www.usip.org/pubs/peaceworks/pwks51.pdf. (Last accessed 26 April 2016.)

Lapidoth, R. 'Jerusalem: Past, Present and Future/Jerusalem: Reflexions D'Ordre Juridique sur son Passe, son Present et son Futur'. *Revue internationale de droit comparé* 48 no. 1(1996): 9–33.

Lapidoth, R. *Autonomy: Flexible Solutions to Ethnic Conflict*. Washington, DC: US Institute of Peace Press, 1995.

Lapidoth, R. and M. Hirsch. *The Jerusalem Question and Its Resolution: Selected Documents*. The Hague: Martinus Nijhoff Publishers, 1994.

Latendresse, A. *Jerusalem: The Palestinian Dynamics of Resistance and Urban Change*. Jerusalem: Palestinian Academic Society for the Study of International Affairs, 1994.

Ma'oz, M. and S. Nusseibeh. *Jerusalem: Points of Friction and Beyond*. The Hague: Kluwer Law International, 2000.

Molinaro, E. *Negotiating Jerusalem: Preconditions for Drawing Scenarios Based on Territorial Compromises*. Jerusalem: Palestinian Academic Society for the Study of International Affairs, 2002.

Nusseibeh, S., B. Sabella and Y. Reiter. *Jerusalem-Religious Aspects*. Jerusalem: Palestinian Academic Society for the Study of International Affairs, 1995.

O'Mahony, A. (ed.) *The Christian Heritage of the Holy Land*. London: Scorpion Cavendish Ltd., 1995.

'Patriarchs Demand Old City Stay United'. *Ha'aretz*, 20 July 2000.

'A Policy of Discrimination: Land Expropriation and Building in East Jerusalem'. *B'tselem*. May 1995. http://www.btselem.org/Download/199505_Policy_of_Discrimination_Eng.doc. (Last accessed 26 April 2016.)

Quigley, J. 'Old Jerusalem: Whose to Govern?' *Denver Journal of International Law and Policy* 20, no. 1(1991): 145–166.

Qutob, I. *Neighbourhoods in Arab Jerusalem*. Jerusalem: Palestinian Academic Society for the Study of International Affairs, 1997.

Reiter, Y. (ed.) *Sovereignty of God and Man: Sanctity and Political Centrality on the Temple Mount*. Jerusalem: Jerusalem Institute for Israel Studies, 2001.

Rock, A. *The Status Quo in the Holy Places*. Jerusalem: Franciscan Printing Press, 1989.

Romann, M. and A. Weingrod. *Living Together Separately: Arabs and Jews in Contemporary Jerusalem*. Princeton, NJ: Princeton University Press, 1991.

Segal, J.M. et al. *Negotiating Jerusalem*. Albany, NY: State University of New York Press, 2000.

Sharkansky, I. 'Governing a City Some Would Internationalize'. *Jerusalem Journal of International Relations* 14, no. 1(1992): 16–32.

Shragai, N. 'Solving the Puzzle in the Old City'. *Ha'aretz*, June 18, 2000.

Smock, D.R. (ed.) *Interfaith Dialogue and Peacebuilding*. Washington, DC: United States Institute of Peace Press, 2002.

Sorkin, M. (ed.) *The Next Jerusalem: Sharing the Divided City*. New York: Monacelli Press, 2002.

Statistical Yearbook of Jerusalem. Jerusalem: City of Jerusalem.

Wasserstein, B. *Divided Jerusalem: The Struggle for the Holy City*. New Haven, CT: Yale University Press, 2001.

7

MANDATE ELEMENTS FOR THE OLD CITY SPECIAL REGIME

David Cameron, Arthur Hughes, Michael Bell,
Michael J. Molloy and John Bell

Executive summary

The Old City encompasses all aspects of the Israeli–Palestinian conflict. With overlapping claims, systemic distrust, multiple stakeholders, deep religious divides and the impracticability of physical division, we believe options splitting Old City governance are problematic. We do not believe agreement on sovereignty is likely in the foreseeable future, although we would prefer agreement between sides to this end.

Yet, if there is no sustainable, practical solution to the problem of Old City governance, there will be no peace between Israelis and Palestinians. We are therefore proposing, as a transitional mechanism, a Special Regime, led by a Chief Administrator, operating under the authority of a Palestinian/Israeli-based Governance Board and responsible to it.

Core elements of the Old City Special Regime include:

- The Old City as a distinct unit with a distinct legal personality under the executive authority of a single Chief Administrator accountable to a Governance Board;
- The Governance Board as the oversight authority of the Special Regime;
- The Chief Administrator appointed for a fixed renewable term by the Board, the latter consisting of senior representatives of the Israeli and Palestinian governments and select other countries and institutions as may be agreed by Parties;
- Special Regime responsibility for specific aspects of governance including policing, heritage, archaeological oversight, access, planning, zoning, property registration and transfer and ensuring equal status for all residents and visitors;
- Chief Administrator consultations, as appropriate, with:

a   a Religious Council which will provide guidance and facilitation related to management of ritual worship, access, and Holy Sites;

b   international advisory bodies on cultural heritage, in close coordination with Palestinian and Israeli authorities and institutions;

c   expert committees to develop legal and regulatory frameworks;

d   Palestinian and Israeli intelligence and security authorities;

e   the governments of Israel and Palestine and the municipalities of Al-Quds and Yerushalayim.

- All powers not specifically allocated to the Special Regime being the responsibility of the Parties;

- Direct Palestinian and Israeli responsibility for particular functions respecting civil matters affecting their respective nationals *inter alia* education and family law;

- Israeli and Palestinian residents to carry either Israeli or Palestinian citizenship, with their political rights secured through participation in the political processes of their country of citizenship;

- Freedom of worship secured and guaranteed, according to established practice;

- A Police Service with a Chief of Police, heading a unified command structure accountable to the Chief Administrator; members of the service recruited individually according to a list of countries agreed by the Parties;

- Israelis and Palestinians to participate in the Police Service as 'community liaison officers';

- Police Service responsibilities to include maintenance of public order, counter-terrorism, entry and exit control to and from the Old City, enforcement of criminal and specific civil laws, security and intelligence responsibilities and community policing;

- Close Police Service liaison with Israeli and Palestinian police and security services;

- The Old City as a 'weapons-free' zone, excepting the Police Service.

We recognize that the Special Regime will not fully satisfy all the objectives of the Parties, but are convinced such a Regime can go a considerable way to accommodating their respective needs and ensuring a secure and sustainable future.

There continues to be variance among both our local and international partners respecting components of the plan. Our goal has been to encompass as many common elements as possible and add to them, or modify them, only where we believe sustainability, the *sine qua non* of success, would be otherwise compromised.

The documents published by the Jerusalem Old City Initiative since its inception reflect the evolution of our thinking. This Mandate paper is the most recent expression of our ideas. We have taken the view that our work is best understood as a kind of 'rolling draft' subject to change as new ideas come to the fore and as circumstances require.

Our efforts have been greatly enhanced by David Cameron of the University of Toronto and Arthur Hughes, formerly of the US State and Defense Departments, and currently the Initiative's Washington Coordinator, who skillfully drafted the document which follows.

Mandate elements for the Jerusalem Old City Special Regime

1) The Peace Treaty

a   In their peace treaty the Parties (Israel and Palestine) will create a Special Regime to govern the Old City (that part of Jerusalem within and including the existing walls both above and below ground) as a single entity.

b   The Special Regime will not prejudice the claims of either party regarding sovereignty over the Old City.

c   The Special Regime will replace Israeli governance.

d   The Treaty provisions (including the associated documents) together with a UN Security Council resolution of endorsement will be the Source of Authority and constitute the Mandate for the Special Regime.

e   The Treaty will create a Governance Board to be the oversight authority of the Special Regime. The Board will appoint a Chief Administrator as executive authority.

f   The Parties will agree to fund the Special Regime with assistance from the international community.

g   The Parties will agree that neither will attempt in any way, by action, verbally or by means of a third party, to assert or implement their respective claims of sovereignty.

2) The Special Regime

a   The Special Regime is the practical means by which the Parties will jointly address their responsibilities and interests without prejudice to their respective claims of sovereignty over the Old City.

b   The Special Regime will have its own legal personality.

c   The Special Regime will have a Chief Administrator with specific authorities and powers, appointed by the Governance Board, to ensure effective and just governance and administration of the Old City, the rule of law and equality under the law for its residents and visitors, as well as security, public order and safety.

d   The Old City will be a weapons-free area, except for the international members of the Old City Police Service.

e   Freedom of religion and worship will be guaranteed by law.

f   The Special Regime will work closely and actively with religious groups and institutions to:

      i   protect and preserve the religious sites;

      ii maintain decorum and public order;

      iii uphold the status quo and agreed customary practice;

      iv promote religious tolerance and respect.

g   The existing arrangements, roles and responsibilities of the religious authorities and custodians of the religious sites will continue as provided by the Parties in their peace treaty.

h   The Special Regime will be responsible for security, public order and safety, city planning and zoning consistent with the preservation of the character of the Old City, real property registration and transfer, environmental protection, archaeology, including the preservation of historical sites, the provision of essential public services and any other domains as the Parties may decide.

i   All powers and functions not specifically allocated to the Special Regime shall be the responsibility of the Parties, including education, family law, religious practice, health, tourism promotion, culture, contract law and commercial law except insofar as they involve security matters.

j   The Special Regime will have its own distinct legal personality limited to the mandated responsibilities enumerated in 2) h. above and will work with Israel and Palestine to ensure that their legal systems, and that of the Special Regime, constitute a coherent overall legal framework for the Old City.

k   Residents will be invited to form advisory bodies to provide information and counsel to the Special Regime on the issues affecting them which fall under the authority of the Special Regime.

l   Citizens of Palestine and Israel who are resident in the Old City will exercise their political rights by means of participation in the political processes of their countries of citizenship.

3) The Governance Board

a   The Governance Board will be the oversight authority of the Special Regime.

b   Palestine and Israel will create the Board within 90 days of signature of the peace treaty between them.

c   The Board will consist of representatives of the Parties and of such other states and international organizations as may be agreed by the Parties.

d   Membership will be for three years, renewable.

e   Within 90 days of the creation of the Board, it will appoint a Chief Administrator as its agent and representative to exercise the executive and regulatory powers of the Special Regime. The Board may seek suggestions for this position from the international community.

f   The Board will also:

      i hold the Chief Administrator accountable for the execution of the Mandate contained in the peace treaty;

    ii require the Chief Administrator to appear before it on matters affecting interpretation of the Mandate;

    iii approve the legal regime proposed by the Chief Administrator and exercise decision-making authority over any modification of the legal regime recommended by the Chief Administrator;

    iv be available to the Chief Administrator;

    v exercise specific other authority as specified in the Mandate such as the approval of the appointment of the Deputy Administrator, the Police Service Chief and the Police Monitoring Board;

    vi undertake the financing of the establishment and operation of the Special Regime, funding to begin upon appointment of the Chief Administrator;

    vii approve the annual budget of the Special Regime;

    viii have the authority to replace the Chief Administrator, should it so choose.

g   The Governance Board will not involve itself in the day-to-day operations of the Special Regime nor in the direct governance of the Old City.

h   All decisions of the Governance Board will be taken after discussion and deliberation among all members of the Board. Decisions relating to the authority and Mandate of the Special Regime, as stipulated in the Treaty and associated documents, will require the agreement of the Parties (constitutive decisions). Other decisions (management decisions) will require a simple majority vote of the members of the Governance Board.

i   Any member may delay voting once on any issue until a subsequent board meeting that may be held only after 15 days have passed.

j   Each member will have one vote. A quorum will be a majority of the membership including both Parties.

k   The Board will decide its procedural rules and the Parties will provide administrative and technical support.

4) The Chief Administrator

a   The Chief Administrator will be appointed by and be accountable to the Governance Board.

b   The Chief Administrator will be responsible for implementation of the Mandate contained in the peace treaty, its associated documents and the related UN Security Council resolution. He shall also be responsible for the direction and functioning of the Special Regime in the fulfilment of its responsibilities to the Parties and of those to the residents, visitors and institutions of the Old City.

c   He will be guided by the principles articulated in the entirety of the treaty.

d   He will have executive and regulatory powers.

e   He will present formal reports to the Board semi-annually regarding the functioning of the Special Regime. Such reports will include a review of the operations of the Special Regime in the reporting period, annual outside audits of the finances and internal controls, and annual proposed budgets. Governance Board decisions related to these matters will be regarded as management decisions, as described in 3) i. above.

f   The Chief Administrator will appear before the Board upon its request and it will meet with him at his request.

g   The Chief Administrator will not be a citizen of Israel or of Palestine.

h   The term of office will be five years, renewable for one additional term.

i   The Governance Board may replace a Chief Administrator before the end of a term.

j   The Chief Administrator is authorized to make and enforce regulations, to establish the Police Service and administrative apparatus and to engage staff, to institute legal proceedings, to contract, to acquire and dispose of property and to take whatever other actions as may be necessary and proper in fulfilment of his responsibilities.

k   The Chief Administrator may, as appropriate, invite the establishment of advisory bodies composed of residents and others who have ongoing links with the Old City. Such bodies will be invited to offer advice that the Chief Administrator may take into account as he carries out his executive and regulatory responsibilities.

l   The Chief Administrator may consult and cooperate with members of the international community, including diplomatic missions accredited to Palestine and Israel, on matters of interest or concern to the Old City, its institutions, and to its residents and visitors.

m   The Chief Administrator will appoint, with the agreement of the Governance Board, a Deputy Administrator who, in the absence of the Chief Administrator from Palestine, Israel and the Old City, will have the authority of the Chief Administrator. The Chief Administrator will notify Israel and Palestine in advance on the occasions when such a transfer of authority will occur.

n   The Chief Administrator will appoint, with agreement of the Governance Board, the Chief of Police Service.

5) Religious matters

a   Freedom of access, religion and worship for all residents of and visitors to the Old City will be guaranteed by law, with appropriate access to the Holy Sites, based on customary practice. These rights shall be subject to the requirements of security, safety, public order and decorum.

b   The Special Regime in itself will not affect existing bilateral or international agreements of the Israeli or Palestinian authorities regarding religious matters, nor the present arrangements for residency of religious persons within the Old City.

c   The Special Regime will have no responsibility for the internal management of the Holy Sites, but will be responsible for security, ensuring respect for customary practice, public order and safety, including the structural soundness of the sites.

d   Management of the sites will remain the province of the custodians and religious groups and communities they represent and serve.

e   Religious groups, communities and authorities will be invited to establish an Advisory Religious Council to foster cooperation and development of constructive relations among them and to coordinate matters of common interest with the Special Regime administration.

f   The Special Regime will maintain close discussions and liaise with the Council on appropriate matters pertaining to religious affairs in the Old City, including security, preservation, maintenance of access to and sanctity of the Holy Sites, and planning for major religious observances and festivals.

g   The Special Regime shall work closely with the Council and other religious institutions to promote tolerance.

6) Security, public order, and safety

a   The Old City will be a weapons-free area except for Old City Police Service officers. Any divergence from this will require permits from the Police Service.

b   Israel and Palestine will ensure that the Old City is weapons free upon entry into force of the Special Regime.

c   The Special Regime will have an Old City Police Service responsible for enforcing laws, regulations, ordinances and directives in effect in the Old City.

d   The Police Service will have full authority to investigate, question, arrest, detain and transfer to the appropriate Palestinian and Israeli authorities suspects in accordance with law, accepted international norms and human rights standards.

e   As soon as possible after his appointment, the Chief Administrator will appoint, with agreement of the Governance Board, a Police Service Chief.

f   The Police Service Chief will not be Israeli or Palestinian.

g   The Police Service Chief will report directly to the Chief Administrator.

h   The Police Service Chief will design and recommend a Police Service to the Chief Administrator with emphasis on neighbourhood policing with community partnerships and the ability to monitor and control entry into and exit from the Old City, in close cooperation with Israeli and Palestinian services.

i   The armed Police Service will consist only of international officers, thereby excluding citizens of Israel and Palestine. These international officers will be recruited by the Special Regime from countries agreed by the Parties.

j   The Special Regime will recruit Palestinians and Israelis to serve alongside their international colleagues as unarmed Community Officers. All will be under the command of the Police Service Chief.

k   Palestinian and Israeli police, security and intelligence services will have no authority within the Old City. The Old City Police Service will have a cooperative relationship with those services and will work closely with them on matters of interest to them.

l   The Parties will agree to post Israeli and Palestinian liaison officers at Old City Police Service Headquarters and establish real time communications protocols to ensure close cooperation and effectiveness.

m   The Police Service will maintain close liaison with services of relevant countries and of international organizations such as INTERPOL.

n   The Police Service will give special attention to ensuring respect for the sanctity of the Holy Sites in cooperation with the custodians of the sites.

o   The Police Service will have integral rapid reinforcement capability, including expert units for special circumstances. The Police Service will also have criminal, counter-terrorism, intelligence, explosives training and support units.

p   The Chief Administrator, on the advice of the Police Service Chief and with agreement of the Governance Board, may conclude agreements for special units that could be called in should the Chief Administrator and Police Service Chief determine the existence of extraordinary requirements not manageable by integral Police Service units.

q   When requested by the Chief Administrator, the Parties will agree to facilitate entry into staging areas and movement of these units with their arms and equipment through their territories to the Old City.

r   The Chief Administrator will establish, with agreement of the Governance Board, a Police Board to monitor the Police Service and its operations. Monitoring will include public meetings and independent assessments.

s   The Parties agree to provide fire safety and first responder services to the Special Regime, including specifically ambulance, rescue and firefighting capability. These functions will be coordinated by means of the Israeli and Palestinian liaison at Police Service Headquarters.

t   The Parties will ensure that incitement or actions against the Special Regime and the Old City will not occur from their territories.

7) The legal system and civil issues

a   The Parties will have jurisdiction over their respective citizens for all matters not falling under the authority of the Special Regime.

b   For third country nationals, the law of the country from which persons enter the Old City will apply, with the exceptions specified in section 7) d.

c   With the endorsement of the Governance Board, a distinct legal personality for the Special Regime will be established by the Chief Administrator and apply to those matters falling under the Special Regime Mandate listed in section 2) h.

d   The legal system will include a mechanism to determine jurisdiction in cases involving citizens of both states, cases involving Old City residents and third country nationals, and cases involving exclusively third country nationals.

e   In developing the legal system for the Old City in the areas of responsibility specified in section 2) h, the Chief Administrator will appoint a panel of Palestinian, Israeli and international experts. In selecting members of the panel, the Chief Administrator will give full consideration to suggestions from the Parties.

f   The panel will develop, for recommendation to the Chief Administrator, a legal system based on existing law, Palestinian law and international law as appropriate.

g   During the interim period, that is the time between appointment of the Chief Administrator and entry into force of the distinct legal system of the Old City, existing legislation deemed relevant by the Chief Administrator and the Governance Board will continue to apply.

h   Existing legislation prejudicial to the interest of either Party such as that pertaining to absentee property, residency and the annexation will become inoperable within the Old City on the coming into force of the peace treaty.

i   Under his authority and responsibility for public order and safety, the Chief Administrator will develop dispute resolution mechanisms, utilizing existing mechanisms as appropriate.

j   The Chief Administrator will develop regulations for residency and presence in the Old City. Denials for either Palestinians or Israelis will require advance consultation with appropriate officials of the relevant Party.

k   Changes in the Special Regime legal system may be required from time to time. Such changes will be formalized on the decision of the Chief Administrator and the endorsement of the Governance Board.

8) Archaeology and excavation

a   The Chief Administrator will develop and enforce regulations, procedures and institutions to include standards, consultative processes, assessment applications for licensing, monitoring and excavation and, if necessary, suspending such activity.

b   The Chief Administrator will appoint a panel of experts to provide analysis and advice based on UNESCO and other established international standards.

9) Planning, zoning and property

a   Prior to the establishment of a distinct legal system for the Special Regime there will be no property or land purchases, change of usage or transfer of ownership without the approval of the Chief Administrator, who will establish a committee of experts to advise him. Those aspects of the legal system affecting these issues should be developed on a priority basis.

b   The Chief Administrator will develop and implement, subject to the concurrence of the Governance Board, a comprehensive urban development and conservation plan for the Old City that balances the needs of residents, improves living conditions, addresses environmental concerns, conserves heritage buildings and structures, maintains an appropriate commercial environment and accommodates pilgrims, tourists and other visitors.

c   The Chief Administrator will create a multidisciplinary Planning and Zoning Department. Under his direction that department will assume responsibility for the issuance of building permits, structural safety inspection, heritage protection and environmental standards enforcement. It will advise the Administrator respecting urban infrastructural and utilities issues.

d   The Chief Administrator will consult the various stakeholders to determine the feasibility of creating an Old City property registry.

10) Urban services, utilities, infrastructure, and environment

a   The Special Regime will cooperate with Palestine and Israel and their respective municipalities to ensure that effective public services, utilities and infrastructure are constructed, maintained, updated and provided on a reliable basis.

b   Operations and annual and long-term capital and maintenance budgets will be prepared jointly by the Parties and the Special Regime.

c   The Parties will meet the costs of such budgets.

d   The Special Regime will ensure environmental regulations and practices of a high standard.

11) Administration, economic matters, liaison and facilitation

a   The Special Regime will not apply duties on goods and services entering or leaving the Old City.

b   Licenses, charters, permits and other authorizations issued by Palestine and Israel for banks, insurance companies, law firms and attorneys, notaries, guilds, labour unions, chambers of commerce and other institutions necessary for economic activity will also be valid in the Old City.

c   Palestinian and Israeli currency will be legal tender within the Old City.

d   The Parties agree that their respective authorities and agencies will cooperate fully with the Chief Administrator and his staff in the fulfilment of Special Regime responsibilities. To this end they will designate appropriate officials to act as interlocutors with the Chief Administrator and his staff.

e   The Chief Administrator will establish a liaison system to ensure prompt and ongoing dialogue, collaboration and cooperation with appropriate officials of the Parties and their respective municipalities.

f   The Parties will facilitate the work of the Chief Administrator and Special Regime, *inter alia*, by facilitating passage through their territories to and from the Old City of Special Regime staff and contractors.

g   The Parties will provide radio and television frequencies at no cost both for the internal use of the Special Regime and for public service broadcasting.

h   The Parties will assist with the importation of equipment including arms and special equipment for the Police Service.

i   The Parties will not restrict the entry of goods, including letter and package mail for Special Regime use and that of its staff and direct contractors.

j   The Parties will not levy taxes, fees or any other charge on purchases including imports by the Special Regime for use by the Regime or any of its staff or its direct contractors.

k   Postal and telecommunications services will be offered by the Parties or their licensees and Israeli and Palestinian post offices will be open for public use.

l   The Parties shall make available to the Chief Administrator public property, facilities, records, and archives within or relevant to the Old City as requested by the Chief Administrator to fulfil his mandate.

m   The Chief Administrator will establish his office and if possible, the greater part of the Special Regime administration within the Old City. Because of space constrictions and special needs, such as for Police Service training and other facilities, the Chief Administrator may also acquire facilities including housing outside the Old City within Palestine and Israel. The Parties agree to facilitate such acquisitions, which will be free of all taxes, fees, levies and assessments.

n   The Chief Administrator will reside within the Old City.

o   The Chief Administrator may establish administrative and support systems to provide for and sustain the operations of the Special Regime. This may include a vehicle fleet registered and licensed by the Special Regime and a procurement system based on best practices and transparency. The Chief Administrator will seek to focus purchases in Israel and Palestine but there will be no quotas, and purchasing will be conducted according to the norms of tender law.

p   The Chief Administrator and his staff and direct contractors of the Special Regime will enjoy privileges and immunities in accordance with common international diplomatic practice, including while outside the Old City within the territories of Israel and Palestine. The Chief Administrator will issue appropriate identification documents for this purpose and notify Palestine and Israel accordingly. Such persons' entry into and exit from Palestine and Israel and passage into and out of the Old City will not be hindered in any way by the Parties.

q   All premises of the Special Regime whether in the Old City or within Palestine or Israel will be inviolable.

12) Entry into effect

a   The Special Regime will assume authority and remain in effect until such time as the Parties may agree on successor arrangements for the Old City.

b   The Parties will invite all members of the international community to acknowledge the unique role and status of the Special Regime and to offer support to Palestine and Israel to ensure their ability to provide the services to the citizens of the Old City for which they are responsible.

8

GOVERNANCE DISCUSSION DOCUMENT

A Special Regime for the Old City of Jerusalem

Michael J. Molloy, Michael Bell and John Bell

Executive summary

The Old City of Jerusalem is the central focus of the national aspirations of both Israelis and Palestinians. This small, densely populated space embodies every aspect of the Israeli–Palestinian conflict, including overlapping political, demographic, security, economic, social, and religious claims. The area is also a central focus for Jews, Muslims and Christians worldwide. Palestinian and Israeli negotiators will have to deal with and master the complexities of Old City governance if they are to achieve a viable, comprehensive solution to the Israeli–Palestinian conflict. To do so will present extraordinary challenges, including overcoming the systemic distrust that pervades the Palestinian–Israeli relationship.

The heart of the problem is this: Israelis and Jews see the Old City of Jerusalem as their birthright from of the time of King David some 3,000 years ago. The Temple Mount within the Old City with its Western Wall is the holiest site in Judaism, and the Wall is the most sacred place of Jewish worship. Muslims also see Jerusalem as their birthright dating from the first Muslim presence in the seventh century. The Haram al-Sharif is their third holiest site, the place from which they believe Mohammad ascended into the heavens. Both vigorously dispute ownership of the Haram/Temple Mount and its foundation wall, all of which are overlapping parts of the same construction. Given the overwhelming importance of this common sacred space and its place in religious and national narrative, neither side shows any willingness to concede to the other's claims, for to do so would undermine their own legitimacy. Although the city today is less of an issue of religious and political contention for Christians, they also look to Jerusalem as the centre of their faith, the place of the crucifixion and the resurrection of Jesus.

These challenges demand special governance arrangements. Based on extensive consultations and study, the Jerusalem Old City Initiative has concluded that the optimal solution is an Old City 'Special Regime', founded on agreed norms of international law, established at the direction of both Palestine and Israel. The envisioned mandate would remain in force until the parties achieve a negotiated agreement that establishes a new system of governance for the Old City.

The proposed Old City Special Regime would neither resolve nor seek to resolve competing claims to sovereignty over the Old City and its Holy Sites. Rather, it is designed to permit the achievement of a peace agreement even in the absence of such a resolution facilitating the smooth functioning of life within this highly contested space without prejudicing the sovereignty claims of either side. To be sure the Special Regime would not be assigned sovereignty but would be tasked by the Israeli and Palestinian governments to perform specific functions on their joint behalf. Establishment of this Special Regime would require the full approval and participation of both Israel and Palestine, something that would not be achievable unless both sides were convinced that the envisioned arrangements would be open to the resolution of sovereignty claims in the future.

Key characteristics and functions of the Special Regime

The proposed Special Regime, headed by a Chief Administrator, would be responsible for the efficient and equitable management and governance of the Old City, including ensuring the sanctity of and access to the Old City's Holy Sites. In doing this, it would have to take into account the needs, interests, aspirations and sensitivities of all stakeholders including not only residents but also workers and business people living outside the Old City walls, as well as tourists and religious pilgrims.

The regime's mandate would extend to those aspects of life that are, by their nature, uniquely grounded in the Old City: security and policing, entry and exit, movement and access within the Old City and to its Holy Sites, heritage and archaeology, residency and property ownership, zoning and planning, and environmental regulation. Aspects of life linked to nationality (e.g. political rights, education and family law) would be the province of the national authorities, Palestinian and Israeli. That said, to the greatest degree possible the Special Regime would need to preserve the urban fabric connecting the Old City and the rest of Jerusalem, meaning that arrangements for the Old City should not be divorced from Jerusalem as a whole. Moreover, some functions – including legal, environmental and those related to infrastructure and utilities – would involve a degree of shared authority, requiring ongoing coordination between the Special Regime and the relevant national and municipal authorities.

To meet these responsibilities, the Special Regime would require an empowered autonomous bureaucracy – one whose leadership has the confidence of both Israel and Palestine and one that is vested with both the authority and the capacity to administer, manage, and police specific aspects of the Old City and its inhabitants.

Our discussions have shown that the Israelis express their concerns mainly in terms of security while the Palestinians frame their concerns in terms of fairness and equity. To be sustainable, the Special Regime would have to balance both. Given the importance of security concerns in the Israeli–Palestinian arena, a key function of the Special Regime would be to ensure equity, law, and order. Security will be the test of any peace agreement: if order in the Old City breaks down, any Israeli–Palestinian peace agreement itself will be at risk. Moreover, equity and security are the *sine qua non* for sustainable governance: no regime can be sustained if it cannot provide both, including, in the special case that is the Old City, ensuring access to Holy Sites for residents and visitors. In terms of equity, the Special Regime must ensure equality of treatment for all residents and visitors to the Old City in all its functions. Furthermore, the structure and nature of the executive authority will need to respect and preserve the dignity and rights of all residents and visitors.

Thus, the Old City Special Regime would require a robust security force, with the capacity both to deliver even-handed law enforcement and justice and to confront successfully large-scale security threats, including potential efforts by extremists from the various camps seeking to undermine an Israeli–Palestinian peace agreement. Substantial third country participation in such a force would be vital, helping to overcome the deep mistrust that exists between the sides. Close liaison and coordination with Palestinian and Israeli police would also be crucial. The Special Regime would also have an independent legal system and dispute resolution mechanism for specified issues of adjudication and resolution.

The proposed Special Regime would require substantial financial support from Israel and Palestine, as well as from the international community, to fulfil the mandate. While the regime would have some fundraising capacity (through taxation, fees and bonds), it would not, on its own, have sufficient resources to carry out all its responsibilities. International support for the Special Regime would be all the more imperative given the Old City's meaning and symbolism worldwide and the threat to any peace agreement that would ensue were the regime to fail.

The characteristics and functions of the Special Regime are more fully explained in parts I and III of this chapter.

Governance structure of the Special Regime

The Special Regime would be created and supported by the parties themselves – Palestine and Israel – with the support of the international community. Structurally, the regime would be anchored in an Old City Board, consisting of senior representatives of the Israeli and Palestinian governments, as well as representatives of select other countries agreed to by the parties. The principal functions of the board would be to appoint, on behalf of the Israeli and Palestinian governments, the Special Regime's Chief Administrator and to maintain oversight of the application of the mandate.

The Chief Administrator, an experienced and internationally respected individual who is neither Israeli nor Palestinian, would be the Special Regime's executive authority. The Chief Administrator would have overall independent responsibility for policing and security and also specified public administration and governance functions. This authority would extend to appointing a Police Chief, accountable to the Chief Administrator, and establishing offices to liaise with the Israeli and Palestinian authorities at the senior and working levels. The Chief Administrator and staff would also work with existing and new local and international bodies, representing the stakeholders. Prominent among these would be the Advisory Religious Council, to provide advice on the management of the Holy Sites.

Other bureaucratic bodies (see Annex A) would develop organically under the authority of the Chief Administrator, in order to respond to the various needs of the stakeholders. When the Special Regime is initially put into place, it is recommended that the Chief Administrator establish specialized transitional commissions the administrator believes warranted.

The full governance structure of the Special Regime is detailed in Part II of this chapter.

Conclusion

Traditional thinking about solutions for the Old City has been restricted to zero-sum options (i.e. either Israeli or Palestinian sovereignty over the entire area) or unwieldy plans to divide sovereignty (e.g. the Clinton parameters, the Geneva Accord). In this document, the Initiative is offering another option.

Typically, analysis of possible solutions to the conflict over the Old City of Jerusalem looks at three options: 1) sovereignty and control in the hands of Israel, 2) sovereignty and control in the hands of the new Palestinian state, and 3) the division of the Old City between the parties as, for example, in the Clinton parameters and the Geneva Accord. Options 1 and 2, where sovereignty and control are exclusively in the hands of one party or the other, will not result in a peace agreement. Option 3, a simple division of sovereignty within the Old City, given the unhappy history of cooperative efforts by the parties and the legacy of a century of conflict, would, in our view, be untenable as well, for the foreseeable future.

Recognizing that it is very difficult for governments to undertake this kind of study, this discussion document represents our best attempt to present a 'fourth option' for the Old City, neither control by one party at the expense of the other nor split governance. While we are convinced the prospects for peace and reconciliation exist and can be realized with good will and hard work, we do not believe that the Old City can be governed effectively by the two parties alone until trust builds over time with the successful implementation of the peace treaty.

Our proposed solution, which grants full control to neither party and leaves sovereignty questions open, is based on two things: 1) the recognition that zero-sum options are incompatible with a peace agreement, and 2) the firm belief that it is impossible, for the foreseeable future, to divide sovereignty and governance within this small, densely populated area, with its overlapping sacred spaces. Short of a peace agreement that resolves, to the satisfaction of all stakeholders, competing claims to the Old City and its Holy Sites, we believe this proposal is the best and perhaps only option that will permit the achievement of peace.

Indeed, a key advantage of this option is that, if adopted, it would ensure that Palestinian–Israeli peace would not be held hostage to the final resolution of claims to the Old City and its Holy Sites. The importance of this point should not be underestimated. Given the national and religious sentiment attached to the Old City and its Holy Sites by both the Palestinian and Israeli communities, it is likely that even the most promising peace negotiations could easily fall apart over these issues.

Finally, our proposal would give any resulting peace agreement the breathing room it needs to succeed. It would provide time for peace between the two peoples to be consolidated so that when the parties try, at some future time, to find a permanent solution for the Old City, they can do so in an environment of shared interests and trust and with a much greater likelihood of success.

Rationale

For decades the Israeli–Palestinian conflict has taken lives, destroyed opportunities, and hindered the national development of Palestinians and Israelis. It has obstructed the acceptance of Israel as a legitimate and integral member of the Middle East state system and blighted its relations with much of the international community. It has delayed the entry of Palestine as a recognized and viable state into the international community. Resolution of this conflict is critical to relations among the Islamic, Jewish and Christian worlds.

Jerusalem – its Old City in particular, is the central focus of Israeli and Palestinian national aspirations. At its very core, the conflict is about control over Jerusalem's Holy Sites, the most important of which, the Haram al-Sharif/Temple Mount, the Kotel/Western Wall and the Church of the Holy Sepulchre, are located within the stone walls of the Old City. Most importantly, the sacred space of the Haram al-Sharif and Temple Mount are physically overlapping and indivisible.[1] These sites are powerful religious, cultural and emotional symbols that must be administered with fairness and equity if the profound needs of stakeholders are to be met. Without the sustainable, effective and equitable management of the Old City's status, enduring peace between the Palestinians and Arabs, on the one hand, and Israelis, on the other, will be unattainable.

The Old City of Jerusalem is a microcosm of the Palestinian–Israeli conflict, encompassing political, demographic, security, economic, social, religious, territorial and environmental elements, among others. The search for a solution to the conflict is complicated by the systemic distrust that exists between the sides, in particular with respect to Holy Sites, their surroundings, ownership, security, access and human dignity. Israeli and Palestinian negotiators will have to master the complexities of Old City governance if they are to achieve comprehensive peace.

The Jerusalem Old City Initiative was established to develop creative governance and management options for the Old City, based on a two-state solution and two national capitals in the Jerusalem conurbation. For over four years we have worked in close consultation with Palestinian, Israeli, regional and international experts and advisors to this end. The recommendations in this document are intended to provide negotiators, political leaders and policy planners with creative ideas for practical solutions that can bridge gaps and spark imagination. Our recommendations contained in this document aim to offer workable solutions. They are based on preliminary ideas first formulated in *The Jerusalem Old City Initiative Discussion Document: New Directions for Deliberation and Dialogue*, published in late 2004.

As a result of our research and our consultations, we have come to believe that governance solutions based on the notion of dividing the Old City between Israelis and Palestinians are problematic, given overlapping claims and aspirations coupled with their charged history. With an area of just 0.9 square kilometres, the Old City is too small, too densely populated, too architecturally linked, and too riven by systemic distrust to be managed viably by a number of separate authorities that would carry, perforce, a legacy of acrimony and be imbued with mutual suspicion and distrust.

The attachment to religious and national symbols is so intense and the wounds so deep that they will require a very long time to heal. We see no evidence that ingrained bias, resentment and prejudice will erode in the near term simply by the act of signing a peace agreement. Changing human and community behaviour patterns requires the effort and experience of decades.

We believe, however, in the context of a two-state solution, sustainable governance arrangements can be agreed upon by both sides, treating the Old City as a single entity under a Special Regime led by a Chief Administrator. The Old City Special Regime proposal is designed to offer negotiators a detailed, realistic, integrated model for addressing the myriad challenges of Old City governance. The solutions offered in the proposal would ideally be adopted as a whole – which we believe to be the optimal solution – but could also be adopted in parts or in some combination, according to the needs and preferences of the negotiators.

We envisage the parties – Palestinians and Israelis – constituting the Chief Administrator's Source of Authority. It is they who would determine the Special Regime's mandate and they who would choose the administrator. The arrangement we propose is unique because it is the parties themselves who will create the governance mechanisms.

To ensure fair and appropriate access to the Holy Sites for Muslim, Jewish, and Christian believers, access, movement, safety, and security requirements must, in our view, be met by a single impartial authority so that rights can be exercised equitably without fear of retribution or intimidation.

Virtually every issue today has the potential to develop into a serious crisis among differing individuals, believers and communities. Sustainable arrangements must create peace, order and good governance by ensuring that a single, impartial authority, in this case the Chief Administrator, enjoys a clear mandate from the parties and the strong support of the international community, thereby enabling the incumbent to ensure orderly access, equitable law enforcement and public order. The administrator should be made responsible for ensuring the rights and dignity of all.

The Old City Special Regime will necessarily exist as a separate governance entity surrounded by Israel's capital in West Jerusalem, Yerushalayim, and Palestine's capital in East Jerusalem, Al-Quds. The need, however, to maintain the urban fabric and contiguity of the Jerusalem conurbation as a whole is also critical.

The nature of governance in such a complex, intertwined, urban area would, of course, require close coordination on municipal and broader issues with the two national and municipal governments concerned.

The discussion developed herein is the culminating document in a series of papers detailing the characteristics of the Special Regime and examining various possibilities and arrangements within that framework. Earlier documents examine and propose a variety of possible solutions focused on this concept. In particular, the 'Jerusalem Old City Initiative Security Assessment', released by our SWG in November 2007, lays out in considerable detail the requirements for law enforcement and security systems. The 'Jaffa Gate Crossing Facilities Study' by Saya Architecture and Consultancy provides innovative ideas for implementing an efficient security system at one of the Old City's busiest gates. It is from them and from innumerable meetings, workshops and conferences that we have developed our proposals. To all those who contributed, we owe a great debt of gratitude. Responsibility for the conclusions drawn in the document, however, and for any errors, rests with the authors alone.

Part I: Overview of the Old City Special Regime

1.1 Core features

Any successful Special Regime must take into account the needs, interests, aspirations and sensitivities of all stakeholders. It must put in place a system that can effectively manage and facilitate the normal functioning of the Old City and protect residents, visitors, Holy Sites and other symbolic venues. It must be capable of coping successfully with crises and it must do this in a manner that is effective, fair and equitable, and is seen by the parties, Israel and Palestine, to be so.

The Old City Special Regime should contain the following key characteristics:

a. Israeli/Palestinian ownership A regime for the Old City would have to be created and embraced by both Israel and Palestine, the source of its authority. The Special Regime and its mandate should, in our view, be integral parts of a peace treaty between Palestine and Israel. These two parties, acting together, would need to create what we have called an Old City Board to which the Chief Administrator would ultimately be accountable.

b. Mandate The mandate, which would be the basis of the Special Regime, would be drafted and issued by the parties as an integral part of a peace treaty and its associated documents. The mandate would lay out the functions of the Special Regime and invest authority in the Chief Administrator, stipulating agreed-on functional limits. The peace treaty would establish the Old City Board and delineate its functions.

c. Relevance under different sovereignty scenarios We recognize the significance of physically overlapping sovereignty claims by the two parties to territory and sacred space within the Old City. Agreement on the primordial question of sovereignty

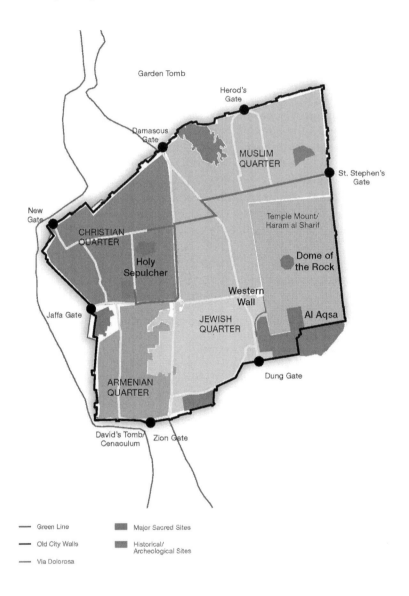

MAP 8.1 The Old City
Source: Courtesy of Terrestrial Jerusalem.

would clearly be the most desirable outcome of any negotiation. We consider, however, that the prospect of early resolution is remote.

We believe that existing claims to sovereignty are so exclusive and based on such deeply felt national and religious identities and community narratives that bilateral Palestine and Israel governance options cannot be realized except through the role of an interim third party. Through the third-party presence, with growing trust and experience, confidence between Israelis and Palestinians can be established and reinforced over time, making feasible what today seems impracticable.

In the unlikely event that the parties are able to reach agreement on sovereignty, this will not mean that suspicion, distrust, competition, and prejudice would disappear. It seems likely to us that, particularly in the initial years, provocateurs and spoilers may do their worst in the hope of promoting the collapse of the agreement. If a bilateral system were to break down over issues such as archaeological excavation or tunnelling, let alone access to and conduct at Holy Sites, the entirety of any peace treaty could fall apart. Such is the emotive force of sacred space. Therefore, a Special Regime with appropriate modifications and scaled to the magnitude of its responsibilities might still remain the optimal system for the interim management of the most contentious elements involved. We believe that conclusive Palestinian–Israeli agreement on sovereignty over the Old City would be optimal, yet even in this case, a third party role would still be necessary to ensure stability.

For the purposes of this document, however, we have assumed the more complex scenario of a Special Regime installed in a situation where the assignment of sovereignty within the Old City has been postponed. Under this scenario, our research conducted by the Jerusalem Old City Initiative suggests a Special Regime would have to take on a broader range of functions than if most sovereignty issues were resolved.

d. Third party support and participation A strong third party role would be central to the regime's ability to meet the legitimate equity and justice, safety and security, emotional and psychological, and religious and material needs of the Old City's stakeholders. We realize that this third party element may raise concerns respecting perceived or real impacts on sovereignty. We thus emphasize again that our proposals do not seek to resolve, or in any way prejudice, sovereignty claims, which remain within the total purview of the parties. The Special Regime, as we conceive it, will be created and owned by the parties, who will appoint the Chief Administrator and issue the mandate. This mandate would assign specific tasks or functions to the Special Regime, but not sovereignty. What is more, the Special Regime would be sustained by the participation of Israel and Palestine in the Old City board. Such an arrangement would be unique and would in no way constitute internationalization or a *corpus separatum*, concepts we reject.[2]

e. Sustainability and legitimacy To be effective, the Special Regime's governance arrangements would need to strike a careful balance between sustainability, which requires autonomy of decision making for the Chief Administrator, on the one hand, and coordination and consultation with the parties, on the other. The administrator would require clear and unimpeded lines of authority and management, coupled with the capacity to maintain public order and react rapidly and effectively in case of crisis. Given conflicting national aspirations and claims, the profound, systemic distrust between the parties, the almost inevitable activity of 'spoilers', and other factors, including the Old City's complex and diverse society, any successful administration by a third party would also require ongoing support and active participation by local representatives of the Old City's existing social, religious and institutional bodies. The Chief Administrator would have to establish consultative mechanisms to this end. The regime's legitimacy would begin with the fact that its mandate is rooted in the Israeli–Palestinian peace agreement, and in the fact that Palestinians and Israelis would shape the rules that guide it. Support from the international community, including a supportive United Nations Security Council resolution, would strengthen that legitimacy. However, in the end, the character and skills of the individual chosen as Chief Administrator will be critical.

   f. The urban fabric To the greatest degree possible the Special Regime would need to preserve the urban fabric that connects the Old City to the rest of Jerusalem. Arrangements for the Old City cannot be divorced from the Jerusalem conurbation as a whole. Relatively few residents live their lives strictly within the confines of the walls; most have family, social and economic relations beyond. Conversely, many of those who earn their living in the Old City reside elsewhere. The walled city's symbolism, as well as its infrastructure, economic and social realities, and the legions of tourists and pilgrims eager to visit their Holy Sites, make it inseparable from Jerusalem as a whole. Very few stakeholders – Jerusalemites, Israelis, Palestinians, Muslims, Christians, or Jews – will accept the Old City as an isolated enclave. Meaningful and strong linkages with the Israeli and Palestinian capital cities Yerushalayim and Al-Quds are therefore both natural and necessary. The participation of the Special Regime in any future arrangement to coordinate services, infrastructure, standards and utilities would be imperative.

   g. Focus on place The Old City, defined by its walls, demands special governance arrangements. However, such arrangements must recognize that the inhabitants are part of larger communities extending beyond the walls, and that these communities already have and will have in place legal, social and cultural structures to address many aspects of their daily lives. Residents of the Old City would overwhelmingly be citizens of the new Palestinian state or of Israel.[3] In many cases, in civil matters Palestinian residents would be subject to Palestinian law, Israeli residents to Israeli law. A workable Special Regime must thus seek to focus more on place – and critical issues of friction related to place – than on people. It should address those functions that are quintessentially of the Old City, for example the security of the Holy Sites and worshippers. It should leave undisturbed natural linkages, including national political rights, education, and family law, which would remain the domain of a resident's country of citizenship, Palestine or Israel.

1.2 Guiding principles for place and people

Functions and activities within the Old City can be divided into two categories: place and people. The relation of the Special Regime to each function and activity should depend on and be governed by this categorization.

a. Place functions under the authority of the Special Regime Place functions include all those related to Holy Sites, heritage and archaeology, as well as all aspects of security and policing (see section 1.4). Because of their highly contentious nature and their interlinkage, these functions must be under the authority of the Chief Administrator. Indeed, successful oversight and management of these functions is the core mission of the Special Regime. Beyond this there are other require-ments, which, due to their location-based connection to the Old City and their potential to generate conflict, would best be placed under the authority of the special regime.

The extent of this authority should, in part, reflect the extent to which issues of sovereignty have or have not been resolved by the parties. These could include issues such as residency permits, planning and zoning, and local infrastructure and services – areas that will likely remain matters of political contention between the parties and whose management affects peace and security. In many of these cases, there is a need for degrees of reference to and coordination with national and municipal bodies.

b. People functions under the authority of national governments People functions include those grounded not in the Old City itself, but in the approximately 35,000 people who inhabit it, as well as those who work in it, or visit it. Under the pro-posed Special Regime, most residents would be citizens of either Israel or the new state of Palestine, and they would exercise their political and social rights and duties in the context of their own states and national capitals. Israeli residents would vote in the national and municipal elections of Israel and of their capital, Yerushalayim. Palestinian residents, who are currently permanent residents of Israel, would nor-mally become citizens of the Palestinian state. They would participate in the elections of that state and of their capital, Al-Quds. People aspects of the lives of residents including education, family matters, health, social programmes, and religious prac-tice would fall under the authority and jurisdiction of national governments and the laws and regulations of their respective states.

Following the Israeli occupation of East Jerusalem in 1967, Palestinians in that part of the city were accorded Israeli 'Permanent Resident Status', unlike those in the West Bank and Gaza. This status carries with it access to Israeli welfare and health insurance benefits as well as freedom to travel and access to employment on a level denied to other Palestinians. Like Israelis, Palestinian Jerusalemites pay for these services through taxes. These services are highly valued and consequently place Palestinian Jerusalemites in a privileged position.

Some of our Israeli and Palestinian research partners involved in the Initiative have recommended that the Special Regime create an alternative to the National Insurance programme for Palestinian residents in the Old City. We have reservations. This is a Jerusalem issue, with important ramifications for both Israel and the new Palestinian state; it is not an Old City issue. It is doubtful that the international community would be willing to fund a programme that privileges one small portion of the Palestinian population at the expense of the rest. Furthermore, this is an issue that has stability, security and legitimacy implications for any two-state solution and must be addressed within the context of final status negotiations. The challenge of how to handle situations of this sort equitably, taking into account not only people's expectations but also the rights they accrue from contributing over time to pension and health insurance funds, for example, is one where there is considerable international experience and a wealth of examples to draw on.

1.3 Mandate, geographic scope, and duration

Certain defining elements would need to be specified in the agreement between the parties that creates the Special Regime, as follows.

1.3.1 The mandate

The mandate issued by the parties to the Chief Administrator would *inter alia* establish responsibility for the management and administration of matters of particular sensitivity and friction, especially policing and law enforcement, access to the Old City and the Holy Sites, and protection of the Holy Sites and worshippers, along with heritage protection and archaeological oversight. On the assumption that sovereignty issues are deferred, the Chief Administrator would be assigned responsibility for residency permits for inhabitants living within the Old City. The mandate would also include a regulatory role respecting planning, zoning and construction permits, property matters, infrastructure, environmental and safety issues. The Special Regime should have a basic legal system including dispute resolution mechanisms to resolve disagreements. Agreed norms of international law will act as a foundation for this system.

1.3.2 Geographic scope

The Special Regime is designed specifically to meet the challenges of the Old City. Limiting the application to the Old City, within and including the walls, has significant practical advantages, including well-defined boundaries and a clear capacity to control exit and entry into the area.

If the two sides were to agree, it might be possible to expand aspects of the system beyond the Old City to other sites of substantial friction and religious claims, such as the Mount of Olives and the City of David settlement in the Palestinian village of Silwan. There is no reason to rule this out *a priori*. After much consideration, however, we have concluded that such an extension may be difficult to manage and sustain, given the challenge of defining clear authority for the Special

Regime in this larger area and the differences that would arise between the regime authorities and sovereign governments. The many Holy Sites outside the Old City can be managed, we believe, through other creative options, including the application of World Heritage Site regulations, similar to those applied inside the walled city today.

1.3.3 Duration

The duration of the Special Regime has been the subject of continuous debate through the life of this project. Recommendations range from as little as five years to centuries. The critical factor is that the Special Regime must be in place for sufficient time to permit a comprehensive peace agreement to be consolidated, or until the parties jointly come to another solution. Although some of our partners had differing views, we believe that the parties need to consider the advantages of a mandate that would remain in force for a generation, giving sufficient time for peace between the two peoples to become a reality and also sufficient time to discourage efforts by elements on either side from attempting further land grabs at the expense of the other. The Special Regime could continue thereafter, pending agreement by the parties to an alternative. Indeed, it could be ended sooner, if the parties agree on an alternative arrangement. The Special Regime is the creation of the two parties, and should not impede possible further agreements regarding sovereignty.

1.4 Equity, justice and security

1.4.1 The importance of equity

After decades of mistrust and violence, a Special Regime must be capable of delivering equitable, even-handed law enforcement and a justice system that would provide safety to all, based on the rule of law rather than national agendas. Equally importantly, it must provide equitable treatment to all residents and visitors and respect their dignity in all aspects of its functions. It must not be perceived as merely replacing one occupying authority with another. Thus, the role of the third party and the implementation of its mandate are critical in terms of equity for all residents and visitors to the Old City.

1.4.2 Security as the sine qua non for sustainable governance

In the absence of an equitable, reliable, effective security system that has the confidence of the parties and their citizens, no Old City governance arrangements will be sustainable. Both Israel and Palestine require a system that offers the best possible security and safety for their citizens, for the Holy Sites, and for tourists and pilgrims. The system must ensure that the Old City will not become a base of operations or incitement against the parties or the peace agreement. Nor can it become a haven for criminal activity. Governance arrangements must ensure that treatment without bias or favour is accorded to all residents and visitors.

1.4.3 Security as the test for any peace agreement

There is a broader context within which a security system that protects all residents must be viewed. A comprehensive peace agreement between Palestine and Israel will almost certainly be a package deal in which the parties will make compromises and agree to tradeoffs among core issues, including the Old City. Under any peace agreement, if security in the Old City breaks down, the agreement itself will be at risk.

Part II: Governance structure

2.1 Overview

The Special Regime would be composed of the following central elements.

2.1.1 The Old City Board

As an integral part of their peace treaty and its related documents, the parties would create an Old City Board consisting of senior representatives of the Israeli and Palestinian governments and representatives of select other countries agreed to by the parties. The principal functions of this board would be the appointment, on behalf of the Israeli and Palestinian governments, of the Old City Special Regime's Chief Administrator and the oversight of the regime's mandate.

2.1.2 The Chief Administrator

Executive authority would be vested in a Chief Administrator, an experienced and internationally respected individual appointed by and reporting to the Old City Board. The administrator would have overall independent responsibility for assuring equity, security and specified public administration and governance functions. The requirement for fair-minded legitimacy means the Chief Administrator should *not* be a citizen of either Israel or Palestine because of the mistrust and expectations this would create. The administrator should be appointed for a fixed, renewable term.

2.1.3 Inter-authority liaison

Effective liaison between the Special Regime and national and municipal governments is fundamental to successful operation. There should be rapid access and consultation in case of crisis. Liaison offices should be established for this purpose. Senior-level liaison officers would facilitate direct and immediate communication between the Chief Administrator and the Palestinian and Israeli presidencies, prime ministries, and key ministries responsible for security and defence along with the mayors of the two capitals. Working-level liaison officers would connect the various departments of the Special Regime with their national and municipal counterparts.

2.1.4 The Old City Police Service

The Chief Administrator would have responsibility for establishing and overseeing an internationally staffed Police Service functioning under a unified command structure. The service would be headed by a Police Chief to whom all on the force will be accountable. In turn, the Police Chief would be accountable to the chief administrator, who would appoint the Police Chief with the concurrence of the Old City Board. To ensure stability, fairness and equity, the Police Service's mandate would include community policing, the maintenance of public order, counter-terrorism, Old City entry and exit control and monitoring, the enforcement of civil and criminal laws, security and intelligence. The Police Service would liaise closely with Palestinian and Israeli security services as well as with community groups functioning within the walls. The Old City would be a weapon-free zone except for the Old City police.

2.1.5 Old City legal and dispute resolution systems

The Special Regime would include a basic, independent legal system and a dispute resolution mechanism for specified issues of adjudication and resolution.

2.1.6 Transitional commissions

At the outset the Chief Administrator would establish a number of specialized transitional commissions to review more complex issues and make recommendations on frameworks for their management.

2.1.7 Consultative councils and bodies

The Chief Administrator would also work with existing and new local and international councils and bodies, representing the various stakeholders. Of critical importance would be the Advisory Religious Council, independent from the Special Regime, which would provide advice on the management of the Holy Sites and related issues. The composition of this body should take into account the views of the existing Council of Religious Institutions of the Holy Land and the heads of the various religious communities and institutions resident in the Old City.

2.2 The Old City Board

2.2.1 Definition

The Old City Board would be established jointly by the Israeli and Palestinian governments and embedded in or appended to their peace treaty. The board's primary purposes would be to appoint the Chief Administrator, maintain oversight of the mandate, and be the administrator's formal point of contact with the parties. Each party would designate a senior official or officials as its representatives on the Board.

2.2.2 Composition

The inclusion of outside members, selected by the parties, could help bridge differences and resolve issues, as distrust between Israeli and Palestinian members may be considerable. Furthermore, third parties on this board could help defuse political pressure on Palestinian and Israeli representatives and their governments, particularly from elements within their own countries including domestic constituencies. In addition, international membership would underpin the legitimacy of the Special Regime and enhance the parties' ability to raise funds and recruit technical expertise and personnel for the regime's operations. The presence of selected outside representatives is not intended to detract from the responsibility of the parties – the signatories to the peace agreement – but rather to support them. The outside members should direct their efforts to reinforcing confidence between the two sides.

The structure and composition of the board would be decided by the parties in their peace negotiations to avoid possible disagreement during implementation. Various options have been considered regarding the structure of the board. While the board should be small enough to be manageable, its size should be determined by the parties. Membership would consist of equal numbers of representatives of the Palestinian and Israeli governments and representatives of a small number of additional countries and/or institutions acceptable to them and chosen by them. Old City Board meetings would include all members; however, decisions should require the concurrence of the two parties to ensure their continuing ownership of the process.

2.2.3 Functions

The primary purpose of the board would be to provide Palestine and Israel with a mechanism to recruit and appoint the Chief Administrator, to oversee the mandate and act as the authority to which the administrator would be accountable. In addition, the board's role would include ratification of the Chief Administrator's nominee for Police Chief.

During the start-up phase, the board would be consulted regarding the structure and establishment of Special Regime institutions and the resources required for them, the mandating of any transitional commissions, the review and confirmation of recommendations issued by those commissions, and establishment of the legal framework including guidelines for heritage, archaeology and conservation, along with residency and property. Once the Special Regime is in place, the board would review and approve the annual operating budget, review the Chief Administrator's annual reports, and take the lead in fundraising to support the regime's operations. *In extremis* the board would have the power to remove and replace a Chief Administrator for reasons of misconduct or incapacity. It must be stressed, however, that the board should not be involved in the day-to-day operations of the Special Regime, as otherwise the mandate we envisage could not be fulfilled.

2.3 The Chief Administrator

2.3.1 Definition

The Special Regime model we are proposing calls for the recruitment and appointment of an internationally respected individual as Chief Administrator. The administrator would be appointed for a fixed, renewable term of five years. Any shorter period would inhibit the occupant's ability to ensure continuity in practice and policy and ultimately could affect the quality of the peace.

2.3.2 Authority

The Chief Administrator would have executive responsibility and authority, rooted in the mandate negotiated and adopted by the parties. Such authority is a requirement to enable the administrator to manage responsibilities equitably and to react effectively and rapidly to ensure the security and stability of the Old City, for the benefit of its inhabitants and visitors, as well as other stakeholders, most particularly Palestine and Israel. The Chief Administrator must be empowered to act quickly and decisively in the face of threats to public safety, to Holy Sites and heritage sites, and to the peace treaty as it applies to the Old City. In the absence of an empowered administrator, relatively small problems would have the potential to become major crises with consequences for the Old City, Israeli–Palestinian relations and beyond.

2.3.3 Responsibilities

In order to ensure that the core of the Special Regime's mandate is fulfilled, the Chief Administrator and authorized officials should possess authority over several key areas. Regarding security, these responsibilities should include monitoring and, when necessary, controlling access and egress through the gates, delivering effective security and equitable police and justice services, protecting lives, property and public order and detaining suspects and making arrests.

Regarding the key issue of heritage sites and Holy Sites, the Chief Administrator should have the authority to protect the Holy Sites and those using them, and ensure appropriate access, to license, inspect, and, if necessary, suspend archaeological excavations, and to regulate construction, repair and restoration especially where heritage buildings and structures are concerned.

Furthermore, other key areas of contention would require that the Chief Administrator have authority over planning, zoning, building permits, building and environment inspection, and land and property transfers. As well, the administrator and staff would regulate, monitor and contract for urban services and utilities.

2.3.4 Reporting relationship

During the initial period, it would be useful for the Chief Administrator and the board to meet frequently to discuss the setting up of the Special Regime's institutions. Once the Special Regime is up and running, the chief administrator should meet formally with the Old City Board on an annual basis and consult with the board as required on issues the administrator believes advisable. The chief administrator should submit an annual formal report that includes an external financial audit.

2.3.5 Personal and professional qualities

To satisfy the requirements for transparency, impartiality, accountability and sustainability in this new governance arrangement, it will be important that the Chief Administrator establish legitimacy by demonstrating exemplary values and ethics, proven leadership skills, excellent interpersonal abilities, respect for diversity, and sensitivity to real or perceived conflicts of interest. Strong management and communication skills and financial prudence would be essential. Given the small size of the Old City, the Chief Administrator's capacity to establish cordial personal relationships with residents is critical. The administrator should reside within the walls and be a visible presence in the Old City community. To assure the perception and reality of impartiality, the administrator should not be either Palestinian or Israeli; distrust is too deep to permit mutual confidence in equitable governance.

2.4 The liaison function and consultative bodies

2.4.1 Rationale

The Chief Administrator and staff should coordinate as appropriate with Israeli and Palestinian national authorities and with authorities from the Yerushalayim and Al-Quds municipalities. Certain issues, such as protection of Holy Sites, would fall under the authority of the Special Regime, in close consultation with the Advisory Religious Council. Other functions, such as the provision of health and education services to inhabitants, would fall wholly under national or municipal authorities. There would be other issues involving, for example, planning and zoning standards or common municipal utilities and infrastructure, where the interests of all would be served by cooperation and coordination. It is important that such communication not impede but rather facilitate the resolution of issues, the priority being to provide equitable governance.

2.4.2 Liaison offices

Each of the parties should establish liaison offices with required staff to act as links between the Chief Administrator and the Special Regime with the national and municipal governments. This would ensure rapid access for the Chief Administrator and staff to authorities in case of a crisis as well as during the normal course of events. Similar liaison would be required with the municipalities over aspects of zoning, planning, property and infrastructure, although these functions most often should be at the technical level. There should be close liaison and cooperation among the respective security and Police Services.

2.5 Legal provisions

The exploration of the legal aspects of the Special Regime has been particularly challenging. One option is presented here but more work should be done to yield a design that reflects more fully the views of the number of legal experts whose opinions were sought in the course of the present exercise.

The underlying principle guiding this present proposal is that the Special Regime should function with as few changes as possible to current practice. Rather than create a comprehensive legal system that would address every aspect of the Old City residents' lives, the jurisdiction of the Special Regime should, in our view, be limited to matters that concern the unique or essential characteristics of the Old City fabric, particularly those that are issues of friction and contention.

Legal provisions that would be developed would therefore address such administrative matters as archaeological excavation and heritage protection, planning, zoning, and construction permits, whereas education, family law and health would fall under the respective municipal jurisdictions of Yerushalayim and Al-Quds or the national jurisdictions of Israel and Palestine as appropriate. The Special Regime would also have to create the necessary legal mechanisms that would guarantee the full and equitable application of the law.

In our view, a special transitional law reform commission should be created for these purposes. This commission, appointed by the Chief Administrator, would establish the criteria that would serve to determine jurisdiction and law under the Special Regime, as well as the legal mechanisms needed to implement the new system. It would be composed of a number of Israeli, Palestinian and international legal experts.

2.5.1 Application of law

In most cases, Palestinian and Israeli national courts would enjoy *ratione personae* jurisdiction, i.e. personal jurisdiction. Accordingly, Israeli law would apply to Israeli nationals residing in the Old City, while Palestinian law would apply to Palestinian nationals. With the exception of crimes listed below such as inter-ethnic crimes or 'crimes against the Old City', an Israeli who committed a crime in the Old City would be brought to court in Israel and a Palestinian in Palestine.

The Transitional Law Reform Commission would have to define those exceptional matters over which the Special Regime would enjoy *ratione materiae* jurisdiction, i.e. subject-matter jurisdiction. Special regime courts of special jurisdiction would be created to this end and would apply Special Regime law, as opposed to Israeli or Palestinian national law.

Special regime law would be necessary to resolve cases involving 'crimes against the Old City' (see below), regulatory and administrative disputes arising as a result of the application of the regime, and labour disputes arising between the Special Regime and its employees. Both a Special Regime Criminal Court and a Special Regime Administrative Court should therefore be established. The decisions pronounced by these courts would be subject to appeal to a Special Regime Court of Appeals that would have both a criminal and an administrative section.

One of the main priorities of the Special Regime would be to establish clear jurisdiction regarding the above-mentioned subject matters to which the parties would agree. However, due to the inherent sensitivity of many of those matters, conflicts of jurisdiction between Special Regime courts and Palestinian or Israeli national courts would inevitably arise. For example, both courts could consider themselves competent to hear the same case, or either of the two could consider the other not to be competent.

Consequently, it would almost certainly be necessary to create a competence tribunal that would pronounce on these conflicts as well as on inter-ethnic crimes. The competence tribunal could be composed of five judges or legal experts (two Israelis, two Palestinians and an international) who would apply international private law norms in order to determine jurisdiction. We recommend that the decisions of the tribunal be adopted by qualified majority voting, i.e. four out of five votes, under the condition that the vote of the international judge be one of the four votes required. This modality has the advantage of avoiding a decision without the consent of at least one Palestinian and one Israeli judge. The tribunal's decisions would not be appealable.

The commission should also develop dispute resolution mechanisms that could be resorted to voluntarily. These mechanisms should comply with international mediation and arbitration norms and could be used when the dispute is civil or commercial in nature, or when it concerns the jurisdiction of the Special Regime.

2.5.2 Ratione materiae *jurisdiction and Special Regime courts of special jurisdiction*

The Special Regime would have full or partial jurisdiction in the following matters.

a. Crimes committed against the place The transitional law reform commission would establish an exhaustive list of crimes that would be defined as 'crimes committed against the place'. Cases involving such crimes would be heard by the Special Regime Criminal Court. The commission would determine both the procedural and substantive rules that the court would have to adhere to. In case of a conflict of jurisdiction arising between the Special Regime Criminal Court and an Israeli or Palestinian national court, the competence tribunal would determine which has jurisdiction.

b. Inter-ethnic crimes Cases involving inter-ethnic crimes would be referred to the competence tribunal, which would determine jurisdiction according to international private law norms. We suggest that inter-ethnic crimes of a particularly sensitive nature be defined as 'crimes committed against the place' (e.g. attacks against a specific religious or ethnic group of the Old City) and therefore subject to the jurisdiction of the Special Regime Criminal Court.

c. Crimes committed by third country nationals Crimes committed by third country nationals would be subjected to the law of the gate of entry regardless of the nationality of the victim. Accordingly, a third country national who entered the Old City via Israel and subsequently committed a crime would be subject to Israeli law and such a case would be heard by an Israeli court. However, if the victim of a crime is Israeli and the 'gate of entry' Palestinian, or vice versa, the question of the application of the law of the 'gate of entry' despite the nationality of the victim should be studied further.

Crimes committed by third country nationals against the place would constitute an exception to the application of the 'gate of entry' law and would fall under the jurisdiction of the Special Regime Criminal Court, which has *ratione materiae* jurisdiction.

d. Municipal and local matters Matters such as constructing a building in the Old City without a license or excavating without a permit would fall under the jurisdiction of the Special Regime courts. Parking tickets, local taxes and the sale of prohibited materials or other issues related to public health in the Special Regime area should also fall under Special Regime court jurisdiction.

e. Civil and commercial disputes Except for those cases where those involved in a civil or commercial dispute decide to resort to one of the dispute resolution mechanisms created by the Special Regime, we recommend that civil and commercial matters continue to fall under the jurisdiction of Israeli and Palestinian courts. In case of a conflict of jurisdiction, the competence tribunal would determine jurisdiction.

f. Property related disputes As we suggest in section 3.4.2b, a transitional commission composed of Palestinian, Israeli and international experts could be established to design a framework to oversee and deal with property transactions and disputes. Due to the complexity of these issues, we recommend that, at least initially, the responsibility for dealing with property transactions and disputes rest with an expert committee established by and responsible to the Chief Administrator.

g. *Disputes related to the application of the Special Regime* Disputes related to the application of the Special Regime would be administrative in nature, involving the Special Regime on the one hand and the residents of the Old City on the other (e.g. planning or zoning decisions), or arising between the Special Regime and its employees (e.g. application of a Special Regime employment contract).

The Special Regime Administrative Court would have *ratione materiae* jurisdiction over those administrative matters that would be defined as falling under the jurisdiction of the regime (e.g. planning and zoning regulation). The commission would determine what regulatory law norms would apply to these cases. In addition, the administrative court would have *ratione materiae* jurisdiction over labour-related disputes arising between the Special Regime and its employees. The commission would have to develop separate labour laws that the court would apply.

2.5.3 Appeal to the Special Regime Court of Appeals

The decisions pronounced by the different Special Regime courts would be subject to appeal to the Special Regime Court of Appeals. This court would have both a criminal and an administrative section and would be composed of five judges (two Israelis, two Palestinians, and an international) who would resort to qualified majority voting.

2.5.4 Dispute resolution mechanisms

The main advantage of dispute resolution mechanisms in a context of mutual mistrust between the two parties to the peace treaty – as well as with regard to misunderstandings and distrust among local citizens and regime employees, on the one hand, and the Special Regime, on the other hand – is that they allow for a free choice of law regarding both procedure and substance, in addition to the free designation of the arbiters or mediators. This flexibility is particularly attractive for parties to a civil or commercial dispute, but could be particularly useful in the resolution of disputes related to the application of the Special Regime, where efficient governance requires fast solutions.

The commission would therefore develop dispute resolution mechanisms that those involved in a dispute could voluntarily decide to resort to when the dispute is civil or commercial in nature, or when it concerns the application of the special regime.

2.6 The transition from status quo to Special Regime

The transition from existing arrangements will pose considerable challenges, requiring careful planning and preparation. The actual transfer would occur in phases while establishing confidence, on both sides, in the Special Regime's efficacy and purpose. Suspicion and distrust will be high after the many failures of phased approaches in the past. Many of the steps suggested below should therefore proceed concurrently so that the concerns of all sides can be addressed in a balanced and effective manner. Given other instances, such as the Israel–Egypt peace treaty that provided for full implementation within three years of signature, there needs to be adequate time to arrange these matters.

Below is an illustrative list of steps required:

- Agreement between Israel and Palestine to establish the Special Regime.
- Negotiation of the terms of the mandate.
- Issuance of the mandate and establishment of the Old City Board.
- Appointment of the Chief Administrator.
- Initial mobilization of international political, technical and financial support.
- Creation of preliminary rules and guidelines to be effective as of the dates of the appointments to the Old City Board and of the Chief Administrator, allowing for a reasonable interval to create more comprehensive provisions.
- Establishment of bilateral and multilateral linkages between the Special Regime and the Old City's religious communities and custodians of the Holy Sites, including the Advisory Religious Council.
- Establishment of transitional commissions to identify options, standards, and regulations for the management of complex issues.
- Consultations with Old City community leaders regarding preferred methods of consultation with the Special Regime and the Chief Administrator.
- Establishment of the Special Regime's infrastructure including the Police Service.
- Establishment of a coordinated process of transition from Israeli control to Special Regime control, particularly regarding security and access.
- Establishment of preliminary legal and dispute resolution mechanisms.
- Decisions on the recommendations of the transitional commissions.
- Formalization of coordination and liaison mechanisms with national governments and municipalities.

In marshalling international funding and expertise and in the interests of sustainability, it is important to recognize that at present conditions of parity do not exist between the parties. There is no Al-Quds municipality and the body of trained Palestinian urban planners, city administrators and the like is small. Therefore, particular consideration should be given to international support for capacity building on the Palestinian side so that the Palestinian national government and the Al-Quds municipality develop the abilities necessary *inter alia* to support and participate in the Special Regime.

Part III: Functions of the Special Regime

3.1 Security and law enforcement

3.1.1 The Jerusalem Old City Initiative Security Assessment

The Security Working Group of the Jerusalem Old City Initiative, working with Palestinian and Israeli experts, developed 'The Jerusalem Old City Initiative Security Assessment', containing concepts, ideas and detailed proposals for a comprehensive security system. The security arrangements described in that assessment are designed to ensure freedom of worship, dignity, access and equity. This point cannot be emphasized enough, given the experience of some who view the word 'security' as indicative of repression rather than as a service for the community. While no arrangement can absolutely guarantee security, a sound system is achievable through coordination and the commitment of Israeli and Palestinian authorities.

3.1.2 The Old City Police Service

The security system should take the form of an Old City Police Service along the following model:

a. Structure and authority The Police Service should be headed by a Chief of Police appointed by the Chief Administrator, with agreement of the Old City Board. The authority of the Police Service should be rooted in the mandate the parties entrust to the Chief Administrator. Under this arrangement, the Old City would be a weapon-free zone, except for the armed elements of the police. A Police Board would hold the chief and the Police Service publicly to account. Public meetings and independent assessments including public opinion surveys would assist the Police Board in monitoring Police Service performance against public expectations and an annual policing plan.

b. General responsibilities The Police Service would work to ensure the safety and security of the Old City, including routine policing, entry and exit monitoring and control, and public-order rapid response. It would be responsible for enforcing laws, ordinances and directives of the Old City Special Regime. Neighbourhood policing would be a major function, with neighbourhood partnerships an important element. The Police Service would need a public-order rapid deployment unit to deal directly and quickly with disturbances.

c. Resources An effective and respected Police Service would require significant resources, financial, personnel, training and equipment from the international community.

d. Composition The Police Service would, at least initially, include only international officers, given the lack of trust that exists between the parties. However, officers seconded from Palestine and Israel, serving as community relations officers, would perform a variety of functions to assist third party police officers in specific neighbourhoods. They would initiate the active development of community partnerships at the neighbourhood level. This could include community meetings, the assessment of community needs and wants, and advice on local contacts and partners. As trust develops, regular officers could be recruited from the parties, at the discretion of the Chief of Police and the Chief Administrator.

e. Area of operation The Police Service's area of operation would be within the confines of the Old City's walls, with two exceptions:

- The police would need to operate entry and exit facilities, bearing in mind that, due to space limitations at the gates, some facilities would need to be at least partially located outside the walls.
- There would have to be periodic and unchallenged police inspections of the exterior of the walls.

f. Special responsibilities The Police Service would have particular responsibility for the protection of the Holy Sites and for the safety of pilgrims, worshippers and visitors. The Chief Administrator and the Chief of Police would work closely with the parties, the religious communities and institutions, and the Advisory Religious Council to establish measures to guarantee appropriate access while maintaining public safety and order. They would also work closely with these groups to define the conditions under which armed Police Service units would have the authority to enter Holy Sites with care, respect and appropriate sensitivity. In a broad sense, while the Special Regime would have authority over all institutions in the Old City, regarding the Holy Sites its focus would be to support the religious authorities and custodians as they meet their responsibilities.

Physical security of the Holy Sites would begin at the gates to the Old City. The police role in monitoring and controlling access at the gates *inter alia* needs to be understood in that context. The degree of control would depend on the Special Regime's current threat assessment and would be designed to be minimally intrusive.

Given the centrality of Holy Sites and the issue of access to them by both locals and third country nationals, a special Holy Sites Police Unit seems essential. The unit would maintain close relations with the religious authorities at key sites and with the Advisory Religious Council. The composition of this unit and the special training of its members require careful consideration. We do not envision that Police Service offices would normally be stationed within the Holy Sites.

g. Criminal operations and intelligence units The Police Service would need Criminal Operations and Intelligence Units. Both would work closely with Israeli and Palestinian police and intelligence services. Both would include seconded Palestinian and Israeli intelligence officers working in the Old City Police Service Headquarters in order to facilitate effective communication and information sharing. The Police Service would maintain ties with the relevant agencies of other countries and with INTERPOL, and would have its own training, logistics and administrative capabilities.

h. Maintaining public order The Police Service should also have capabilities for responding on short notice to crises and would maintain a public-order rapid deployment unit. Various alternatives exist for reinforcing this unit and are explored in greater detail in the Security Working Group's Security Assessment.

i. Residency in the Old City For reasons of security, special residency cards may be required that, under specific situations, would be verified by the Old City Police Service, especially at points of access.

3.2 Holy sites

3.2.1 The problem of defining Holy Sites

A key to the Special Regime's success would be its ability to protect, preserve and maintain the Holy Sites, manage heritage preservation and archaeological activity, and provide security and safety for visitors and residents. Given conflicting claims, the Special Regime should adhere to a definition of Holy Sites that is clear and flexible.

Our commissioned reports have confirmed previous research demonstrating that simply defining a Holy Site can be contentious. Many sites are defined as holy by one community but not recognized as such by others or by secular authorities. Furthermore, the number of sites identified by the various communities as holy to them has proliferated over time, at least partially in response to political developments. Today, estimates of the number of sites in the Old City claimed as holy by one or more communities range from 225 to more than 300.

3.2.2 A functional approach to the Holy Sites

The Special Regime should consider Holy Sites in terms of security, heritage and archaeological significance. Rather than entering into the debate of which site is deemed holy by which community and how that designation is justified, the Chief Administrator and the Chief of Police should view their responsibilities through the lense of public order and safety. Sites that are contested or most frequented would be the sites of particular concern; less contested or less frequented sites would normally require less focus.

3.2.3 Responsibilities toward the Holy Sites

The challenges to meeting the Special Regime's mandate regarding Holy Sites include the following.

a. Ensuring respect for sanctity Maintaining the sanctity of all sites deemed holy by particular faiths involves ensuring that whoever gains access follows established customs with regard to decorum and treats the site with the respect its custodians require. This includes ensuring that any excavation, maintenance, conservation or repair undertaken in or adjacent to these sites is carried out after consultation and in accordance with international benchmarks. It also means managing, through careful coordination and exercise of authority, activities or forms of worship by one community that may be perceived by another as impinging on the sanctity of the site or the rights of other worshippers.

b. Protecting access Access routes must be open to worshippers and visitors who must not face intimidation or harassment. This entails establishing effective mechanisms to accommodate rituals, pilgrimages and processions to and from the sites on particular festival days. It also requires the realization that there is often a tension between access and sanctity in the minds of believers, and that access is not an absolute right. There are times, places, circumstances, and occasions where public order and safety may require restrictions, as is already the case at certain Holy Sites elsewhere. This would be a matter for close consultation between the Special Regime and custodians of Holy Sites.

c. Preserving the status quo Technically, the term '*status quo*' refers only to the arrangements established by the Ottoman authorities in the eighteenth and nineteenth centuries.[4] Because of the long history of disputes over the control and use of the Christian Holy Sites, a series of understandings evolved (or were imposed) to regulate use, access and decorum. This *status quo* was recognized in diplomatic agreements and was enshrined in the law of British Mandate Palestine after World War I. However, the term is often used more loosely to describe the entire body of rules, customary practices and understandings that govern issues of access and usage with regard to the Holy Sites including those sacred to Jews and Muslims. Taken together, this body of arrangements and understandings permits the differing faiths and religious communities to operate in the Old City and its Holy Sites with a significant degree of order and predictability. The role of the Special Regime should be to ensure that these arrangements are respected and equitably administered. Any evolution of their scope and form over time must be peaceful and respectful of differing interests.

d. Building tolerance and trust It will be important to pre-empt trends towards intolerance and radicalization by fostering a culture of respect for the three faiths and the development of the Holy Sites as inspirational symbols of faith, spiritual growth and religious harmony.

3.2.4 The relationship between the Special Regime and religious communities

In exercising executive authority, the Chief Administrator would liaise actively with a range of religious and secular authorities. Supporting the chief administrator in delivering these core mandate functions would be the Old City police

service along with a Religious Affairs Department and a Heritage and Archaeology Department integral to the regime. These departments would be
responsible for liaison with:

- the Advisory Religious Council,
- the relevant ministries in the Palestinian and Israeli governments and in the
  municipalities of Al-Quds and Yerushalayim on matters of national or municipal
  relevance,
- the Old City's religious communities including the formal custodians of the
  Holy Sites, and
- international religious and cultural heritage organizations.

3.2.5 The management and security of Holy Sites and heritage

The model we propose has five components for the management and security of
the Holy Sites and heritage, which are described here.

   a. The Advisory Religious Council The religious communities and their leaderships
have a legitimate interest and concern about how a Holy Site's management and
security framework would be established and operated. The existing coordination
mechanism for the three religions is the Council of Religious Institutions of the
Holy Land. To ensure inclusiveness, we anticipate that this council would play an
important role in establishing the Advisory Religious Council as a vehicle for
communication and coordination.

   However, to avoid deadlock and politicization of every issue, decision-making
authority would rest with the Special Regime. The Chief Administrator and the
relevant departments of the administration would inform and consult with the Advisory Religious Council on all matters pertaining to the religious affairs in the Old
City, including special planning related to holidays and festivals. The council
would also participate in training for the Holy Sites Police Unit and would act in
an advisory capacity to the police force. The council would also liaise with national
and international religious and cultural heritage organizations over the development
of the Old City as a place for spiritual growth and religious harmony.

   b. The existing custodians of the sites Holy sites should remain under the authority
of their existing custodians and their duly appointed successors. The internal management of Holy Sites should remain the exclusive province of those custodians
and the communities they represent and serve.

   c. Relevant departments within the Special Regime The Chief Administrator would
be responsible for facilitating respect for the sanctity of the Holy Sites, including,
by supporting the sites' custodians. The Chief Administrator would also ensure
access to the sites, to the satisfaction of the religious communities subject to the
requirements of public order.

   The relevant departments within the Special Regime, in particular the Religious
Affairs Department and the heritage and archaeology department, would be the
primary instruments through which the Chief Administrator would liaise with

the custodians and the Advisory Religious Council to monitor whether this responsibility is being met. While the Chief Administrator would be the primary point of contact with the Advisory Religious Council, the Religious Affairs Department would interact directly with the appropriate religious institutions and their respective Holy Sites custodians at the working level. The Religious Affairs Department would also liaise with counterpart organizations within national governments as appropriate.

d. *The Old City Police Service* The Police Service would be responsible for protection, as needed of the Holy Sites and for ensuring the access and safety of pilgrims, worshippers and visitors. A unit within the Police Service would be dedicated exclusively to the Holy Sites.

e. *Mechanisms for special issues* Our research has identified five areas where enhanced coordination on Holy Sites and religious activity would be desirable:

- the exchange of information on religious activities,
- the improvement of the aesthetics of Holy Sites and religious properties in the Old City,
- the promotion of tolerance and respect,
- the coordination of heritage maintenance and archaeological activity, and
- the facilitation of dispute resolution between religious communities.

3.3 Heritage and archaeology

In Jerusalem, the past is often recruited into the service of conflicting political agendas. Excavations and maintenance of archaeological sites can represent real or perceived attacks on the sanctity of another community's heritage and religious and national patrimony. Such situations can rapidly deteriorate. The responsibilities and activities of the Special Regime must be developed accordingly.

3.3.1 Responsibilities of the Special Regime

a. *Managing archaeology* To manage points of friction, the Chief Administrator will need a professional Heritage and Archaeology Department that would work initially with a heritage and archaeology transitional commission, staffed by Palestinian, Israeli and international professionals. The commission would establish a framework of rules and best practices to guide the activities of the Chief Administrator and staff. The Heritage and Archaeology Department would inventory and review ongoing archaeological and heritage projects and practices. It would be responsible for establishing priorities, procedures, and criteria to ensure that the evaluation, licensing and monitoring of projects meet UNESCO standards including the relevant Hague and New Delhi conventions. This department would develop institutional relationships with Israeli and Palestinian professional and academic institutions and with UNESCO and other relevant international bodies.

b. Preserving heritage In recent years there have been controversies resulting from damage to various ancient structures as a result of climatic, environmental and human factors. In the context of a peace agreement and the urban development and increased pilgrimage and tourism that will follow, the need to monitor the stability and safety of the walls and buildings takes on a new urgency. Working with the religious institutions, property owners, heritage organizations, UNESCO, and other appropriate bodies, the heritage and archaeology department should ensure regular inspection of structures. These inspections should be designed to detect and address maintenance, conservation and safety problems and to identify sources of expertise and appropriate technical assistance. The department should also undertake to ensure that UNESCO be consulted and involved where appropriate. It should ensure that any material alteration at or adjacent to Holy Sites takes place only after extensive consultations and conforms fully to international norms.

c. Authority The Chief Administrator should have the authority to license archaeological excavations and the repair, renovation, or reconstruction of archaeological and heritage sites. The administrator should have the authority to suspend or terminate such activities if they fail to comply with appropriate norms or when, in the judgement of the Chief Administrator, they constitute an actual or potential threat to public order and inter-communal harmony. These provisions include tunnelling of whatever sort.

3.4 Planning, property and infrastructure

3.4.1 Planning and zoning

a. The current situation Our research suggests that the complex political struggle for control over the Old City, the unequal application of laws and regulations, and chronic overcrowding, especially in the Muslim quarter, have resulted in *ad hoc* and extra-legal construction, degradation of ancient buildings and structures, and overtaxing of inadequate infrastructure, not to mention destructive pressures on families and communities. In many cases it is difficult, if not impossible, to provide definitive evidence of property ownership. Many holdings over 200 years old have neither title nor deed and are passed on without documentation. Other property is divided among various parties informally. This has significant implications for property ownership, zoning, planning, public health, taxation and the environment.

b. The responsibilities of the Special Regime The administration should create and implement a comprehensive urban development and conservation plan that strikes a balance between meeting residents' needs and improving living conditions, addressing environmental concerns, maintaining an appropriate commercial environment, preserving heritage and accommodating pilgrims, tourists and other visitors.

c. The Old City Planning and Zoning Department The Chief Administrator would need a small, highly professional, multi-disciplined planning and zoning department, bringing together qualified international, Israeli and Palestinian city-planning experts under an international chief planner. This department's priority would be to create an urban development plan for the Old City. The planning process would require substantive consultations with the relevant units of the adjacent municipalities, and also with the inhabitants, the major property owners, including the religious institutions, and the business community. The planners will also need to create institutional linkages with UNESCO and organizations such as the International Council on Monuments and Sites (ICOMOS) to ensure that international standards are applied.

d. Mandate of the Special Regime's Planning and Zoning Department This Planning and Zoning Department should take the lead in creating an urban development plan wherever possible in coordination with the planning and development programmes of Al-Quds and Yerushalayim. It would assume responsibility for the issuance of building permits, and no building or renovation would be allowed without a permit from the Chief Administrator. The Special Regime would also take responsibility for the enforcement of zoning, heritage, construction, environmental and safety standards, which would be carried out by a small, empowered, internationally supervised team of inspectors.

3.4.2 Land and property registry

a. The current situation The Old City has no independent land or property registry recognized by the parties. The majority of buildings have neither title nor deeds. In many instances, this has not prevented normal patterns of property purchase or rental, or the resolution of disputes and claims in the courts. There are, however, cases of claims that derive from or affect the national conflict, which will have to be addressed directly by the Special Regime.

b. The role of the Special Regime At first glance it would seem sensible to remedy what appears to be a chaotic situation by creating a land registry. Those of our advisors with the most direct experience in property issues have advised strongly against this. Since, however, land and property issues are among the most complicated and contentious matters and since a perception of corruption in property transfers exists among some, we do not believe the matter should be allowed to lie. Rather, we advise that during the initial phase of the Special Regime there should be no property or land purchase, change of usage, or transfer of ownership allowed without approval from an expert committee established by and responsible to the Chief Administrator. This would serve to regulate and legitimize property transfers. It would, moreover, be a means of maintaining order and controlling politically motivated property changes that could threaten stability, while still allowing flexibility. This subject requires further study and is a case where the administrator may wish to establish a transitional commission to study the situation and recommend a set of rules for regulating future property transaction.

3.4.3 Utilities and infrastructure

a. The current situation The provision of services and maintenance of basic infrastructure are uneven and inconsistent, and are provided by a mix of private and public entities. In general, the Jewish Quarter enjoys much higher standards in terms of services provided by the existing municipality, compared to the rest of the Old City. The need for the creation of a more equitable situation is self-evident in consolidating a peace agreement between a Palestinian state and Israel and in enhancing the Old City as an asset to both countries and communities.

- Services provided by the municipality: The current Jerusalem Municipality is responsible for sanitation, including street cleaning and trash removal (usually through private contractors), the water network and the sewage system. In general the quality of water and sewage service to the Jewish Quarter is of a high standard. Elsewhere, lack of investment in infrastructure, poverty and overcrowding result in considerable leakage and unknown damage to the ancient layers below the streets. Access to safe water for domestic uses is a serious issue. Our research indicates that the sewage system, which connects to the current municipal system, needs major renovation. The rainwater drainage system covers only parts of the Old City and the resultant run-off is responsible for serious structural problems. The current municipality maintains, cleans and repairs the parts of the road system that are used by vehicular traffic and walkways that are used by the public.
- Services provided by the private sector: Currently the Jerusalem Municipality plays no direct role in the provision of electricity in the Old City. Rather, electricity is provided by two private companies: JEDCO, which serves the Muslim, Christian and Armenian quarters, and IEC, which serves the Jewish Quarter. JEDCO's infrastructure is said to be in serious need of upgrading. It has an inadequate number of transformers. The public lighting system is substandard. Telephone, television and internet services to the entire Old City are provided by the Israeli firm Bezeq.

b. The responsibilities of the Special Regime The chief administrator would establish a utilities department, responsible for issuing contracts or licences, as appropriate, to providers of services to the Old City, and would seek to privatize service provision wherever feasible. This could include contracts for street cleaning and trash removal, electricity, telephone and cable/internet services. In addition, the utilities department of the Special Regime would be responsible for ensuring that contractors and licensees meet their obligations through monitoring, inspections, and public consultations. The department would also need the authority to sanction service providers who fail to meet agreed standards or contractual commitments.

c. Sharing responsibility for infrastructure Infrastructure, including roads and water as well as sewage and rainwater drainage systems, requires considerable upgrading and ongoing maintenance and repair. The question of formal responsibility over this infrastructure is a difficult one. The Special Regime would need a considerable source of funding to assume such responsibility over the long term and would need the authority to float bonds to finance infrastructure improvements.

d. Coordinating mechanism If the decision is made to create two capitals out of the present city of Jerusalem, there may be a requirement to create an effective coordination mechanism to plan and oversee common utility, service and infrastructure projects and processes, not to mention the economically critical issue of tourism planning, promotion and services.

Part IV: Finance and economics

4.1 Finance

A model must be developed that recognizes that the Special Regime will never have sufficient resources to fulfil its mandate through the Old City's own resources, even though the Old City Special Regime would have some fundraising capacity through taxation, fees and bonds. Good governance will require substantial support from Israel and Palestine, as well as the international community.

Support from the global community is all the more imperative, given the Old City's meaning and symbolism worldwide and the threat to the Israeli–Palestinian treaty that would ensue were the Special Regime to fail in discharging its mandate. In the wake of an agreement by Palestine and Israel to create the Special Regime, the Old City Board would need to organize a donors' group to ensure necessary resources and funds.

4.2 Economics[5]

General estimates indicate that, as a result of a peace agreement that includes the recognition of two capitals in Jerusalem by the international community and the implementation of a Special Regime, the situation would yield more than 9,000 new jobs in the Jerusalem conurbation. This situation would result from increased international involvement and a stable environment in Jerusalem. Approximately two-thirds of these jobs would, we estimate, go to local residents, with each new job in turn fuelling the local economy through the consumption of goods and services. Using a multiplier of two, more than 18,000 jobs would be created for Jerusalemites in the service sector. The total number of new jobs for the local population would be close to 24,000, an approximate 10 per cent increase in employment for the conurbation. New jobs as a result of construction have not been factored into these estimates, since a building boom would be less predictable in duration. Specifics of anticipated growth include the following.

4.2.1 Diplomatic representation

The economic impact of the movement of 85 existing embassies from Tel Aviv to Jerusalem, establishment of full embassies to the new Palestinian state in Al-Quds and the opening of new embassies from Arab and Islamic countries in the wake of a peace agreement could result in as many as 150 embassies, 3,000 foreign diplomats and dependants, and as many as 5,000 new jobs for Jerusalemites.

4.2.2 Old City administration

The establishment of a Special Regime would involve the arrival of several hundred expatriates, a concomitant requirement for accommodation, goods and services, and as many as 500 new jobs for local inhabitants.

4.2.3 Tourism

Our research points to the arrival of between 3 and 5 million tourists in the Holy Land annually once peace is established. The Israeli Ministry of Tourism calculates that each additional million tourists create 45,000 new jobs. If the 5 million figure is realized the Jerusalem share could be as high as 28,125 new jobs.

4.2.4 Impact

The growth that can be anticipated with the signing of a peace agreement would include several essential improvements – to the existing and planned road and rail systems, to infrastructure in East Jerusalem and the Arab sections of the Old City, and to effluent management systems – as well as expansion of the water distribution system and the electrical grid. Taken together these pose serious planning and environmental challenges, which would require the creation of new coordinating mechanisms between the states and the municipalities. They also would demand serious investment and create additional employment.

Part V: Conclusion

Typically analysis of possible solutions to the conflict over the Old City of Jerusalem looks at three options: 1) sovereignty and control in the hands of Israel, 2) sovereignty and control in the hands of the new Palestinian state, and 3) the division of the Old City between the parties as, for example, in the Clinton parameters and the Geneva Accord. Options 1 and 2, where sovereignty and control are exclusively in the hands of one party or the other, will not result in a peace agreement. Option 3, a simple division of sovereignty within the Old City, given the unhappy history of cooperative efforts by the parties and the legacy of a century of conflict, would, for the foreseeable future be untenable as well.

Recognizing that it is very difficult for governments to undertake this kind of study, this discussion document represents our best attempt to present a 'fourth option' for the Old City, neither control by one party at the expense of the other nor split governance. While we are convinced the prospects for peace and reconciliation exist and can be realized with good will and hard work, we do not believe that the Old City can be governed effectively by the two parties alone until trust builds over time with the successful implementation of the peace treaty. When that time comes – earlier or later – we believe that a third party role, scaled to the tasks it is assigned, would still be needed to assist the Parties to implement their agreement.

The area within the walls goes to the heart of the Muslim, Jewish and Christian belief systems. An atmosphere of systemic distrust has dominated issues, as in the whole of the Middle East conflict. The significant difference in the walled city is that sacred space is indivisible, whereas territories that have been the subject of dispute between Israel and Egypt, or between Israel and Jordan, for example, are divisible – and have been divided – by borders. Elements among the parties can therefore be expected to expend considerable effort to profit at the expense of the rights and needs of the other for some time after a peace agreement is signed.

The Old City is seen by each national community as the centre of its identity. We recognize that to invite outside participation in governance within the walls requires great trust and flexibility. We fear that without such a fair-minded governance mechanism, the Old City would soon be at risk and any peace agreement with it.

We also realize that many on both sides would prefer a string of joint consultative mechanisms to protect and maximize their interests as issues arise. This, as well, we understand. We believe, however, that in the absence of a clear-cut decision-making authority, where responsibility is recognized and untrammelled, no system will be sustainable and no comprehensive peace achievable. For this reason, we put forward what we believe to be a creative option for both sides and for those across the world interested in stability and tolerance in this most sensitive of places.

It should be reiterated that while we consider the option of the Special Regime is best taken in its entirety, this proposal is designed in such a way that it can be used in whole or in part. Rather than an explicit blueprint, it offers a model that can be followed or adjusted as seen fit by the parties.

Further study is required regarding the complex issues of property ownership and the legal system; however, we believe this document provides the details and options under such a model, especially regarding critical matters of security, the Holy Sites, and the overall governance structure of an Old City Special Regime.

Annex A: Organization Charts

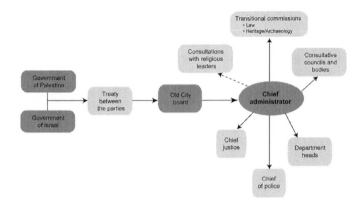

FIGURE 8.1 Establishing the Old City Special Regime (Process)

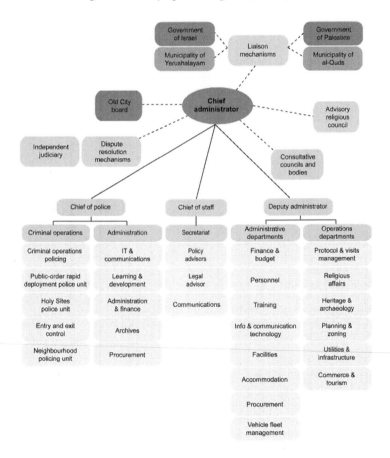

FIGURE 8.2 Final state detailed (structure)

Notes

1 Old City Holy Sites are often referred to interchangeably by their Arabic, Hebrew, or English names. We recognize the sensitivities inherent in using one term over another, and must stress that the usage in this document in no way represents a bias. We have thus chosen the terms most common in academic literature. We elected to use the term 'Western Wall' to refer to the Kotel (Hebrew)/Al Buraq (Arabic), and the terms 'Temple Mount' and 'Haram al-Sharif' (Arabic) instead of the lesser known term 'Har ha-Bayit' (Hebrew).
2 'Internationalization', to us, implies that the Old City would be governed by an external authority under an international jurisdiction, for example a commissioner appointed by and accountable to the United Nations or some other outside body. The *corpus separatum* designed under UN auspices in 1948 to exclude Jerusalem from both Israeli and Arab control, called for in Resolution 194 of the United Nations General Assembly, is an example of an internationalization model.
3 We recognize, of course, that a number of foreigners have lived, do live, and will continue to live in the Old City. Special arrangements already exist for them. Responsibility for them would be transferred to the Special Regime.
4 Scholars consulted during our research prefer to confine the term '*status quo*' to its original meaning and utilize the term '*modus vivendi*' or '*modus operandi*' to describe the contemporary body of rules, including those put in place under Israeli rule since 1967, and which apply today to the Holy Sites, Christian, Jewish and Muslim. Some scholars apply *modus operandi* only to the rules that apply to Muslim and Jewish sites.
5 Economic issues have been studied in detail by Joseph B. Glass and Rassem Khamaisi in the 'Report on the Socio-Economic Conditions in the Old City of Jerusalem'. We have based our preliminary estimates on the results of this work.

References

Unpublished Papers, Jerusalem Old City Initiative, Windsor, ON, Canada

Al Mustakbal Foundation. Old City Governance, 2007.

Bell, M., M. Molloy, J. Bell and M. Evans. *The Jerusalem Old City Initiative Discussion Document: New Directions for Deliberation and Dialogue*, 2005.

Bell, M., M. Molloy, J. Bell, D. Cameron and J. White. *The Jerusalem Old City Initiative Guiding Assumptions*. Rolling Draft, 2005 updated in 2007 and 2008.

Berlinquette, R., J. de Chastelain and A. Hughes. *The Jerusalem Old City Initiative–Security Assessment*, 2007.

Breger, M. *International Law of Holy Places in the 'Old City' of Jerusalem*, 2008.

Dajani, Y. and J. al-Bakri. *Security Arrangements in the Old City of Jerusalem*, 2007.

Dumper, M. *International Norms and the Preservation of Culture and Heritage in the Old City of Jerusalem: A Study of the Role of UNESCO*, 2008.

Dumper, M. *Jerusalem Old City Initiative: A Security and Management Framework for the Holy Sites of the Old City*, 2008.

Glass, J.B. and R. Khamaisi. *Report on the Socio-economic Conditions in the Old City of Jerusalem*, 2004.

Greenfield-Gilat, Y., K.L. Bar-Sinai and SAYA Architecture & Consultancy. *Jaffa Gate Crossing Facilities: Spatial Study*, 2007.

International Peace and Cooperation Centre. *Challenges for an International Administration of Urban Functions in the Old City of Jerusalem*, 2007.

al-Jubeh, N. and D. Seidemann. *Mapping Factors of Stabilization and Destabilization in the Old City*, 2006.

al-Jubeh, N. and D. Seidemann. *Conflict Resolution in the Old City Past and Future*, 2008.

Kassissieh, I. and N. al-Jubeh. *Jerusalem Security Principles: The Old City*, 2006.

Meidan-Shani, P., A. Amit and M. Cristal. *Security Mechanism in the Holy Basin*, 2005.

Meidan-Shani, P., P. Golan, R. Berko and M. Cristal. *Security Mechanism in the Holy Basin – Phase II*, 2006.

Meidan-Shani, P., P. Golan, R. Berko and M. Cristal. *Security Mechanism in the Holy Basin – Phase II/2*, 2007.

Oliel, M. *Property Rights and Ownership in the Old City of Jerusalem*, 2006.

Qupty, M. *The Legal Framework for a Special Regime: The Old City of Jerusalem*, 2007.

Qupty, M. *Dispute Resolution under the Special Regime of the Old City of Jerusalem*, 2008.

Reiter, Y. *Options for the Administration of the Holy Places in the Old City of Jerusalem*, 2007.

Seidemann, D. *Events Surrounding the Mugrabi Gate: 2007 Case Study*, 2007.

Sher, G., J. Gillis and A. Kadari. *The Legal Parameters of the Old City of Jerusalem Special Regime*, 2005.

Sher, G., J. Gillis and N. Vestfrid. *A Plan for Governance in a Special Regime in Jerusalem*, 2007.

Sher, G., J. Gillis and N. Vestfrid. *The Adjudicatory Regime and Dispute Resolution Mechanism*, 2008.

9

THE JERUSALEM OLD CITY INITIATIVE SECURITY ASSESSMENT

Roy Berlinquette, John de Chastelain and Arthur Hughes

Executive summary

1. The Old City of Jerusalem is the central focus of the national aspirations of both Israelis and Palestinians. The Old City of Jerusalem is perhaps the most contentious issue in the Arab–Israeli conflict. Its sovereignty, administration and control are questions of great dispute, and its Holy Sites resonate powerfully in the hearts and minds of Muslims, Jews and Christians. If questions respecting the Old City remain unresolved, stability in Jerusalem cannot be assured and peace between Israelis and Palestinians will be impossible.

2. The Jerusalem Old City Initiative aims to develop creative options for the effective governance and management of the Old City, including security arrangements addressed in this chapter. This goal is predicated on ensuring the integrity of the Old City and its holy space; the area is too small, densely populated and architecturally linked to be managed viably by a mix of different authorities and police forces.

3. Special governance arrangements are therefore proposed (dealt with in detail in a separate governance paper), treating the Old City as a single unit under an Administrator with executive authority, accountable to a Governance Board composed of the parties themselves and international stakeholders acceptable to both. These arrangements would be within the framework of an agreement between the parties, with two national capitals, Al Quds and Yerushalayim. It should be stressed that this initiative is not designed to resolve the conflicting claims of the parties respecting sovereignty over the Old City and in no way prejudices them. Rather, the initiative outlines practical mechanisms which can be implemented under various sovereignty options.

4. These proposed security arrangements are designed to address the fundamental security and law enforcement needs of the Old City and its residents,

while ensuring freedom of worship, dignity, access and equity of treatment for all stakeholders. They require close coordination with Israeli and Palestinian authorities. Indeed, their success will depend on the ability of Israelis and Palestinians to agree on the implementation of such special governance arrangements and to develop conditions that permit coexistence in this most contested and sacred of cities.

5.   Within such a framework, and after careful consideration of the recommendations of Israeli and Palestinian security experts, the following security recommendations have been developed:

a   The Administrator should be accountable to an international Governance Board composed of international stakeholders and the Parties themselves;

b   A single Old City Police Service should be established, reporting to the Administrator, who should have ultimate responsibility for security arrangements in the Old City;

c   The Administrator should be responsible for naming a Chief of Police, in consultation with the international Governance Board, to serve for a fixed period of service;

d   The Police Service should function under a unified command structure headed by a Chief of Police to whom all on the force will be accountable;

e   The Police Service should be professional, effective, impartial, accountable and integrated, and composed of international officers from countries acceptable to the Parties and with clear hiring criteria consistent with international standards. The issue of whether Palestinians and Israelis should be taken into the Police Service should be examined by the Administrator and the Chief of Police in the context of the satisfactory implementation of the agreement and the establishment of trust between the Parties. Their deployment should be determined by the Chief of Police;

f   Police responsibilities should include community policing, enforcement of civil and criminal laws, implementation of security arrangements affecting movement and access to and through the Old City, security and intelligence functions, counter-terrorism, and protecting the rights of all the City's residents and visitors. The Police Service should be organized and staffed to be able to deal with all contingencies;

g   The police should have the authority to investigate, question, arrest and detain suspects in conformity with accepted international norms, and to remand them to the custody of Israeli or Palestinian authorities, or, in appropriate cases to be defined, to an Old City judicial system;

h   The Police Service should, by necessity, coordinate its efforts closely with Israeli and Palestinian security authorities, including in matters of 'pursuit' and access control to the Old City;

i   A special emphasis should be placed on learning, training and develop-
     ment, as keys to achieving professionalism and performance success
     in the Police Service, given the unusually complex and sensitive
     environment; and

j   Arrangements touching on the sanctity of Holy Sites and access to them
     should be dealt with to the satisfaction of the religious communities,
     subject to the requirements of public order. Special security arrange-
     ments should be developed for these sites in close coordination with
     advisory religious and heritage bodies.

6.   From our reading of the papers produced by Israeli and Palestinian partners,
     and our consultations with them, we are aware that there is not full agree-
     ment respecting these proposals. It is our strong belief however that the points
     of difference are resolvable and an effective, fair-minded and sustainable
     security system for the Old City is achievable.

7.   It is possible that a situation of major unrest could occur that includes the
     complete breakdown of the Palestinian Authority in the region prior to any
     agreement being reached to set up the Special Regime for the Old City that
     we are proposing in this paper. We believe that such a circumstance would
     make it extremely unlikely that the Special Regime could be activated, and it
     is not considered further here.

Glossary

CCTV	Closed Circuit Television
CLO	Community Liaison Officers
CROPS	Criminal Operations Unit
DCOP-Adm	Deputy Chief of Police – Administration
DCOP-Ops	Deputy Chief of Police – Operations
EECU	Entry and Exit Control Unit
EOD	Explosive Ordnance Disposal
ERF	Emergency Reserve Force
EU COPPS	European Union Co-ordinating Office for Palestinian Police Support
HSPU	Holy Site Police Unit
ILCTU	Intelligence, Liaison and Counter Terrorism Unit
JOC	Joint Operations Centre
JOCI	Jerusalem Old City Initiative
LTD	Learning, Training and Development
NPU	Neighbourhood Policing Unit
PORDU	Public Order Rapid Deployment Unit
PSNI	Police Service of Northern Ireland
RCMP	Royal Canadian Mounted Police

Introduction

1. This assessment examines security, the core issue in the challenge of how Jerusalem might be addressed in the final status negotiations between Israel and Palestine (known as the Parties). Without an equitable, reliable and sustainable security arrangement for the Old City, we believe that no final status agreement is possible. This assessment is the result of our study, examination and discussion of what such a security arrangement might be. We were guided by a desire to be comprehensive – to offer detailed proposals where possible and to flag other issues that would need further consideration – and also by the conviction that any security system for the Old City could work only if it were part of a governance arrangement created and supported by the Parties themselves. This paper does not address the issue of sovereignty. However, we believe that this assessment constitutes a useful resource for policy planners, negotiators and decision makers as they deal with the single most difficult and contentious issue among the myriad questions relating to Jerusalem.

2. The Old City of Jerusalem and its Holy Sites resonate powerfully in the hearts and minds of Muslims, Jews and Christians around the world. The Jerusalem Old City Initiative's approach to the Jerusalem conundrum is to recognize the full range of factors that affect resolution, including security, the symbolic importance of the Old City, the strong religious feelings of Jews, Muslims and Christians around the world, economic sustainability, the needs of the Old City's residents, and the interests of the Palestinians and Israelis more broadly. Fundamentally, we believe that a special governance system – what we call the Old City Special Regime (henceforth called the Regime) involving an international role fully agreed by Israel and Palestine – is required to achieve equity and long-term sustainability in this most sensitive of locales. Indeed, an agreed international presence in the Old City may also serve as a disincentive for the Parties to turn national mechanisms into instruments for territorial gain or struggles for power.

3. Any security mechanism within such a system must take full account of Jerusalem as the focal point of individual and group identities, and the sensitivities and mistrust this engenders. Taken together, these physical and symbolic factors make the Old City a soft target for those seeking to disrupt Muslim–Jewish and Israeli–Palestinian co-existence. Disruptions could range from provocative political action to outright terrorism, which would not only cause death and suffering, but also threaten their bilateral political agreements and indeed the general peace.

4. The Israelis and Palestinians taking part in this process of engagement on the Old City, while they may differ on specific issues, share the view that, without guarantees of a fair-minded security mechanism, no agreement respecting the Old City will be sustainable.

The process

5. The Jerusalem Old City Initiative (JOCI) has been engaged in consultations and studies on this question for over three years. Today, the initiative is pursuing a series of papers and studies focusing on governance (including the management of Holy Sites), security measures, symbolic issues and the political economy of the Old City. This chapter looks specifically at the security dimension assessing options for negotiations between the Parties.

6. The importance to all stakeholders of security, in perception and actuality, and the potential urgent needs of decision makers, have led JOCI to pursue security first. The ideas presented will, however, ultimately be contingent on administrative and governance arrangements, especially regarding the Holy Sites. These will be presented in detail in subsequent documents to be published in the near future.

Aim

7. The aim of this paper is to assess the factors that members of the Security Working Group believe should form the basis of a security system for Jerusalem's Old City, under the authority of an Old City Special Regime.

Outline

8. This assessment will be structured under the following headings:

    Background;
    Premise and Source of Authority;
    Mandate;
    Duration;
    Organization;
    Command and control;
    Operations;
    Learning, training and development;
    Infrastructure;
    Administration and logistics;
    Oversight; and
    Conclusion.

Background

9. This document's authors have extensive professional experience in the areas of policing, diplomacy, the operation of international policing organizations and military and peacekeeping operations. None of us is an expert on Jerusalem's security requirements, but we have each spent considerable time familiarizing ourselves with the situation in the Old City. It is not for us to decide what

security system should be adopted by the Old City Special Regime. Nevertheless, we have examined the special nature of the security requirements in Jerusalem's Old City, and we have been informed by detailed papers prepared on the subject by Israeli and Palestinian experts and by comprehensive consultations with individuals on both sides (for details, see References). Based on their opinions, as well as on our experience, we have identified what we believe are some important factors to consider in establishing a security system under the Regime.

10. We accept that the security situation in the Old City of Jerusalem presents special challenges. But while some of them are unique to the Old City – particularly with regard to the Holy Sites – some of them are also found in conflict situations elsewhere. We have paid close attention to the setting up of new Police Services in post-conflict circumstances in Northern Ireland, Bosnia and East Timor, and we have attempted to apply lessons learned from these situations, where they apply, to the concept of a new security system for Jerusalem's Old City.

11. We start from the belief that no security system can provide one-hundred percent assurance of inviolability. The system existing in the Old City today is as effective as any, yet security incidents still occur. But we believe that once the Parties have agreed to establish a Special Regime in the Old City, with an internationally mandated responsibility to provide security for residents, worshippers and visitors, a security system – one that merits the confidence of the people and that has a good chance of success – can be put in place. The chances of success will be enhanced if:

    a   The Regime is created and sponsored by the two Parties and supported by the members of the Security Council, as well as other major nations;

    b   Israeli and Palestinian, as well as international, involvement in the security system will demonstrate the will to make it work;

    c   The existence of two national capitals in West and East Jerusalem, with all their accruing international recognition and financial advantages, serves to boost the Old City's prestige and economic prospects; and

    d   The knowledge that failure of the Regime will likely cause a breakdown in the Israel–Palestine Treaty – and also spell a return to violence and a loss of hope for the future – elicits support from those initially sceptical of the process.

12. In making this assessment we have put special emphasis on the Learning, Training and Development (LTD) component of the security system and we include a special annex on this subject (Annex C). In the annex, we discuss how the LTD component is not an end in itself, but represents a key long-term investment to achieve policing professionalism and performance success.

13. The context of the creation of this LTD process presumes a fundamental change in the socio-political relationship between Israel and Palestine, which is

also the basic concept on which the establishment of the Old City Special Regime is predicated. The intention of the two Parties must be to make the Regime (and hence the Old City Police Service) work. It will involve the beginning of interdependency between the communities in the Old City and the police officers who serve them. It is a determination to create community-led, partnership-policing based on a firm commitment to the investigation, detection and prevention of crime, the enforcement of the rule of law, the maintenance of peace and order, and the protection of life and property. Implicit in this commitment is the need to protect and respect human rights. The goals, core values and principles of such an approach permeate the suggestions in this study.

Premise and Source of Authority

14. The Jerusalem Old City Initiative (JOCI) has developed a set of working assumptions, premised on a framework that envisages two independent states, Israel and Palestine, with the city of Jerusalem divided along an agreed line into Al Quds and Yerushalyam, with the Old City the subject of a special governance system. This Regime will be based on a formal agreement between Palestine and Israel and endorsed by the United Nations Security Council in a manner to be agreed by the Parties. The Regime will be administered by an Administrator who is neither Israeli nor Palestinian, appointed for a fixed renewable period by a Governance Board (with functions to be further defined) composed of members agreed to by Israel and Palestine, to which the Administrator will be accountable.

15. The Parties will prepare the mandate and issue it to the Administrator. The mandate will delegate to the Administrator authority over many Old City matters, including a security system.

16. The security system should be constituted in the form of an Old City Police Service, (henceforth called the Police Service), headed by a Chief of Police appointed for a fixed period by the Administrator, with the agreement of a Governance Board composed of representatives of the parties themselves – Israel and Palestine – and international stakeholders acceptable to both. It will be critical for the Police Service to have a close ongoing cooperative relationship with police as well as intelligence and other relevant agencies of Israel and Palestine. This can best be done by having attached Israeli and Palestinian liaison officers seconded to Police Service Headquarters in the Old City. In addition we believe that the Administrator and Chief of Police should establish formal cooperative relationships with the security agencies of other countries and with INTERPOL.

Mandate

17. The mandate for the security system, issued by the Parties to the Administrator, should be to preserve law and order in the Old City and to ensure the equal and fair treatment of all who live or visit there. This mandate should be confined to the area of the Old City – a universally accessible city,

indivisible within the walls – whose gates lead directly into Israel or Palestine. But allowance should be made for the security system's members to operate in those areas outside but close to the walls, where the implementation of effective entry and exit security measures make such exceptions necessary. Consideration should also be given to allow periodic inspections of the exterior of the walls by Police Service members.

18. Given the existence in the Old City of Holy Sites of great importance to the three Abrahamic religions, special concerns relate to security within the walls. The security system should be based on a Police Service charged *inter alia* with carrying out conventional day-to-day policing functions and enforcing the law. It should also provide the measures necessary to ensure access to, and the security of, the Holy Sites as well as response to potential mass demonstrations and violence related to those sites. To ensure the protection of, and access to, the Holy Sites, the methods in effect now should be continued until new procedures, made in consultation with the religious authorities, can be effected. At the point during the handover period when the Old City Police Service has a preponderance of personnel in position and taking charge of security roles, we envisage the Police Service taking control of the security of the Holy Sites from the Israelis, working in conjunction with whatever traditional security elements are agreed to have a continuing role in them.

Duration

19. As long as the Regime continues to exist, its security system will have to exist also. Given the proposal that the mandate continue for an indefinite period pending agreement by the Parties on an alternative arrangement, consideration of tour length will become an important factor.

20. It is clearly advantageous to have security system members remain in place for as long as possible, as effectiveness in their role will improve with experience. On the other hand, countries may be unwilling to release their nationals for service in the Police Service for lengthy periods, and independent individuals seeking involvement may not wish to engage in lengthy contracts. In particular, training requirements for members will have to be tailored based on anticipated tour lengths and these will be discussed below under Learning, Training and Development. As a rule, however, we believe that to provide an effective security system in the Old City, tour lengths for its members should be open-ended, but members must commit to serve for a minimum of three years after training has been completed.

Organization

21. ***General*** The security system will be headed by the Chief of Police who will report to and receive direction from the Administrator, who will be responsible to the Governance Board.

22. ***Old City Police Service*** The basis of the Old City security system should be an Old City Police Service. This service should be designed to carry out a number of functions necessary for the safety and security of the Old City, including routine policing, protection of the Holy Sites, entry and exit control, and public order rapid response. The Police Service should be responsible for enforcing laws, ordinances and directives of the Administrator. While neighbourhood policing will be one of its major functions, the Police Service should also have:

   a   A Criminal Operations Unit (CROPS) to address serious crimes such as murder, organized crime, drug operations, smuggling and kidnapping;

   b   A viable intelligence organization, well connected to the intelligence organizations of the two Parties – by means of seconded officers from those organizations – that is capable of alerting the Administrator to potential threats or difficulties in a timely fashion;

   c   Close connections with other national intelligence agencies and with INTERPOL; and

   d   An internal training division as well as a logistical and administrative organization, capable of addressing the needs of the Service's members and their dependents.

23. ***Structure*** In Annex A we include an organizational chart depicting our assessment of how the Police Service could be structured to meet or exceed international standards of policing. While it will be the Chief of Police and his advisers who recommend the final organization of the Police Service to the Administrator – including its suggested size and structure – we believe that the outline offered in Annex A can provide the basis for initial planning.

24. We suggest that the Chief of Police should have two deputies, a Deputy Chief of Police Operations (DCOP-Ops) and a Deputy Chief of Police Administration (DCOP-Adm). The Chief of Police should have his own legal section reporting directly to him, as well as a public relations unit emphasizing outreach. All functions required to make the Police Service workable should be grouped under the two DCOPs.

25. The structure we propose is intended to take account of fundamental policing needs as well as potential security threats in the Old City. There are several aspects to this goal:

   a   ***Public order*** The objective is to have police contribute to a sense of normality, taking account of the special nature of the Old City with its Holy Sites, and the need, at times, to monitor entry and exit into and out of the two neighbouring states. It anticipates the possibility of having to react at short notice to unexpected events, and includes a full-time Public Order Rapid Deployment Unit (PORDU) within the Police Service for this purpose;

   b   ***Extreme emergency***

  i Given the potential volatility of crowds during religious occasions, the large numbers that can be involved in such events, and the history of violent reaction to incidents on or around the Holy Sites, we believe there will be an on-call requirement to increase the strength of the security forces within the Old City, at relatively short notice, by a factor of three or four;

  ii The role of such an Emergency Reserve Force (ERF) will be to provide the necessary trained manpower to flood the Old City with security forces and maintain this heightened presence for a period of up to several days. While in the short term, numbers can be provided by deploying the complete strength of the Police Service simultaneously, such a measure cannot be maintained for long. Hence the need for large numbers of additional reserves;

  iii Clearly, such a large formation in place full-time would be prohibitively expensive as well as difficult to maintain when not required. But we think it is important that such an element – intended for operations only within the Old City – should be available to be drawn from outside sources rather than from existing units and resources belonging to the Parties. This formation will not be part of the Police Service and will be called on only when an emergency makes its presence necessary, at which point it will deploy to Jerusalem (into staging areas agreed by the Parties) and come under command of the Chief of Police for operations in the Old City only; and

  iv We believe that the Administrator and the Chief of Police should consider how best to provide for this requirement. One option might be to make arrangements with one or two countries acceptable to the Parties, and that are deployable within two to three hours (such as Italy and Turkey), to earmark trained and professional units for emergency intervention. Another option might be to call on formed manoeuvre units already deployed in the Mediterranean, such as NATO.

c The need to anticipate events that may require the deployment of the PORDU or the ERF makes it essential that the intelligence apparatus within the Police Service be structured and maintained at a consistently high level and that it have access to existing outside intelligence sources;

d Since such problems described above could originate outside the Old City but within the territories of the two Parties, it is essential that the Parties be committed to energetic and constructive action to preclude such developments; and e   It is possible that a situation of major unrest could occur that includes the complete breakdown of the Palestinian Authority in the region prior to any agreement being reached to set up the Special Regime for the Old City that we are proposing in this paper. We believe that such a circumstance would make it extremely unlikely that the Special Regime could be activated, and it is not considered further here.

26. **Organizational steps** We envisage several steps in the deployment and development of the Police Service. At the outset we foresee the employment of professional police officers from countries agreed to by the Parties. These officers will undertake an initial familiarization course and then assume responsibility from the Israeli security forces. In the second step, international candidates will be recruited and trained to the basic level of qualified police officers. Third, these newly qualified officers will be introduced into the Police Service while the international officers brought in at the beginning – with the exception of some in leadership roles – will be successively relieved of their duties. The culmination of this process will be a police service almost entirely composed of international members specifically recruited and trained for the Old City Police Service.

27. **Police service composition**

a   *Concept*

i   Our initial conception of the Old City Police Service was that, once fully established, it would incorporate not just international candidates but Israelis and Palestinians recruited specifically for the Service. We believed that doing so would give both Parties a feeling of greater involvement in the policing of the Old City and would pave the way for whatever security system is put in place once the Regime's mandate expires. However, we were advised of the difficulties that would arise from employing Israelis and Palestinians as police officers in the Police Service at an early stage in the operation of the Regime, and we have adjusted our thinking accordingly. Nonetheless, we believe that at some future time, in the context of satisfactory implementation of the Israeli–Palestinian agreement and the building of mutual trust, the Administrator should re-examine this option with the Parties; and

ii   Our agreed conception therefore is that the Police Service should include international police officers only, but with trained and qualified unarmed Israeli and Palestinian Community Liaison Officers (CLOs) engaged as part of the Police Service. The CLOs will be assigned to the Police Service stations throughout the Old City and will work closely with the international police officers in the neighbourhoods and with their various ethnic and religious groups. As we see it, the need to get the Police Service up and running as swiftly as possible – once the decision is made to adopt it – requires that it be initially made up of experienced international police officers. These will have to undergo a course that familiarizes them with the special circumstances of the Old City. Once deployed, they will be accompanied by CLOs, either Israeli or Palestinian, as circumstances warrant.

b   Recruits While the trained international police element is providing security in the Old City, international police recruits will undertake basic police training to prepare them to take their place as qualified police officers in the Police Service. Candidates will be recruited from countries agreed to by the Parties and will need to reflect an appropriate mix of responsible international players. As this latter group completes its training and is deployed into active Police Service, the original international contingent may, with the exception of some leadership elements, be gradually drawn down, decreasing the burden placed on the initial contributing countries; and

c   Our recommendation that the Police Service be composed solely of international police officers is not an argument against attaching Israeli and Palestinian intelligence and counter-terrorism officers, seconded from their respective services, to the Police Service. Indeed, we feel that such an attachment is vital to the effective functioning of the Police Service. The subject is discussed below in connection with the establishment of a Joint Operations Centre.

Command and control

28. All members of the Police Service will be under the command of the Chief of Police who will report to the Administrator. As mentioned earlier, we believe the Chief of Police should appear regularly before the Governance Board, either at the Board's or the Chief's initiative. We believe the ability of the Chief of Police to have regular access to the members of such an organization, and they to him, is essential to the efficient conduct of the Police Services and security role in the Old City.

29. Other factors relating to command and control within the Police Service include:

a   *Seconded Israelis and Palestinian police officers* The Liaison, Intelligence and Counter-Terrorism Unit should be grouped under the DCOP-Ops and it is here that we envisage the secondment of experienced members of the Israeli and Palestinian police organizations needed for these roles. While these officers will work closely with the Police Service during their secondment, they should remain under the command of their parent organizations;

b   *Access to other intelligence agencies* The Police Service will need assured access to the Israeli and Palestinian police and other relevant agencies, by means of a formal liaison system;

c   *Special status* Whether or not members of the Police Service should have some form of special status conferred by Israel and Palestine, as presumably other members of the Regime will have, is something that should be determined during the planning stage of the Regime;

d   *Ease of movement* A number of Police Service units (e.g. logistics and training) and their headquarters will be located outside the Old City. The PORDU and the ERF (when deployed) will also be located outside the walls. Some of these units may be stationed in Yerushalyam and some in Al Quds, as agreed between the Administrator and the Parties. Regardless of their location, it is essential that these units be given unimpeded access in and out of the Old City in the performance of their duties.

30. Headquarters location

a   We envisage Command of the Police Service being executed from an Old City Police Service Headquarters located within the Old City, with subordinate headquarters or stations located where necessary to control the different functions of neighbourhood policing, Holy Site security and entry and exit control;

b   We see the DCOP-Ops exercising command from his headquarters located in the Old City, with most of his units' headquarters located there also. We see the DCOP-Adm exercising command from his headquarters located outside the Old City, with all of his units located there in areas to be negotiated by the Administrator with the Parties;

c   We see the PORDU being located outside the Old City but with easy access to it; and

d   The ERF (Emergency Reserve Force), when deployed, will be placed temporarily in holding areas to be negotiated in advance with the Parties. To conduct operations it will be deployed into the Old City.

Operations

31. General

As mentioned earlier, we envisage the Police Service being formed and readied for operation in several stages:

a   First, the Chief of Police and his principal commanders will do the preliminary staff work to set up the organization including deciding on structures, determining the required numbers, acquiring the necessary equipment, infrastructure, communications and supplies, and setting up the necessary recruiting and training apparatus;

b   Second, the experienced international police officers who will initially comprise the Police Service will commence familiarization training that prepares them to take over policing in the Old City from the Israeli security forces. Simultaneously, prospective international candidates will be recruited and start basic training courses, and the Israeli and Palestinian CLOs (Community Liaison Officers) will be recruited and trained;

c   Third, the trained international police officers will take over the security of the Old City from the Israeli security elements, and CLOs will be deployed with them as necessary. As recruits complete their training and become qualified police officers, they will be introduced into the active Police Service. To minimize the time between the Regime's formation and the start of Police Service operations, it is likely that the numbers of trained international police personnel initially deployed will be high. As more recruits are trained and take their place, the initial numbers of trained international police personnel can be reduced; and

d   The Chief of Police will undertake to form Local Neighbourhood Policing Partnerships. Their purpose will be to provide the Chief of Police and the neighbourhood police commanders with views on matters concerning the policing of local areas. Implicit in this concept is that it will build cooperation and increase trust between the police and area inhabitants, encouraging the latter to assist in maintaining law and order where it most concerns them.

32. **Standard operating procedures** The Chief of Police should be responsible for all operations conducted by the Police Service. To this end he will approve the operational structures needed to exercise his mandate. He should also be responsible for developing the necessary procedures to permit the Police Service to function. These procedures will have to take account of procedures already being followed in the Old City – e.g. Holy Site security (see also below) – so that disruption of day-to-day life resulting from the change of security systems is minimized. The procedures will be particularly essential given the various international elements that make up the initial structure of the Police Service. Firmly enforced procedures will be necessary to ensure that officers from different national Police Services operate as a cohesive organization from the outset. Separate procedures will also have to be established for each of the Service's personnel, administrative and logistics units.

33. **Operational handover** Of particular importance will be the way in which the handover of the security operation in the Old City is managed between the Police Service and the Israeli Security Forces. There will need to be an agreed period of time between the establishment of the Regime and the point at which the Police Service is ready to assume the complete security operation from the Israeli security elements. In that interim period the latter should

continue to maintain control of security operations in the Old City and gradually hand over responsibility to the Police Service as its personnel and units become ready to assume it. The Chief of Police must be responsible for advising the Administrator of the length of time this interim period will take, and for making the appropriate phasing arrangements with the Israeli security authorities.

34. *Policing division* The Policing Division should be responsible for routine policing in the Old City, for Holy Site security, for entry and exit security, for rapid deployment, for intelligence, liaison and counter-terrorism and for serious crime prevention:

a   Routine policing

     i   The neighbourhood police unit (NPU) will be responsible for the enforcement of routine policing within the Old City. We envisage this function being sub-divided into responsibilities for different neighbourhoods within the Old City, with foot patrols being the preferred method of maintaining law and order and of contributing to a sense of security among inhabitants and visitors;

     ii   Patrol composition

         • We believe such patrols should involve international Police Service officers, along with Israeli or Palestinian CLOs to demonstrate the special nature of the Police Service's mandate as well as the determination of the Administrator and the Parties to see that it works. The patrols' composition should follow principles of equity in the treatment of residents and visitors alike, and should be put together according to the demographic needs of the various Old City areas. When necessary, these patrols will allow for arrest of inhabitants or visitors in the most effective and efficient way possible; and

         • No matter the nationality of the individual involved, officers of all nationalities should be available to act in the most effective way possible and as required by the circumstance. For example, if there is an incident in an Israeli home, we envisage that international officers and Israeli CLOs will engage directly with the residents involved. If there is an incident in a Palestinian home, we envisage that international officers and Palestinian CLOs will respond.

         • *Serious crime* Routine policing must include the investigation of serious crime, which will be conducted by the Criminal Operations Unit.

b   Holy site policing

    i   The matter of the Holy Sites will be the subject of a separate study. In general, however, the Holy Site Policing Unit (HSPU) will be responsible for policing sites within the Old City. We envisage that the present procedures for protecting the sites should continue pending review by the Administrator and the Governance Board. This function should include assuring undisturbed access to the sites and preventing incidents or damage to them;

    ii   Crucial to such policing will be the need to maintain close relations with the religious authorities that currently have responsibility for the sites, and to involve them to the degree considered appropriate in executing the task;

    iii   While special attention will have to be paid to the most sensitive of these sites, including the Haram al-Sharif/Temple Mount and the Western Wall/Kotel, the HSPU should consult with religious authorities to catalogue and prepare plans for the protection of all sites considered at risk;

    iv   Particular consideration should be given to specially composed detachments of the Police Service for the Temple Mount/ Haram al-Sharif/Western Wall/Kotel. The nature of these sites and global attachments to them are such that the symbolic value of the carefully chosen and trained police units to be deployed at them needs to be seriously assessed; and

    v   One method of dealing with these most sensitive sites might be to have two concentric rings providing security there. The inner ring would be composed of unarmed Muslims at the Temple Mount/Haram al-Sharif and unarmed Jews at the Western Wall/Kotel. The outer ring, further back but readily available to intervene if necessary, would be composed of armed Police Service officers – presumably international officers accompanied by Palestinian CLOs at the one, and international officers accompanied by Israeli CLOs at the other.

c   Entry and exit policing

    i   Concept

       •   We understand that there is inherent conflict between normal access to a city with free and unhindered entry and exit, and the imposition of security checks. Nonetheless, an unavoidable part of providing security in any confined location is the requirement to control entry and exit there when necessary;

- After an evolutionary period to build confidence and experience and within an atmosphere of orderly implementation of the Israel–Palestine Treaty, we believe that security checks will become minimal; and
- The two Parties will have a significant interest in ensuring that persons of ill intent do not enter the Old City from their respective territories, and one can posit that the two will act decisively to ensure that does not happen since serious disruption of the Regime would have highly negative consequences for treaty implementation.

ii   Control points

- The Entry and Exit Police Unit (EEPU) will be responsible for supervising and controlling entry into and exit from the Old City. This task requires control points at each of the seven open gates, with special attention at those gates allowing both vehicle and pedestrian traffic;
- We envisage one control point at each gate, with members of the EEPU and representatives of the appropriate Party being co-located. While the Parties have indicated that they do not envisage individuals passing from one state to another through the Old City, we expect that they will wish to have their own agents located at their respective gates in the event there is a dispute over exit from, or re-entry into, their countries; and
- The EEPU's aim must be multifaceted: to build confidence among the inhabitants and to ensure minimum interference with the flow of pedestrian and authorized vehicle traffic, while taking account of the security needs of the moment. To this end a system that will allow a range of control measures, from minimum or no checking, to strenuous personnel and vehicle monitoring, should be put in place. Suggestions as to how this might be accomplished – at the Jaffa Gate, for example – are included in Annex B. Similar suggestions can be developed for other gates as considered necessary by the Parties and the Administrator.

iii   Residents. We believe that the Administrator, in concert with the Parties, will be responsible for determining who is a resident of the

Old City and for issuing identity cards to them. These cards will facilitate exit or entry by Old City residents; and

iv   Passage time. In normal circumstances we anticipate that a pedestrian will transit entry/exit points in a matter of seconds.

d   Public order rapid deployment (PORDU) will be responsible for rapid response to incidents or events beyond the ability of routine policing units to handle. It will maintain a level of readiness commensurate with this requirement and be deployable in anticipation of such events. The unit will be trained in special tactics including riot and crowd control and will have the arms and equipment necessary for its role. The Explosive Ordnance Demolition (EOD) capability of the Police Service will be located in the PORDU. While the PORDU should be located outside the walls to accommodate spatial limitations and facilitate deployment, it may have advance elements permanently stationed at sensitive locations such as Holy Sites and the main access gates;

e   Intelligence, liaison and counter-terrorism

i   The Intelligence, Liaison and Counter-Terrorism Unit (ILCTU) will function as the Police Service's intelligence and liaison unit as well as the planning unit for counter-terrorism measures. It will also be responsible for carrying out risk assessment on a daily basis. While for the most part the unit will be composed of international Police Service officers, it is here that we envisage experienced Israeli and Palestinian police and counter terrorism experts being seconded;

ii   The unit will establish regular communication with other international intelligence services and will provide the main liaison function between the Police Service and the Israeli and Palestinian police organizations. Its location will be determined by the Chief of Police and the DCOP-Ops and may include sites both within and, with the Parties' concurrence, outside the walls;

iii   While it will be for the Chief of Police to decide how he will organize his resources to best meet his mandate, we believe he will want to consider setting up a Joint Operations Centre (JOC) which will be the focal point for controlling and planning all operations conducted by the Police Service, and the Emergency Reserve Force if deployed. The seconded Israeli and Palestinian officers, and the liaison chain to outside police and other security elements, will be optimally placed in a JOC; and

iv We recommend that the Chief of Police and other senior officers of
the Police Service keep in frequent contact with their Israeli
and Palestinian counterparts.

f Arrest and handling of suspects

i *Authority* The Police Service will have full authority to investigate,
question, arrest and detain suspects in accordance with law
and accepted international norms. The arrest and handling
of suspects will normally be carried out by Neighbourhood
Policing Unit officers assisted by Community Liaison Officers. We believe that suspects should normally be turned
over to the appropriate national authorities as soon as possible, or, in exceptional cases, to the Old City's judicial
system. They can be held temporarily in the Old City at
one of the police stations in the appropriate neighbourhood.
Further work on the judicial system will be developed in
the JOCI study on governance;

ii *Israelis and Palestinians* While the exact judicial process remains under
study, we believe that the judicial process for Israelis and
Palestinians arrested in the Old City and brought to trial
will normally take place in either Israel or Palestine, as
appropriate. Another option that remains under study is to
develop some judicial capacity for the Governance Board;

iii *Others* Suspects arrested in the Old City who are neither Israeli nor
Palestinian will be handled by the Police Service in accordance with accepted international standards. The question
of which courts will be used to deal with cases involving
such individuals will be determined by the Administrator in
consultation with the Parties;

iv *Pursuit* We expect that there will be occasions when suspects in the Old
City may flee Police Service officers seeking their apprehension
in accordance with law. Such individuals may attempt to leave
the Old City. However, every Old City gate will have control posts staffed by Police Service and Israeli or Palestinian
authorities. These can take the fugitive into custody pending
arrival of the pursuing Police Service officers. If for some reason
the fugitive is able to flee the Old City, consideration should
be given to authorizing pursuit jointly by Police Service officers and the Israeli or Palestinian national police. Alternatively,
those who flee could become the object of the Old City
Special Regime's judicial arrest warrants and sought by the
Palestinian or Israeli police as appropriate. Similar arrangements could be made for circumstances where fugitives
from Israel or Palestine seek refuge in the Old City;

v   *Old City Police Service officers giving testimony* While members of the Police Service will have no jurisdiction outside the Old City, we believe that those officers who are involved in arrests should be able to appear in court outside the Old City in an official capacity to give evidence.

g   *The carriage of arms* We believe that Police Service officers on duty within the Old City should be armed in a manner to be determined by the Chief of Police and they should be the only individuals permitted to own or carry arms inside the Old City. The Old City free of weapons in private hands is critical to calm and stability. We believe that Israel should work with the Administrator and the Police Service to ensure the turnover of a 'weapons-free' city to the Regime.

Learning, training and development

35. **General** The learning, training and development strategy we propose is based on a philosophy of learning that emphasizes core themes including human rights, situational training, continuous learning culture and international experience. These themes are cornerstones to implementing a successful training strategy that will develop a new Police Service, one that is all-inclusive when dealing with different cultural backgrounds, and that promotes policing in cooperation with the community in its neighbourhood policing approach. For recruiting to be successful, service in the Old City Police Service must be seen to constitute a satisfactory and rewarding experience, with remuneration at internationally recognized rates and with work conditions that compare favourably with those in use elsewhere. This must be the case both for the trained international contingents brought in to start the process, and for those individuals recruited for long-term service.

36. **Transition team** As mentioned earlier we envisage a staged deployment of police units or squads in the Old City each of which will have its own training requirements. Details of the proposed Police Service training programme are included in Annex C, but in general we anticipate a two-month period of conversion training for the Transition Team of trained police officers who will constitute the initial deployment of the Police Service. This conversion training will include an introduction to the rule of law that will govern the Old City, instruction in the special circumstances of its religious and cultural differences, and some basic language training for those with no knowledge of Arabic or Hebrew. We do not anticipate lengthy language training for either these or the follow-on members of the Police Service. We feel that each should have some very basic instruction at the outset, and for those who will spend longer periods in the Police Service, additional courses can occasionally be given to improve capacity and fluency. At the same time as the Transition Team undergoes its conversion training, we envisage a course for the Israeli

and Palestinian Community Liaison Officers. The CLOs would be recruited on an individual basis and trained in the basic function of the Police Service and their role in it, and they would be deployed with the Transition Team as appropriate from the outset.

37. *Follow-on members* The follow-on, individually recruited international candidates should undergo a six-month introductory programme that mirrors basic police training. The programme should include some elemental language training for those who need it, to be followed by a six-month period of probationary Police Service deployment, with each new officer participating in an international police tutor programme, i.e. under the watchful eye of a trained international police officer.

38. *Steady state* Such a training programme envisages that once the decision to establish the Regime is made, there will be at least a two-month preparation period before the initial international police deployment begins and – at the earliest – a subsequent four-month period before the first of the recruits start being introduced into the system. As more newly qualified officers complete their probation, more and more of the initial international cohort can be replaced, although there will continue to be a need to retain some officers at the more senior supervisory levels. Once a steady state has been reached, there will be an ongoing requirement to run training courses for a variety of purposes including basic training for new recruits to address attrition, as well as advanced and specialty courses. In the latter case it is envisaged that officers who already have specialty qualifications, such as Explosive Ordnance Disposal (EOD), should be recruited directly at the outset to fill the required positions.

Infrastructure

39. The Police Service will require 'bricks and mortar' infrastructure to support its operational, training and administrative functions. Arrangements will have to be made to acquire this infrastructure immediately after the decision to form the Regime so that the initial deployment of Police Service staff and training personnel can commence their work. Such infrastructure needs will be determined by the Chief of Police and the DCOP-Adm, but they will likely include:

a   Operational infrastructure within the Old City

    i   A main headquarters to be located in the Old City;

    ii   Substations located in each of the different neighbourhoods with temporary holding facilities in each;

    iii   A number of police posts located within the Old City from which detachments can be dispatched at short notice to deal with incidents. In conjunction with the use of electronic measures such as Closed Circuit Television (CCTV), this system will allow swift reaction to problems requiring police attention; and

    iv Specialized pedestrian and vehicle installations at certain gates to control access to and exit from the Old City.

  b Operational infrastructure outside the Old City

    i A Police Service training and education centre;
    ii Offices for the various branches of the Police Service;
    iii A Quartermaster facility, including a magazine;
    iv Facilities for the PORDU; and
    v Facilities for EOD and other specialist organizations.

  c Non-operational infrastructure outside the Old City

    i Quarters for single officers;
    ii Married quarters for Police Service officers and their families; and
    iii Recreation facilities.

Administration and logistics

40. **The DCOP-Adm** will be responsible for planning and implementing the administrative and logistic organizations needed to support the activities of the Police Service. In the possible structure proposed in Annex A is a suggested outline of these organizations. It will be for the DCOP-Adm to ensure they are manned with appropriately trained personnel from the beginning of operations. Procurement contracts should be let on the basis of open bidding with no fixed quotas. The Police Service should actively seek local vendors in conformity with procurement regulations issued by the Administrator. The Police Service personnel and training branches will each be responsible for the recruiting and training of the Police Service personnel and for providing the administrative services necessary for them and their families.

41. **Uniforms** An important issue is the subject of visual identity. It is vital that Police Service officers are easily identifiable to residents and visitors within the Old City, and it may also be considered important that each individual carries some identifying symbol of his or her country of origin. It will be up to the Chief of Police to make recommendations to the Administrator regarding this subject.

42. **Equipment, arms and facilitations** The Police Service will require free, uninhibited and unrestricted entry into its operational area of equipment, arms and communications and other items needed to carry out its functions, exempt from all duties and taxes. The same should apply to personal mail, including packages for personal use, by Police Service members. No charges shall be levied by the Parties for any of the above.

43. **Communications** The Parties shall commit to assign radio frequencies to the Police Service in accordance with its requirements. The Police Service may also wish to install cable or low-power television transmitters for use in training and recreation. The Parties' execution of this commitment should be

reviewed by the Governance Board, with input from the Administrator and the Police Service.

44. **Financing** There will be considerable costs in developing and implementing the operation of the Police Service. While financing is not a part of this study, we expect that such costs will be agreed to as part of a final status agreement between Israel and Palestine, and that the international community will fund the set-up of the Police Service and the Emergency Reserve Force.

Oversight

45. As mentioned earlier we believe that a Police Board should be established to oversee the operation of the Police Service and its members. We believe that the Administrator should appoint a representative to be Chairman of the Board – which could be done on a rotational basis – and that the Board might include:

    a   Members from the Old City neighbourhoods;
    b   Representatives from each of the Abrahamic religions; and
    c   Representatives from each of the Israeli and Palestinian authorities.

46. To be effective, and to build public confidence in the operation of the Police Service, we believe that the Police Board should meet on a regular basis, with the Chief of Police called to attend and to respond to questions from members, and that the proceedings should be open to the public.

Conclusion

47. The concept of the Old City Special Regime and its security system depends on agreement being reached between Israel and Palestine to authorize its creation and to determine its functions and duration. The purpose of this assessment has been to outline what our experience and our knowledge up to this point leads us to believe are factors that could contribute to the successful operation of a security system in the Old City as part of the Regime.

48. From our reading of papers produced by our Israeli and Palestinian partners, and our discussions with each of them alone and together, and with many others, we are aware that there is not total agreement on a number of the issues, but that there is agreement on some. It is our belief that the points of difference are capable of resolution. We believe that an effective security system to address the special circumstances of the Old City is achievable.

Annex A to JOCI Security Assessment November 2007

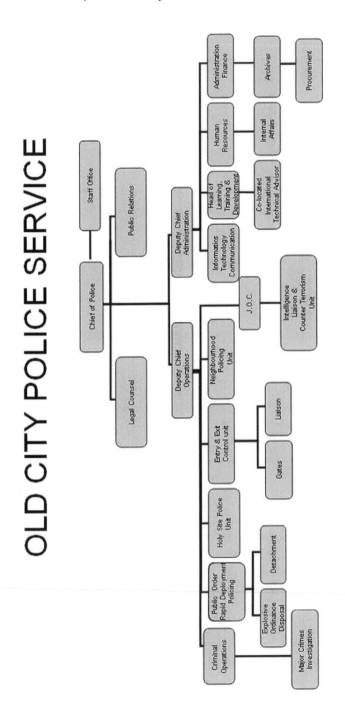

Annex B to JOCI Security Assessment November 2007

Options on entry and exit control in the Old City

Proposed system for Jaffa Gate

Introduction

1. We believe that one of the key aspects of security in the Old City will be the importance of controlling entry and exit to and from it. The ability to prevent undesirables (terrorists, criminals, etc.) from entering the Old City, and the ability to arrest those who have committed crimes there, will call for security measures tailored to the special circumstances of the Old City and potential threats to it. Balanced against this requirement is the need to preserve an atmosphere of normality and to provide for the unhindered access and egress of the regular inhabitants and visitors. A further consideration is that in making whatever adjustments to existing infrastructure that may be considered necessary, care has to be taken not to interfere with the historic and aesthetic nature of the Old City's gates and thoroughfares.

2. To examine the challenge of providing security in the Old City during periods of low to high security threat-levels, we concentrate on examining the provision of appropriate security measures at the Jaffa Gate, given its key location as a major pedestrian and vehicle entry and exit point. While we focus in detail on the Jaffa Gate, we also look at general requirements for control over entry and exit across the whole of the Old City.

3. We endorse the need for a similar study to be conducted on a gate leading into what will be Al-Quds and the State of Palestine. We have not attached the *Jaffa Gate Crossing Facilities Study* as an Annex to this paper given its length, but it should be referred to as an integral part of the work of the Security Working Group, and can be found in volume two of Routledge's three-volume series on JOCI.

Aim

4. The aim of this annex is to cover some of the key points concerning the physical and architectural aspects of entry and exit into the Old City, with particular reference to the Jaffa Gate, and the conclusions we draw from them.

Outline

5. The discussion will address the following issues:

   a   Threat;
   b   General principles;
   c   The gates;

d Entry and exit options;

e Vehicle policy; and

f Architecture.

Threat

6. As we noted earlier, the Old City is a key focus for those who wish to disrupt Israeli–Palestinian co-existence as well as Jewish–Muslim interaction. Events within the Old City can attract interest from political and religious factions around the world and lead to attempts to incite violence or attack religious sites within the City. Religious or political-based terrorism is therefore a major potential threat. Similarly, the location of important religious sites within the City attracts large numbers of pilgrims at various times of the year. Massive crowding within the constrained area of the City, coupled with the limited pedestrian and vehicle routes inside the walls, pose particular problems for crowd control and the danger of injury caused by panic.

7. These threats to safety and security must be met by the ability, when necessary, to impose an escalating range of control measures over those entering or leaving the city. Planning must allow for the worst case scenario, and measures and infrastructure must be put in place to counter it. Other measures must be planned to cater to diminishing threat levels, so that in a steady state, the minimum disruption to pedestrian and vehicle traffic is imposed. While the ideal would be to have a minimum threat level posture as the steady state (Condition Green, say), there must be an ability to move rapidly into the most severe threat mode (such as Condition Red). It is taken as a given that since the Regime will be in place at the agreement of the Parties, both will do all they can to assist the Police Service in foiling any attempt to pose a threat to, or disrupt the running of, the Old City.

General principles

8. Since entry to and exit from the Old City involves the two Parties as well as the Regime, we have examined the subject based on four general principles:

a Entry and exit points into and from the Old City should be staffed by the Police Service with the presence of the authorities of the state involved;

b In order to facilitate movement into the Old City, each Party should take such measures at the entry point in its territory as to ensure the preservation of security in the Old City. The Police Service will monitor the operation of the entry and exit points;

c Citizens of either Party and tourists may exit the Old City only into the territory of the Party for which they possess valid authorization to enter; and d   Residents of the Old City, or special permit holders, will be able to enter with special checking regulations. A special procedure for such individuals will be defined by the Administrator, based on advice from the Parties, in an independent protocol.

The gates

9. Of the eight gates in the Old City, seven are open and are used to enter and exit. Five of the gates (Dung Gate, Zion Gate, Jaffa Gate, New Gate and Lion's Gate) have some access for vehicles and all, including the pedestrian-only Damascus Gate and Herod's Gate, are widely used year-round.
10. Of note is the existence of the ring road around the Old City – which leads into the five gates that have vehicle-access – and the area between the road and the walls. A suggestion has been made that this area be regarded as a 'buffer zone' in which the Regime shares responsibility with the authorities of the appropriate Party. While we do not fully agree with this suggestion, we do agree that in certain cases, where the architecture of the security apparatus controlling exit and entry into the Old City calls for it, the Police Service should have the ability to operate there in the execution of its access-control mandate and given the need to inspect the exterior walls. The infrastructure we propose for the Jaffa Gate extends beyond the walls and Police Service officers will be required to work there.

Entry and exit options

11. We have looked at various levels of providing security at the gates and considered a number of options as to how that may be achieved depending on the status of the threat at the time. One option is the procedure used at many airport terminals, with passengers presenting their passport – or pass – upon entering or leaving the country. This latter system provides as little restriction as possible to local citizens and visitors alike, and is the most likely to facilitate tourism and pilgrimage into the Old City.
12. Under whichever system is finally accepted, special arrangements will have to be in place to treat full-time residents of the Old City with appropriate consideration. Also, if the system is to work smoothly and to best advantage, there will need to be particular emphasis on cooperation between the Police Service and agencies of the two Parties in their exercise of control at the gates. It seems to us that ultimately the Administrator will have to decide what documentation will be required that will provide the least impediment to ease of movement but at the same time assure the necessary level of security. As mentioned above, the study we commissioned considers a variety of options and we believe it should be up to the Administrator, in concert with the Parties, and based on advice from the Chief of Police, to decide how they wish to address this issue.

Vehicle policy

13. Some suggestions have been made that all vehicles should be excluded from entering the Old City. Other suggestions are that only official Regime and Police Service vehicles (including emergency vehicles) should be allowed access. We believe that none of these suggestions is advisable. As we have mentioned elsewhere, we consider it important that a state of normality be encouraged in the Old City under the Regime and excluding or placing restrictions on a majority of vehicles – other than in a situation of heightened security – would not support that end. That said, we see the need for putting in place some measures to control the vehicles that are permitted to enter (e.g. emergency vehicles, commercial vehicles, Regime and Police Service vehicles, and some private vehicles).

14. Under present arrangements, vehicles entering the Jaffa Gate must exit through the Zion Gate or the Dung Gate. While there is space available to locate security control installations for vehicles entering the Jaffa Gate, there is no such space available for similar installations to check vehicles exiting at the Dung Gate. A compromise, whereby public transport vehicles only will enter and exit by the Dung Gate, traveling as far as the roundabout, while some public transport will also use the Jaffa Gate for both entrance and exit, might be considered. Private vehicles could enter by the Jaffa Gate and exit by the Zion Gate and emergency vehicles could both enter and exit by the Jaffa Gate (see Appendix 1). In both cases the infrastructure at the three gates mentioned will have to allow for the checking of both vehicles and passengers or pedestrians.

Architecture

15. In proposing the necessary infrastructure for security control at the Jaffa Gate, we have underlined the importance of installations that provide the required capability to check the various categories of vehicle traffic entering or exiting there (e.g. private, commercial and emergency), as well as the various categories of pedestrians or passengers (e.g. inhabitants, visitors, business personnel, worshippers, pilgrims, tourists, etc.). At the same time we have emphasized the importance of avoiding structures that might mar the appearance of the Gate itself and the surrounding walls, and we have noted that special efforts should be made to preserve those parts of the area that have archaeological significance.

16. Proposed vehicle security control arrangements for the Jaffa Gate are shown in Appendix 2, which also demonstrates why the controlling infrastructure must be located outside the wall. It is for this reason that we recommend the Police Service be given authority to operate outside the walls in such control situations.

Conclusion

17. We have examined the various challenges in providing security-control measures for those entering and exiting the Old City and considered options for

meeting those challenges. We believe there are a number of workable ways in which measures can be put in place to provide security control at the gates to cover a spectrum of threats, each of which will have to be agreed between the Parties and the Administrator to make the system work. Amongst the solutions we consider workable are several that have been proposed by the study we commissioned on this issue. We suggest that this study's recommendations be examined as a means whereby the Administrator and the Parties can put in place effective entry and exit mechanisms at the Jaffa Gate and at other gates.

Jaffa Gate Crossing Facilities Study. The Old City Initiative, SAYA Architecture & Consultancy. Yehuda Greenfield-Gilad and Karen Lee Bar-Sinai, May 2007.

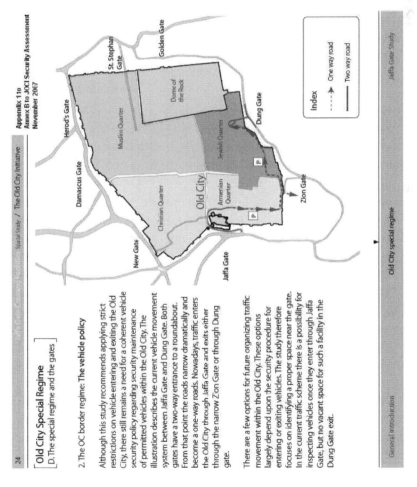

Appendix 1 to Annex B to Joci Assessment November 2007

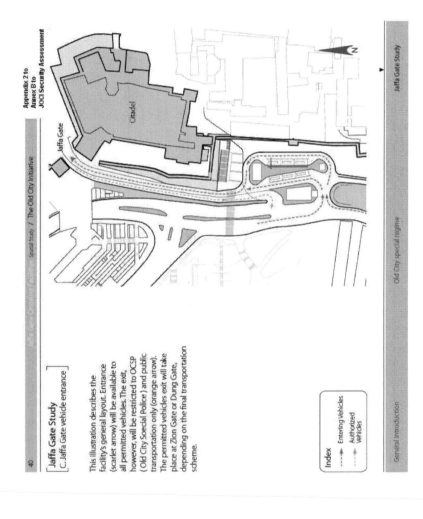

Appendix 2 to Annex B to Joci Assessment November 2007

Annex C to JOCI Security Assessment November 2007

Learning, training and development strategy for policing Jerusalem Old City Police Service

Introduction

1. The learning, training and development (LTD) strategy for members of the Old City Police Service is to produce officers capable of providing an effective Police Service that meets the special requirements of Jerusalem's Old City. Principal factors among the special requirements are dealing with the different backgrounds and sensitivities of residents, protecting the sanctity and availability of the Holy Sites, and controlling and assisting the varying numbers of tourists, worshippers and pilgrims who visit the Old City on a regular basis. While the protection and recognition of the human rights of all who live in or visit the Old City is a major part of the Police Service's function, the primary role will be enforcing law and order in the Old City.

2. It will be up to the Old City Chief of Police and his training experts to define the LTD strategy needed to produce a police service equal to the requirements. We believe that the Police Service should comprise officers of exemplary integrity who can enjoy broad public support and whose discretion and skills in negotiation, reasoning and mediation are sufficient to ensure an environment in which public safety and respect for human rights are maintained. The LTD strategy adopted by the Police Service should be designed accordingly.

Aim

3. The aim of this annex is to outline the factors we believe the Chief of Police and his staff should consider when developing the training programme for Police Service members.

Outline

4. This annex is organized as follows:

    a   A general assessment of the requirements;
    b   The goals and needs of policing in the Old City;
    c   Core themes of policing;
    d   Guiding principles of effective and accountable policing;
    e   Community policing;
    f   Core competencies;
    g   Organizational structure;
    h   Training functions including:

        i   Familiarization training;

    ii   Basic training;
    iii Field training;
    iv Management and executive training;
    v   Outside agency training;
    vi Diversity and language training.

  i   Evaluation

General assessment of the requirements

5.   In any context there are complexities associated with policing. These are even more apparent in setting up a policing organization in the circumstances envisaged for Jerusalem's Old City Special Regime, where the pace of change is increasing, restructuring is constant, established practices are being subjected to critical analysis, and new technology and equipment are being introduced. Moreover the volume of legislation is at times overwhelming, while front-line operational performance is subject to constant scrutiny. The LTD process will require careful planning, effective policy development, structured implementation plans and adequate resources if positive benefits are to be fully realized.

Goals and needs

6.   A comprehensive and coherent LTD strategy, linked directly to the goals and needs of policing the Old City will:

  a   Cultivate community policing and partnership policing;
  b   Demonstrate that stakeholders are getting the best value possible for their investment in Police Service training;
  c   Inculcate continuous learning and knowledge-development as the basis for maintaining a dynamic learning organization;
  d   Imbed throughout the learning organization the appropriate values, attitudes and behaviours;
  e   Ensure a continuous improvement in the quality and performance of Police Service members and training staff;
  f   Demonstrate and imbue the organizational cohesion necessary for a successful Police Service.

Core themes

7.   The LTD process will promote core themes throughout its curriculum that emphasize the importance of:

  a   Human rights theory and practice;
  b   Community policing;

c   Community safety;
d   Diversity and professional practice;
e   Problem-solving policing;
f   Professional standards and ethics;
g   Health and safety; and
h   Best practice, best value.

Guiding principles

8.   The pursuit of the core themes in LTD will greatly assist in meeting the guiding
     principles that ensure Police Service officers function professionally and accountably:

    a   In a way that actively promotes and protects human rights in accordance
     with all relevant internationally recognized rules and practices, by
     ensuring that respect for human rights is emphasized in training
     curricula and is imbedded in all courses given by the Police Service;

    b   With integrity, impartiality, courtesy, compassion and courage, through
     the alignment of LTD under one philosophy delivered in support of
     core competencies;

    c   Treating everyone fairly, regardless of ethnic origin, political or religious
     belief, gender, sexual orientation, disability, age or social back-
     ground, with the LTD strategy designed to reflect the organization's
     vision and aspirations for the future;

    d   Efficiently and effectively through partnership and in concert with the
     two governments and the Jerusalem Old City Administration, with
     the LTD strategy shaped by the vision of community policing that
     implies internal and external partnerships and problem-solving at the
     front line of policing;

    e   In a way that is adaptable and – through consultation – reflects local
     priorities acceptable to local communities and partners, with LTD
     emphasizing the processes of 'how to learn' and 'problem-solve' to the
     benefit of the communities that the police serve;

    f   In dealing speedily and transparently with police wrongdoing in coop-
     eration with the Police Board, with the concept imbedded in the
     LTD curriculum that there are consequences to all police actions;
     and

    g   Respecting and safeguarding the right to life and the protection of
     property with an LTD strategy based on life-like situations and the
     reality of the circumstances in the Old City and the Region.

Community policing

9.   One of the fundamental principles of community policing is to gain the trust
     of community members and to engage them in helping to develop a situation

in which law and order prevails, with the community assisting in keeping it that way. Foremost is the need to assure the community that the police will be firm in the enforcement of the law, and will do so in a fair and impartial manner. The community also needs to be convinced that the recognition of human rights will be respected and applied equally to all members.

10. It follows, therefore, that in addition to training members of the Police Service in the basic elements of law enforcement, training in human rights standards must be fully integrated into the LTD process at all levels, in cadet training at the Police College, in field training, and during other in-service training courses and exercises. The respect of human rights must be included in training in the use of force and the use of firearms, as well as in exercises that demonstrate its application in life-like situations peculiar to the Old City. Special training in this area will be necessary for members of the Public Order Rapid Deployment Unit (PORDU), whose deployment will normally be in response to incidents where the usual methods of law enforcement have been insufficient to meet the need.

Core competences

11. The training programme for the Police Service will provide the cornerstone for building an effective relationship between the police and the Old City community (and in this sense the 'community' comprises the visitors and pilgrims as well as the residents). To be effective in building the confidence necessary for effective community policing, certain core competencies should be included in the training programme.

    These include:

    a   Integrity;
    b   Leadership;
    c   Client-orientation and service-delivery, including cultural sensitivity;
    d   Action-management;
    e   Thinking skills;
    f   Continuous knowledge enhancement.

Organizational structure

12. To deliver the LTD strategy that we are proposing requires a broad organizational structure, based on modern international Police Services that can be amended to suit the circumstances, a structure that we believe can meet the training requirements of the Police Service. In view of the complexity associated with developing the infrastructure for the delivery of the LTD strategy, we are recommending that a suitably qualified International Technical Advisor be co-located at the senior level of the Police Service training structure. His or her function would be to serve as a senior advisor to the Head of Learning,

Training and Development and provide the expertise to meet commitments. See the organizational chart included in Appendix 1 to this annex. In Appendix 2 are details of some of the terms used in the chart and an explanation of the roles and responsibilities envisaged for the Police Service training structure.

Training functions

13. We believe the training model should have curricula and course standards based on the core competencies. The model should involve a problem-oriented approach that includes theory, as well as situational exercises stressing the importance of problem identification based on the complex Jerusalem Old City reality. Exercises that emphasize team problem-solving, negotiation, mediation, consensus building and role-playing activities should be included. The Police Service should adopt a model used by a number of major Police Services worldwide. In this so-called SARA Model, problem solving incorporates a sequential Scanning, Assessing/Analysing, Response, and Assessment approach (SARA). We believe that such training can go a long way to provide the candidates with required core skills as well as an understanding of the fundamental concepts of policing within the community.

14. As in any large organization, training must be designed to reflect the organization's vision and purpose. In this case, it must also take into account that Police Service members will initially be taking over responsibility for policing in the Old City from the Israeli Security Forces, at the same time as developing untrained international recruits to serve as full-time officers. As mentioned in the main paper, this process will involve the initial deployment of a cadre of trained professional international police officers who assume responsibility for policing in the Old City until the main element is trained and ready to deploy. This cadre, though consisting of trained professionals, will still require a familiarization course to inform its members of the special circumstances of the Old City as well as the structure and procedures of the organization in which they will serve.

15. To meet this one-time requirement it will be necessary to have the initial cadre undergo familiarization training at the same time as the basic course starts for the newly recruited international candidates and the Israeli and Palestinian CLOs. Thus the training structure will be required to cater temporarily to an unusually large number of personnel, but only for as long as the familiarization course is run. Once the initial cadre has finished its familiarization training and deployed to its role in the Old City, the training structure can be adjusted to the level required by a steady-state recruit training intake.

16. We believe that an Old City Police Service Police College should be the organization that delivers the main elements of the LTD programme. We recommend it be located outside the Old City, since space for lecture-rooms, student accommodation, logistical needs and training area requirements will

not be available within the Old City's perimeter. The College's sole role will be to train Police Service personnel; its staff and students will have no police powers outside the Old City's walls. We also see an advantage to locating the PORDU with the school, both to share accommodation and, if appropriate, to assist in the training role. The steady-state student capacity of the Police College will depend on the approved strength of the Police Service – a responsibility of the Administrator, based on recommendations from the Chief of Police – but we envisage it to be in the region of 300 to 350 students at a time.

17. The types of courses or programmes we suggest will be needed to meet the Police Service's requirements are as follows:

    a   *Familiarization training course* This should be designed to introduce trained international police officers to the special circumstances of the Old City as well as to inform them of the Chief of Police's Standard Operating Procedures. We believe the course should last about two months. While it will be given by the Police College Training Staff, it would benefit from the involvement of some Israeli and Palestinian instructors. The aim will be to prepare the international cadre to take over responsibility for policing in the Old City from the Israeli security elements;

    b   *Basic training programme* This should be approximately six months long, providing candidates with the introductory training necessary to reach the level of basically trained police officers, while incorporating the topics covered in the Familiarization Course. The aim is to prepare candidates to carry out policing duties under supervision in the Old City;

    c   *Field training programme (field coach programme)* We believe that Police Service field commanders should be responsible for conducting this programme, including its delivery, monitoring, assessment and evaluation. During the first six-month period in which newly trained officers are deployed in the Old City, they will be supervised by trained superiors as they put into practice the knowledge and skills learned in the classroom;

    d   *Management and executive training programme* This programme should focus on core competencies and knowledge of the environment, public policy trends and skills related to leadership. It should promote unity of purpose and a working environment committed to service, teamwork, innovation and creativity, professionalism and accountability. While senior management courses will be given at various levels of command or authority, we believe they should each address the issues of:

        i   Leadership;
       ii   Managing human resources;

    iii   Managing fiscal resources;

    iv   Managing information and technology; and

    v   Managing the External Environment, e.g. neighbourhood relations, community policing, and public order restorative policing.

e   Outside agency training Even though we envisage that most of the training of Police Service personnel will be given in-house, it will be necessary to send some officers for specialist training that is either not available within the Police Service's resources or not cost-effective to develop there. This training might be available using Israeli or Palestinian resources or in other countries that support the Regime's work. The LTD programme should take account of such requirements. Indeed, it should be arranged that each officer spend some time in both Israel and Palestine (i.e. outside of Jerusalem) to become fully acquainted with the culture of each nationality as well as to become familiar with each nation's security and intelligence agencies.

f   Diversity and language training A central LTD objective should be to educate Police Service personnel in working with and providing Police Services to people of diverse national, religious and social backgrounds. All Police Service officers must learn to understand the differing relationships that exist within the Old City as well as the differing community needs. This requires a course curriculum informing officers of these challenges and equipping them to meet them effectively. While each officer cannot be expected to be fluent in the different languages that are used within the Old City, a good understanding of English and some understanding of key phrases in both Arabic and Hebrew is important to develop good relations as well as to communicate. Time should be set aside in courses at all levels for some language training.

Evaluation

18. Evaluation of the effectiveness of training within the Police Service should be carried out regularly by Police Service staff, with the Chief of Police establishing measures to achieve this aim. These performance measures should seek to define not only quantitative but qualitative indicators. It is important to have in place qualitative measures related to effectiveness of the LTD programmes and how the training is transmitted to the community by front line policing. We believe that other measures such as the conduct of public attitude and opinion surveys, as well as occasional validation visits from outside Police Services invited by the Chief of Police for that purpose, could be helpful in evaluating the success of the Old City Police Service training programme, and suggesting improvements where appropriate.

Conclusion

19. The introduction of the Jerusalem Old City Police Service will constitute a new beginning for the more than 35,000 residents of the Old City. In our assessment of the requirements for a security system to provide effective policing in the Old City we have gone to some lengths to demonstrate our belief in the importance of portraying the Police Service as a 'Service' rather than as a 'Force'. We believe it is important that the Police Service officers be viewed by the Old City's residents and visitors as trained professionals whose role is to maintain law and order and to provide them with assistance and advice when needed. We believe that success will follow once the Police Service is viewed as having the ability to investigate, detect and prevent crime, protect property and persons and arrest and hold in custody perpetrators of crime. While the principal role of Police Service members must always be to enforce the law within the Old City, we believe this training programme will help ensure they do so in a manner that will win and then keep the confidence and respect of the people there.

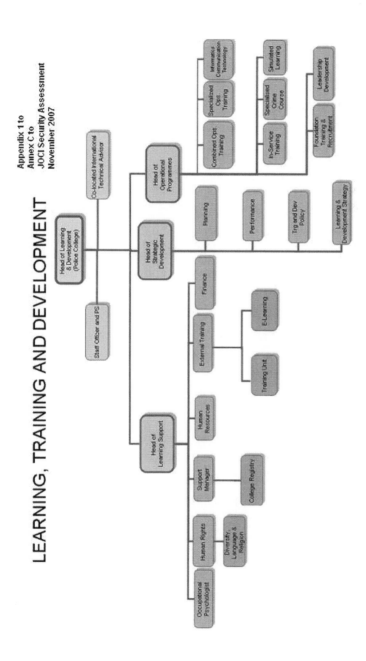

LEARNING, TRAINING AND DEVELOPMENT

Appendix 1 to
Annex C to
JOCI Security Assessment
November 2007

Appendix 1 to Annex C to Joci Assessment November 2007

Appendix 2 to ANNEX C to JOCI Security Assessment November 2007

Learning, training and development organizational structure

1. The intention of this proposal is to suggest a broad organizational training infrastructure for the Police Service. It is a proposal that can be altered or amended for effectiveness or for efficiency reasons.

Authority

2. All LTD programmes will be the responsibility of the Head of LTD who will report to the Deputy Chief-Administration and Support (DCOP-Adm), who will chair a Training Policy Group that will incorporate organizational needs and, more importantly, the Police Service's operational side.

Architecture/methodology

3. The proposed LTD strategy is designed to meet the needs of the Police Service through a systematic and consistent approach to LTD services organizationally and strategically as well as at an individual and team level. To make optimal use of training time, technology and alternative means of delivery should be employed, including classroom-based training, distance learning packages, internet and intranet focus on interactive computer-based training, video presentations, pre-read materials, on-the-job training, problem-based scenario training, and partnership development training with other Police Services and emergency services as well as other criminal justice and social agencies in the community. Most importantly, the LTD should be focused on workplace problems related to the Old City's unique environment.

4. To ensure a firm link between the Police Service's goals and the LTD's capacity to meet those goals, a continuous evaluation process should focus on future needs, while performance indicators are developed to measure the relationship between training and Police Service performance.

5. The organizational chart in Appendix 1 reflects a structure we believe capable of delivering an effective LTD strategy. Based on modern international police service structures, it is flexible enough to be amended to suit the special circumstances of the Police Service. A number of positions central to this structure are explained in the following sub-paragraphs:

    a   *Head of learning, training and development* This position will report to the DCOP-Adm and will be responsible for Police Service organizational LTD policy development. This area of responsibility will need the right people with expertise in LTD to develop timely and standardized training policy.

    b   *Head of learning, training and development (Police College)* It is our contention that the Head of LTD will also serve in this position, thereby assuming responsibility for the operations of the Police College. This allows for one policy centre and eliminates redundancy. The College will be responsible for basic foundation training, in-service training and specialized training programmes.

c   *Branches* There will be three branches reporting directly to the Head of the Police College including:

    i   Learning support;
    ii Strategic development; and
    iii Operational programmes.

d   *Head of learning support* This position will be responsible for the following support areas:

    i   Human resources (College Registry) and finance (Budget Comptrollership);
    ii Occupational psychology;
    iii Human rights and diversity;
    iv Culture and language training;
    v   External training (outreach programmes to other institutions); and
    vi E-learning programmes.

e   *Head of Strategic Development* This position will be responsible for LTD organizational policy incorporating 'best value training' with 'best practice training' to meet the Police Service's institutional and operational requirements. There are four major components under strategic development, including:

    i   Planning;
    ii Evaluation, performance, measurement and quality assurance;
    iii Training needs, assessment and development policy; and
    iv LTD strategy.

f   *Head of Operational Programmes* This position will be responsible for combined operational training, including areas such as firearms training, first aid training, public order policing, tactical training, close protection unit and driver training. He will also be responsible for:

    i   Familiarization training;
    ii Basic training;
    iii Leadership development;
    iv Simulated learning (information and communication technology training); and
    v   Specialist operation branch training (evidence and disclosure training, photography, and surveillance techniques, etc.).

Future considerations

6. The Old City Police Service Police College, in addition to being the institution that provides the development and training programmes required by Police Service members might conceivably be developed at some stage to become a Law Enforcement Training Centre providing courses for non-Police Service members of the Old City Special Regime. Consideration might eventually be given to inviting representatives of other nations with an interest in the Israeli and Palestinian supported Old City special initiative, to attend lectures and seminars at the College. The latter might constitute a practical approach to convince other nations to support and provide resources for this initiative.

References

Unpublished papers, Jerusalem Old City Initiative, Windsor, ON, Canada

Bell, M., M. Molloy, J. Bell, D. Cameron and J. White. *The Jerusalem Old City Initiative– Guiding Assumptions*. Rolling Draft, April 17, 2007 (Updated).

Bell, M., M. Molloy, J. Bell and M. Evans, *The Jerusalem Old City Initiative Discussion Document New Directions for Deliberation and Dialogue*, November 2005.

Dajani, Y. *The Jerusalem Old City Initiative Governance Working Group*, Palestinian Paper (Skeleton) For Discussion Purposes–First Draft, February 2007.

Greenfield-Gilad, Yehuda and Karen Lee Bar-Sinai. *Jaffa Gate Crossing Facilities Study*. The Old City Initiative, SAYA Architecture & Consultancy, May 2007.

Joint Assessment Mission. *The Government of Timor-Leste, UNMISET, UNDP and Development Partner Countries for the Timor-Leste Police Service*, January 2003.

al-Jubeh, N. and D. Seidemann. *Mapping Factors of Stabilization and Destabilization in the Old City*.

Kassissieh, I. and N. al-Jubeh. *Jerusalem Security Principle The Old City*, September 2006.

Meidan-Shani, P., A. Arieh and M. Cristal. *Security Mechanism in the Holy Basin Guidelines for the Security Elements of the Old City Special Regime (OCSR)*, September 2005.

Meidan-Shani, P., P. Golan, R. Berko and M. Cristal. *Security System in the Holy Basin – Phase II*, November 2006.

Meidan-Shani, P., P. Golan, R. Berko and M. Cristal. *Security System in the Holy Basin – Phase II, Part 2*, April 2007.

Meidan-Shani, P., P. Golan, R. Berko and M. Cristal. *Security Mechanism in the Holy Basin – Phase II, Part 3*, August 2007.

Seidemann, D. *The Events Surrounding the Mugrabi Gate – 2007 A Case Study*, June 2007.

Published Reports

Amnesty International-Briefing to Security Council, Members on Policing and Security in Timor-Leste, 2003.

Capacity Building in Bosnia The Role of the United Nations Civilian Police, 2003.

Centrex, Course Portfolio, Developing Policing Excellence, 2005–2006 Northern Ireland Policing Board Policing Plan, 2007–2010.

Bayley, D.H. *Changing the Guard Developing Democratic Police Abroad*. Oxford: Oxford University Press, 2006.

Monitoring of the Police Service of Northern Ireland Training, Education and Development Strategy. Policing Board of Northern Ireland, August 2003.

National Police of Timor-Leste, PNTL Training Model, June 2003.

Northern Ireland Policing Board Report-Monitoring Human Rights of the Police Service of Northern Ireland, 2006.

Office of the Oversight Commissioner for the Police Service of Northern Ireland, Report 19, May 2007.

Palestinian Civil Police Development Programme, Transformational and Operational Plans, EU COPPS, 2005–2006.

Police College of Northern Ireland Prospectus, 2004–05.

The Royal Canadian Mounted Police–Cadet Training Program–Cadet Training Handbook.

The Royal Canadian Mounted Police International Training Services.

The Royal Canadian Mounted Police Training Strategy, 2006.

Strudley, D. *Police Service of Northern Ireland, Learning and Development-Monitoring Framework Reporting Areas,* October 2006.

Summary Proceedings of the South Caucasus and Central Asia Consultations, September 2001.

United Nations Civilian Police Handbook.

United Nations Civilian Police Principles and Guidelines.

United Nations Police Peace-keeping Operations.

EPILOGUE

It is a common habit to suggest that Track Two policy development processes, such as the Jerusalem Old City Initiative (JOCI), are destined for the bookshelves. Indeed, as this epilogue was being written, Israelis and Palestinians had attempted and failed to resolve their longstanding conflict through negotiation, and violence had begun in Jerusalem. In light of these developments, an answer for Jerusalem, one of the thorniest issues of contention, seems distant. A Special Regime for the Old City of Jerusalem, as we have put forward, is therefore all the more necessary.

The work developed through JOCI contributes to the understanding of the complexities of the city, and demonstrates that workable and practical answers do exist and can be implemented if the political will exists to do so. Such a policy process can be of benefit for negotiators during any future talks and, more importantly, it serves as a statement of the possible for Jerusalemites, Israelis and Palestinians, and the many interested in the fate of the city from across the world. Today, as contention over Holy Sites in the city is rising, this assertion may be more important than ever.

Over the past few years, the need to create a Palestinian state has taken on greater urgency, and international pressures on Israel appear to be on the rise. One of the critical goals of future negotiations will therefore be the basic act of creating two states, 'drawing a line' between Israel and Palestine. Despite denials, this border will inevitably and effectively be based on the Green Line of 1967 and UNSCR 242, and trade-offs and swaps on that basis. This process will meet its greatest point of contention over Jerusalem, where the symbolic and emotional attachments are far stronger than along the rest of the potential border (and especially for the Old City and its Holy Sites).

If the question of Jerusalem is to be broached in future negotiations, the answers will range between a strict division of sovereignty between the two states, Israel and Palestine, to a total internationalization of the city, which, at this point, is unrealistic. There are many options in between, and many accept that some third party engagement is necessary and to the benefit of a city as complex as Jerusalem. The debate is over the nature, extent and scope of an international role. Even the Geneva Accord, which proposes a sovereignty split of the Old City (and has often served as a counterpoint to our ideas) provides for an international management system for the Temple Mount/Haram al-Sharif and an international 'Implementation and Verification Group' to oversee the implementation of the overall deal. Others have suggested joint Israeli–Palestinian control in Jerusalem, instead of an international role, for certain functions and areas. We share this ideal, and believe it may be possible for municipal functions for the larger Jerusalem; however, we believe that some international component will be required to ensure security and freedom of worship at the Holy Sites and for the Old City, where most of the key sites stand.

We came to the idea of a Special Regime for the Old City with the intention of finding a solution that met the national ambitions of both Palestinians and Israelis as well as the needs of all believers who sought access to the many Holy Sites. These concerns are the primary drivers of developing a 'special' governance structure in Jerusalem, i.e. one beyond national jurisdiction. In the JOCI Special Regime, the two parties mandate a third party to take on certain functions in the Old City for the sake of maintaining peace. The decision to limit the concept to the Old City was a recognition that both sides required Jerusalem as a national capital, and would not necessitate a large role for a third party in other aspects of managing the city. As well, this option took advantage of the natural limits and security of the Old City's walls, while still addressing the key Holy Sites.

The JOCI Special Regime is not the first attempt to introduce an international element into the governance of Jerusalem. There have been many such ideas ranging from the United Nations' proposal in 1949 to create a 'Corpus Separatum' stretching from north of Jerusalem to Bethlehem, to Adnan Abu-Odeh's 1992 article in *Foreign Affairs* that suggested internationalizing the Old City. The idea of special arrangements for the Holy Sites, or in our case a Special Regime for the Old City, was also under consideration in the talks between former Prime Minister Ehud Olmert and Palestinian President Mahmoud Abbas. The parties did not then enter into details regarding such arrangements, and the forms of special arrangements or regimes remain many. Yet, all have in common the need for a third party and an international role in the management of the city.

The great strength of the Jerusalem Old City Initiative is in detailing what such a role can look like at a robust and comprehensive level. JOCI describes what functions a third party can take on, and what degree of control is required for each function. Great care was taken to consider the needs of all sides, to meeting them in a balanced way, while maintaining functionality and effectiveness of the third party presence. There is little use in creating a role for a third party if it is to be simply a casual presence or, worse, an inert impediment in a tense and conflicted environment. Given the history of the region and the high levels of distrust, we opted in many cases for a robust capacity for the Special Regime. In many ways, this may also be useful to negotiators as it is easier to 'claw back' from this level of third party role rather than work up to it.

This model can serve negotiators in many ways. It provides a set of ideas that can either be taken as a whole, as is our intention, looked at in modules (e.g. security, governance, archaeology and heritage issues), or only certain elements can be used. It can even serve as a foil and a reference for debate and the development for new forms of a third party role that could arise during the thick of negotiations.

One of the strengths of this initiative, and also a source of criticism, is that JOCI did not tackle the question of sovereignty. This was an intentional decision by the organizers based on the view that this was for national negotiators to decide, given the profound sense of historical attachment on both sides. Unlike what some have presumed, we did not indicate a preference for deferred sovereignty. Instead, we took a view that the Special Regime is 'sovereignty-neutral' and could be applied under conditions of agreement on sovereignty or not. Some have argued that there would be no need for a Special Regime if there were agreement on a sovereignty split in the Old City. We believe this critical third party role will be required to maintain peace and stability, and is best implemented over a coherent whole, such as the Old City, rather than piecemeal over disparate fragments of Jerusalem.

Given the difficult nature of any future negotiations, and the temptations not to conclude a final status deal (with all its attendant political sacrifices), there is a risk of temporary arrangements being put forward. Indeed, it is very possible that, in any upcoming negotiations, agreement may be found on a border between Israel and Palestine everywhere but in Jerusalem. The temptation may be there to utilize the Special Regime or special arrangements as a stop gap in such a temporary circumstance; however, the reality is that, without a final status deal, such arrangements would effectively be created under remaining Israeli control of the city.

The Special Regime, however, is designed for a final status agreement between the two sides and presumes a division, hard or soft, between the two capitals 'Al Quds' and 'Yerushalayim'. It is our view that a comprehensive re-examination of our current proposals would be required for such an interim arrangement (that could be seen by many as a continuation of the status quo).

Despite the avoidance of the central sovereignty question, we do believe that the critical third party and international role outlined in the Jerusalem Old City Initiative is a step towards the future constellation of arrangements required for a sustainable solution to Jerusalem and its Holy Sites. An agreement by the sides to derogate elements of their sovereignty to an international body, such as through a Special Regime, would be a reflection of innovation and maturity regarding the very concept of sovereignty. It would be an evolution away from the classic territorial sovereignty, that fuels the dispute between the sides, and towards layers of sovereignty that reflect complexity and the many needs in a city like Jerusalem. There is likely no other place in the world that requires such layers and complexities as much as Jerusalem. We believe the Jerusalem Old City Initiative provides one step further in managing this complexity, encouraging a more flexible approach towards this critical issue.

Finally, we would be remiss if we did not point to the mutual benefit that this very process may have provided to us and our many partners – Israeli, Palestinian and international. This volume, and the two which follow, is a result of their direct output, and an amalgam forged in many intense discussions and consultations with many of them. By holding the concept of a Special Regime through the fire of debate and disagreement, of research and redrafting involving dozens of partners over many years, a rich policy debate was created, as well as a product that, we hope, will leave a mark on sustainable governance for the Old City of Jerusalem. The sum of this process is the papers and studies found in the three volumes. What may be more important, however, is what remains in the minds and convictions of the many talented individuals who shared with us this considerable journey of seeking to find a solution for the intractable – but not impossible – question of Jerusalem.

JERUSALEM OLD CITY INITIATIVE: CHRONOLOGY

2003	December – initial meeting – Ottawa
2003	Michael Bell, Michael Molloy and John Bell decide to establish a peace process
2003	Project on Jerusalem's Holy Basin
2004	February – institutional base – Toronto
2004	Munk Centre agrees to host Holy Basin project; designates Marketa Evans to provide administrative and academic support
2004	May/June – research – Jerusalem
2004	Met dozens of experts in Israel, Jerusalem and the West Bank Decided to focus on Jerusalem's Old City, and not the Holy Basin
2004	July – research – commissioned study
2004	'Socio-economic Conditions in the Old City of Jerusalem', Glass and Khamaisi
2004	August/September – research – Jerusalem
2004	Workshops on legal, constitutional and symbolic issues; urban issues; inter-faith issues; perceptions of young Palestinian leaders; and Track II realities in the Middle East
2004	October – consultations – Washington
2004	Initial consultations with US government institutions and foreign policy organizations
2004	November – research – UK
2004	Chatham House Workshop on Post Conflict Issues and Security
2005	May – planning – Windsor
2005	Decision to commence drafting of *Discussion Document*
2005	May – research – Jerusalem
2005	Consultations with senior Israeli and Palestinian officials and Jerusalem experts; agreement regarding conference late 2005 (Istanbul). John

	Bell named resident Director of NGO Search for Common Ground, Jerusalem
2005	June – consultations – Washington
2005	Discussions with officials and experts
2005	August – institutional base – Windsor
2005	Transfer of JOCI to the Department of Political Science, University of Windsor. Dr. Tom Najem joins team as Project Manager with responsibilities for academic and administrative matters
2005	August – drafting – Windsor
2005	Review of advanced draft of *Discussion Document*
2005	September – research – commissioned studies
2005	'Security Mechanism in the Holy Basin', Meidan-Shani
2005	'Legal Parameters of the Old City Special Regime', Sher
2005	October/November – consultations – London, Washington, Jerusalem
2005	In preparation for the Istanbul conference
2005	Art Hughes and Dan Kurtzer join JOCI Project
2005	December – publication – Toronto
2005	JOCI/Munk Centre publishes *The Jerusalem Old City Initiative Discussion Document – New Directions for Deliberation and Dialogue*
2005	December – conference – Istanbul
2005	Israeli, Palestinian, and international experts (the Jerusalem 'A-Team') review *Discussion Document* and identify priorities for a Track II process
2006	January/March – planning/fundraising – Ottawa/Windsor
2006	Briefings and negotiations with potential funders
2006	January – planning – Princeton University
2006	Discuss cooperation between institutions
2006	March – workshop – Windsor
2006	Track II: Theory and Practice – Dr. Peter Jones
2006	March – consultations – Jerusalem
2006	Initial discussions regarding establishment of Security Working Group (SWG). Decision to recruit John de Chastelain, Roy Berlinquette, and Art Hughes as core international members of SWG
2006	March – research – commissioned study
2006	'Jaffa Gate Crossing Facilities: Spatial Study', Saya Architecture
2006	June – research
2006	Commissioned study 'Security Arrangements in the Old City of East Jerusalem', al-Bakri and Dajani
2006	SWG workshop – Durham University, UK
2006	SWG inaugural meeting; Kurtzer suggests 'Rolling Draft' to record and track evolution of basic concepts; need to develop a more flexible process
2006	August – SWG planning – Ottawa

2006	Follow up Durham meeting and discussion of security-related research and development of security paper
2006	September – research – commissioned studies
2006	'Jerusalem Security Principles: The Old City', al-Jubeh and Kassissieh
2006	'Mapping Factors of Stabilization and Destabilization in the Old City', al-Jubeh and Seidemann
2006	'Security Mechanisms for the Holy Basin, Parts 1, 2, 3', Meidan-Shani
2006	September/October – planning – Windsor/London/Jerusalem
2006	Decision to establish Governance Working Group (GWG); consultations in London and Jerusalem regarding GWG research, methodology and participants
2006	November – SWG workshop – Windsor (Willistead Manor)
2007	February – JOCI Newsletter #1
2007	February – SWG meetings – Jerusalem
2007	March – research – commissioned studies
2007	'Options for the Administration of the Holy Places in the Old City', Reiter
2007	'A Plan for Governance in a Special Regime in Jerusalem', Sher
2007	'Old City Governance', Al-Mustakbal Foundation
2007	March – research – Jerusalem
2007	Inaugural research trip of GWG (David Cameron, Art Hughes and Jodi White – core international members of GWG); work on 'Rolling Draft' resumes
2007	March – consultations – Washington
2007	Consultations with US officials and experts
2007	March – SWG drafting
2007	First comprehensive draft of SWG report circulated for comment
2007	May – JOCI Newsletter #2
2007	May – GWG and SWG research and consultation – Jerusalem
2007	June – commissioned study
2007	'Event Surrounding the Mughrabi Gate 2007 – Case Study', Daniel Seidemann
2007	July – GWG meetings and research – Ottawa, Jerusalem
2007	August – JOCI Newsletter #3
2007	August – consultations – Washington
2007	September – SWG workshop – Waterloo (Centre for International Governance Innovation)
2007	September/October – consultations – Jerusalem, Amman, London
2007	October – SWG workshop – Istanbul
2007	Penultimate review of JOCI security document
2007	October – consultations – Washington
2007	October/November – GWG research and consultations – Jerusalem
2007	November – JOCI Newsletter #4

2007	November – commissioned study
2007	'The International Law of Holy Places in the Old City of Jerusalem', Breger and Hammer
2007	November – London Caucus Meeting 1 – London
2007	High level review and articulation of JOCI basic principles
2007	November – SWG paper
2007	'The Jerusalem Old City Initiative Security Assessment', de Chastelain, Berlinquette and Hughes
2007	December – GWG drafting – Ottawa
2007	Drafting of *Governance Document* commences
2007	December – London Caucus meeting 2 – London
2007	High level review of JOCI basic principles concludes; 'Rolling Draft' becomes 'Guiding Assumptions'
2008	January – GWG drafting – Windsor
2008	Shira Herzog proposes 'people vs place' paradigm
2008	February – advocacy – Washington/Ottawa
2008	JOCI Israeli partners Sher and Meidan-Shani reinforce support for JOCI in Washington and Ottawa
2008	February – SWG paper
2008	'The Jerusalem Old City Security Assessment' publication revised
2008	March – JOCI Newsletter #5
2008	March – commissioned studies
2008	'Dispute Resolution in the Old City', Donais
2008	'A Plan for Governance in a Special Regime in Jerusalem', Sher
2008	'The Legal Framework for a Special Regime: The Old City of Jerusalem', Qupty
2008	'Conflict Resolution in the Old City, Past and Future', al-Jubeh and Seidemann
2008	April – advocacy – Jerusalem
2008	JOCI low-key advocacy campaign commences with presentation at Jerusalem Institute for Israel Studies conference
2008	June – consultations – Jerusalem/Madrid
2008	Final consultations of Governance paper with Israeli, Palestinian partners and officials, and discussion of paper with religious leaders
2008	July – commissioned studies
2008	'International Norms and the Preservation of Culture and Heritage in the Old City of Jerusalem: A study of the role of UNESCO', Dumper
2008	'A Security and Management Framework for the Holy Site of the Old City', Dumper
2008	August – JOCI Newsletter #6
2008	September – advocacy – Washington
2008	Presentation to the Middle East Center for Peace
2008	November – GWG paper

2008	'Governance Discussion Document: A Special Regime for the Old City of Jerusalem', Molloy, Bell, Bell, Cameron, Hughes and White
2008	November – consultations and advocacy – Jordan
2008	December – JOCI Newsletter #7
2009	April/May – GWG workshops and consultations – Jerusalem
2009	Legal system, dispute resolution and Holy Sites
2009	June – advocacy – European Union, Brussels
2009	Presentation to European Union Middle East Peace Process Committee
2009	July – planning – Toronto
2009	Decision to commission a paper by Cameron and Hughes to develop the 'Guiding Assumptions' into a Mandate for the Special Regime
2009	November – advocacy – Amman, Ramallah, and Jerusalem
2010	January – research – economics project
2010	Michael Bell to coordinate research on economic aspects
2010	January – commissioned study
2010	'Implications of Alternative Israeli-Palestinian Trade Agreements on the Jerusalem Old City Special Regime', Halevi and Kleinman
2010	January – research – archaeology project
2010	John Bell to coordinate JOCI research on political aspects of archaeology in the Old City
2010	Lynn Swartz-Dodd recruited as international expert on archaeology issues
2010	February – JOCI papers – Mandate
2010	Completion of paper 'Mandate Elements for the Old City Special Regime', Cameron, Hughes, Bell, Bell and Molloy
2010	February – JOCI papers – Proposals
2010	Bound compilation of JOCI Proposals for the Old City of Jerusalem, including the Security, Governance and Mandate documents
2010	May – research – property project
2010	Mike Molloy to coordinate research on property issues in the Old City
2010	Anneke Smit and David Viveash recruited as international experts on property issues
2010	May – advocacy – Washington
2010	Presentation held at the Mayflower Hotel to formally unveil the Special Regime model to 400 plus representatives from government, think tanks and foundations. Event hosted by Middle East Institute
2010	June – property project research – Jerusalem
2010	July – advocacy – UN New York
2010	Presentation to the International Peace Institute
2010	Meeting with Arab Heads of Mission to the UN

2010	August – archaeology project research – Jerusalem
2010	August – commissioned studies
2010	'Land Use and Ownership in the Old City', al-Jubeh and Seidemann
2010	'Archaeology and an Old City Special Regime', al-Jubeh and Seidemann
2010	October – property and archaeology consultations and meetings – Jerusalem/Windsor
2010	October – JOCI Newsletter #8
2011	May – property and archaeology workshop – Jerusalem
2012	February – JOCI workshop – London
2012	Final meeting between JOCI management and regional and international partners to review the project and discuss future advocacy and transfer activities
2012	October – final report of the archaeology project
2012	'Sustainable Management of Archaeology and Heritage, Jerusalem's Old City', Swartz-Dodd
2013	August – final report of property project
2013	'Property under the Old City Special Regime', Smit and Viveash
2013	September – advocacy – Washington
2013	JOCI proposals and research papers forwarded to US State Department Middle East Peace Negotiation Team
2013	October – advocacy – Washington
2013	JOCI team briefed the Peace Negotiation Team

INDEX